INSTITUTION AND PASSIVITY

Northwestern University
Studies in Phenomenology
and
Existential Philosophy

Founding Editor †James M. Edie

General Editor Anthony J. Steinbock

Associate Editor John McCumber

INSTITUTION AND PASSIVITY

Course Notes from the Collège de France (1954–1955)

Maurice Merleau-Ponty
Foreword by Claude Lefort

Text established by Dominique Darmaillacq, Claude Lefort, and Stéphanie Ménasé

Translated from the French by Leonard Lawlor and Heath Massey

Northwestern University Press
Evanston, Illinois

Northwestern University Press
www.nupress.northwestern.edu

English translation copyright © 2010 by Northwestern University Press. Published 2010. All rights reserved. Originally published in French as *L'Institution-La Passivité: Notes de cours au Collège de France (1954–1955)* (Paris: Éditions Belin, 2003).

10 9 8 7 6 5 4 3 2 1

Library of Congress Cataloging-in-Publication Data

Merleau-Ponty, Maurice, 1908–1961.
 [Institution, la passivité. English]
 Institution and passivity : course notes from the Collège de France (1954–1955) / Maurice Merleau-Ponty ; foreword by Claude Lefort ; text established by Dominique Darmaillacq, Claude Lefort, and Stéphanie Ménasé ; translated by Leonard Lawlor and Heath Massey.
   p. cm.—(Northwestern University studies in phenomenology and existential philosophy)
 "Originally published in France as L'Institution-La Passivité: Notes de cours au Collège de France (1954–1955) (Paris: Editions Belin, 2003)."
 Includes bibliographical references and index.
 ISBN 978-0-8101-2688-6 (cloth : alk. paper)—ISBN 978-0-8101-2689-3 (pbk. : alk. paper) 1. Phenomenology. 2. Ontology. 3. Philosophy—History—19th century. 4. Philosophy—History—20th century. I. Lefort, Claude. II. Darmaillacq, Dominique. III. Ménasé, Stéphanie. IV. Lawlor, Leonard, 1954– V. Massey, Heath. VI. Merleau-Ponty, Maurice, 1908–1961. Institution dans l'histoire personnelle et publique. English. VII. Merleau-Ponty, Maurice, 1908–1961. Problème de la passivité, le sommeil, l'inconscient, la mémoire. English. VIII. Title. IX. Series: Northwestern University studies in phenomenology & existential philosophy.
 B2430.M3763I5813 2010
 194—dc22
                                                                   2010000279

Contents

Foreword by Claude Lefort — ix

Editors' Note to the French Edition — xxxiii

Translators' Note — xxxv

Part 1. Institution in Personal and Public History

Introduction — 5

Institution and Life — 16

Institution of a Feeling — 28

The Institution of a Work of Art — 41

Institution of a Domain of Knowledge — 50

The Field of Culture — 58

Historical Institution: Particularity and Universality — 62

Summary for Thursday's Course: Institution in Personal and Public History — 76

Endnotes for the Course on Institution — 80

Part 2. The Problem of Passivity: Sleep, the Unconscious, Memory

Philosophy and the Phenomenon of Passivity — 117

For an Ontology of the Perceived World — 133

Sleep — 138

Perceptual Consciousness and Imagining Consciousness — 146

Symbolism — 151

Dreams — 156

The Freudian Unconscious	162
Delusions: *Gradiva*	170
The Case of Dora	177
The Problem of Memory	191
Appendix: Three Notes on the Freudian Unconscious	199
Summary for Monday's Course: The Problem of Passivity: Sleep, the Unconscious, Memory	206
Reading Notes on Proust	210
Reading Notes on Freud	216
Endnotes for the Course on Passivity	233
Bibliography of Texts Relevant to the Courses on Institution and Passivity	253
Index	257

Foreword

Claude Lefort

Translated by Leonard Lawlor and Heath Massey

This volume contains the notes that Merleau-Ponty composed for the courses that he presented at the Collège de France in 1954–55. At the Collège, one was required to teach two courses. The first was the principal course; the other could be converted at the professor's discretion into either personal projects or commentaries on texts. If we judge by the abundance of notes on which it is based, and the number of quotations copied over onto separate pages, *The Problem of Passivity*, given the circumstance of it being the second course, bears witness to a minute preparation and does not appear to be less important in Merleau-Ponty's eyes than *Institution in Personal and Public History*. All things considered, the two chosen themes for that year were closely related. Thus Merleau-Ponty warns at the beginning of his course on passivity that there will be no introduction and refers his audience to the introduction for the principal course. In *Institution*, he notes that "time is the very model of institution: passivity-activity, it continues, because it has been instituted, it fuses, it cannot stop being, it is total because it is partial, it is a field."[1] The notion of field will turn out to be essential throughout the lectures. Not that we think that passive and instituted are equivalent, and still less that the argument of one of the courses fits in nicely with the other. They encroach simultaneously on one another (referring sometimes to the same authors) and follow divergent paths, moving in the direction of a new ontology.

The *Institution* Course

What sense does Merleau-Ponty give to the concept of institution? The course summary specifies: "Therefore by institution, we were intending here those events in an experience which endow the experience with durable dimensions, in relation to which a whole series of other experiences will make sense, will form a thinkable sequel or a history—or again the events which deposit a sense in me, not just as something surviving or as a residue, but as the call to follow, the demand of a future."[2] In fact, there in the course summary Merleau-Ponty only reproduces in more concise terms a passage from his introduction. There is no doubt, therefore, that he feels as though he has discovered the right words in order to indicate the framework for his investigations. These investigations do not bear on one field of existence, one field of action, or one field of limited knowledge. They are guided by the idea that we can discern, in whatever field we consider, a singular mode of the structuring of events, events which, while being wholly locatable "in" time—as the very word "in" indicates—show themselves to be constitutive of a time that is properly temporal. Or still, we could say that the events present the index of an interiority of time. In effect, the events cannot be separated from one another; the oldest let themselves be identified only because they have turned out to have been generators of the ones that came next, and the most recent allow themselves to be identified only because, if we judge them as innovators, they bear the trace of their gestation in the past. Thus, where a dimension common to distinct experiences unconceals itself, regardless of the duration that separates them, we are referred from a simple observation of the difference between times to the thought of an *ontological genus* (following the expression introduced in order to account for the phenomena of passivity) where an efficacy of the instituting is conserved in the instituted.

It is not necessary to pause over the new use Merleau-Ponty makes of the term "institution" by exploiting its ambiguity. He takes it in its double sense—the action that provides a beginning and a state of the thing established, for example, the state of being social, political, or juridical—but with this essential difference, that institution as foundation is not considered as the product of an act and that institution as establishment contains at the same time the possibility of its perpetuation, by means of repetition, indeed, the possibility of its petrification as well as the possibility of the reactivation of the instituting force. The philosophical scope of this reformulation of the concept of institution is explicit. Merleau-Ponty distinguishes immediately the problematic of institution from that of constitution (in the Kantian sense). He rejects, along with the idea of a constituting consciousness, that of a world in which nothing would be discovered that had not been constituted by its operations. Understood in its double sense, institution presupposes a non-coincidence between the institutor and the instituted. This is what

FOREWORD

makes him say that time is the model of institution. If institution is *openness to*, openness to is always produced *on the basis of.* There is no call to the future which does not imply a decline of the past.

In the passage we quoted from the course summary, Merleau-Ponty speaks of events that *deposit a sense in me.* However, if we follow his analyses, the reference to a "me" is unnecessarily restrictive. In fact, in a first part (whose theme surprises us, since the course's title does not prepare us for this), Merleau-Ponty indicates that certain characteristics of institution are already discovered in the order of life. The development of the organism, far from being entirely derived from an innate structure, as we have believed for a long time, testifies to a certain plasticity. The development is accomplished only by means of reactions that "make sense" (within the framework of the species, of course). On the other hand, the study of animal behavior demonstrates that behavior is not fixed by instinct. Its orientation is decided by means of the effect of an "impregnation" of the new that comes from its fellow creature. Moreover, the animal is likely, when it lacks this decisive event, to discover a substitute in a partner of a different species, or even in the observer (if he knows how to mystify the animal, as Lorenz does). According to Merleau-Ponty, the notions of reference to sense, response to *expressive* stimuli, fruitful events indicate in the processes that we assume to be natural a mode of development which is not pre-given, a mode of development that implies a history or, more precisely, an institution—a mode of development that does not give way to the invocation of a teleology. This brief incursion into the domain of life comes to Merleau-Ponty by way of Raymond Ruyer's study of instinct, which was published a bit earlier in *Les Temps Modernes* (under Merleau-Ponty's initiative), a study whose argument he follows closely (as Dominique Darmaillacq shows in the careful extract of the texts on which Merleau-Ponty bases himself). We recall in passing that Merleau-Ponty was already interested in the function that the image of the individual of the same species plays in the formation of behavior in animals. He discusses this function in a course he taught at the Sorbonne where he evoked Chauvin's work on crickets, and he devoted a large part of his *Nature* course (1957–58, the second course) to a lengthy reflection on animality by referring directly to Lorenz, Uexküll, and Portmann.

Before coming to the main point of the *Institution* course, Merleau-Ponty focuses on a phenomenon which, more than any other, leads us to discern a schema of institution, this time, in the life of the human being: puberty, which we had thought could be reduced to a physiological process. This emergence from childhood, which cannot be dissociated from the fact that it arises out of Oedipal conflicts, reveals that there was an anticipation of the future in the first period, an experience of the impossible (to take the place of his father) which was accompanied by a "putting in reserve." A reactivation and an overcoming of the first cathexes of the Subject are produced—without it being the case, moreover, that this overcoming signifies a complete break with the past.

These first descriptions persuade us, if we had any doubt about it, that the notion of institution is put forward in order to make us recognize a fundamental modality of time. It is true that the three studies devoted, respectively, to the institution of a feeling, the institution of a work, and the institution of a domain of knowledge are placed under the rubric "personal and interpersonal history." But they do not bear only on the self-transformation (or the self-encounter) that love involves, or on the discovery by the painter of the sense of what he creates, or on the inventive power of the mathematician. They bear on the historicity of the feeling (its attachment to some apparently contingent events, where the feeling is formed, carried on, unmade, and restarted, up to the moment when, having passed, it inhabits memory forever). Or they bear on the historicity of the painting as such (they testify, for example, to the permanence of the problem of perspective and the diversity of its solutions). Or they bear on the historicity of mathematics. Nevertheless, under a second great rubric, Merleau-Ponty goes so far as to broach the very question of History, in the conventional sense of the term, by wondering what History means insofar as it can have within it "an access to another time on the basis of one time" or insofar as, despite abandoning the idea of progress, we must grant the possibility of the formation of a culture which is open to the knowledge of all the other cultures—the formation of a humanity that probes the depths of its past.

Probably, Merleau-Ponty's project can be clarified if we remember the criticism he made earlier of History such as it is conceived by philosophers and historians. In regard to the event-oriented viewpoint that dominates narrative history, he does not delay at all in putting it on trial, so much so that narrative history looks to him as if it were guided by a naive faith in the objectivity of the observer. The practice of Charles Seignobos—to whom less than one page is devoted in *Sense and Nonsense*—seemed to him to provide the best illustration of narrative history.[3] Yet, during this time prior to his course, Merleau-Ponty sought to make a double criticism of what we can later call conceptual history—Max Weber's—and of Marxist-Hegelian philosophical history. This was the point of one of the two courses he gave at the Collège de France the year before, *Material*

FOREWORD

for a Philosophy of History, and, to a large degree, this was the point of the book he had written precisely at this time, in 1955, *Adventures of the Dialectic*. If he admires Weber, if he judges fruitful and appropriates the idea of an "elective affinity" between the events which arise from distinct areas, indeed, from domains that appear foreign to one another (the puritan ethic and the spirit of capitalism), Merleau-Ponty contests the separation that is established by the historian between the reality that we assume to be unformed, "a pure diversity" which is also then ungraspable, and the object of knowledge constructed by the historian, which bears, certainly, the imprint of his values and of those of his time. Within the limits that the arbitrariness of the selection of facts imposes, this construction brings to light a network of intelligible relations whose validity is imposed universally. On this basis, the criticism is harsh: "Weber lets the universe of knowledge and the universe of practice subsist side by side without any communication." In other words, Weber does not recognize his own inclusion within the field that he explores, and the only thing he does is transpose the Kantian idea of a constituting consciousness into his method. And, let us add in passing, Weber does this without taking into consideration the effort that Kant made in order to disclose within certain events "signs of history." (Kant did this, notably, with the French Revolution, which, at one moment, presented itself as a spectacle for the entire world.) In the same course from 1953–54, Merleau-Ponty credited Lukacs with the elaboration of a theory which, while remaining faithful to Marxism, would renounce as a myth the idea of a necessity imprinted in the course of history. Lukacs' theory would limit itself to recounting the work of the negative, the movement of the contradictions displacing themselves as far as the moment in which the fundamental contradiction appears undisguised and renders its overcoming possible for the first time. Nevertheless, this attempt appears to Merleau-Ponty to maintain the illusion that negativity can at any time incarnate itself in a "historical carrier." In short, this is the illusion that transcendental history can invest itself in an empirical class, the proletariat. Thus, the course summary that we are discussing finishes with these words: "This question should now be resumed."

One is tempted to think that by devoting himself to detecting and describing the phenomenon of institution, Merleau-Ponty engages in this *resumption*, that is, he has made use of this criticism of ideas of History in order to open a new path. He is seeking now in the *Institution* course to extract from what we confusedly call History (whatever the domain of investigation may be) sequences in which a *generativity* manifests itself. This project does not turn away from the consideration of events, but it seeks events, we might say, that form a sequel, and which make sense only if we grasp how they function in favor of a foundation, a preservation, a resumption or a mutation. As Merleau-Ponty says (in a place where he contests Lévi-Strauss's idea of haphazard series of events for which only a theory of probabilities would account), it would be an abuse to assign every non-natural event to a process of institution as soon as that event would have had considerable importance by means of its consequences. The invention of the potato or that of corn, these inventions are of another order than those events that we call "historical" because they look to be matrix events. On the other hand, such a project does not give itself over to the illusion of realism. It implies a work of interpretation that is guided by the investigation of the genesis of sense in the events, and, by the same token, that requires of the one doing it that he interrogate himself about his own place in the present and the relation with time that this place has provided for him. This is a remarkable fact: while Merleau-Ponty explores the institution of a feeling, that of a work, that of a domain of knowledge, and somehow discovers what is in the strict sense *historical,* outside of the conventional domain of History, he never stops thinking about how his analyses will affect the Marxist philosophy of history. Sudden references to the notion of permanent revolution, to Marx's thesis that humanity poses only questions that it can solve, references to Daniel Guérin or to Trotsky emerge here and there (for example, the considerations concerning the crisis of puberty and the history of a love affair give way to a long digression called "Parallel with the Philosophy of History"). This is intriguing for the reader, but the reader cannot know whether Merleau-Ponty developed them for his audience.

Nevertheless, the idea of institution cannot be derived directly from a reflection on the problems of history. In fact, it is necessary to remember how Merleau-Ponty used this term in *The Prose of the World,* a work whose writing was interrupted shortly before Merleau-Ponty entered the Collège de France.[4] In the chapter called "Indirect Language" (the chapter that will provide the essential part of the study published in *Les Temps Modernes,* "Indirect Language and the Voices of Silence"),[5] he says of the painter that "what is at issue for the painter is only to push farther the groove already sketched in the world as he sees it in his pictorial works or in those of the past . . . to convert a custom into an *institution.*"[6] His work is judged to involve a triple resumption by which "he continues while going beyond, conserves while destroying, interprets by deforming, and infuses a new sense into what nevertheless called for and anticipated this sense." Besides, Merleau-Ponty is already concerned to show at once the historical dimension of pictorial work and that of the painting. Whether it is the issue of one or the other, or more generally the issue of all that arises from "the order of culture," we must recognize there, across events, the trace of an advent. Merleau-Ponty asserts that "the order of the advent must not be derived, if it exists, from pure events."[7] But "the advent" nevertheless does not "dispense with the event."[8] The reflection on art looks to him to be an invitation to rethink history: "we would rediscover probably the concept of history in its true sense," he writes, "if we got used to forming it as we propose on the basis of the example of the arts or language."[9] Such a thought, he judges, is the one that Hegel has sketched in his best texts. Let us emphasize this point, for Merleau-Ponty thus sees in the dialectic the formula of a movement such that to emerge from oneself is simultaneously to reenter oneself, and this movement is what expression accomplishes.

In regard to the chapter of *The Prose of the World* called "The Algorithm and the Mystery of Language," Merleau-Ponty already develops the argument that will be found in "Institution of a Domain of Knowledge" by grounding it in the same example, that of the anchorage of mathematics in the definition of the first series of whole numbers. Merleau-Ponty does not yet elaborate a theory of institution, but he lays out its elements. Thus he writes, in words that are close to the ones in his notes:

> What is essential to mathematical thought . . . lies in the moment when a structure is decentered, opens up to an interrogation, and reorganizes itself according to a new sense that is nevertheless the sense of this same structure. The truth of the result, its value independent of the event, consists in its not involving a change in which the initial relations dissolve, to be replaced by others. . . . Rather, the truth lies in a restructuring which, from one end to the other, is known to itself, and is in agreement with itself.[10]

What Merleau-Ponty owes to Husserl is clearly acknowledged. He writes:

> Husserl has used the fine word *Stiftung*—foundation or establishment—to designate first of all the indefinite fecundity of each moment of time which, precisely because it is singular and passes, can never stop having been and thus being universally. Above all he has used *Stiftung* to designate the fecundity, derived from that of a singular moment of time, the workings of culture which open a tradition, which continue to have value after their historical appearance and which require beyond

themselves other operations and operations that are the same as the first workings.[11]

However, we should go farther back in Merleau-Ponty's itinerary in order to locate the schema of institution and refer to his first great philosophical essay, "Cézanne's Doubt," published in the journal *Fontaine* in 1945 and clearly revised later. Certainly it was during this time—when Merleau-Ponty was already familiar with Husserl, but was in the process of examining Cézanne's path—that he was led to discover a sense-becoming of the work, a structuring of moments that bear traces of anticipation and of multiple resumptions.

Therefore, in what way is the *Institution* course at the Collège de France innovative? The idea of institution emerges now, and likewise the idea of the theory of history and theory of expression in which the idea of institution was being traced out.

Here is an instructive landmark. In the "Report" addressed to Martial Guéroult, in order to justify his candidacy to the Collège de France, Merleau-Ponty mentions two works in progress, the one in which he will elaborate a theory of truth, and the other where he will elaborate a theory of intersubjectivity. Never moving beyond the planning stage, the first was to be called *The Origin of Truth;* the second, which was never completed, was *The Prose of the World*. Indicating that he had already established some of the foundation in different essays ("Cézanne's Doubt," "The Novel and Metaphysics," and *Humanism and Terror*—a book which therefore he does not disavow), he specifies that, before undertaking the analysis of formal thought and of language, he had already revised half of *The Prose of the World* and proposed to advance a new idea of expression. We see, in fact, that his teaching at the Collège aimed first at "The Sensible World and the World of Expression" (1952–53), then "The Problem of Speech," and, as we have already indicated, "Material for a Theory of History" (1953–54). We imagine therefore that, when he takes up the theme of institution (in connection with that of passivity) and thereby gives a new orientation to his investigations, he noticed that the attempt to extend the phenomenology of perception through a theory of expression (the project he announced to Guéroult) left him still dependent on the philosophy of consciousness. Moreover, it is by means of a criticism of the idea of a constituting consciousness (from which, Merleau-Ponty notes in passing, Husserl had been slow to separate himself) that his new course opens. This criticism is going to open out immediately onto a reformulation of the relations of the Subject "to the world, to others, to action and to time."

FOREWORD

As we noted earlier, Merleau-Ponty confronts the question of History (in the conventional sense of the term) only after having presented the characteristics of institution by means of examining a feeling, a work, and a domain of knowledge. In fact, the question of history has been opened indirectly. By discovering the historicity of a love affair (in Proust), even though a love affair is most often considered irrational or artificial, and the historicity of arithmetic, even though arithmetic seems to provide atemporal truths, Merleau-Ponty has brought to light in the two circumscribed fields, which are as different as possible, an indestructible connection between contingency and logic. His proposal now no longer consists so much in criticizing the belief that is at the source of an idealist or materialist philosophy, the belief that one is able to possess the sense of history taken in its totality. On the one hand, he is opposed to those who think that every attempt to find an intelligible orientation in accidental changes in the past is arbitrary, a view that goes as far as contesting the validity of the project of historical science as soon as it goes beyond the collection of established facts. On the other hand, he is opposed to those who judge that the difference between times cannot be overcome, because they are—with some justification—careful not to dissolve the experience of one epoch within an assumed evolution of humanity or, and this amounts in fact to the same thing, are careful not to interpret the behaviors and beliefs of another time on the basis of our own categories.

We could rely on the references that Merleau-Ponty makes, in this last part, to the events that, we know, furnish him with a theory of institution (for example, the events that set up the development of capitalism and indicate the possibility of either its transformation or its petrification, or the events which arise from the dynamism unleashed by the French Revolution). But it is also important to him to go to the place that lies ahead of descriptions of this kind in order to clarify the place from which the philosopher speaks, the place from which the very idea of institution is formed. We apprehend in fact a society as *other*, in its particularity, from within the present culture, from within a temporal field. And we gain the experience of a "communication" between two times in the exercise of knowledge, provided that we do not lose the notion of our implication in a history that is being made.

Anyone who reads the *Institution* course notes will see the argument displayed (the argument for the self-implication in a history being made) throughout the criticism of Lévi-Strauss and in the commentary on a work by Lucien Febvre which at best looks to demonstrate the irreducibility of beliefs found in another time to the categories that fashion the modern state of mind (*The Problem of Unbelief in the Sixteenth Century: The Religion of Rabelais*). Merleau-Ponty discerns in the skepticism that

Lévi-Strauss professes, just as in the claim to an absolute knowledge, the sign of a Subject detached from the world, the sign of a denial of the historical condition of the observer: "The absolute opacity of history, like its absolute light, is still philosophy conceived as closed knowledge. The one who observes the opacity sets himself up outside of history, becomes a universal spectator."[12] The criticism is all the more severe insofar as Merleau-Ponty shows that skepticism when history is at issue, and relativism when ethnography is at issue, go together with the program of a pure science capable of establishing the laws from which all social structures would be deduced, that is, the program of a systematic sociology.

Nevertheless, Merleau-Ponty considers Febvre's *Rabelais* to be an exemplary study with much philosophical weight. Note that he had already highlighted this book and had already commented on it in "The Metaphysical in Man" (collected in *Sense and Nonsense*).[13] What he saw there was the definition of the historian's task: "We must reawaken the past, to put it back in the present, to reconstitute it . . . without imposing any of our own categories upon it." And he had already introduced the idea of a communication of particularities: "We will arrive at the universal not by abandoning our particularity, but by turning our particularity into a way of reaching others, by virtue of that mysterious affinity that makes situations mutually understandable." In *Institution*, Febvre's worth consists in showing that access to another time is possible. In such a case, we gain access if—instead of wondering whether Rabelais believed or disbelieved by looking, in his writings, for obvious or hidden signs of his "opinions" (it doesn't matter which kind of sign)—we put him back in the milieu of his contemporaries, if we compare his propositions with a number of others, if we seek to find out how his readers would have understood him, if therefore we make ourselves sensitive to a "field of culture," and if we go as far as doubting the very possibility of being an unbeliever in the sixteenth century. Whoever is acquainted with Febvre's work knows that he does more than doubt this possibility; he judges that the "mental toolbox" of the people living during this time did not provide them with the means of conceiving what we call atheism. But, far from being content with admiring in Febvre the sole attempt to restore another time by taking advantage of a sort of decentering and of bringing us into confrontation with the difference of times, Merleau-Ponty observes that this decentering is possible only because we are not enclosed in our own time. Our time provides us with the resource of a communication with the past precisely when we do justice to its difference. He goes farther than Febvre when, while admitting that Rabelais could not be an unbeliever in the sense that we give to the term now,

FOREWORD

Merleau-Ponty imagines that the distance that Rabelais manifests in regard to religion was a sign of an openness to the future. Perhaps then Merleau-Ponty gives to Febvre an idea that he did not formulate, but lacking it, we would not be able to understand how a world so thoroughly dominated by Christianity would be able to change. (The title of the last section, "True Meaning of the Febvre Study" authorizes this hypothesis.)

The questions raised in this last part come together finally. We can neither conceive a universal history nor fall back upon the observation of the difference between times. In one place, Merleau-Ponty notes that philosophy becomes the knowledge "of particularities which unite." This is what was coming out earlier in his reflection on institution.

The *Passivity* Course

Merleau-Ponty poses the problem of passivity by means of the examination of phenomena which do not form themselves according to the model of institution. If the notion of institution is indissociable from the notion of history or historicity, if it confronts us with an instituting activity and an instituted state related in such a way that the institution—the foundation, the birth—always assumes something pre-given and the instituted state involves an openness, indeed, a call to the future, if this is the relation presented in the notion of institution, then in contrast the examination of passivity apparently excludes the dimension of time. We notice that Merleau-Ponty analyzes a feeling—love—within the framework of *Institution*, but he analyzes a delusion—the one that Freud describes in the reading of Jensen's *Gradiva*—within the framework of *Passivity*. Isn't it the case that this delusion is developed as an effect from events about which one can say that they form "a succession"? Undoubtedly. But nothing of what affects the Subject comes to alter the first belief that the Subject has formed. Strictly speaking, there is no history of a delusion.

What is at stake in a reflection on passivity? The summary for the course, which has passivity as its object of study, tells us that what is at issue is to overcome a fundamental alternative which is already implied by perception: "The explication of perceptual experience must make us acquainted with a genus of being with regard to which the subject is not sovereign, without the subject being inserted in it." Thus the course's project allows us to lead an attack against the root of modern ontology—an attack that is still better than the one in the *Institution* course—in its subjectivist version and in its objectivist version. If we pay attention to it, passivity must not be conceived as a state. It is a modality of our relation with the world. What we do not intend, as the sentence we just cited might lead us to believe, is that there is another genus of being in which the subject would be sovereign. Passivity is seen, however, to be assigned the function of being something revelatory, something even more valuable because the phenomenon has been neglected by most philosophers—the body being charged with providing the reason for a dependence of the soul in regard to the world.

Concerning perception, knowledge, and action, Merleau-Ponty has already maintained that they do not derive from the operations of a Subject. We donate sense to what appears only by responding to a solicitation from the outside, following an orientation that a certain "field" imposes on us, a field that involves levels and dimensions and that opens onto horizons. The things themselves are given only under perspectives and, although we want to describe them, they exceed the limits of the observable. They turn out to be inexhaustible. In regard to the perception of others, only an obstinate defensive position in a problematic that leaves no choice between the status of the subject and the status of the object can hide from us the fact that we project ourselves into others at the same time as we perceive ourselves in others. (Merleau-Ponty notes that such a position always has for us something mythical about it.)

Before describing the phenomena which particularly deserve attention, Merleau-Ponty leads his audience back to the base of his phenomenology: perceptual life. The life of perception teaches that if we endow with sense all of what happens to us, this is done, from the moment of our birth, by means of the experience of something irreducibly earlier, of an irreducible exteriority, and of an alterity that is as well irreducible. Although an introduction to the *Passivity* course is judged superfluous, as we indicated, the preliminary comments take up a large amount of space. The first propositions are sudden and quasi-familiar in the sense that Merleau-Ponty alludes to the fashion that leads young people to seek a master, for example, to expect from a psychoanalyst that he provide them with his knowledge. This is a form of "passivism" that blinds us to what passivity means. Or again, he alludes to a type of political commitment (of course, it's Sartre and the Sartreans whom he has in mind) that allies the idea of a freedom of radical choice of the Subject with that of its complete submission to the proletariat or to the masses who are the most needy and who alone are able to decide the sense of history. This is another form of passivism, we could say, this time indissociable from activism. But the tone changes as soon as the appreciation of the climate of the epoch gives way to a reflection on the resistance in contemporary philosophy to phenomenology and to the revision of classical ontology for which it calls. In a dozen pages of exceptional density, Merleau-Ponty works to explicate what he intends with the "perceived," the reason by which Being and perceived-Being are unified. In the first place, he wants to respond to objections that were formulated from a Cartesian viewpoint by Ferdinand Alquié and from a Kantian viewpoint by Pierre Lachièze-Rey. Merleau-Ponty is careful to distinguish his own notions of the phenomenal body and of the pre-objective world from the use that Alquié has made of them as the correlatives of consciousness, instead of admitting that with their introduction the very definition of consciousness is put in question. He is even more careful to dismiss Lachièze-Rey's argument according to which the description of a body that is removed from the distinction between thought and extension leads to finalism or to vitalism. Consequently, Merleau-Ponty engages in a criticism of certain interpretations of Raymond Ruyer that are apparently quite close to his own (his interpretation is already explored in the first course). Finally, he comes for the first time—if we are not mistaken—to separate his conception of phenomenology from equivocations to which it might be prey.

Here it is necessary to quote:

> 1) World side: do not limit oneself to the static image of the perceived world taken at an instant. Consider, not abstract perceptions in an isolating attitude, which I have done too much (hence, overestimation of sensing or of the quality as mute contact with an endpoint), but take up the analysis of the perceived world as being more than sensory. For example, my whole perception at each moment is only the relation of a human action, absolute plenitude is the result of isolating analysis. [The] sensible world [is] full of gaps, ellipses, allusions; objects are "physiognomies," "behaviors,"—[there is] anthropological space and physical space.
> 2) Subject side: do not consider only the "natural" body, consider everything that is sedimented above and describe the subject resolutely, not as consciousness, i.e., coincidence of being and knowledge, or pure negativity, but as the X to which fields (practical no less than sensory) are open. —In particular, it is necessary to introduce imaginary fields, ideological fields, mythical fields—linguistics and not only [the] repletion of sensing.[14]

These quotations indicate clearly that the problem of passivity is not a regional problem.

The *Phenomenology of Perception* had already taught us this. This was the conclusion to the chapter on temporality: "We are not in some incomprehensible way an activity joined to a passivity, an automatism overcome by a will, a perception overcome by a judgment, but wholly active and wholly passive, because we are the upsurge of time."[15] This wide-sweeping judgment was stated at the end of a double criticism of intellectualism and empiricism, a criticism which appears to be still dependent on the conventional framework of the philosophical debate. Yet, the course at the Collège de France proposes to open the problem of passivity straight on, instead of defining it by its antonym. In order to do that, Merleau-Ponty is going to examine phenomena which seem, in principle, to exclude the decision of a Subject: sleep, dream, the unconscious, and memory. Some years later he will return to this project, without referring to it explicitly, in a working note to *The Visible and the Invisible*:

> Philosophy has never spoken—I do not say of passivity, we are not effects—but I would say, of the passivity of our activity, as Valéry spoke of a body of the mind: new as our attempts may be, they come to birth at the heart of being, they are connected onto time that streams forth in us. . . . The soul always thinks: this is in it a property of its state, it cannot not think because a field has been opened in which something or the absence of something is always inscribed.[16]

He added this fine sentence that he wrote more than once: "It is not me who makes me think, no more than it is me who makes my heart beat." At the very beginning of *The Visible and the Invisible*, he writes with a similar care: "Everything comes to pass as though my power to reach the world and my power to entrench myself in phantasms only came one with the other; even more: as though the access to the world were but the other facet of a withdrawal."[17]

These sentences only make more explicit the idea that he formulates in his *Passivity* course. When Merleau-Ponty suggests that the access to the world could be only the other facet of its withdrawal, he understands by "world" common space and common time, the shared experience of what is by means of language. It is from this world, in which we acquire the status of a Subject, that, simultaneously, each makes his withdrawal. That each diverges away from this common world does not, however, mean that he is detached from it. If, with his access to the world, a field is opened for him in which something or the absence of something is always inscribed, then the traces of what is impressed in him subsist in the divergence away: impressions that are distributed, classified, mixed in a singular way independently of the constraints that the norms of the perception of space and time and those of communication impose. In order to emphasize the innovation of the course, let us say that passivity no longer points merely at the fact of the unperceived that our perception involves, to the fact of the unthought that the activity of thinking involves. The course aims to distinguish two *regimes* of thought, for, far from leading the phantasms, the dream itself, back to a chaos of images, Merleau-Ponty speaks of a "*dictatorship* of the visible" (my emphasis), or, in order to account for the effects of censorship, he speaks of the institution of a "dictatorship of figuration." It is really under these conditions that we could evoke a sovereignty of the Subject, except that the concept of the Subject, even if we modified it, is no longer adequate.

The course's entire argument depends on the idea of a distinction between the common world and the private world, in other words, the world for me. This distinction would make no sense, however, if we converted it into a separation, since the world for me is constituted on the basis of events that have affected me, events that continue to affect me in the life that I lead in the middle of others, and since there would be no common world unless there is a multiplicity of subjects whose relation implies not only that each is different from the others but also that the identity of each is not abolished in communication. Let us note that what Merleau-Ponty is making us understand here should not prompt us to reduce his philosophy to a theory of intersubjectivity.

When he examines the conditions under which the subject gains access to the world, through perception, through knowledge, and action, he draws our attention to a passivity which is not, as we might believe, the opposite of activity, but is the obverse side of it. Yet, when he examines the conditions under which the subject removes himself from the world, Merleau-Ponty does this in order to discover an activity that is the obverse of passivity. In sleep already—this is a limit case that is particularly embarrassing for someone like Sartre, who does not turn sleep into a purely physical phenomenon—we must admit that the notion of a presence of the world subsists. If we did not make this admission, we would not be able to understand that the one who is sleeping, when he awakens, knows immediately that he is finding himself again in place, sometimes in the very position in which he had fallen asleep. We also could not understand that in certain circumstances the one sleeping manifests the capacity of waking up at the time that he has decided to wake up, indeed each time that a foreseen task solicits him to awaken. (Freud gives the example of the nursemaid.) Merleau-Ponty intersects with Freud, who judged that "during the whole duration of our sleep we know that we were in the process of sleeping." In regard to the dream, it does not proceed from an eclipse of the subject in the sense that consciousness would stop intending the object that is adequate to its intention and would become "empty," and would let itself be fascinated by ever-expanding images. The dream takes a hold of the events that are produced during our life—or at least it takes a hold of a certain number of them. At times we do not even have the memory of these events, but they have nevertheless affected us, have made infantile desires vibrate, and suddenly the desires are reactivated, without us knowing that they have been reactivated, by an event that happened while we are awake, an event that is often insignificant.

Freud's thought holds a considerable place in the *Passivity* course. Merleau-Ponty had already referred in passing to psychoanalysis in *The Structure of Behavior* and less briefly in the *Phenomenology of Perception* (see the chapter on "The Body in Its Sexual Being").[18] He had stressed the fruitful contribution that analytical work has made to the study of child psychology during his courses at the Sorbonne.[19] Nevertheless, it is at the time of his preparation for the *Passivity* course that he reads or rereads Freud's *Interpretation of Dreams*. He annotates it abundantly and copies out several passages (which are reproduced in "Reading Notes on Freud" in the present volume). There is no doubt that this reading had really made an impression on him. It revealed a Freud to him that he had not before sensed as so close to himself, and at the same time the reading provoked Merleau-Ponty to clarify what he understood by "perceptual consciousness." As the reader of these notes will see, the more Merleau-Ponty tries to slice Sartre's philosophy apart from his own—Sartre's theses appearing to him wholly dependent on a conventional idea of consciousness and seeming to take nothing into account that cannot be determined by the alternative of being and nothingness—the more he concerns himself with drawing on Freud's descriptions in order to defend the idea of an "existential field." This is the idea of an existential field in which one can never take account, in the contact with the event, of the sense with which we endow it and of the sense that the event imposes on us, nor are we able to discover entirely in what way the event enters us.

The subject who dreams is the same as the one who is awake. Merleau-Ponty makes this judgment based on the fact that the content of a dream, as strange, indeed, as absurd as it may seem, turns out, under analysis, to be made of materials extracted from the history of the one who had the dream. It is not possible, therefore, to make a cleavage between the real and the imaginary. But it is also necessary to dismiss such a division for another reason. In fact, if we observe the conduct of the Subject in "real" life, in other words, when the Subject is awake, we

FOREWORD

cannot fail to observe that the relations that he entertains with others are largely cut out from an imaginary fabric, this fabric formed from the start by the intersections of their projections and their introjections. Merleau-Ponty had already indicated this. But this truth was still abstract. The other, in fact, can never be isolated. The other is perceived in a particular situation which has a sense for me. His physiognomy, which is such a distinctive feature, his purposes, the relations that I see and know him to have with those who are other than himself, all of this produces the effect that, if I am affected, disturbed, alarmed by some sign that is connected to his person, this sign will be capable of returning by means of some event which will involve some such element of the constellation that was impressed in me.

It is not enough, then, to admit that the dream cannot be entirely dissociated from perception. It is necessary to recognize, on the basis of the same movement, an oneiric consciousness of wakefulness. This oneirism indicates the persistence, during the participation in the common world, of the world for me. The persistence of the world for me is manifest in the uncertain relation I maintain with the other, but we also see it in what we call our interior monologue. This is the pseudo-monologue that Maurice Blanchot denounces when he speaks of "the incessant flux of speaking speech," of a private speech, truncated in a way that we understand it, but it does not understand itself.[20] What distinguishes the dream from the oneiric consciousness of wakefulness, Merleau-Ponty tells us, is that the dream is formed because of sleep. Freud, of course, says moreover that the dream is the guardian of sleep insofar as it satisfies the subject's desire by sheltering it from excitations from the outside. What is most important here is that the closing off of the body to the world—the closure of the gates of the senses and the immobility—have the result of making discrimination impossible, the very discrimination that perception, knowledge, and language require. In passing we can say that Merleau-Ponty brings up very quickly the connection of perception to the capacity for movement and for orienting oneself in the sensible world. Thus the body as the source of an "I can" is essentially the agent of the adaptation to the outside, and therefore of the distinction between the real and the imaginary. In the quasi-absence of the "I can," the dream is born and maintains itself on the basis of a "dedifferentiation" of the elements of the existential field of the Subject. This concept, however, cannot be maintained without any reservation. After having posed at one moment the question of who is the Subject of the dream, Merleau-Ponty responds later by saying that "what dreams in us is our existential field." This is a clarifying response only if we remember that the field is not uniform. It involves levels and it is structured, at these different levels, by "existentialia," a term, as we know, that Merleau-Ponty uses in order to avoid those of the categories. It is a term he uses to express that what is at issue are events for which one is not able to impute a definite origin, but on the basis of which a certain type of behavior is engendered, a structure of responses to problems that the Subject poses in the relation it has with others in the variety of the circumstances of its life. Merleau-Ponty also speaks about matrices of events or hinges or pivots. No matter what, his concern is to show that the loss of criteria for the discrimination that defines wakeful consciousness, the fall into indifferentiation, does not entail the confusion of everything with everything else (this is the thesis he attributes to Sartre). Instead, by means of the structure of the existential field, the loss of means to discriminate and differentiate make association, combinations, and condensation of disjoined elements of prior perceptions emerge, elements that were subjected to the need to maintain a world for me.

Merleau-Ponty announces the objections that Freud's theory of dreams inspires in him. The theory requires that we presuppose two texts, the one constituted by the manifest content of the dream, the other constituted by its latent content. We also have to presuppose two Subjects: the first conceives indecent thoughts, thoughts that cannot be formulated as such, and the other forms images whose sense it is incapable of understanding. Finally, we must admit that the interpretation of a dream would consist in reconstituting, on the basis of the data that the patient supplies, the originary thoughts, and this would be done by apprehending the data as elements of a rebus, that is, by reordering them in such a way as to make them legible. This picture, as artificial as it seems to him, does not, however, discredit for Merleau-Ponty the conception that Freud makes concerning a distinction between the conscious and the unconscious and the function of the dream. In fact, what is essential for Merleau-Ponty is the discovery of a structure of oneiric thought, the structure of what he calls successively a *positive symbolism* and a *primordial symbolism*. It is positive in the sense that the symbolism is not inadequate or is not manufactured on the basis of the residue or the leftovers of language. It is primordial in the sense that the symbolism has its source in infantile desires and always accompanies, in each of us, the perception of others. In addition, and this point must be emphasized, the symbolism does not derive from the repressed but is utilized by the repressed. Freud, he tells us, has methodically explored this symbolism in *The Interpretation of Dreams*. Now, if Freud had drawn the consequences of his discovery, he would not have found himself hindered by the difficulties that a duality of subjects and a duality of dream contents have made come about. The problem has emerged from the idea that thought could be attributed only to consciousness in the conventional sense and that it could be expressed only by the processes of language in the conventional sense. Such an idea implied necessarily a division between the "I think" and the oneiric production, a division between an agency that holds knowledge back and the dream in the strict sense, which becomes deceptive by virtue of the rejection of unavowable thoughts. Yet, if we admit that there is a primordial symbolism, there is no need to imagine a subject hidden deep within us. Since our perception of things and in particular our perception of others are never reduced to a knowledge that works under the imperative of a strict distinction within the elements of the sensible field, the hypothesis of this supposedly knowing subject is a fiction; and if we imagine a text whose explicit meaning would be deliberately converted into unintelligible images, this text is another fiction. Likewise, it is erroneous to suppose that the work of the analyst consists in moving back from the content of the dream narrative to the thoughts which are its origin. Freud himself warns that by moving back from the manifest to the latent we do not retrace the path that was followed but go now in the reverse direction, for the thoughts mobilized by the event which triggered the dream are really a lot more than those that will find their way into the dream. It looks, then, as though the task of the interpreter is not so much to grasp fully the sense of a dream communicated by the patient as it is to clarify a part of the network of the dreamer's oneiric life by means of—to use Merleau-Ponty's interesting phrase—a sort of hermeneutical reverie.

Merleau-Ponty's attachment to Freud's work is seen in his concern to distinguish his own reservations from the objections that Georges Politzer made. In his *Critique of the Foundations of Psychology*, Politzer was the first to reject the prejudice according to which all of our experience derives from operations of consciousness, in the conventional sense used by philosophers—in order to make way for a symbolic order.[21] Nevertheless, he consequently seems to want to blur the distinction between the unconscious and the conscious to the point where we cannot find any bearings. While rejecting the definition of the subject as pure self-presence, Politzer seeks, paradoxically, to lead the repression back to the experience we have of ideas, the experience we have of images about which we can only admit that we have conceived them. Repression, as Merleau-Ponty comments, is then nothing but a moment of the drama that we always live in the "first person," and thereby the dream symbolism is nothing but a procedure of bad faith. Merleau-Ponty says explicitly that the study of the structure of oneiric thought must not be made against repression or in order to do away with repression. However, a question remains: can we admit repression without conceiving—even if we reject the idea of a censorship—some sort of unconscious barrier that makes a current of thoughts flow again and makes it ready to irrupt under the impulse of desire and which forces the thoughts to borrow canals whose ways make the tenor of these thoughts unrecognizable? Obviously, Merleau-Ponty is not attracted to this kind of metaphor. Although he appreciates the transition that Freud makes from the topological to the dynamic in the last chapter of *The Interpretation of Dreams*, his reticence cannot be missed. If we follow his attempts to maintain the idea of repression and the idea of the unconscious without admitting, let us say, even a "cleavage," or at least a fundamental difference between two modes in the way thought works, we can in principle wonder whether Merleau-Ponty is tempted to turn the unconscious (such as he recognizes its signs in the dream work) into a simple circumscription within the field of oneiric life. Oneiric life would be produced under the effect of a regression provoked by sleep, when the flow of excitations originating in the outside is momentarily interrupted. But we would have nothing more to discover in oneiric life than in the perceptual experience. Thus we read in one place in the course notes that "consciousness is side by side with its dream" or that, characterized by the norms of waking life, "this unconscious is not distant, it is quite near, as ambivalence." These assertions are very different from those of Politzer. But probably the surest signs of Merleau-Ponty's hesitation are staked out in his silence concerning the existence of a *primary process* that Freud uncovers when he examines the phenomena of displacement, condensation, and the figuration characteristic of the dream. This is a silence that agrees with the refusal to accept an intentional dressing-up. Pontalis had already insisted on this point, a long time ago, in a very insightful article called "The Unconscious in Merleau-Ponty."[22]

Merleau-Ponty indeed notes on one occasion that condensation is not merely a procedure of dissimulation in service to the censors, but he abstains from examining the cases where condensation becomes a procedure of dissimulation. Moreover, he does not take into account the process that Freud judges to be the most apt to distort the sense of the dream: decentering, that is, the movement to the periphery of the most important theme and the movement to put the anecdotal on the first level. Now, by not recognizing the idea of a primary process, is Merleau-Ponty not led to reject the idea of an unconscious? By restoring to perceptual consciousness all its thickness, does Merleau-Ponty not do away with the attempt to find in the dream anything other than a "logic of implication and of promiscuity"? In the course summary, Merleau-

Ponty judges that "what is essential in Freudianism is not to have shown that beneath appearances there is another reality altogether, but that the analysis of a given behavior always finds in it several layers of signification, that they all have their truth." Yet, the course notes for *The Problem of Passivity* do not justify this conclusion, and they do not let us think that he is done debating it with Freud and with himself. The exploratory study of the case of Dora, the examination of the interpretation of Gradiva, or that of dreams that foretell the future quite indicate the concern to pursue the question of the unconscious in contact with the details of Freud's analyses.

Research for a New Ontology

As valuable as they may be, the course summaries that we have mentioned do not give a fair idea of the nature of the work that Merleau-Ponty accomplished during his third year of teaching at the Collège de France. Revised after the fact, they present the state of the philosophical motivations of the choice of the subject matter treated. The notion of institution, he specifies, has been selected in order to look for "a remedy to the problems with the philosophy of consciousness." The notion of passivity should lead us to conceive a genus of being that shows the deficiencies of the traditional conceptions of the Subject. Thus the phenomena that have been the main object of investigation seem, if they don't have the function of being examples, at least to provide materials in service of an ontology that is liberated from the opposition of the In-itself and the For-itself. These course summaries give us a very mild version of the research being done in both the courses. The word "research"—we're using this word on purpose—must be understood here in its true sense, and even in its strongest sense: in this case, in the sense of something adventurous. As I have tried to show, Merleau-Ponty has already uncovered in his earlier works events which "form a succession"; we can attribute neither chance, nor material necessity, nor even spiritual logic to the structure of this succession. But he does not possess truly the notion of institution. He invests in this notion a philosophical meaning only when he recognizes the same schema of generativity over areas that are quite different.

Why would we cover over the fact that there is something extravagant in the movement that leads Merleau-Ponty from his incursion into Proust's universe and the analysis of the liaisons and breakups between Swann and Odette and between the narrator and Albertine to the exploration of belief in the sixteenth century, following the path that Lucien Febvre has taken? This extravagance bears fruit; there is no sign of arbitrariness. One imagines that the inquiry could have taken other routes; none are imposed absolutely. Thought searches to assure itself by means of exposing itself to the unusual.

Notes

1. The quotation is from page [4] (3) below. One of the great benefits of these course notes lies in the fact that they render this research completely visible, the blunt side of Merleau-Ponty's thought which is often masked in his books by the elegance of his prose. Another benefit lies in the fact that they show what role the dialogue with authors has in his work, the dialogue in which he searches to extract the best from them before criticizing their theses. Merleau-Ponty's art of reading Sartre, Proust, Freud, and Febvre will not let itself be forgotten.

2. The course summaries were published in the Annuaire du Collège de France and reproduced by Gallimard in 1966. See Maurice Merleau-Ponty, *Résumés de cours: Collège de France 1952–1960* (Paris: Gallimard, 1968); English translation by John O'Neill, as "Themes from the Lectures at the Collège de France 1952–1960," in *In Praise of Philosophy and Other Essays* (Evanston, Ill.: Northwestern University Press, 1988).

3. Maurice Merleau-Ponty, *Sense and Nonsense*, trans. Hubert L. Dreyfus and Patricia Allen Dreyfus (Evanston, Ill.: Northwestern University Press, 1964), 131.

4. Maurice Merleau-Ponty, *The Prose of the World*, trans. John O'Neill (Evanston, Ill.: Northwestern University Press, 1973).

5. "Indirect Language and the Voices of Silence" was then collected in *Signs*. See Maurice Merleau-Ponty, *Signs*, trans. Richard C. McCleary (Evanston, Ill.: Northwestern University Press, 1964).

6. Merleau-Ponty, *Prose of the World*, 67 (my emphasis). The phrase including the word "institution" does not appear in the English translation.

7. Ibid., 79.
8. Ibid., 80.
9. Ibid., 85.
10. Ibid., 127.
11. Ibid., 68.
12. See page [74 verso] below.
13. Merleau-Ponty, *Sense and Nonsense*, 83–98. The discussion of Febvre occurs on *Sense and Nonsense*, 92.
14. See page [217].
15. Maurice Merleau-Ponty, *Phenomenology of Perception*, trans. Colin Smith, rev. Forrest Williams (London: Routledge and Kegan Paul, 1981), 428.
16. From translators: Maurice Merleau-Ponty, *The Visible and the Invisible*,

trans. Alphonso Lingis (Evanston, Ill.: Northwestern University Press, 1968), 221. Lefort's quote has "time" instead of "field" (*temps* instead of *champ*); we have restored the quote to its correct form.

17. Ibid., 8.

18. Merleau-Ponty, *Phenomenology of Perception*, 154–73.

19. See Maurice Merleau-Ponty, *Psychologie et pédagogie de l'enfant, cours de Sorbonne 1949–1952* (Paris: Verdier, 2001). Parts of this large volume are available in English. See Maurice Merleau-Ponty, *The Primacy of Perception*, ed. James M. Edie (Evanston, Ill.: Northwestern University Press, 1964); for "Phenomenology and the Sciences of Man" and "The Child's Relation with Others," see Maurice Merleau-Ponty, *Consciousness and the Acquisition of Language*, trans. Hugh J. Silverman (Evanston, Ill.: Northwestern University Press, 1973).

20. From translators: The title of this essay is in fact "The Death of the Last Writer" ("Mort du dernier écrivain"), which can be found in the English translation by Charlotte Mandel: *The Book to Come* (Stanford, Calif.: Stanford University Press, 2002). Lefort seems to be referring to the discussion found on page 222: "Interior monologue is a coarse imitation, and one that imitates only the apparent traits of the uninterrupted and incessant flow of unspeaking speech." Lefort's point seems to be that as a "*coarse* imitation," interior monologue is not unspeaking speech but speaking speech.

21. Georges Politzer, *Critique des fondements de la psychologie* (Paris: Presses Universitaire de France, 1967 [1928]); English translation by Maurice Apprey as *Critique of the Foundations of Psychology* (Pittsburgh, Pa.: Duquesne University Press, 1994).

22. See J. B. Pontalis, "The Problem of the Unconscious in Merleau-Ponty's Thought," trans. Wilfred Ver Eecke and Michael Greer, in *Review of Existential Psychology and Psychiatry* 18 (1982–83): 83–96.

Editors' Note to the French Edition

The course entitled *L'institution dans l'histoire personnelle et publique* has been transcribed by Dominique Darmaillacq, on her own initiative. The course entitled *Le problème de la passivité* has been transcribed by Stéphanie Ménasé, on her own initiative. Claude Lefort has reread the manuscripts. The text of the first course has been established by D. Darmaillacq and C. Lefort, and that of the second by S. Ménasé and C. Lefort.

The set of Merleau-Ponty's manuscripts can be found at the Bibliothèque Nationale in Paris. Those which contain preparatory notes for the courses given at the Collège de France in 1954-55 make up volume 13. The dossier which concerns *L'institution* involves in total 104 sheets, of which the 67 that are numbered by the author constitute the course notes, properly speaking. The dossier which concerns *La passivité* involves 160 sheets, of which the 64 that are apparently numbered by the author form the course notes.

The concern of the editors of this volume was to make the reading of the text as easy as possible—that is, the concern was to make Merleau-Ponty's thought accessible—without making the text lose its character of being notes (this is obvious in the abridgements, the elliptical propositions, the condensations, the allusions, and also the repetitions). It was important to leave the syntax alone, but at times it seemed good to insert an article, a conjunction, or a verb which frees the reader from a useless hesitation. The words added are always between brackets.

The editors have had to make a choice, which was at times difficult, in two cases. In the first case, we had to make a choice when we were confronted with two versions of the same argument. The other case was when the course notes demanded clarifications or even assumed the knowledge of commentaries or quotations that we would then discover in the course notes' dossier. We made these choices, however, without always being able to determine what use Merleau-Ponty was to make of these quotations and what extension he was giving to them. Priority was given to the intelligibility of the text.

In the first case, what was at issue, most often, was two successive versions of an argument, where the second had the same enumeration as the first, except that the number on the second was accompanied by an asterisk. The first has been conserved only when it appeared to contain some direction of thought or some reference that it would have been unfortunate to neglect. The deletions have been indicated in the endnote, and, at times, some sentences of an eliminated passage have been restored. The boldest intervention has consisted in replacing the first eight sheets of *La passivité* with seven sheets of one note found in the dossier. There is no doubt that the second seven pages constituted a new revision of the beginning of the course, which is clearer and more concise. The reader should not be surprised at seeing a break in the Bibliothèque Nationale pagination at this point.

In the second case mentioned, it has been decided to include in the course notes, each time that it seemed necessary, and, of course, by indicating it, the quite rich content of complementary notes, on which Merleau-Ponty was basing himself. Thus we have not hesitated to insert the case of Dora, that of the heroes of *Gradiva*, or that of Frau B., who obtained the interpretation of "dreams that foretell the future." Without this information, the reader who is not very familiar with Freud would not be able to follow Merleau-Ponty's argument in the last part of the course.

Each course is followed by its summary. The references are collected at the end of the *Institution* course, and there one will find a selection of the passages which Merleau-Ponty mentions but does not explicitly cite. *The Problem of Passivity* includes Merleau-Ponty's reading notes on Proust and Freud and an appendix consisting of three brief texts on "The Freudian Unconscious." At the end, there is a bibliography of texts relevant to both courses.

At the beginning of each section of the two courses, the titles, which are in uppercase italicized letters between brackets, are not from Merleau-Ponty. They are simple landmarks in order to lay out the design of the text and thereby make it easier to read.

The double numbering of the sheets is indicated as follows: in brackets, there is the Bibliothèque Nationale's pagination; between parentheses, there is Merleau-Ponty's pagination of the sheets. For example, [2] (1) means page 2 of the Bibliothèque Nationale, and page 1 of Merleau-Ponty's manuscript. As we mentioned earlier, the appearance of asterisks indicates that we are using Merleau-Ponty's second version.

The italics indicate, besides the titles of works, terms that are subtitles, or expressions underlined by Merleau-Ponty. The appearance of a question mark between square brackets indicates that we were unable to decipher Merleau-Ponty's handwriting.

Translators' Note

Certain terms presented problems which we solved in the following ways. The term *reprise*, which appears frequently in these notes, a term which is central to the idea of institution, connotes the idea of taking up and of repetition. So we have usually rendered this term as "resumption," but at times as "taking up" or "recovery." We have rendered *événementielle* as "event-based," *imagines* as "imaginings," and *dépasser* as "to surpass" or sometimes "to overcome." In regard to Merleau-Ponty's discussion of memory, we have rendered *souvenir* as "recollection" and *mémoire* as "memory." We have tried to make use of Strachey's translations of Freudian terms. So when Merleau-Ponty has used the word *désir* in his discussion of Freud, we have generally rendered this word as "wish," but sometimes as "desire," as for instance in the *Institution* course when he speaks of love. For *complaisance* we used "compliance" in the context of Freud's concept of "somatic compliance," but elsewhere we used "indulgence." In general we rendered *sens* as "sense" or "meaning," depending on the context; occasionally we have rendered it as "direction." We rendered *signification* as "signification" or "significance" (following Lingis's practice in the English translation of *Le visible et l'invisible*). And usually we have rendered the famous term *écart* as "divergence" or "deviation." In both courses, but especially in *Institution,* Merleau-Ponty frequently uses the word *recherché*. Depending on the context, we have rendered the word as "research" or "search" (the context of Proust) or as "investigation" (the context of Kafka). In order to make the notes more readable in English, we have also modified Merleau-Ponty's punctuation by sometimes replacing punctuation with a word, or sometimes by changing one punctuation mark to another (a colon to a period, for example). Finally, text in reduced font indicates portions of Merleau-Ponty's notes that were composed apart from the lecture notes and inserted at another time.

We would like to thank Anthony Steinbock, who supported this project from the beginning. We are also grateful to Jenny Gavacs, Henry Carrigan, and Serena Brommel at Northwestern University Press for steering it to its completion. Joe Balay also deserves our thanks for compiling the index and checking citations. Renaud Barbaras and Mauro Carbone, as well as Darian Meacham and Davide Scarso, helped us clarify certain difficult passages in the courses. A research group in Montreal, made up of David Morris, Lisa Guenther, Shiloh Whitney, Noah Moss Brender, and Donald Beith, read through the entire *Institution* course and made many helpful and interesting comments about our translation.

INSTITUTION AND PASSIVITY

Part 1

Institution in Personal and Public History

Transcription by Dominique Darmaillacq. English translation by Leonard Lawlor and Heath Massey. Notes by Dominique Darmaillacq, Leonard Lawlor, and Heath Massey.

[INTRODUCTION]

[2] (1) Personal life considered as the life of a consciousness, i.e., a presence to the whole for which the other is empty negation [and] indifferent action, or, at the least, making sense only for me, through closed signification: the past exists for this consciousness only as consciousness of the past, i.e., as a picture that is overcome; a mode of presence that is entirely spectacular; doing something functions by means of an end, i.e., by means of a represented result, and [as] realization through the body of gestures and words which procure the past, [it is] the fiat of a signification. The decision [is] maintained, against the background of indifference, of the end.—Why do we maintain it? Descartes' [response]: we cannot do one thing and not do it; i.e., the action goes outside where it has to be or not be, a minimum of coherence is necessary so that we have tried, so that there is a teaching of this action, but we are never what we do because we are not it and because it is necessary that this signified non-being comes into the world.

Is this so? Are we this immediate presence to everything before which the things that are possible are all equal—all the things that are impossible? This whole analysis presupposes a prior reduction of our life to the "thought of . . ." living. This is to say 1) a distinction of form and content: *hyle* and *Auffassung als . . .*[1] 2) a distinction which has the purpose only of extracting the content, of turning it into an ob-ject for the "thought of" . . . , the signifying activity, considered as the sole thing that is concrete.

But, both this real form-content analysis and the position of the form as the a priori condition of the content are illusory. Both the empiricism of successive "sensations" or of "Abschattungen" and the idealism that rectifies the empiricism falsify the experience. When we approach an object or a recollection, there is no numerically distinct *Abschattungen*[2] and no *Auffassung als . . .* representation of one selfsame intelligible core, there are no instants and their ideal and signified unity, there is the consciousness of [the] thing and of its traces *on the basis of the thing*,[3] traces which will be differentiated if I reflect on the thing, but whose distinction is contemporaneous with the ideal unity—there is the consciousness of *Zeitpunkt*[4] which cannot cease having been, because it has been in impressional consciousness and not because it is identified as an ideal unity of temporal perspectives. Husserl's hesitation: the original, philosophically first mode, of consciousness, is it the *Auffassung als* (i.e., empty and [relative] consciousness, entirely outside of itself but exactly coextensive with being), or is it in fact the *Urempfindung*[5] (i.e., consciousness that is not [surmountable?] because it is that of a present whose past and future are modalizations, but in which I am surpassed, [since I experience the] thickness of the sensible, of the present, the thing-itself.)

[3] (2) With this notion of the subject, [we conceive a] change in the

1) *relation to the world*

[There is] immediate non-presence, but perspective understood as opening its beyond, leading to it by its very thickness, [which presupposes] relief, obstacles, configuration.

Someone will say: it is through relation to a project. If you like, but there is a non-decisionary project, not chosen, [an] intention without subject: living. This project [implies the] existence of norms or levels, uncrossable mountain, upright objects or not, paths. This does not mean that what I am doing is determined: I can learn to cross these "obstacles" or not. But it is on the basis of the given obstacle that I will learn. I can learn to know the surroundings better through science, but this will always be the reworking of the perceived world, the employment of its structures.

Therefore [there is an] instituted and instituting subject, but inseparably, and not a constituting subject; [therefore] a certain inertia—[the fact of being] exposed to . . .—but [this is what] puts an activity en route, an event, the initiation of the present, which is productive after it—Goethe: genius [is] "posthumous productivity"—which opens *a* future.

The subject [is] that to which such orders of events can advent, field of fields.

2) [relation] *to others.*

[The other is] not constituting-constituted, i.e., my negation, but instituted-instituting,[6] i.e., I project myself in the other and the other in me, [there is] projection-introjection, productivity of what I am doing in the other and of what he is doing in me, true communication through lateral practicing: [what is at issue is one] intersubjective or symbolic field, [the field] of cultural objects, which is our milieu, our hinge, our jointure—instead of the subject-object alternation.

3) [relation to] *doing*

not pure efficiency, which is the obsession of spectator consciousness, and assumes end + fiat.[7] Doing takes place in the same world as see-

INTRODUCTION

ing: it is my substance (gestures, words) which is directed towards the fissures of the landscape, towards the to-be done (just as a movement takes up the frozen movements of things). Doing knows that it is in the eyes of others, that it too is symbolic activity: it is not therefore the positing of an end and choice, but an operation according to a style, response to the *Sache*[8] not enclosed in a jealous signification, thereby it too institutes: Marx [says]: I am not a Marxist, Kierkegaard, the Christian does not say: I am a Christian. Sense as divergence, difference, not closed.

[4] (3) With [the notion of a] subject of the field of presence, renewal of [the conception] of time.
4) *time*
Is it necessary to say that time flows from the past, or that it flows from the future? Is time objective, enveloping—or, idealist reversal—consciousness of time, i.e., movement of negation of the past, pure in itself, in the name of a future which, itself, is not, i.e., time enveloped by my non-being? Time is not enveloping and not enveloped: there is from me to the past a thickness which is not made of a series of perspectives or of the consciousness of their relation, which is an obstacle and liaison (Proust). Time is the very model of institution:[9] passivity-activity, it continues, because it has been instituted, it fuses, it cannot stop being, it is total because it is partial, it is a field. One can speak of a quasi-eternity not by the escaping of instants towards the non-being of the future, but by the exchange of my times lived between the instants, the identification between them, the interference and static of the relations of filiation (cf. Guérin)[10] (neither an objective filiation nor the choice of the ancestors). Lateral kinship of all the "nows" which makes for their confusion, their "generality," a "trans-temporality" of decline and decadence. [But] the originary trans-temporality is neither decline and decadence nor moreover the presence of the future in the present (Permanent Revolution), but it is institution in the nascent state. Institution is neither mimicry of the past (Guérin) nor fulguration of the future (Trotsky). These two notions, moreover, are correlative (the mimicry of the past and the anticipation of the future; all the revolutions resemble one another; the bourgeoisie as instituted recognizes itself in the *ancien régime* as instituted and disavows the instituting bourgeoisie).[11] Originary time is neither decadence (delay back upon itself) nor anticipation (advance forward upon itself), but it is on time, the time that it is.

By these ways ([by discovering the] subject of the field of presence and its relation to the world, to others, to doing) we have encircled the philosophical content of the notion of institution.

[5] (4) Here [we introduce the] crucial notion of institution:

This word makes no sense for consciousness or, what amounts to the same thing, everything for consciousness is instituted in the sense of being posited. [The] relation with others [is conceived] as pact or contract. And even if we take account of the spirit of the contract, what is still contractual is that the prisoner is his jailer, that he is not subjected to the force of the other himself, but by his decision to constitute the other.[12] To constitute in this sense is nearly the opposite of to institute: the instituted makes sense without me, the constituted makes sense only for me and for the "me" of this instant. Constitution [means] continuous institution, i.e., never done. The instituted straddles its future, has its future, its temporality, the constituted depends entirely on the "me" who constitutes (the body, the clock).[13]

The relation to the past is different also: consciousness has no consciousness of being *born*. Birth: [it is] the passage from the moment where nothing was for X to the moment where everything is also for X. Such is the translation that consciousness makes of it, i.e., birth [means] first of all the openness of a future, from a background of non-being from which what was projects itself—[hence]: "born to." Birth is an act, and, like all acts, arises from nothing. Being was in itself (i.e., for the others) and suddenly effected in a new growth. So Colette's saying that this person has not come in through the door. Consciousness will say that this person came in through the door by means of the mother's body, this person did not come in through the door in the sense that he did not know it, and that later he will know this relative change of place of his body and of his framework, he will turn it into a positing of an end. Does the difference consist merely in that? Motility proper is not merely consciousness of means and ends. The crawling baby "gets away," the sleepwalker "goes out,"[14] in the sense that they are possibilities of the spatial situation, *exposed*, solicited by hunger, cold, weight, lights, something can happen to them, there is the openness of a field, i.e., from the moment of conception and still more after birth, there is an encroachment towards a future which is made from itself, under certain given conditions, and which is not the act of a *Sinngebung*.[15] Birth [is not an act] of constitution **[6] (5)** but the institution of a future. Reciprocally, institution resides in the same genus of Being as birth and is not, any more than birth, an act. There will be later decisionary institutions or contracts, but they are to be understood on the basis of birth and not the reverse.

Therefore institution [means] establishment in an experience (or in a constructed apparatus) of dimensions (in the general, Cartesian

INTRODUCTION

sense: system of references) in relation to which a whole series of other experiences will make sense and will make a *sequel*, a history.

The sense is deposited (it is no longer merely in me as consciousness, it is not re-created or constituted at the time of the recovery). But not as an object left behind, as a simple remainder or as something that survives, as a residue. [It is deposited] as something to continue, to complete without it being the case that this sequel is determined. The instituted will change but this very change is called for by its *Stiftung*.[16] Goethe: genius [is] posthumous productivity. All institution is in this sense genius.

What does that mean?

I. *Personal and Interpersonal Institution*
1) The institution of feelings
a) Prehistoric institution (which is uncovered for us only through archaeology)

Animal institution as "impregnation" ("imprint"). Difference from human identification [in which] the historical is reserved.[17] Problem in suspense and avoidance of the problem. How the question is reframed? Corporeal "causality" [puts] the problem back on the agenda. [Example of] institution as reactivation and transformation of a preceding institution: puberty. This institution can be either permanence of a ritual or true institution. And that depends on what the initial Oedipus complex has been: pathological or formative. "Investments," "cathexis."[18] How are we to understand these metaphors and the mode of presence to the subject of this entire subject that has been instituted?

b) Historical institution: birth of a love affair

The crystallization, or *cathexis* by means of someone. To find the path, between love as constituting, substance which is developed—and love as constituted,[19] i.e., choice of being seen in the other, of what one says and promises to him, of what he announces, of his response which produces sorcery because it announces to me what I will be—in short, love as the voluntary phantasmagoria of the other.

Swann in Love: the "errors" that generate love, errors committed because of the obsession with the other and from jealousy and from the need of being recognized by this unknown, who is a mirage because either too human and valueless or truly the other and negation of me. [Take up this] interpretation of Swann's love: the objection [according to which] this singular mode of love goes in the direction of the error (through predominance of the other and imaginary fulfillment **[7] (6)** of this other—general love in relation to which the object is contingent).

This objection is worthless, since all love is in each love. In Proust, there is also the masochistic component, wanting to love, and not only the sadistic component, wanting to be loved, to be complete again.[20] In *The Fugitive*, the disappearance of Albertine is not only the highest point of privation, the narrator recognizes that one is deprived only of what one loves, that it is he who has made Albertine into a liar and fugitive, that, in this jealousy, he has joined up with and made Albertine herself, made therefore the irreality, the non-realization of their love,[21] and that that is to love—a way of loving. Likewise, the one who did not want to be loved recognizes in the privation that he did not want to be loved because he was loved, that he counted on this love, that he rejected it only by knowing that it was acquired. Therefore the whole "irreality" of love is due to the fact that one is never anything but oneself, but there is a reality of love that is due to the fact that this self has, however, married the form of another presence, or even has given birth to it such that the form of the other presence showed itself.[22]

Institution [means] that this body, these gestures, these words, this life becomes the retort or the inverse of mine, and that happens beyond what is willed, experienced, known, since words have more senses than we give to them. To love, placed before analytic and spectator consciousness, *is only* to want to be loved because the other [for this form of consciousness] is only a not-me, constituting-constituted, and because to love can be only to become oneself again. The instituting subject invests itself, i.e., animates itself with another meaning, transforms itself by means of its love, i.e., succeeds in making a meaning which is transcendent to him dwell in his *I think* and in his body, as a meaning dwells in the book and the cultural object.

2) The institution of works

Therefore the visible institution is only the support of a spirit of the institution, certainly not immutable (love changes constantly, like a separation), but whose very change is a reaction of the event upon the instituted. An instituted is necessary so that there is an open register, history.

Likewise in [the] institution of a work. This is not the fact of a closed signification, or, if there is one, it changes en route. [There is an] emptiness in the writer or painter prior to beginning. It is by writing or painting that one discovers. Not by means of associative relations of language or of colors. But insofar as the book advances we discover things that are consonant. This is because the partial view was a total view. But this silent project is known only through its partial realizations (in some

INTRODUCTION

such chapter). A book is a series of institutions and makes obvious that every institution tends toward being a series. This is where the impression comes from that the book produces itself. What does the "total" signification mean? It exists only at infinity as the sum of encounters of other minds with the work. But institution [8] (7) nevertheless has an internal sense and has an external sense only because of this internal sense. Badly understood, but understood. This internal sense precisely induces the external sense because it is open, because it is a divergence in relation to a norm of sense, *difference*. It is this sense by divergence, deformation, which is proper to institution.

Noticeable in the action of the work on the author.[23] What is at issue is not the simple help of memory, recording, depositing. The author is not reread or cannot be reread because there is precisely not this imposition of a "beyond" of the signs which is realized with others. The "beyond" of the signs, the author has it already. The work does not have its relief in front of him. However, to have written or painted this or that changes him. To the point that he would not be able to make it again precisely because he has made it. Or he remakes it differently. Is this exactly progress of ideas? Formation of new concepts? But in this case [the] subsequent works should *form a sequel;* but this is often not the case: change of manner of the painter; change of the writer (we always prefer his book before the last one). This is because what is written has realized certain instruments, operational concepts, defined by their use value, type of praxis, and not as essences. The book is instituted, established as (private) institution—insofar as to organize the signs in a way that results in a book of magic; this is to set up the difference, the personal divergence in the norm, to turn it into a new norm, in relation to which other divergences are possible. This is where new polarization of the field and change come from. The repercussion is exercised according to the unknown equivalences of the painter, but equivalences which will be able to be recognized after the fact when the repercussion will be in its turn instituted. So that there is a genuine development, research (and not semblance of development), it is necessary that the new means become truly norms of the praxis, of the theoretico-practical landscape, and that the new lived-experience is measured in relation to them. Revolution and institution: the revolution is reinstitution, resulting in the reversal of the preceding institution. (Cf. puberty: immanent problem recovered and resolved by rupture.)

3) The institution of a domain of knowledge

To apply the notion of institution itself to knowledge, and not only to knowledge through language, but to knowledge through algorithm.

Here, however, it seems that what is at issue is the conquest which is resumed in concepts, i.e., in possession of intelligible beings: the algebraic number, the irrational number, etc. The surpassing seems to render useless what is surpassed. Therefore, not institution, i.e., open sense of a certain apparatus, but a timeless system of ideas from which little by little we form knowledge but which stands in the eternal.

It is true that there is a surpassing, but at the same time as this relation, [9] (8) there is an inverse relation according to which what is surpassed is not only the condition of the existence of the surpassing, but in a sense remains its model. The surpassing surpasses only through recurrence. Certainly, there is no need to reactivate everything in order to make use of the surpassing, it has its own evidence, it is not only the conservation of what has been surpassed and abbreviation, but the revolutions themselves will be made by means of putting back in question the *field* defined by what has been surpassed and therefore reactivation.[24] For example, when one passes from Cartesian mathematics to later mathematics. This is to say that there really was a particularized and a partial institution, burdening a whole development with partiality. Revolution is a return to the sources, reawakening of what surrounds the founding idealizations, of their context, future which has passed, which is a more profound understanding of the past, which is *gestiftet* by this past in an ambiguous way.[25] Double aspect of institution: it is itself and beyond itself, restriction and openness. This is where the definition of truth through a double relation comes from (Wertheimer).[26] This is not only the inclusion of a concept in a larger essence (the inclusion of the arithmetical number in the generalized number), it is also a sort of immanence of the larger essence in the particular cases by means of which the essence manifests itself first.

Institution therefore [is] neither perceived nor thought as a concept. It is the wherewithal on which I count at each moment, which is seen nowhere and is assumed by everything that is visible for a human being, it is what is at issue each moment and which has no name and no identity in our theories of consciousness.

II. *Historical Institution*

Apparently clear sense: the "body" of the State, organic laws, subjected to special procedures of revision—and the apparatuses that they set up.

Nevertheless that accentuates (in the psychoanalytic sense) institution as the letter without the spirit of the institution. Which mutilates institution. Institution [is not only] what has been fixed by means of contracts, but that plus functioning.

INTRODUCTION

True institution [is the] actual framework of the dynamic of the system, whether it is official or not. It is often in the latent content that we find what is most important, the reason for the *Stiftung*[27] (example: abstract idealism made in order to maintain [the] power of the bourgeoisie or in any case is systematic with it).

Thereby the very general sense of institution is not the opposite of revolution; revolution is another *Stiftung*.

Thereby the double aspect of institution.
1) universalizing 2) particularizing.

1) Universalizing [10] (9)

[It would be] excessive to call every non-natural event an institution: [the introduction] of the potato, of corn. Already the "Neolithic Revolution," or the Industrial Revolution of the eighteenth century, are institutions in a more pregnant sense: not only events of great consequence, but event-matrixes, opening a historical field which has unity. Institution [is] what makes possible [a] series of events, [a] historicity: in principle event-ness.

To be discussed: Lévi-Strauss's [thesis]: [28] no difference [between the events]. The series of events are probabilities and chance. [Here and there an] agglomeration of events [has taken place]. Institution [is] residue, sum of the parts. Kinship [is the] play of certain elements of social life that chance reunites (example, binary structure, reciprocity, etc.). Humans mount "cultural affairs,"[29] but only chance makes the results. [Between] cumulative history and static history [the] difference [is] merely relative. [Thus] h[istory] is produced where there is a number of diverse factors ([in the case of] Europe at the moment of the discovery of the New World), providing a greater probability; [conversely] history is relatively static [when] the institution [is still] isolated.[30]

Question: isn't there a foundation for this diversity itself and for the cumulative capacity? Max Weber: in fact, a fortuitous meeting is necessary, but on the basis of these conditions a system which has its logic (Cosmos) is engendered. Example, capitalism [proceeds from the conjunction of elements concerning different domains]: law, State, religion, science—"free" labor, accountability, etc. But all of that forms a cosmos, and other elements that are assembled do not form one. Lévi-Strauss indicates precisely that the pre-Columbian civilizations have "advanced" traits, but have "gaps."[31] Institution in the strong sense [is] this symbolic matrix that results in the openness of a field, of a future according to certain dimensions, and from this result we have the possibility of a common adventure and of a history as consciousness. Why does something advent? (Lévi-Strauss says that it is because you are not inside that it seems to you that nothing happens.) But it is still the case that the event-ness of Western history is recognized by others.[32] Relativism gets carried away. It is a Western conception (of Lévi-Strauss) and one which [11] (10) includes all the others and itself, while the primitive Brazilians weep for pity to think of the sufferings he must have endured so far away from them.[33] We cannot judge the given in the name of the event-basis. It is not by accident that there is no trace of most of the civilizations and that on the contrary we attempt to restore the history of them.—Someone will say: but that is merely because we have created means of transportation in order to explore, writing, ink, paper, learned societies, science ... it is the cooperation of circumstances which provides us with more of an event-character.

But is there only coincidence, or, as Weber says,[34] a *Rationalisierung* which turns all the facts into *Wahlverwandschaft*?[35]

2) Particularizing

But, at the same time, institution is always particularizing; even the thought of the eighteenth century or of the nineteenth century is ingeniously dogmatic. The true history, the true institution, has to know precisely this particularity (Lucien Febvre and Rabelais).[36] The triumph of universality consists precisely in making me capable of understanding differences. But then, how are we to understand them truly? (Malraux, Febvre).

Is there a single horizon of all the institutional horizons? Does history understand on the basis of the nonhistorical?

Institution therefore has a double facet and thereby holds this last question in reserve.

Novelty of this conception, therefore, in regard to [a] philosophy of history founded on consciousness (Hegel).

Capital [must be] considered as an institution and not as a shadow, hollowed-out trace of a socialist production, of a classless society, i.e., of the absolute consciousness where each is each only by being all. Thereby [the] Marxist revolution (which is the eminent product of Western historicity, since it is the idea that the entire history is instituted *for* a future that is already there) changes its sense when [the] Revolution is itself conceived as institution,[37] for this is to say that it is not 1) the end of history[38] and 2) not even the surpassing of the institution, institution of the non-instituted or of the out-of-balance creator, i.e., permanent revolution.

A sort of Marxist idealism inherited from Hegel.

[Our] philosophical perspective: not idealism of absolute consciousness, but truly openness and truth as mystery. Existence turning back upon itself but without succeeding in carrying itself away.

History and intersubjectivity **[12] (11)**

[The idea of an] originary rationality in private history: History [becomes] "the relation between people mediated by things." Understanding is always resumed by someone. Therefore by studying [the] relation of [the] person to public history and [to the] anonymous institution, we will be able to determine [the] sense of public history's rationality.

But the person himself [must be] understood as institution, not as consciousness of . . .

From then on strange relation. No *separation* between private institution and public institution. The Oedipus complex [looks to be both] private and public, cause and caused. Our whole society imposes it (culturalism, the care for children) and it sustains our society (coincidence of historical, cumulative, and Oedipal "civilizations"). Truly this is not causality. It is two symbolic systems in which each makes sense of the other. The private and the public connected not through commitment in the event, but through echoes, exchanges, symbolic accumulation[39]—therefore it is true that such a morality, such an ideology is reactionary and conversely such a mode of labor sustains spirit.[40]

That freedom and truth are [indissoluble?]. The freedom of pure negativity is a signification, just as the verbalized cogito is derived from the tacit or instituted cogito. We have no experience of it. Experience in the Cartesian sense (*sunt quaedam quae quilibet debeat apud se experiri potius quam rationibus persuaderi*)[41] and Spinozist sense (eternity) are not the originary experience which is that of instituting.

[INSTITUTION AND LIFE]

Institution—Animality—Life[1] **[13] (12)**
***

The instituted in opposition to the innate (as what is acquired), in opposition to natural maturation ([as] learning), to the internal environment ([as] external environment), to the physiological ([as] psychological [and] social).

The instituted cannot be defined in this way. For there is no pure innate, no pure endogenous maturation, no pure internal environment, no pure physiology.

Proof: animality which, with instinct, should have all of that, and which is in reality below (fragmented instinctive themes,[2] the non-solidity of instinct) and above (relative plasticity of instinct, resemblance to human attitudes). And even the organism: pure physiology cannot be defined (embryology: [the] functional viewpoint [is] necessary in order to explain [the] structure itself).

Hence, [the] problem: [since there is an] environment of animal life (instinctive "gnosis,"[3] "localized" learning),[4] [there is an] environment of the organism (finalism) ("non-pure" purposiveness:[5] cf. dream half-causal, half-logical).[6]

No matter what interpretation (trans-spatial "form in itself," neo-finalism—or philosophy of the perceived world) (we shall return to that in the other course),[7] [we must] start from this usage in order to discover the true sense of human institution.
***

I. Institution and Life **[16] (12*)**
1) *The Organism*
The graft of a paw adapts itself to the territory in which it is inserted in order to become a right paw or a left paw. But if already determined as right, [it] can't adapt itself: "There is . . . in the determination of the destiny of an organic outline a very fleeting moment of lability in which what the outline will become is irreversibly fixed by the place in which it is found" (Ruyer).[8]

Therefore 1) plasticity; 2) limited by consideration of place. Destiny instituted in the sense that 1) it is not absolutely given with the internal innate structure; 2) it is never independent from the givens (time and place).[9]

In general for the embryo: 1) the development is already a behavior;[10] 2) the behavior develops by way of organic outlines.

1) the embryo is regulated by semicircular canals, respiratory movements (absorb and expel amniotic liquids). Function [is not the] simple effect of structure.[11]

INSTITUTION AND LIFE

2) [the] behavior first follows the tracks of the organization. Gesell: twins picking up pills with the same postural attitude, position of the hand, etc.[12]

No precise limit between organization and life (Bergson). "Side by side" determination, causality, determination: triggers of "reaction,"[13] "signals"; trans-spatial feedbacks: what acts in reverse upon the cause is not only the deviation between result and the existing, material aim[14] ([?]), but deviation between result and "idea" or "mnemonic theme."

Organism: not only irreversible duration (accumulation, aging, stages of life)—not only cyclical history that the duration produces—but history and institution in the sense of: reference to a sense. Simply this sense is fixed by the species or by "competence" for certain territories. There is the fruitfulness of the event but between two limits: 1) the species, 2) monstrosity. Another use of the event at inferior degrees.

2) *Animality*

Imprint: "Imprinting," "Prägung."[15] Geese in incubators refuse to be fixated on the geese couple and follow the observer. Starred heron in the Amsterdam Zoo adopts the guardian, leaves and chases the other herons away in favor of the guardian and tries to attract him into its nest (unpublished text by Ruyer).

Relation of the being to the encounter: simultaneously it is pretraced. The geese follow the human in such a way that the angle of sight remains the same as for the parents. The human swims, **[17] (13*)** the geese get close, are upright, lost; the human must move forward crouched down; Lorenz and the bicycle. The imprint exists "upon a foundation of general innate and expected themes."[16]

*The imprint connected to a certain "pace" of the trigger,[17] "expressive," "significant" stimulus. The experimenter must move and speak. No cathexis by means of a stuffed duck. And in contrast, cathexis by means of supra-normal stimuli, experimental Platonism,[18] sensitizing to themes (eggs that are unnaturally spotted, darker females).

The human, moreover, will never be treated as a being that needs to be protected (the jackdaw bird protects only young jackdaw).—But at the same time the encounter is the decisive factor. A goose which is raised with chickens rejects the gander and will make advances to the rooster. The white peacock who, when placed inside the tortoise room at the [Schönberg?] Zoo, becomes aroused only with the tortoises and is deaf and blind to peacocks.

Therefore here [the] relation of the being and the event [is not] only contamination of the being by the "competence" of a place or by the mnemonic theme of the species. But *Prägung* by means of the encounter that is external and outside of the species.

Hence, even in normal cases

1) Appearance of a determinator of sexuality which is the alter ego. Sexuality developed by life in common: the retrospective and prospective species.

2) Recommencement of this initial "choice" a lot later: analogous capacity of adult choice. Falling in love:[19] "This male jackdaw bird . . . purchased by Lorenz when it was already an adult is taken with Lorenz and treats him exactly like a female of its species. The bird tried to draw him into the hole which was serving as its nest and which was only a few inches in size. The bird also sets about nourishing Lorenz (as a male does for its female in order to woo it) by pushing some grains of bread which the bird had stuck together with its saliva, pushing them at him towards the mouth or the ear." Monogamy of a lot of animals.

The weight of these events is even much greater in species that are more "premature."

3) Cathexis not only from the other (and from another that is not fixed once and for all) but also from the world as the place of the encounter with the other: the "territory." Election of a territory by mammals and birds. Hometown and hometown girlfriend; sweet heart and sweet home.[20]

***

3) *The human*[21]

This activity of life or of "animality" will really make an echo in humans. Not [that] human societies [are] termite nests,[22] but inversely [there are] human behaviors in the animal: quasi-Freudian "displacements" in the animals: the woman who "makes the baby."

Elective love and falling in love[23] in animals as in humans. The gosling has the human "in its skin"—the property [is] the territory [. . .?].

The human is animal instinct ever ripe. Embryonic brain at birth.

[15] (14) Fruitful moments when "the mind turns to girls," when the man marries "the girl of his youth" (Ecclesiastes) [?] Conrad in the West Indies for months. Genius lives from certain imprints.[24] Is respiration a "mechanism" or does it not live from respiratory themes?[25]

However, immense difference: not that the human *does not have* animal institution, but because of *the use that he makes of it* and that usage transforms institution genuinely.

Not only because the human codifies it, legalizes it, creates social symbols. That is not the *first* difference.

But in that, even considering only the individual imprint independently of cultural patterns, the human turns it into something else.

The first imprint is a "symbolic matrix," that is, it resurrects chain reactions not only at some given moment, not only by means of mechanical reactivation

INSTITUTION AND LIFE

at puberty, but also [then] an *investigation* that distances it, if need be, from itself. Not simply reproduction, but the getting underway of an "investigation" in Kafka's sense:²⁶ the image sensitizes itself.

***

Character of These Behaviors

Prospective and open. More precisely, there are "receptions" which are fruitful and evaluate dimensions (the "territory," the sole love, the "individual of the same species"). Therefore *Stiftung* of a future.

Hence quasi-human behaviors: displacement ("the animal, at once excited and embarrassed, bends this excitation into instinctive acts without relation to or in vaguely analogous relation to the objective cause of the excitation: amorous parading about or pseudo-sleep during a battle in order to defend the territory; a song after a wound; smoothing of feathers or the taking in of nourishment when the bird is bothered by the presence of an observer . . . acting as if wounded or "trance reaction" when there is no enemy present following some sort of frustration").²⁷ This displacement presupposes substitutes, i.e., not only sense, but double sense. Magical equivalences. [18] (14*) Not only articulated universe, but universe of agglutinated causality, which is free in regard to the given universe.

—displacement that is not residual but efficacious, assumption of roles: "a woman who 'makes the baby' in front of a man, and who begs for small symbolic gifts as proof of his power, meets up with a theme that is already well constituted in birds who 'demand symbolic nourishment': a female will pester her male although she finds herself on a manger filled with wheat mites or though she has a mouth full of insects for her little ones. By means of this transfer of food, the female of the bird returns to her youth and resumes the behavior of the gosling."²⁸

But does that make human institution? No. Human institution is not only the utilization of the past or the utilization of an experience as a substitute, or even the creation of a register of substitution (birdgosling). Human institution is still the integration of this past into a new signification. The animal-human difference is not [between] causality [and] prospection. Already in the animal there is prospection; there is never pure prospection in the human.

But human institution is nevertheless clear. It is the past becoming a symbolic matrix.

Therefore the animal-human relation: why do animals haunt us, interest us (children—primitives—religions—[?] [?]).²⁹ Freud: they are only substitutes. We think about animals in order to disguise the human, as we think about the upper half of the body in order to disguise the lower. Negative explanation. Animality as variant of humanity

(Husserl)—La Fontaine: disguise the criticism. In order to take account of the positive interest, one must not conceive [the] animal [as] machine and [the] human [as] consciousness, nor even [the] animal [as] instinct and [the] human [as] consciousness [plus] instincts. We must conceive animal temporality as being already open to a future (domestic animals), therefore providing an image touching on the human, an image of the human who does not understand, weak human. [Therefore] the gentleness of the superego towards him, the humor of animality as parody of humanity. Thereby [think] not the animal-human, not the human-animal, but truly the one being the alter ego for the other, because we do not have the one *inside* time and the other *outside* of time. The surpassing preserves. Kinship of finitudes. Our displacement onto the animal reflects the animalization of the human by the animal.

3) *Vital Institution and Human Institution*

Therefore past-future relation: symbolic matrix, and research that conforms to it (cf. Kafka: investigations of a dog).

But the investigation is precisely of another kind. Which?

[Problem] to study in relation to institution: sexuality

1) of the pre-genital or of the phallic in the latent Oedipus complex
2) of the latent Oedipus complex **[19] (15)**
3) of the latent in puberty
4) involute transition: menopause

Speak especially about 2 and 3.

a) Of the latent Oedipus complex: Institution of the phase of latency: proper mode of human temporality

On the basis of Freud: *The Passing of the Oedipus Complex* (1924)[30]

Freud indicates two interpretations:

1) the Oedipus complex disappears by means of maturation. Cf. baby teeth. Hereditary and phylogenetic conditions. It must disappear "when the next pre-ordained stage of development happens."[31]

2) it is surpassed by means of experience:

a) disappointment: [the] girl believes that she is really loved by the father and is punished. [The] son believes that he is really loved and sees that he is deprived of being given exclusive attention (a new child). Fear of castration [gives rise to] internalization and the ebbing of the first thrust.

b) Even when there is no disappointment: absence of gratification, "continuous frustration" of the will to have a child (i.e., to be the parent of the same sex). "The Oedipus complex becomes extinguished by its lack of success, the result of its inherent impossibility."[32]

Freud refuses to choose. He concedes both. Even if there is a *schedule*, it is necessary to study "the way in which the innate schedule is worked out."[33]

This is typical of Freud: in appearance physiologism, phylogenetic explanation which is standard during Freud's time. (Since even the phagocytosis of baby teeth today [is not considered as a] *schedule*, but as a dynamic moment. Cf. dehiscence of fern spores: "achievement" substituted for the dynamic of formation. Therefore the ontogenetic factor of phylogenesis is needed and every development is actual dialectic. No engrams.)

In fact, retaining both and speaking of a *working out* of the *schedule*, [Freud has a] profound intuition: not only "psychological explanation" and ideal dialectic, but also concrete dialectic.

We see it in what he says about *passing* on the basis of experience: immanent impossibility.[34] That consists in the fact that he cannot be his father, they are distinct. The Oedipus complex as the will to **[20] (16)** the impossible. As pre-maturation. Imaginary sexuality. [The] child's own body [is] perceived by means of that of the parents, in a relation of identification with their bodies. Disappointment, frustration [are implied in the] rupture of this unity. Castration [means the] reduction of one's own body to one's own body. That is made out of the structure whose incidents (the parents' threats, etc.) are only a punctuation or an illustration. Therefore Freud is not against (dialectical) structure and for the empirical explanation by means of events.

The regression and the passage to latency [mark the] end of a premature, imaginary pseudo-integration, [the] failure, [the] non-institution, [the] return to the ego [from which comes the] development of the ego and of techniques, curiosity disguised by knowledge, [thus] the preparation of a detour.

b) Puberty

How are we to represent resumption and institution?

The *schedule* of the body? Physiological, hormonal development, etc. Yes. But how is this *schedule worked out*? There is a working out which is 1) supported by the corporeal dynamic and not by the corporeal calendar; 2) where all the experiences and in particular the experiences earlier than the Oedipus complex intervene, the acquisitions of pre-maturation.

The formative event or institution [is not] merely corporeal, not merely psychical, but a nexus of the one with the other.[35] The "premature" is now mature, not according to a *schedule*, but when the materials of behavior are truly capable of receiving the anticipated form. Institution [is] at the crossing over of an anticipation and of a regression.

Premature: phallic (auto-erotic) love: immediate, infinite pleasure, and then sadistic and aggressive love giving way to an object by means of identification with the parent of the same sex. But this identification even as the Oedipus complex was realizing it was still with the immediate, encountered impossibility. It is necessary once again to learn to distance oneself in order to achieve infinite pleasure.—Reactivation of all of that at the moment of puberty [with] the resumption of the Oedipus complex and the displacement onto [an] object which is an object: a living being of the other sex who is outside [the] family. Pre-maturation and reactivation mean presence of the universal in the first symbolic matrix and the permanence of the particular in the new institution. Institution [is therefore] advent of a sense which is oblique and which is not a pure surpassing, not a pure forgetfulness. It is the forgetfulness which would be false (prepubescent) maturity.

[**21**] (17) Is it the body, is it the mind that becomes pubescent? Corporeal tracks? No. Psychological tracks, [that is to say] knowledge? No. Social tracks, the learning of the Oedipus complex by means of the attention given by the parents. This is a particular case of the lived Oedipus complex, of the mirror play between mother and child, of identification—likewise the social tracks of puberty are nothing as long as there is no elaboration in one's own life, in one's own body, resumption. No tracks, but elaboration of an "inherent possibility" or human institution. What defines human institution? A past which creates a question, puts it in reserve, makes a situation that is indefinitely open. Therefore at once the human [is] more connected to his past than the animal and is more open to the future. The future by means of a deepening of the past: fruitful moments: acquisition of certain schemas that the artist develops indefinitely. Conrad in the West Indies only for a few months. Institution [is] neither chance nor entelechy. One does not change and never remains the same. One is absolutely free and absolutely prefigured.

Human institution: [it is] chained integration, a whirlwind where everything converges, where everything succeeds; the *Deckung*[36] of an anticipation and of a regression and the founding of a true *now* that is full.

Human institution always resumes a prior institution, which has posed a *question*, i.e., a question which was its anticipation—and which has failed. It reactivates this problem and human institution reunites its givens in [a] totality that is centered otherwise. Instituted [means] segment of a history.

The mode of existence of the question, like that of the answer, is not psychological. It is not a state of consciousness (anxiety) and it is not an object of consciousness. The modes of existence of the question and answer are *dimensions* of a field, dimensions in which all of what is lived is distributed, but which are not lived for themselves.

[The] mode of existence of institution, like that of the reactivated "past" and of the "anticipated" future, is not yet a content of consciousness.

In regard to the institution of puberty [22] (16*)

1) We were examining [the] latency phase. At once the failure of the Oedipus complex, failed institution, and a properly human phase is being put in place: latency, which is going to be the development of the ego, of means, of techniques for living, after the failure of the immediate identification with the parents, after the rupture of the imaginary identity, immediacy of the bodies, earlier than the proper/objectal impulse of life.

2) By means of this failure and this detour, we see that the institution of puberty presupposes

—1) Anticipation, pre-maturation, immediate transport toward the goal, being capable of the imaginary and not only being capable on the basis of articulated relations.

Failure by means of the immanent impossibility of this immediacy. The child is not the parent of the same sex.

—2) And [he] can become the parent of the same sex only in an internal way, by means of putting it in reserve, mediation, acquisition of the means, and not only capitation, but also oblation, or a truly objectal relation. Puberty would be the ramification of life over all the latent acquisitions: new impulse of desire which comes to animate the apparatus of the Ego.

3) Therefore human institution [is] the transformation which preserves (resumption of the Oedipus complex, regression of the pre-puberty) and surpasses. (The Oedipus complex failed only because it was "pre-maturation." It set up a movement towards the future.) Oscillation of pre-puberty between infantilism and aggressive futurism. The true institution of puberty [is] the past referred to its place and [the]

future truly open to the individual. Synonymy of institution and truth: truth which becomes. I.e., institution condenses and opens up a future. Not simply an imprint, but fruitful imprint. Growth by successive waves, or by means of detours.

4) Question and answer: question or investigation immanent to the history of the individual, and which finds then an answer. The answer is not given with the questions (in Marx's sense: humanity poses only questions that it can answer). The answer is truly new, but it is not so new that it creates the question (like the decision which precedes the deliberation, in the choice or pure creation.)[37] The question is earlier like something that haunts, consciousness of a determinate-indeterminate, which **[23] (17)** neither the wholly objective conception of the development (*schedule*, Marx's conception in this phrase) nor [the] conception of the development by choice and creative consciousness sees. Choice in the psychoanalytic sense is going to be the passage from [the] question in itself, latent, to [the] solution, the junction of the proper becoming and of certain learned themes. There we find institution and we have to make it more precise.

5) Medium of institution (of puberty): [what is it?], and at the same time, are there tracks?
Body? Hormones, growth? All of that is necessary but not sufficient. Creates disequilibrium or anxiety. But no resolution just from oneself. Acts like a blind thrust against external and internal obstacles, but which can as well and alternatively result in regression, i.e., in the resumption of an attitude of pre-maturation which refers to aggressiveness.
Experience? [namely] experience acquired over the course of the latency? Relations to friends, knowledge of social stereotypes by means of language and literature. All of that certainly plays into it. It is the conscious extension of cultural initiation from the beginning: parental concerns, which are the inverse of a conception of the human; the cultural objects of the adult world (furniture, etc.) arouse in the child [a] homological answer (whether it be negative or positive). Therefore B.P.S.[38] But what would all of that be if there were no relation with the Oedipus complex as it is lived?[39] Reciprocal relations certainly. Social roles and family roles learned together. But [the] social roles [are not] a simple imprint. What is decisive is the elaboration which turns these anonymous "significations" into moments of a personal drama. Therefore no social tracks, no deep or real centering.

INSTITUTION AND LIFE

What is essential to experience is therefore the Oedipal history as the openness of the register in which all the rest comes to be inscribed. The absolute love of childhood as the anticipation. The institution is made in this same medium. As the "passage" of the Oedipus complex results from its immanent impossibility, the beginning of puberty is going to be the immanent possibility of the relation to others, with all of its components, both archaic (state of the Oedipus complex and traumas), **[24] (18)** and notional (acquired significations and techniques). Cf. stairway that one constructs oneself. Cf. writer learning to speak with his own voice, by speaking first. Institution is the recentering of all of that around a new pole, [the] establishment of a system of distribution of values or of significations, a system which is *practiced* like the phonematic system of a language (principles of discrimination), but which is not acquired notionally, because the notional is always based in the positive and because the diacritical is always deeper. For example, the internalization of the parents, which brings along relaxation and helps the passing of the Oedipus complex, [is not] the presence of significations in the subject. But rather, it is the systematic extraction that the subject works precisely upon that of which it is conscious, a consciousness that does not want to recognize itself. It perceives the world as if through other eyes. That avoids conflicts with the external parents, but there is likewise a trace in it of the primitive identification: the struggle with the parents is transformed into a struggle with oneself. Therefore, since there are no tracks, but the reaction of a history upon itself, and the originary impulsion of pre-maturation, institution does not absolutely liquefy what preceded it.

Medium of institution: the libido. It is the becoming of the total relation with the world and others insofar as actual and not official, not imaginary. The true history of our cathexes, of our polarities. Lived and unrecognized like every dimension (cf. Wertheimer's experiment). Institution: the establishment of a dimension.

6) Institution and personal history

Institution is therefore real and never finished.

Real: there is change that is truly observable, there is "normal" puberty, [that is,] sufficient quantity of libido invested in objectal love of the opposite sex, so that the adult history is not the simple substitute of the childhood history recommenced.

But this "reality," this "Endstiftung," resumes an "Urstiftung,"[40] and, for this reason, is never an absolute beginning, extends and "interprets" the initial mode of the Oedipus complex, does not therefore erase it. The "liberation" is therefore always relative, and the cases of simple repetition and of pure creation are limit cases of the more substantial relation. Therefore institution does not get carried along as if it had a date and followed a certain past. "Normal" puberty is incomplete. It is masked as much as it is truth, it is acquired only on the terrain of the anonymous. Pre-maturation is never entirely eliminated and neither is the possibility of regression. It is not the end of history, nor even of prehistory; it opens another history which is going **[25] (19)** to be again a "search": the history of a love affair. The exploration of this past is not finished, never will be finished, because it is pre-maturation, absolute and impossible love.

7) Parallel with problems in the philosophy of history:
[There is a] common concept of revolution as the state that surpasses prior contradictions. *Schedule* of objective historical development. There would be an objective point of maturity in which the revolution is inscribed in the true, factual state of history. But in fact [the] revolution [is produced] in backward countries: prematuration. Is it therefore objective maturity?

Examined more closely: there is the anticipation of the Revolution. It is already in [the] "internal mechanism" of premature forms. Consequence: it results in there being a historical deterioration, since the proletarian revolution demotes the 1793 "bourgeoisie" revolution and identifies it with the Ancien Régime, after 1793 the proletarian revolution puts something non-progressivist in the "bourgeoisie" revolution. If the Revolution is anticipated, it is also the case that it is repeated, and we can wonder if it was ever "pure." Therefore we have the second sense of "permanent revolution": to be redone in the direction of the revolution itself. Process, not state. But that means in the end [that the] revolution [is the] institution of a regime in which nothing is instituted, the institution of an out-of-balance creator. That would synthesize [the ideas of] revolution always in advance of itself and always too late for itself. Institution is the *Selbstaufhebung*[41] descending into history.

But that means true self-criticism, i.e., internal and loyal opposition. In the fact [of revolution, the opposition] stops functioning: no internal opposition. Therefore no *Selbstaufhebung*, no realized negativity, we have a positive regime.

Therefore real but relative revolution. Real: the social relations are no longer the same; [it is] absurd to want to return to the former regime; classes are no more. But relative: this is not the end of history nor even of prehistory, because this is not the *Aufhebung* of history by means of itself, absolute truth of absolute consciousness, because there is still a lot to criticize and because we are not criticizing it. [The] revolution is really the surpassing of social infantilism, pre-maturation. But not an absolutely new history, without any relation to the prehistory, terminated. [Therefore] relative justification of the revolution. But the justification which it does not want.

[INSTITUTION OF A FEELING]

Institution of a Feeling [26] (20)
Cathexis or crystallization. How does a feeling "take hold"? Common idea of a preordination, of a nature calling forth a feeling. And consequently the idea of a reality and growth of the feeling as if it were an organism.

To which is opposed: no truth, nor falsity of the feeling. As soon as it is felt, it is true. And it is never true as conformity to a nature or to a destiny.

It is created by oath, decision, i.e., promised behavior. But we throw ourselves into it, i.e., we end up feeling, and not only acting, according to the promise. If we did not feel according to the promise, it is because we have not truly decided or promised, a half-decision is a decision to be double. The true decision results in the feeling.

What supports it and helps it is that the other person is the mirror of my decision. Answers me according to what I say to him. Each spoken thing receives the support of this answer, but it is the echo of this speech. I fashion the other person. Nevertheless, the "answer" looks to be a miracle, preordination, destiny. Alain: the Chartreux's rule of silence. Man is a sorcerer for man. Man forgets that the other is, like him, the fortunate freedom of being destitute, of being handed over to destiny. He sees a preordained correspondence in the other. And forgets the freedom of the other is like his own. Therefore [the] mirage of common life, which is sewn together by this double illusion. In truth there are two lives, each of which is constructed freely. What defines love, what makes its fate legendary is 1) [the] secret consciousness of this freedom; 2) [the] consciousness that freedom is threatened by the other person; that I am not merely what I am for myself; 3) [the] will to confirm what I am by means of the other person, to be recognized by him, to be complete again; 4) [the] "common" life as if it were constituted on this basis: I forget that I call the tune and that the other person calls his own, and I figure a) that he recognizes me truly, which is not true since he also wants only to be recognized, [and] b) that I recognize him [27] (21) truly, which is not true since he wants only to be complete again. This double illusion is constitutive of "us." The I and the Thou always harbor the higher reality. One lives alone since one dies alone. If we forget all of that, this is because we do not let ourselves be taken into the sorcery of the incarnation and of the non-reflective attitude. One believes then that there is truly communication, recognition, instituted future.

INSTITUTION OF A FEELING

From this viewpoint, a whole criticism of feelings showing a) their subjectivity: each person's mental construction; b) indulgence toward this construction, how we let ourselves be fascinated without foundation; c) the elements of contingency or of chance: if I had not run into this person, as the saying goes (Jacques Rivière), constructed like fate . . . —if another person had been discovered there. Elements of generality of every love affair: the age, the circumstances, which have no internal relation with the person, have made me sensitive to her.

All of these criticisms [are] true. But do they exhaust the question?

No love without indulgence. It's true. But is that enough to decide to be in love? Why *this kind* of indulgence for this person? Why *this kind* of bad faith?—Without words, there would be only emotion, Alain says. Of course. But does that mean that what the words make flower is always artificial as well? Every time we feel that we are in love, it is true as decision and false as destiny. Is this correct? Difference between hysterical feeling and relatively authentic feeling. Where does it come from? Others, incarnation, are lies.—But what is this lie that accompanies me from my birth?

Proust: a whole criticism of love as subjective, fortuitous, madness or overwhelming illness, as founded upon the mirage of the other person, valued insofar as inaccessible, imaginary, [for] if I were inhabiting this other life I would find it banal and valueless: the repeated illusion of faces. Love is happy to die and is reborn only on the basis of privation and jealousy. **[28] (22)** Love as impossible: or suffering with no cure, or disgust—and no reality of love. Hence *The Captive*.

But Proust catches a glimpse that this is only half of what is true.

For to want to be loved supposes that one loves. Sadism presupposes masochism. Me and my plenitude presuppose that this plenitude might be unmade by the presence of the other person. Illusion or phenomenon? In any case, it is necessary to find out what loving means in order to want "to be loved." If one can lose autonomy to the point that one *is the other*, what allows us to say that autonomy is the *truth*? Whatever the circumstances, the chances, the indulgences may be, is it the case that what is born from these, the common life, is it the simple by-*product* of these chances? [The narrator] believes that he does not love Albertine since it bores him that he has to find her again. Instant by instant love is intermittent and appears to be artificial. But when he has lost her, [he] sees that that is love. However, a question: is it the absence that truly creates this love? The best proof of the theory that love is an illusion? But on the other hand, how would absence create this illusion on the basis of nothing? Is it not the case that the criterion that love is instantaneous is false? Is there nothing more than the instantaneous? Instituted which is not only external and conventional?

Swann in Love [30][1] (**22***)
Criticism of love: love does not go to Odette.
Contingencies: at her age[2]—flattered by being loved
habit of love, a trail already carved
Reality of Odette: kept woman,[3] who has the habit of men, who knows that all the affairs end the same way, who wants to marry him because of his money, who is kept.
Subjectivity of love: quotation[4] from "Swann in Love"[5]
But is that all?
That holds only against a naively realist idea. Cf. the discussion by Proust of the "external world." Of course, in one sense one does not exit from oneself. But is this the self that one perceives or that one loves? And consequently is there not an institution of a *between* the two? Love phenomenon of a reality? Contradictory perhaps, but real because of this?

1) Reality of the desire as contradiction
And first the reality of the desire. Swann possesses Odette not because he desires it but because he happens to miss her at the Verdurins' home. Quotation from "Swann in Love."[6] The pleasures of self-love are only the occasion of this "agitation,"[7] of this lack, of this anxiety, which are negative realities. Possession does not lead up to satisfying them, for they need the other qua other, qua "marvelous." Therefore desire itself is contradictory, but, because of this, real. It inaugurates a drama which is going to be real. Anxiety, the need for the other as other, will survive desire and will reanimate it. (Quotation from "Swann in Love.")[8]
The nature of desire: by means of the body, there is a need for the other as other. "Affinity" with the love for the bodies: insofar as the bodies are instituted life, gaze, existence exposed to others, which can be loved by others, and gives us the illusion of being able to possess all of that. This is the illusion, for they are all of that only insofar as nonpossessed. But the illusion is in the accomplishment, not in the project which is real by means of the fact that we truly become the other, that the other invades us. One does not love a person, one does not love a body, one loves a life established in a body. [The] body [is] neither first

nor second. [The] mind neither second nor first. The individual [is] the passage of a freedom. Impossible love, but not unreal. Its reality is going to be the alternative of pure alienation and a possession which is a little bit bored.

2) Reality of love **[31] (23*)**
a) As alienation: the perhaps "profound" idea of Odette. All of these accusations against me will end up in reconciliation. [That is to say that] love is like jealousy, but it is.

The one who loves turns into the other. (Quotation from "Swann in Love.")[9]

In which we no longer know which of the two is absent.

Love and the problem of personality: perhaps there is no perception of Her, but there is the fact that he is no longer himself. (Quotation from "Swann in Love.")[10]

Love real like Terror (quotation from "Swann in Love");[11] joy at the thought of death.

Self-overcoming, love of the truth (Quotation from "Swann in Love")[12] beyond all hope (cf. Stendhal).

At this extreme point, love resembles the ideas for which the writer searches (and which, like those of music and of painting, are not isolatable, separable from [the] sensible material). The "little phrase" loved because of Odette at first, and now which gives its wisdom to his suffering. (Read *Swann's Way*.)[13]

b) When it is not alienation (and alternatively with alienation), love is the "affectionate," "human" feeling of "common life," of marriage. Odette in her moments of fatigue and weariness is, like every human being, human, and he gets married to this calm Odette. Moreover, we will see later that she was so hard-hearted only because of her humiliation. "Posthumous" realization of her love, which, qua love, is not realized.

Therefore not illusion but well-founded phenomenon.

However, that is not exhibited in "Swann in Love," because there is love [only] from one side.

Love as a two-sided phenomenon: Albertine.

And here a question is going to have to be asked. Swann's love was only able to be narcissistic, negative, the cessation of an anxiety, because Odette did not love him—but, if the narrator's love for Albertine remains narcissistic, is that his fault?

Albertine [**32**] **(24)**
I—The illusion
The fantastic, imaginary Albertine
"To penetrate into a life"[14]—and into a life that is absolutely other.
The life of those young girls in *Within a Budding Grove* as mythological figures of cruelty,[15] figures of all of what he is not. (Quotation from *Within a Budding Grove*.)[16]

When he gets to know her, he finds out that she is the rather shy daughter of merchants.[17] Hence the second idea that is also false: a young girl who is well brought up. This is confirmed by the way that Albertine snubs him when he comes to visit her in her bedroom.

What he loves in her is the Other, a generality, Balbec, and thinks that he is obligated to marry the one with whom he is betrothed "by proxy."[18] Because that is underway.

Albertine in Paris
He no longer loves her. She is the "daughter of the mists of the outside"[19] and he desires her because of that. She accepts that. This is a third Albertine. She appeases his physical needs.

Then she slips away (on the telephone). His "latent" love stirs.[20] As with Swann, this is a diffuse anxiety that crystallizes.[21]

New trip to Balbec.
Cottard's reflections,[22] Albertine's evasions, the hypothesis of sapphism, and the memory of Madame Swann create the construction of Albertine, and the will not to show her that he loves her.

The "binary rhythm" of all love (*Sodom and Gomorrah*)[23]
[He] doubts Albertine's love, does not believe that he is loved, because he doubts his love, because he does not love.

Hence: not to show that he loves, out of fear of no longer being valued, remains other and keeps his distance—to cause pain—conceives love as domination, inquisition and suspicion, jealousy.

What is at the foundation is self-doubt, and that casts a narcissistic color on his entire love. On the basis of that, it's going to look as though the very idea of love as an illusion is itself an illusion and that it is he who makes this love impossible. The turn from *The Captive* to *The Fugitive*.[24]

[**33**] **(25)** But he has not yet understood that and is in a jealous love in a way that is "unrealizable and outside the plane of life"[25]—and without believing himself that this is what love is. This imprisonment in the country prepares him to break it off. He does not break it off because his mother asks him to do it,[26] and because Albertine says that she knows Mademoiselle Vinteuil. Suddenly Albertine is *in him*[27] or rather he is destroyed by her, and he is nothing but the need of her. The *cure is identical*

to the illness: the presence of the being who makes him jealous.²⁸ Says to his mother that he must marry Albertine.

The Illusion of Affirmation **[34] (26)**
We have seen
1) Love is created before anything else by imagining *another* being, mythological figure of cruelty. Love which searches for unhappiness.
This being does not exist. Albertine is only a well-brought-up young girl—or perhaps, in Paris, a rather licentious girl, but in any case not this goddess. Being bored with her. Loves her really, nothing more.
Rebirth of the first love by means of suspicion of her vice. Love [is equivalent] to jealousy, to the investigation of suffering and of absence.

2) We are going back farther.
This jealous and suffering love comes from the fact that the narrator himself doubts his capacity to love. [He] knows the generality of his love,²⁹ that "[their] feelings, [their] actions bear no close and necessary relation to the woman they love."³⁰
Hence, she does not love him either.
Hence, if he has shown tenderness, "human" feelings, this is out of fear of displeasing, out of shame of being cunningly deceived.
Hence, seize on domination; unpleasantness, inquisition, jealousy, alternating with tenderness. Love between suffering and boredom.
All of this is founded on analysis rather than self-esteem, doubt about oneself:
"In a love that is not shared—one might almost say in love, for there are people for whom there is no such thing as shared love."³¹

Real Love as Negation
This results in:
The other and the one who loves: mirrors. It is because we do not love that we believe ourselves not to be loved, and all the rest that follows.
But why do we not love? Because of the intermittences of the heart,³² because of generality, the contingency of love, all of which make us *doubt* love.
What has to be so that we do not doubt love? The *necessity* of this love would have to be, i.e., that we have no body, no generality, no past,

no subjectivity—that this love intends the other herself, happens in her and not in us.

But if that were so, this love would no longer be lived, it would be known, it would not be felt. Is there not a de-valorization here of an incontestable reality in the name of the imaginary?

Is there not an illusion of the immediate which results [35] (27) in our losing sight of a trans-phenomenal reality in the name of intermittences or occasional causes?

The trans-phenomenal reality of love would be, not that of a positive being who is without doubt, but that of a possession or an alienation by the other person: the other person in me, in the form of suffering, of privation—in a way that is "unrealizable," "outside of the plane of life," by means of a lack. Just when it looks as though Albertine knows Mademoiselle Vinteuil, the one who wanted to leave her takes her back to Paris. "Anyone who wished to make a fresh drawing of things as they really were would now have had to place Albertine, not a distance from me, but inside me."[33] Certainly, there is no reception of the other person, nor perception, which reaches the other; it would be necessary to be the other. But the relativist argumentation is false because there is another relation with the other person: the other person as occupying the entire horizon of my life and not as a positive being. Love is the same thing as privation or, if you like, non-love. Albertine offers not to leave him anymore: "She was offering to me [. . .] the sole remedy for the poison that was consuming me, a remedy homogeneous with it indeed, for although one was sweet and the other bitter."[34] The poison: absence, alterity. The remedy: presence as suppression of the absence or of the lack, not as accomplishment.

3) However, is this everything? Negative reality of love as unrealizable, as impossible, because of self-doubt, positive verification impossible, hence doubt of the other.

Consequently, to love is to want to be loved. . . . The other can be present only as horizon, felt in me, in my shame, not perceived. This follows because, her and me, we are perpetual explosions of things that are possible, of discontinuous instants: "I have always been more open to the world of things that are possible than the world of contingent reality."[35] The result is that he can ultimately love her only when she is sleeping. She is other but without fleeing from him and without gazing upon him.

This love being privation, not felt, this is why Proust never says, I love Albertine. But I am not sure that I do not love her. Or, perhaps I am in love with Albertine.³⁶ To love is to seek to kill the privation-love by means of the common life. "We create obligations only towards ourselves."³⁷

Since this love is agonizing, it brings back all the past anxieties, that of the absence of his mother. Because this love has negative reality, it belongs to us and not to the people we love, and all of our loves are mixed together. "This return of my suffering did not provide more consistency to the image of Albertine in me. She was causing my troubles just like a divinity who remains invisible" (*Within a Budding Grove*).

[36] (28) *Is that everything?*
The Illusion of Negation

If doubt about the other comes from doubt about oneself, the belief in myself would result in belief in the other. Perhaps this is where shared love comes from. It is he who transformed Albertine into a liar.

Some people have said that the love for Albertine was a conglomeration of all the other loves. But would one not be able to say that they are all essays and appeals for this particular love?³⁸

Some people have said that the other was a negation: but "it was in my heart, and very difficult to extricate, that Albertine's double was lodged."³⁹

Some people have said: profanation. But is this not because all of these love affairs are one sole love? One sole life? Profanation does not result in the whole reality of love being in the profane.

Some people have said that Albertine is innocent. But Albertine is guilty, like the narrator himself, who believes in so many of the vices only because he has some of them—as if he saw Albertine's vices *like his own*, i.e., wholly natural?

That becomes clear with Albertine's departure: meditation of *The Fugitive*.

I have not believed in my love because it was in "the volatile state";⁴⁰ I had believed in it when it is *crystallized* by Albertine's departure.

Even as egocentric as the point of departure of love is, it becomes something other than a monologue. Hence a year that is as long as a century, "plenitude," "immensity."⁴¹

Even as imaginary as the beginning of a love is, "in exchange for what our imagination leads us to expect . . . , life gives ourselves something which we were very far from imagining."⁴²

Even as general as love is (the echo of Gilberte in Albertine), the love for Albertine is as different from the ones preceding it as the septet was from the sonata (reality of the subjective, quasi-Platonism).⁴³

Must we not say that the starting point has not only revealed the love but also created it? "For very often, in order that we may discover that we are in love, perhaps indeed in order that we may fall in love, the day of separation must first have come."[44]

But no. Conversely, this separation, even Albertine's death, has been played out by them before it has taken place. They were doing it in the mode of the lie (wishing her dead, acting out of the separation—which could not be real), but they were trying (read *The Fugitive*) and already assuming the separation. It is true that they were playing out the separation, and by doing so love was realized only in the separation.

[37] [On some small sheets that Merleau-Ponty did not number he copied some citations from *The Fugitive*.][45]

[38] (29) Decidedly therefore love is not [a] positive, it is [?] negative. And necessarily, because it is the question of the essence of being loved (who was she?), and because this essence is ultimately not simple guilt or innocence to be sure, but both at once. When he learns that she was guilty: "through the intensity of one's pain one arrives at the mystery, at the essence."[46] Moreover, this revelation gives reality to his first love for orgiastic Albertine—at the same time as it emphasizes its impossibility.

Final doubt in *The Fugitive*. There is the erasure, the forgetfulness. When a piece of false news makes him believe that Albertine is alive, this makes him sense the point which his forgetfulness of her is at. [He] wonders if the news of her death has not extended his love. But this very question takes nothing away from the reality of what happened in this way.

What is surpassed is the idea of love as a convention or sum of accidents or appearances, or artifice.

What is not surpassed is the alterity of the other and finitude.

The idea of institution is precisely the foundation of a personal history on the basis of contingency.

[39] (30) *Conclusion About Proust and the Institution of Feelings*
Impossibility of love, "error" of love.

We exist alone, we know only our feelings, the object is only a "sheaf of thoughts" which do not relate to what is, "error of localization" which results in the fact that we put ourselves into another or that we put the other into ourselves.

The Self can have the experience of the other only in her effects upon me. The other [is] present in my anxiety, my lack of her, in her absence. There is no "true" presence that fills in this absence: no possession.

1) Neither in the physical sense: the narrator does not possess Albertine, she extinguishes his anxiety. The body is loved, love has an affinity with bodies only insofar as these bodies (a gaze, for example) (or at least a respiration) are instituted existence, offered to all, desired insofar as public.

2) Nor in the spiritual sense: alternation of "human" feelings and alienation, i.e., joyless bewitchment. Alternation of "banal" other, "familiar" other, even vulgar other (daughter of merchants)—and "marvelous" other, "imaginary" other. No relation between the will to union and union.

This is true all the way to the end. Even at the end of *The Fugitive*, it is not the existence of the other that is intended. Proof: the news that Albertine is still alive leaves him emotionless. The Albertine who was loved was entirely in him, and when these "thoughts" have disappeared, the empirical Albertine is indifferent. Even this news *accelerates* the forgetfulness in him, making him feel that she no longer is alive in him. Perhaps memory and love were prolonged by the death, by the greatest absence. One loves nothing but the absent. Love is a hollow in us, not the presence of the other. Love is "unrealizable," "outside of the plane of life." The remedy is identical to the illness. The presence of the other, which is always the experience of her absence undergone or nothing.

But this very experience of the other is the product of a certain self-feeling. [He] does not feel loved because he does not believe that he is capable of loving: mirror that results in the fact that we fashion the other according to ourselves and ourselves according to this other who is so constructed. No shared loved because no love. But does not love (love that is not substantial, not immediately verifiable, not absolute since one would not always consent to give one's life for the beloved) consist precisely in the establishment of the mirror relation? Isn't love already there exactly when we seek to "verify" it?

It would then be necessary to say that love is not an illusion, but negative reality, actual alienation. The error lies in believing that it is only an error. "She caused my troubles just like a divinity who remained invisible." Yes, but there we have an absence of self, synonym for the presence of the other.[47]

Alienation (the failure) is unified with love, but is its reality. Love entails a beyond oneself, the very beyond of the false desire of possession: we have made the other, we no longer know which one is absent; "poor dear"—the truth [is] beyond what would please me or what would calm my anxiety. Like death, love is what reveals the "personality." It allows us to see everything that someone is, how someone is the world itself, being itself, a world, a being from which we are excluded; in the experience undergone of this pain, one is beyond desire and domination: "through the intensity of one's pain one arrives at the mystery, at the essence." At the mystery: how one can be non-self with all of one's strength. At the essence: revelation that the essence of someone is the non-essence, guilt and innocence, and both at once. Albertine is present at a distance like the little phrase in its sounds, not separable from them and yet intangible, *noli me tangere*.[48] Cf. *Time Regained*:[49] grief teaches you how to see.

On the basis of this viewpoint: [the] contingencies, which lead to that, are reordered; love, not effect, but cause.[50] The other loves [are] calls towards this one, this one is the rebirth of the others. It is death which has prolonged his love for Albertine. But the love for Albertine was the anticipation of separation and of death, the "binary rhythm" was a pre-notion, a "more profound" truth. There is therefore something besides "monologue," there is fullness when we think there is emptiness, the reality of what is not immediately sensed. In exchange for what we had imagined, life gives us something else, and something else that was secretly willed, not fortuitous. Realization is not what was foreseen, but nevertheless what was willed. We advance by recoiling, we do not choose **[41] (32)** directly, but obliquely, but we nevertheless do what we want. Love is clairvoyant; it addresses us precisely to what is able to tear us apart. Albertine was (among other things) the orgiastic Albertine which he thought was an illusion. Illusion by means of a distant vision, but also illusion by means of a vision from up close, in which we do not see the "volatile."

Judgment on This Analysis:
Someone will say: contingencies of Proust.
1) Homosexual love hidden in heterosexual love. Homosexuality [means] jealousy as jealousy.[51]
Objection: but he is precisely less jealous of Saint Loup than of the women that Albertine could love.—The objection, however, turns itself back against Proust: why did he make Albertine a citizen of Gomorrah? If not in order to present a picture of the most irremediable jealousy, the one that intends not the rivals of my sex, but the rivals of the other sex, in order to present a picture therefore of [the] situation of the homosexual who is jealous of the women in whom his male lover is interested. But Proust could respond that, if he is jealous of these women, he is so because he wants to please them, therefore because he is heterosexual. In fact, the narrator loves all the young girls and this is why he is jealous of them. Therefore Proust has really seen [that] jealousy is the substitu-

tion of the jealous one for the beloved in her love affairs and [that] this substitution results in the fact that there is homosexuality in heterosexuality, and the reverse. Polysexuality.

2) Someone will say, however, that homosexual love in itself involves jealousy, flight of the other, not presence, because homosexual love does not involve heterosexual union. Cf. Proust's disappointment: [the narrator] does not possess Albertine, but he gets relaxation from her, solitary pleasure with Albertine while she sleeps, auto-erotic. Does not this provide the explanation of Proust's problems? No. Even heterosexual union cannot pass for the *accomplishment* of love. *Is it the case* that the coupling of physical love is the coupling of life? Necessary but **[42]** (33) not sufficient union. To maintain the contrary would be to hold that there is no body-soul difference, that there is an absolute integration of the body, that there is no contingency.

Thus the particularities of Proust, his contingencies, result in him having, in a particular way, the experience of contingency, of a contingency that is universal. Instead of the psychological explanation removing the universal value from Proust's analyses, it confirms it. Metaphysical significance of all the "facticities."

Universal problem: how would I be the other if not through alienation?[52]

Universal response: but this alienation and fact are not illusions, they presuppose an absence of myself.

The question posed at the beginning: is love real? There's doubt. Love results from the encounter, from circumstances chosen for other reasons. But what would we demand so that it would be real? That it was born from nothing, that it was pure choice. Now, if it were pure choice, construction, it would still not be "real." It would be imaginary as well. This is to say that the requirement is false. Love is not created by circumstances, or by decision; it consists in the way questions and answers are linked together—by means of an attraction, something more slips in, we discover not exactly what we were seeking, but something else that is interesting. The initial *Sinngebung* [is] confirmed, but in a different direction, and yet that is not without a relation with the initial donation of sense. Moreover, all contingency, even what is radically contingent, ends up being willed: evidence of the Thou as naked reality, i.e., as instituted, irrevocable, regardless of what it does. Jealousy, lies, domination are transcended in a desire to die, a desire for truth, abnegation.

We are going to see as well that there is a sense, by way of contingency, an oblique movement of institution in the work of art, that here too the contingencies are recentered by institution and end up receiving a sense that surpasses them—so that we no longer know where in the vital and artistic past of the artist the work of art has begun. We do not even know from where in the tradition the work takes its inspiration, just as all of his loves are enclosed in his initiation to the world, and so that the rupture itself, the separation from this source was already there at the source. Cf. struggle with the predecessors, which is at the same time the initiation by means of them.

[THE INSTITUTION OF A WORK OF ART]

Artistic Creation as Institution **[43] (34)**

[The] first part [considered] institution in private history.—The act of painting is usually a conscious, deliberate relation to public history. [The] task of the painter [is] inherited, [intends a] pictorial telos. Cf. the act of writing or the search for truth. Personal institution that resumes collective institution.

But the insertion into collective institution here is the most personal wish. We see here how [there is] no alternation. This is because the logic of the collective enterprise at once becomes valuable in [the] individual work which locates itself in the collective enterprise, and the collective enterprise is created by the individual work. Since, within the individual work, each attempt proceeds from the preceding ones and cannot be deduced from them, re-creates the whole. [The] kinship is only retrospective. The work of art that is like the daughter becomes the maternal work of art.

Problem: [what is the] mode of presence of the whole in the parts? The parts are neither chaos, nor manifestation of a finality of a ready-made interiority. How do we know what we are making in painting? We do not work by chance. And yet, the entire field of *the* art of painting, and, for each painter, the field of *his* painting, is not truly given. History is retrospective, metamorphoses, and in this sense painters do not know what they are making. And yet, each rediscovers the whole of painting, just as each life discovers all lives. How does the given, perceived world arouse in each this re-creation which is rediscovered?

Blind logic, logic which creates on the way. Retrospectively the ancient painter, the ancient perspective appears as making a way toward Renaissance perspective. But Renaissance perspective in turn as not being the true telos, [but] the particular case of a more general investigation which continues. And likewise, in the meantime. There is logic, but:

1) Not direct. It often happens that the problem around which research is ordered is inaccessible along this path; then there is a turning back or a detour. [The] directing role passes to another procedure

or another art. Return to more "primitive" forms. And, by means of this detour, [the] materials of the work undertaken are resumed and utilized. The distance makes a new creative effort possible (as well in the individual work of art). The result is, there is really **[44] (35)** a teleology of the whole, but without possession of the end; what therefore orients the movement?

2) Not finished. We might think that even the telos manages to appear later as a very particular case to be generalized. For the artist, the work is always an attempt. And for history, painting in its entirety is a beginning.

Therefore how are we to express philosophically this *sense*? The notion of institution alone [is] capable of doing this, as the openness of a field within which we can describe certain [phases]; there is not only a swarming of works and of windfalls, but also systematic attempts—but a field which, just like the visual field, is not the whole, has no precise limits, and opens onto other fields.

Example: the creation of Renaissance planimetric perspective.[1]

I am beginning with the example of collective history because collective history is that of styles or of procedures that can be imitated, participated in, and are sedimented. *Stilmoment* and not *Wertmoment*.[2] Planimetric perspective is neither a necessary nor a sufficient condition for the value of a work of art. Thereby the analysis of this institution does not go all the way to the ground of pictorial institution. There would not be painting if there were only that. But more convenient analysis: the analysis of the available.[3] We will go from the superficial to the profound by going from collective history to individual history.

Ancient perspective: spherical field, angular perspective. The size that it appears to be is not a function of the distance, but of the angle.

Euclid's eighth theorem, which states this, [is] suppressed in the Renaissance translations of Euclid. The Renaissance, [in fact,] opposes a *perspectiva artificialis* to [the] *perspectiva naturalis*. [The Renaissance] seeks not to formulate the laws of natural vision, **[45] (36)** but "to develop a construction that can be used practically of the planar pictorial image" (Panofsky).[4] Planimetric perspective is to be compared to the effort to constitute a perfect language, i.e., being given an idea to express, methodically construct its expression on the basis of "rational" signs, by means of combining these signs. Eliminate the effort of "speech." Likewise [in the] Renaissance, what is at issue is to construct [one] planar image, therefore to abandon spherical visual field since the sphere cannot be developed into a plane.

Antiquity had compromised: several vanishing axes, "fishbone effect."[5] Hence, "instability," "inconsistency." In contrast, [the] single vanishing point allows us [to establish] a constant relation between values of height, breadth, and depth.[6] The dimensions and the distance to the eye from the object being given, its size is *eindeutig festgelegt*.[7]

To this ancient way of expressing space, the following are connected. [The conception of a] non-substantiality of space: it is not beyond the *Körper-Nichtkörper* difference;[8] it is however the *Übereinander* and the *Hintereinander*;[9] it is "what remains between the bodies."[10] It is not a continuum whose spatial relations are variations. There are exceptions to the foreshortening with distance—no sole conception of lighting (we have an *Aggregatraum*,[11] not a systematic space).[12] Therefore it is not a true "impressionism" which "veils" the things and their solidity without suppressing them.[13] As soon as we consider intermediary space (like a landscape), ancient art looks to be inconsistent, oneiric, chimerical, and not harmonious. They do not have the definition of space as "corpus generaliter sumptum" (Arnold Geulincx).[14]

How are we to understand the institution of Renaissance space? The ancient painters who had invented this symbolic form had a certain problem in view: to render, to express the world. But this problem [remained] not *conceived* in its generality, in its systematic sense.[15] If it had, they would have abandoned the spherical visual sphere. The first one who picked up a flint, a piece of charcoal, a piece of chalk wanted to express. But [46] (37) he did not know what it means to express. He saw only a mode of reporting, not the principle of the report. How therefore is the systematic change produced?

Panofsky: the Middle Ages: *Rückschlag*.[16] Recoil.[17] [The Middle Ages] are informed by Eastern influences which are not the cause, but the symptom.[18] The gradations in approximate depth are suppressed: juxtaposition on a plane of heights and breadths, gold background or tin leaf. The objects which are in the background are not cut out, but arranged in order to enter into the background. The surface is not seen through by the gaze but filled.[19] Consequently, the elements of the image lose their relation of mobility and of expressivity.

Recoil but detour, for the objects are inserted into a rhythm of color and gold (or, in sculpture, a rhythm of light and shadow). Hence colored or luminous unity. Cf. metaphysics of light in Christian Neoplatonism. "Space is light" (Proclus). Thereby the world is a continuum. A homogenizing fluid, immeasurable and dimensionless.[20]

Hence, the northwest European "Romanesque style" takes its use of line as a sui generis means of expression. The transition to the surface detaches painting definitively from the third dimension,[21] and prepares anew the expression of the third dimension. Conception of a space that is prior to objects, the surface of the image [being] considered transparent and being transparent, one sees this space through the surface, hence cut-out backgrounds, *Unendlichkeit des Bildes*,[22] *Wirklichkeitausschnitt*:[23, 24] planar section of the visual pyramid (Alberti).[25] [Therefore] system space. Correlatively, the earth is no longer the center of the world, the sky is no longer the limit of the cosmos, infinite world. Perspective has the same function as philosophical critique: connection of subjectivity and objectivity, [of] viewpoint and reality.[26] The later evolution of perspective will consist in denying [a] correlation of this sort and will search for spatiality in the ultra-objective (Italians) or in the ultra-subjective (baroque or ends of the world).[27]

Teaching [47] (38)

1) In what sense does painting know what it is doing? By inventing planimetric perspective through an indirect path, they *also* invent the conception of the picture as *Bildebene*, of perspective as "Durchsehung" (Dürer).[28] Is that willed? No. The consequences and the field open themselves, but we make something which has more meaning than we thought. However, this is not simple chance. Uccello refusing to go to sleep and saying, "Oh, what a lovely thing this perspective is."[29] Cf. Proust: life gives us something other than what we were searching for, something else and the same thing. By means of the question of technique, the very nature of painting itself is in question. It's the *Weltgefühl*[30] at work.

2) However, painting is not a logic of painting; the construction is retrospective (and provisional), what we have found; we do not know exactly what it is going to mean. The parallel with philosophies is acceptable only if philosophies themselves are taken not as statements of ideas, but as inventions of symbolic forms. Shortcoming of Cassirer's philosophy consist in thinking that criticism is the endpoint, that philosophical sense has a directing value even though this sense itself is taken up into sedimentation. Consider criticism itself as a symbolic form and not as a philosophy of symbolic forms.

In order to be convinced about this, [consider the] example of Cézanne: resumption of the entire pictorial problem for each one.

How is planimetric perspective *instituted*?

Mixture of chance and reason: indirect solution. [The] Middle Ages renounce the problem. [It amounts to] Eastern influences (abandoning gradations in depth. Juxtaposition on a plane of heights and breadths—gold background or tin leaf) (the objects in the background are not cut out, but arranged—decoration—filled surface) (consequently, no relation of movement and expressivity between the elements of the image).

Recoil but detour, but objects inserted into the rhythm of color and gold: colored or luminous unity. Metaphysics of light. "Space is light" (Proclus). Christian Neoplatonism. [The] world is a fluid, homogeneous continuum which cannot be measured. Therefore the northwest European "Romanesque style," [the] line as sui generis means of expression. And the detachment of the third dimension prepares a new expression of the third dimension.

[The] invention will consist in conceiving space prior to objects, and not as simple *Übereinander* or *Hintereinander*, not as "what remains between the bodies," henceforth beyond the distinction *Körper-Nichtkörper.* Systematic, continuum space and not an aggregate—*corpus generaliter sumptum* (Geulincx). Constant relation between height, breadth, and depth, and the univocal determination of the size that appears by means of the dimension of the object and its distance from the eye. [The] single vanishing point [allows for] stability, consistency, compossibility, and rationality.

Question: chance and reason in the institution.

Chance: it is not with a view to repeating history that the Middle Ages turned away from the problem of antiquity.

Reason: but there is a resumption of the problem, the substitution of a system for a system. Uccello felt [the] scope of the discovery: Oh, what a lovely thing this perspective is!—In reality this conception of spatiality [implies] a whole conception of painting and of the relation between painting and the world. [The] painting or perspective [is] ([according to] Dürer) *Durchsehung;* [the] surface [is] simple *Bildebene*—and not an object for itself—opening onto a world which itself is conceived as infinite (the earth is not the center, the sky is not the limit of the cosmos) or pure object. Objectivity-subjectivity connection, [which] posits truth. Perspective [treats the] same question [as] Cartesian philosophy or critique.

Reason: do we have to speak of a cunning of reason, truth realizing itself by means of a detour that it ordains?

But planimetric perspective is not truer. No painter applies it entirely (the mathematicians knew about it a long time before the painters); no painter is content with applying it. It is *Stilmoment* **[49] (36)** and not *Wertmoment*. It is to painting what language is to literature. By means of perspective alone, it provides procedures, not painting. Perspective connects *Bedeutungsinhalt*[31] to the concrete sensible sign,[32] i.e., perspective can be communicated. This would be a perfect language which had excluded every effort of expression (Francastel, p. 41).[33]

Therefore this is not the cunning of reason and truth in itself guiding history.

Do we have to say, with Panofsky, "symbolic form," *Weltgefühl,* and assimilate this invention to a historicized, enlarged criticism (Cassirer)? This supposes that we consider at least this kind of perspective as a point of maturity, equilibrium [according to which there is nothing but oscillation towards the ultra-objective (Italian painting) and the ultra-subjective (baroque)].[34] But this is the conventional image of the Renaissance: academic commonplace according to the painters (Francastel, p. 135) (pp. 35 and 38).

Therefore, this is an "aesthetic-social choice" and not a law of nature or even the acquisition of a pictorial, critical consciousness which would be ultimate.

Therefore the question is still one of the *sense* of the process. This sense exists; there is an operative intentionality. But it adheres to concrete investigations, to a pictorial practice, and it is not a free sense, closed, over and against a pure consciousness.

"Aesthetico-social choice" is a notion that needs to be specified.

In reality, is there choice in the ordinary sense? What is in practice is approximation.

Centuries [pass] before we adopt the *Schrägensicht,*[35] the same for the single vanishing point for all orthogonal lines.[36] And moreover, even in the system that is strictly observed, is it the case that the choices which intervene are decisions by means of one of the things that is possible? Example, the horizon: horizon of the content (are the characters seen from ground level, from above, from below)—horizon of layout: (is this horizon of content in the middle, above, below the middle of the painted surface?) (cf. Van Gogh: the perspective of the insect). Example, choice of the distance to the object with a recipe (distance at least equal to the height).

Question: certainly choices are made (motives for which we place **[50]** **(37)** [the] horizon here or there). But the painter does not produce the theory for it, does not know the reason for it. The "motive" [is] a certain expressive divergence in relation to a certain "norm," but not a choice in the sense of positing an *end:*

1) This is a choice in the sense in which a word is chosen. Speaking [does not mean] knowing the systematic structure of a language. Speech reanimates the system and not the reverse.

2) This is why what is sedimented through pictorial gestures is not a *procedure* founded upon a law of nature. If that was the case, we'd have some paintings that were surpassed. Now there is repeated recourse. Of course there is a surpassing in certain regards. But the possibility of not being able to be surpassed and of a perpetual rereading. Not only because of our superficial "metamorphoses" (ancient "impressionist" painting), but because of possibilities of anticipation (Malraux: fragments of works). We learn to paint differently by visiting with the predecessors. Universe of painting. Field of painting. Each painting [is] a matrix of different symbols of what is its own, on the condition that it is seen by a painter.

3) The choice therefore is always an attempt to surpass which preserves, and not a Manichean affirmation which is closed in upon itself.

It is the choice of the hand and the eye: the film [about] Matisse,[37] the slowing down and the impression of a hesitation between the things that are possible. But what or who makes the choice? [There is] motivation that comes simultaneously from colors, light, substance, movement, a call from all of that to a movement of the hand which resolves the problem while being unaware of it just as when we walk or gesture. Implex or animal of movements and of colors. Each partial act reverberates upon the whole, provokes a deviation which is to be compensated by others. Rather than choice, it is necessary to say *labor*. The choices are the trace of this labor of "germination" (Cézanne) (along with nature, along with other pictures). Each choice remakes painting by inheriting it. Each work re-creates the entire work of a painter by inheriting it if it is truly a work. Choice [means] basing oneself on one of the veins of a given pictorial world, turning the vein into the principle of a type of expression, which in turn will undergo the same becoming. Not a choice that breaks but one that slides and opens. Choice [does not mean] making oneself just as one thinks one is; it does not mean anticipating history and the judgment of others, overpowering history. There are certainly—[movement of discovery?], active painting—history of painting, and therefore "chance" in the labor. But in the painter who labors there is re-founded history, universal in which the opposed choices are not really opposed, a world with several entrances, a pluralist universe.

[51] (38*) [The] relation of the painter to [the] total painting and to its history [is] to be understood by means of [the] relation of a part of

his work to the rest. There is a pictorial rationality as there is a rationality of a painter's work, rationality not of completion but of "investigation":

>Example: *Cézanne et l'expression de l'espace*[38]
>After a period where we find traditional space and actual people as figures:
>—[the effort to] rediscover something stable under impressionism. First, a lame compromise: stable space but object figures, or living bodies but living bodies [who] lose contour (seeks to fuse several expressions of the body. Cf. [?]).
>[Then he seeks] how to connect abstract space to the objects and to the living beings ([the] flowers [allows the passage] from the mineral to the living).
>—constructivist period: In the portrait, difficulty. Madame Cézanne in the yellow armchair, posture that we cannot forget although we forget those of the figures in Renoir's portraits. [Questions?] figures. [The] Bathers are [in fact] women. The picture [is] realized by itself.
>—final period of 1894–96. Visible, immediate, sensual brushstroke, and yet synthesis: [discontinuous] painting—with from time to time "germs of crystallization" (watercolors). By means of the style, space and life are reconciled (Tintoretto). Combined play of light as air modulation and brushstroke.
>Success of the portraits: immense success of *Garçon au gilet rouge*.
>[Cézanne] rediscovers the perspective of Dürer and Vinci, without willing it. [He provides] another solution to the Renaissance problem (L. Guerry, pp. 148–49).
>Therefore the "logic" of painting, i.e., the circulation of symbolic forms that can be imitated and participated in, the circulation of general "styles," a circulation that is based entirely on an operation that is the most individual and universal and in this way is created, will be universal only by arising from the other.
>Perspective is germinal in antiquity like interrogation about the vision of a world, a hollow which demands to be fulfilled by painting.

[52] (39) We have, despite appearances, remained in private institution, from oneself to oneself.

We have only sought to catch a glimpse of the fact that public institution extends the relation of self to self.

Institution of a work, like the institution of a love, [intends a] sense as open sense, which develops by means of proliferation, by curves, decentering and recentering, zigzag, ambiguous passage, with a sort of identity between the whole and parts, the beginning and end. A sort of existential eternity by means of self-interpretation.

Indeed. But this unity and this kind of rationality, aren't they forms of unity and rationality that are second? Are there not in linguistic works sedimentation and institution without "movement"? Truth of adequation?

Confrontation with geometry and its growth.

[INSTITUTION OF A DOMAIN OF KNOWLEDGE]

The Institution of a Domain of Knowledge [53] (39*)

The institution of a life (feeling), of a work: [what was at issue was the] establishment of a sense (of a history), not closed, not possessed by the mind, not signification, essence, or end—and yet not nothing (sum of chances), as the fruitfulness of grief shows (Proust, *Time Regained*), the fruitfulness of a painter's labor which takes place, however, not between subject and object but between a seeing person and a painting person. [There is therefore] germination of a life and of a work around "contingent" givens. Connection of event and essence.

But does this make any sense when we turn to knowledge? Knowledge, truth, this time in the full sense—not the subjective "truth" of the person who is in love or of the painter—[but] the truth that is detached from the person, and the truth which integrates and cancels what had preceded it (which painting does not do). Here mustn't we recognize two orders, [the] order of the event—and [the] order of essence or of pure sense, [truth of] adequation, logic?

Moreover, must we not admit that this order claims in principle to subordinate the others under itself (logicism)? The history of painting does not paint itself, it is written, or at least it is born only by means of the creation of the Museum, the reduction of paintings which are traces of life to objects of comparison, historical consciousness, which is not pictorial but true (cf. consciousness of a pain is not painful but true). The sense of a life is truly a sense only through reflection, and this reflection often makes the nascent "sense" descend to the rank of illusion and contingency. Therefore all that preceded it would be psychology, and both knowledge and the truth would not be instituted. Painting [involves] a flickering signification, which is not articulated, which does not go so far as saying itself (and for all the more reason, does not say life). In the order of things said, the pure signification would intervene, which not only organizes cycles of activities and unfolds an obscure-clear history, [but also] belongs to the order of value or of the subsistent, summarizes and surpasses history.

INSTITUTION OF A DOMAIN OF KNOWLEDGE

This is precisely what we are contesting. Certainly there is a difference between knowledge, essence, and event. We are going to seek to specify it. But the true and the essence would be nothing without what leads to them. There is sublimation, not surpassing towards *another order.* The *lekton* is not supported by a logos which would be independent of the "aesthetic world."

[54] (40) There is a historicity of language itself. The writer makes use of his language as the painter makes use of his brush. The signification of the words that he uses [is] what they trail behind them, configurations of his landscape, they receive the signification from this connection to the sense that he has to decipher. Therefore, neither the writer nor the philosopher (cf. Pascal: definitions are only the extracts of usage) is the pure intending of a pure signification. And his reader still less (the words of the writer decenter the habitual signification, and through convergent usages they indicate new senses which are divergences). Precisely in its will to radicalism, philosophy is speaking speech and not spoken speech.

But the demonstration [is] too easy in regard to the way a domain of knowledge makes use of language.—And moreover one could always say that this belongs to the order of the inexact. The rest is the canonical order of exact knowledge where we pass beyond institution. Therefore concentrate [the] analysis upon this order.

We shall do it in two ways:

1) By examining the institution of a true domain of knowledge in the individual in order to see if knowledge is the access to [an] order of the subsistent. Here psychology, which does not inevitably mean psychologism. Is the event of invention or of the comprehending of the sense surpassed by that very sense, reabsorbed, does the event pass to the rank of the circumstances for its disclosure, beyond which are the essences?

2) This individual institution of the true [is] in connection with [an] institution that is more than individual: it takes up an intention which precedes it (the originary *Stiftung* of geometry) and it creates an intention out of it which survives it and will go farther (the actual *Stiftung* of a new sense) and by which there is forgetfulness of origins. [Therefore] traditionality with its two facets. But we will see that it is precisely this traditionality, which makes sedimentation and what appears to be "truth in itself," that is the very core of historicity.

Gestaltists—Husserl[1]

[55][2] **(42)** [. . .] Just as arithmetical numbers, before [the] discovery of algebra, had properties of algebraic numbers (+ more particular, restrictive properties), the trunk of the tree *had* the properties of the circle before the circle was known. This eternity depends on our conception of a *nature*. Nevertheless, this makes sense only retrospectively, and this remark does not only concern the order of invention in opposition to the order of objective dependence. There is truly a retrograde movement of the true[3] (and not only a retroactive effect of the *discovery* of the true). The trunk of the circular tree had equal radii, [which means that] manual operations on it would have obtained results which for us presuppose this equality; but this equality as such does not exist absolutely before geometry. The historicity of geometry [becomes] visible if we apply [it] to the future. Can we say that the properties which will be discovered are already there? No. They will hold retroactively. Abel's theorem is operative in Cartesian algebra, [which] means certain failures which are only failures will appear as consequences of certain relations when mathematical beings which have no intuitive existence will have been invented.

Therefore what there is at each moment [is] "structural truth," connected to perspective, to centering, to structuring. Of course other ways of structuring are possible, formalizations, from which it results that the current way of structuring is surpassed, that the current way of structuring looks to be a particular case, but not an absolute decentering, an indifferent equilibrium, the end of problems, the intelligible world. The history of knowledge is contracted upon itself insofar as it advances, but it never pierces through the order of structures; its light is never entirely in the present: there is a double relation of *Fundierung*.[4] This history creeps along backward like a crab, looks toward the past, does not see the world of ideas directly. The human institution of knowledge, of the "I think that," of the ob-ject, of truth, of the algorithm, of language, is foreign to animality. But it is still an institution, a history, though it has another rhythm, another relation to itself than the animal pseudo-history. Cf. art and life.

The relation of this history to itself is what still remains to be analyzed. The "traditionality" of consciousness [means] forgetfulness of origins, hands over[5] **[56] (43)** a tradition, founds it. And correlatively, [there is] the tradition received, i.e., possibility of reactivation. In this sense the future [is] anticipated in the telos of the first step, *Urstiftung* and *Endstiftung*.[6] We have simplified the relation by speaking of the process of knowledge by means of generalization and integration. Internal relation of the first steps to the future steps. We were not taking account of the halo of sense. It is going to confirm our umbilical cord to the *Lebenswelt*[7] and the past. And in this way distinguish the conclusions that Husserl comes to from those that Brunschvicg comes to. Not philosophy of participation in the one, of intellectual creation, of Spirit, but philosophy of culture.

Institution of Truth [57] (44)

Comparison [between] practical (animal) problem and intellectual problem in order to highlight what properly defines the intellectual problem, the problem of truth.

What is common: [a] problem-situation [brings forth] *Sinngebung* which fills the "gap" by affecting [some] element of the field with new sense.

What properly defines an intellectual problem: the insight,[8] the act of conferring a sense is not a pure event, [it is a] a change of structure which makes one forget the initial structure, but carried out, as is always possible, on the basis of a situation of this type, i.e., logical, i.e., trans-phenomenal, relation. [Thus], the tree branch was a possible stick before I think about it, will remain a stick when I no longer think about it, i.e., there is an order of the in-itself in which the tree branch is by means of itself, categorically, [an] elongated solid whose proper use is to attain [a] goal. The reorganization offers itself as the discovery of a pre-existing, true, objective property, which will never wear out, "subsistent." This is where the idea that there is an order of essence comes from, an order into which the individual somehow gains entrance. Insight[9] [is] reminiscence.

However, this is only after the fact, order of exposition, not of invention, synthetic order, not analytic. The analytic order is not merely an order of existence, is not limited to revealing another order, transcendental, an order of essences. In the future, as at the moment of discovery, in order to put into play the necessity of prior theorems, one will always have to see the present problem *as* a case of application. That is seen only on the basis of the figure (form of the equation to the second degree, or the structure of the triangle); or, if we formalize and replace the triangular object or the equation with a non-intuitive expression, one will always have to make an ascending movement from the situation to the sense; never will the necessity be posited in itself. The necessity will be made only by means of the *forgetfulness* of the analytic step, sedimentation of the result: the triangle will appear right away as having the sum of the angles = 2 right angles.[10] But the sedimentation is the cause, not the effect, of the order "in itself." This is where Bergson comes in: retrograde movement of the true, i.e., not openness of the duration onto a timeless order, but the appearance of a time of the truth.

[58] (45) Time carries itself beyond the succession of nows, a now is given as preexisting itself and in a certain way forever, but it preexists and endures eternally only as sense. [In other words], it is truly a creation which has taken place and it will be preserved only "in substance," i.e., we do not truly enter into the timeless, we enter only into a time which is no longer a simple uprooting, destruction, in which the subject does not encounter simple adversity, but change in an immanent way, change itself, and thereby even the requirement of truth which has first led to today's formulation.

Certainly this temporality is entirely human. This symbolic ("culture," edification of instruments which do not "wear out" in the way that practical instruments wear out, cumulative history in which the "surpassed" still harbors sense) [is] proper to humanity. The monkey discovers only magical relations (optical contact), mediated by manipulator-body, consequently only sediments within strict limits. In contrast, [there is a] human productivity of language and of the algorithm, which means that the sedimentation has [a] different sense, that humans not only manipulate, get used to an environment, but think, institute "cultures." The book exists in a way that is different from the animal pack. The signification is something different from the symbolism.

But the system of significations is not timeless, its light is not that of a *topos noetos,* its light does not merely descend from the principles to the consequences; it is sublimation of a light of the concrete, "idealization," raises itself up above itself by means of recurrence, does not surpass it without preserving it. This is why it is always by means of a return to the concrete that we are able to pursue a fuller truth, and not by developing simple consequences from the first discoveries. Sterility of a science which would forget its origins. *Sinnentleerung.*[11] The existential starting point, the structure of the figure, is certainly surpassed. But the "generalized" sense which is grasped on the basis of this structure is still a structure, only more formalized (this is why it will be surpassed itself, therefore it is essence only relatively), and thereby it retains **[59] (46)** "in its living depth" the initial structure, not because of the noticed fact, *einmalig,*[12] but as that in which idealization is made; [in other words], the

INSTITUTION OF A DOMAIN OF KNOWLEDGE

signification is certainly not supported by a bed of perceptions (as existing, individual facts), but by the perceived world in general; it remains in the field opened by the first idealizations.

In this sense, interpret Wertheimer's remarks and his idea that "the proof itself has its structure."[13] [The] formula for the surface [of the parallelogram], found in relation to [a first] case of the figure, is applied to other cases on the condition that one relates them back to the first, i.e., that we assume Euclidean space, i.e., a being of the parallelogram that is independent from its manifestations, i.e., that the change of structure by means of construction (1) not be connected to this representation, but [constitutes an] internal possibility of the parallelogram, that it is the "*innere* structure"[14] of this "situation." Therefore one does not have subsumption under an essence, and conversely emergence into the intelligible world, but the lateral extension of the privileged case to all the cases.[15] And the light proper to this case is not replaced by another; the history of this situation must be started up again by all those who learn.

When there is a discussion, i.e., generalization, resolution of the privileged evidence of the case of the figure in an evidence that is more general (plane geometry = geometry in the space where one makes a null dimension) (arithmetic = particular case of algebraic relations), the relation is not one of consequence to principle. Formalized algebra is more meaningful than arithmetic, but in a sense it never surpasses arithmetic because it would mean nothing without arithmetic. It exists only as generalized arithmetic, recurrence on the basis of the arithmetical—for what has the arithmetical on the horizon. Formalization, axiomatization pushes aside the illusion of an empiricist borrowing from the perceived fact. But the something in general to which formalized mathematics refers gets its sense from spoken being, and the latter gets its sense from perceived being. Double relation of *Fundierung*. There is a possibility of historical development which defines essence, even if the entire empirical history of the discovery has no need of being present in the result.

[60] (47) Gauss: the sum of n prime whole numbers Sn is equal to $n + 1 (n/2) a$[16]

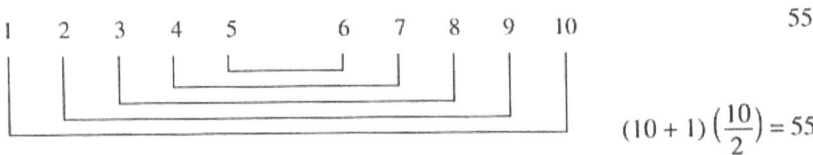

$$(10 + 1)\left(\frac{10}{2}\right) = 55$$

Why? Because this sum is made from $n/2$ numbers of which each is equal to $n + 1$. Now this evidence is accessible only if we formulate $n + 1(n/2)$ in which the double function of n appears:

n as the number at which we have stopped
n as the double of the number of numbers with the value $n + 1$

With the formula $(n + 1/2)n$ we would not see the evidence.

We can logically, formally, pass from one formula to the other; they are equivalent, reversible, reciprocal; they appear to indicate necessity in itself. But the demonstrative light comes to the second from the first.

And even if we happened, on the basis of the formalized definition of whole numbers, and logical calculus, to erase the privilege of the formula $n + 1(n/2)$ we would rediscover in [the] formal beings of the same form [the] privilege of a structure and its recurrence in the others. The idea [that] mathematical being has these properties even before we discover them, [the] passage to the world of essence, this is a retrospective illusion, the realization in advance in a support of what exists only as idealization. The support is in reality natural: "the tree trunks have equal radii before there is geometry." That means nothing, for in the perceived world, there are no radii that are rigorously equal or unequal; there are such things only by means of and for geometry. This means that certain results of manipulation would have been failures or successes that the circle and the equal radii allow us to understand. But there are no equal radii before there is idealization.

[61] (48) This realism
1) Makes no sense in regard to "nature" itself.
2) There is even more reason to think it makes no sense in regard to idealizations that are more distant from nature. Is anyone going to say that our mathematical beings already have the properties that the future will recognize in them? That Abel's theorem existed already in the failures of Cartesian algebra? That Cartesian algebra ran aground on it? No. We must say that mathematical being such that post-Cartesian algebra conceives it did not yet exist, except as the impossibility of Cartesian math[ematical] being. Therefore there is a fitting together of different perspectival views; there is no fitting together of all of them in an absolute knowledge which is completely decentered and final, i.e., an absolute knowledge without the implications of undeveloped sense. Perceptual naivete remains. The passage from the particular to the universal is never finished. And the model of all math[ematical] light, math[ematical] necessity is still the act of *Sinngebung* in a partial context. "Structural truth"

(Wertheimer). The history of knowledge is contracted into itself while advancing, abridges its empirical process, but looks always towards the realized ways that things have fit together, does not see the "essences" face to face. And reciprocally we can say that the first demonstrative step would open a field to which what follows never stops belonging, would inaugurate an "infinite task."[17]

[THE FIELD OF CULTURE]

[66] (49*)[1] [There is a] cognitive process [that is] trans-phenomenal, without being open to essences.

It is openness to the idea.[2] The idea [as] not possessed, but [as] rule for the use of speech (or of the algorithm). The idea penetrates them from a distance just as the moon penetrates the sea.

Consequently historicity of the idea: precisely because it is not included in the phenomena or the words, it exists only in the verbal chain and the perspectives, the apparatuses that make it rigid. And none of them makes it rigid entirely. Therefore, the idea [is] the call to a becoming of individual and inter-individual knowledge.

There is no intelligible world; there is a culture. [That is,] apparatuses of knowledge (words, books, works) which open an ideological field. Exterior and interior of culture: the apparatuses, and their field. In the first relation, there are only discontinuous terms, the one after the other, "cultural objects" and "consciousnesses" which animate them, continuous creation. In the second relation, the idea, we could think, on the contrary, that the past contained the present (retrospective illusion) or that the present actually preserves the whole past in its actuality, its living depth (this is another form of the same illusion). [It is necessary] to think the two relations together, i.e., the idea as field does not contain what will be developed in it, and yet, the idea sends a teleology down a path. The development is not rectilinear, but its zigzags are [a] development, for the rectilinear is *Sinnentleerung*, and the zigzag resumes, reactivates in a different way what has been founded.

Husserl: consciousness is traditionality, and the latter is *understood as* forgetfulness of origins (*Vergessenheit*),[3] i.e., not explication, but appearing of ideas which produce a *step* to be taken, and these ideas were not contained in the past. What is not at issue, however, is to abridge the past in order to leave some space in the mental field for a wholly psychological phenomenon.[4] [As well] what is not at issue is [a] virtue of logic as a separate order, which would in fact contain the whole past. The issue is a survey comparable to that of the perceived through which I know in one sole act that my arm is resting on the table, that I can go over there without articulated means. [There is at once] positive forgetfulness and negative forgetfulness. Conquest of sense and evacuation of sense, realization which is also destruction. Every institution involves this double aspect, end and beginning, *Endstiftung* at the same time as *Urstiftung*. That is what sedimentation is: trace [67] (50*) of the forgotten and thereby a call to thought which depends on itself and goes farther. Evidence, *das Erlebnis der Wahrheit*,⁵ is the experience of this double relation. It is the experience of a resumption which is loss, not totalization, and which precisely for that reason is able to open another development of knowledge. *Wesen ist was gewesen ist*.⁶ But [in a sense] different from Hegel, because it is thought in perceptual terms (*soil* of knowledge, *horizon*),⁷ this becoming can truly anticipate (interdependent *Stiftung* of a symbolic apparatus, founds more than itself: the idea [is to be understood] as a norm of a becoming, and the remedy to *Sinnentleerung* will often be a return to the origins taken in the full sense—[therefore, a] sort of existential eternity of great works), and because conversely the resumption of the past in the present leaves it in its originality, does not truly "surpass" it, does not flatter itself to contain it all [in its entirety], plus something else. In this interiority with escape, this passage from decentering to decentering, without absolute decentering, in this exteriority which does not forbid encroachment, there is truly union of exteriority and interiority, at each moment, while Hegel unifies them only by pushing them to the absolute: absolute real or fact, absolute rational or concept, being unified as absolutes. Empirical history becomes the introduction to Philosophy. [For] Husserl, finally, the transcendental origin cannot be anything other than the empirical origin. There is in the empirical origin an interior, a conceivable history that can be explicated, and which is in the form of a field.⁸

Let us reflect on this idea which is not [that of] an intelligible world.

If there is no system of essences, or pre-personal transc[endental] subj[ectivity], are we not referred to "consciousnesses" with their own "intentional objects," correlative to their "acts"? Where is this surplus of sense that the "field" represents? If it is for the one who is presently thinking, it is one of his intentional objects. If it is not for him, then it is a pure construction of the retrospective illusion: I project into Thales the intentional objects that other consciousnesses have produced in relation to Thales' discoveries. Of course, I think I understand, by means of *Nachvollzug*⁹ and reactivation, the intentional objects of other consciousnesses. But this is only a construction of mine. Within this interlacing, there is no problem, nor is there a phenomenon **[68] (51*)** that surpasses the internal syntheses of one consciousness. No problem of truth, no history of signification therefore: there are only humans, one next to the other, each of which synthesizes, constructs significations that are never objective. The field which contains and does not contain the development of knowledge, the *Nachvollzug* which continues and creates, these are vague thoughts. It has to be the case that the field is neither for Thales nor for his successors, in the inter-world, but then thought by whom?

Answer: this philosophy does not tell us why the consciousnesses claim to understand each other. Why they expect, for example, to know the history of someone in order to judge him. This implies not universal truth, but consciousness of a non-truth of the particular. Certainly history does not provide me with its sense ready-made. I have to remake it, but my interactions with history form me, they give way to a *labor* at the end of which I cannot say that I donate sense, for my criteria are put in question there. External history can give me no criteria, but they can have value against mine. Here to receive is to give, in effect, but to give is to receive. [Such is the sense of the] notion of field and of institution: they give what they do not have and what we receive from them, we bring it to them.[10]

[The] philosophy of the understanding cannot avoid the problem of truth. The philosophy of the understanding is non-philosophy insofar as it takes as given a plurality of consciousnesses having corresponding significations and working in a parallel way, without mediation, without interaction. This view remains within the *Selbstverständlichkeit*[11] of the cogito which is to be founded: how is it possible for me to think that I have reached the universal *cogitatum*? And in particular how is it possible to understand others, history? We have to think about ourselves as substitutable, by means of exchange, my objects must be founded in such a way as to require the assent of others and their objects my assent. We must be inserted into one selfsame world and not the holder of homologous intentional objects.

Then there are not only two modes of existence: the subject for itself, with its intentional objects, and the for others, i.e., the same subject but paradoxically dealt with as if it were an object. There are not only the being for itself, and the being for.

Someone says **[69] (52*)** that the field was not Thales' object, it is the object of successors who resume his works, projected retrospectively into him. It is that or nothing at all. It is necessary that it be the object of Thales or the object of someone else. No. It is at the intersection of the two intentions, the hinge or pivot which has the result that Thales and the others speak of the same truth, just as the perceived world is the same numerically that we all perceive and not simply an intentional object immanent to each. Neither the world nor the objects are behind my back, nor are the hidden facets of things only for me, they are *Wahrnehmungsbereit*,[12] they are not posited as objects. They are objects only if I add the others to myself, others to whom the objects show their hidden facets or to whom they could show their hidden facets, that is, by means of the intermediary of the horizon structure that the philosophy of the understanding wants precisely to reduce.

Then there is an intersubjectivity and not only a plurality of views that are incompossible and connected by their rivalry and their reciprocal destruction. Intersubjectivity: not only do I exist for me, others are for themselves and deny me thereby as myself, and this negation teaches me that they are there and that I am what they think, but we exist *füreinander*[13] as subjects because my objects are worked over by others, objects for him *and* for me, thanks to their thickness. They are not brought back to the "objectified" pellicle.

The notion of "field," of institution, of truth, requires that subjectivity not be for itself at first, but the holder = X of an experience, that the *Sinngebung* be, not the apprehension of this or that under an essence, but the lateral idealization or generalization, by means of recurrence on the basis of a model (this is the *Auffassung als* . . . as open), and consequently that the object is not only the correlate of my *acts*, but also provided with a double horizon by means of which it can become the object for others and not for me alone. The subject gives more than he has because (cf. Valéry) he proposes to the others enigmas that they decipher, with all of themselves, he makes them work, and what we receive, we give it for the same reason, for we receive only an incitement to *Nachvollzug*. The field is, not an order of essences, but cultural cores (phrases, moments of thought) around which this *Nachvollzug* pivots. Being [is not] what is **[70] (53)** in itself or for someone, but what, being for someone, is ready to be developed according to another becoming of knowledge, like a constellation whose figure would be continuously remade according to [a] project which appoints such changes as possible.

We would still have to specify what is invariant, the pivot—in what sense then the future is implied by the institution and the past genuinely integrated into the future. For our description: a work providing an impulse for a labor different and the same, assimilates a history of knowledge to that of painting. Now there is [a] difference. Though the integration is never total, it is more perfect in language. This produces the impression that language is not only, as [in] painting, a construction of a series of quasi-aphasic and mute signifying machines, but the conquest of a free signification, liberated from this gangue, before which the language erases itself. We are not going to consider this, for this is not our subject. It is enough to know that even this (retrospective) possession of a truth comes from institution, and we must therefore return to the institution instead of going more deeply into what properly defines knowledge.

Our problem: is it possible to apply this idea of truth to a history that is other than knowledge? [What is the relation] between personal (and subject) history and total history? Does it involve this perceptual exteriority-interiority? Can we apply the notion of *Stiftung, Ur,* and *Endstiftung* to it?

[HISTORICAL INSTITUTION: PARTICULARITY AND UNIVERSALITY]

Universal history and institution **[71] (54)**

Does institution in the sense above, exteriority-interiority, intersubjective and sociohistorical field, exist anywhere else than in the history of knowledge, i.e., the history of truth?

The history of knowledge results in something other than what it wanted to make, is unforeseeable. But nevertheless algebra realizes the wishes of arithmetic, etc.—Is there this *Urstiftung-Endstiftung* relation anywhere else? Isn't there rather comedy of history, societies which are something other than what they wanted to be and their emblems?

While, in knowledge, to be *this* is to be open to a field that is larger, in general history this would be absolute opacity. While in knowledge the situation is a means of knowing (absolute of the present), in history this would be insularity. There would be no telos. In history, every institution would be emptied of its sense, would be "behind the back" of humans, not resumed by them as a means of dominating or at least of being astride time, still less resumed by others as a phase of a significant whole, but a thing, an opaque structure to be known, which gets developed above the heads of the individuals.

Reaction against Hegel. We react against the idea of real synthesis, which truly accumulates everything, against the idea of a system, of an actual possession of all dispersed existence of humans. Marx already in a sense: by itself, history offers only a "mechanical dialectic." There is a solution only through praxis not contemplation. This solution is itself speculative because praxis is not pure creation, but follows the movement of the history that realizes what bears the negation of negation, universal, self-critical class. A lot of our contemporaries go farther.[1] There is no institution of negativity. There is only a praxis of violence, founded on the basis of the criticism of our society, act of re-creation. There is no *true* society, *true* production, there is only the rational justification of a society as objectively more real, more like a society than another. They are **[72] (55)** incomparable. In reference to that, one can found either a complete agnosticism or a purely moral choice. And thereby weirdly, we intersect with the other Hegel, the one who places the State, the institution, transcendent to the individuals, for in non-knowledge, there is no reason not to consider non-sense as sense.

Therefore a problem: relation of one institutional world to another, relation of a philosopher to the societies on which he reflects—of the individual to the institution.

I. Example of the history of "ideas" (an easier example: what is at issue is no longer science, but we are not yet in the opacity of the social).

II. Example of an institution that is apparently without "truth," accessible to the sole "sociology" (Lévi-Strauss).

III. Example of historical institution, i.e., giving way to resumption and functioning within a horizon of universal history: the Mediterranean.[2]

[74] (supplement to 55)
Reaction against Hegel—which leads back to Hegel. How?

Against the Hegel of the logic of history—For the Hegel of the irony of history. Does Hegel therefore contain two opposite themes?

Logic of history and irony of history are not opposites in him because of his notion of absolute knowledge, of philosophy or of the system.

[In other words] in philosophical consciousness, history is meaningful, rigorous logic. But the non-philosophers do not have this view. They therefore do not know what they are doing (irony of history). However, they are not philosophers. The philosopher knows better than them what they are doing. They are a flaw in the great diamond. The idea of philosophical absolute knowledge, of closure, of exhaustion connects the logic and the irony of history in Hegel.

Our contemporaries disavow the "philosophy of history," absolute knowledge. Therefore, they are for contingency, [the] pure fact.

But this relativism, (Lévi-Strauss saying that it is impossible to confront societies objectively: every society, seen from within, is accumulation and history, seen from without is ahistorical)[3] **[74 verso]**, if we go all the way, results in pragmatism: justified pure creation. Now that restores, in non-knowledge, [the] omnipotence of the philosopher. It is the knowledge that he has of the impossibility of [the] philosophy of history, i.e., still a philosophy, which he uses to justify all "cultural affairs" that are undertaken. The non-philosophers would be led to think that there is a mediation, a rational way to make a hierarchy.

Note that here the thought of Lévi-Strauss marks a stopping point.[4]

It is always philosophical, i.e., closed, consciousness, which in (absolute) knowledge or in non-knowledge, valorizes the irony of history. Thereby [a] kinship with Hegel, and [a] return to Hegel just when we criticize one of Hegel's two aspects. The absolute opacity of history, like its absolute light, is still philosophy conceived as closed knowledge. The one who observes the opacity sets himself up outside of history, becomes a universal spectator.[5]

This is where our path comes in. If there is institution in the sense of a *field*, we are neither for opacity nor for the system. And [the] philosopher, instead of being Cosmotheoros (as he still is in relativism), radical solitude, exhaustive thought, becomes on the contrary and precisely [the one for whom there is] recognition of the particularities which unite. Making his self-critique or relativizing himself, historical relativism or **[75] (supplementary page 3)** skepticism is surpassed. The situation [means] not insularity, not idea-history, but us speaking of other cultures. Cf. Husserl saying that in a sense skepticism concerning perception makes no sense, for I learn about errors only because I know what corrects them. The question would not be asked if it was not, certainly not resolved in advance, but at least asked within a horizon of universality which forbids the opacity and the meaninglessness from hardening into the unknowable.

We propose exactly, with the notion of institution as interior-exterior, the means to exit from philosophical solitude. This can look like the middle line between radical pluralism and logic, but this is [an] appearance, from an external viewpoint. If we really conduct [the] philosophical task of the elucidation of the perceptual sense, the philosophical task will look like a view that is completely positive in relation to which the others are failures.

In any case, let's have some examples of this method.

I. Lucien Febvre **[76] (55 addition)**
Does one time have access to another time?
The problem "is not [. . .] to catch hold of a man, a writer of the sixteenth century, in isolation from his contemporaries, and, just because a certain passage in his work fits in with the direction of one of our own modes of feeling, to decide that he fits under one of the rubrics we use today for classifying those who do or do not think like us in matters of religion. [. . .] The problem is in knowing how men in 1532 heard *Pantagruel* and *Cymbalum mundi* [. . .]. It is, even more, in knowing how these men were absolutely incapable of hearing or comprehending them. We instinctively bring to bear on these texts our ideas, our feelings, the fruit of our scientific inquiries, our political experiences and our social achievements. But those who leafed through them when they were brand-new, under a bookseller's awning on rue Mercière in Lyon or rue Saint-Jacques in Paris—what did they read between the carefully printed lines? Just because the sequence of ideas in these texts confers on them a kind of eternal verity, to our eyes at least, can we conclude that all intellectual attitudes are possible in all periods?"[6]

HISTORICAL INSTITUTION

In order to understand Rabelais, don't take isolated documents (from Rabelais or judgments about him) but enter into the totality of his horizons.

1) Certain contemp[oraries] call Rabelais an atheist.

But [according to] [Pierre] Viret (reformatist from Lausanne), to know God without the Christ is to be an atheist. "For when Saint Paul, in the Epistle to the Ephesians, called the pagans 'atheists' he declared that not merely those who denied all divinity were without God but also those who did not know the true God and follow strange gods instead of Him."[7] Therefore Rabelais's atheism [means] *other* God. The atheist is the one who thinks differently from everyone. The term "atheist" belongs to "objective" thought, i.e., "subjective." Viret thinks that those who do not believe in the God that he believes in are *objectively* atheists, i.e., *for him* atheists. By itself the word encroaches on *the other*. Therefore Rabelais "the atheist" proves the *alterity* of Rabelais, not his unbelief.

But [Cardinal Jacques Davy] du Perron accuses [Martin] Luther of denying the immortality of the soul. **[77] (56)** Was he lying? "Was du Perron telling a cynical untruth, then? Not at all. He had reasoned it out, and correctly, as he saw it. He had made deductions. He had followed an orderly—hence legitimate—chain of syllogisms, each perfectly contained in the other."[8]

But Guillaume Farel, [John] Calvin, accuse [Michael] Servetus of being an atheist because they made a deduction. Because they are deductive. In fact, Servetus does not adhere to their consequences for one principled reason. He is for thought dialoguing with itself. In the clear light of deductive thought [it is] atheism. In the clear light of modern Protestantism, [it is] orthodoxy.[9] Cf. communism: —1) the accusation of "communism" against all "sound reasoning": [they denounce] "the Bolshevik" —2) within communism, the same alterity: [Georges] Friedmann [they say], admitting that Bukharin had been swept up in "the logic of the struggle," objectively taking the side of Hitler.[10] The idea that there is no margin, no *quatenus*,[11] that thought proper *is* universal history. This is what Farel's judgment of Servetus expresses.

2) Rabelais's texts themselves.

A[bel] Lefranc: Rabelais says about his *Grandes chroniques gargantuines:* "For the printers will have sold more of them in two months' time than Bibles bought in nine years." And then in order to testify to his veracity: "I speak of it as Saint John spoke of the Apocalypse: *quod vidimus, testamur.*"[12] And in Rabelais, parodies of miracles, etc.

Febvre: in order to judge, one has to bring together other texts of the time: the *Sermons joyeux* with *Sermons gastronomiques* over *Buvez et mangez*.[13] That resembles the *consummatum est* of Book Three: "he fairly set it on fire, that he might the better say, *Consummatum est*. Even just as since his time Saint Thomas Aquinas did, when he had eaten up the whole lamprey." It also resembles the "Sitio" of drinkers (Rabelais: "I have the word of the gospel in my mouth, Sitio"). That shocks Abel Lefranc, but it does not shock those during the epoch of clerical jokes. "When Madame du Bocage inspired Cardinal Passionei, who was famous for his strict morals, to say something flattering to her, Benedict XIV quipped, 'Et homo factus est' (and he was made man)—which no one used as a pretext to declare him anti-Christian."[14] Our epoch: more rigorously believing (Bérullian believing)[15] or unbelieving in matters of faith precisely because our time is not believing. Cf. the dogs in the churches in olden times and today.[16] "We should be in no hurry to say, with the magnificent rigidity with which unbelievers call on believers to be superhuman (by virtue of their principles), that he was scarcely a Christian."[17] There would also be Christianity, but less, in the fastidious attitude of the moderns. The "purity" of belief would be correlated to unbelief and would produce a system with it. Cf. peremptory, specified theology precisely insofar as there is unbelief. The belief in the immortality of the soul is "in certain of the earliest Fathers . . . vague almost to nonexistence. . . . A Christianity without the immortality of the soul is not, in the long run, absolutely inconceivable, and the proof of it is that it has been conceived" ([Etienne] Gilson cited by Febvre).[18] [Thus] the questions of *opinion* are not the questions of history. A doctrine that has historical significance is not the object of *opinion*. (Examine in Catholicism the attitude of "objective" thought—which condemns over the consequences—which is a reaction, and the counterpart: a justification after the fact of the condemned.[19] With this we are on the terrain of history. Define an ultra-liberalism as being beyond naive liberalism and authoritarianism.) (The true truth would be neither "objective" thought nor the after-the-fact justification, nevertheless the questions of opinion are without interest.)

Closeness of Rabelais to Erasmus. Some have said that Erasmus too stopped being a Christian. But there are sentences in Erasmus which are anti-Christian only for us. For example, frequent communion after the time of Saint Francis de Sales. Erasmus's phrase concerning the Eucha-

HISTORICAL INSTITUTION

rist, according to the translation, is orthodox or against the sacraments. Catholic belief supposes both interiority and exteriority, it wants both, therefore both sincerity and fidelity—and one can therefore always pull in one direction: history [is] choice.[20]

What is in common to both Rabelais and Erasmus is [a] non-chosen Christianity. It is our ideology of choice that falsifies our view of the sixteenth century. It is anachronism (and perhaps it makes us understand our own time badly).[21]

Religion's domination of life[22] even at Geneva.[23] No possible support for irreligion:[24] mental tools, missing words,[25] no perspective, syntax,[26] and vocabulary (language constituting a dam and moreover "backed-up water").[27] Faith and philosophy are certainly not superimposable, but in a relation of exchange.[28] Knowledge by hearsay and compilation,[29] "fluid time, stagnant time." Erasmus did not know his own age, how old he is,[30] therefore no notion of becoming and anachronism, one is in *Urzeit*[31] or history-myth. Does veracity make sense? Century of precursors, men without descendants **[79] (58)** who will have intellectual posterity only two centuries later.[32]

True meaning of the Febvre study **[81] (58*)**[33]

[By maintaining the indictment] against anachronism, apparent "eternity" of the written texts, but [does not conclude in] skepticism; historical agnosticism ("believing" does not have the same sense today as it had in the sixteenth century), [idea of an] insularity of the epochs.

If they were insular, we would not even see their difference.

Febvre's book demonstrates by the fact that we can see the difference. By starting from the whole, by interpreting documents in relation to each other, we reactivate the horizon (for example, fluid time, stagnant time).

And the writer, the precursor, is not only the reflection of others, his "time" is not an island on which he is stranded. He can penetrate outside of himself. Simply, it is necessary to begin by placing him in the historical horizon in order to evaluate what in him anticipates (otherwise, his time would not "change").

[The] labor of historical "objectivity": for the historian, [it is therefore] to be put in question over and against the phenomena, to know its principles in contact with traces, correlatively to determine the other epoch, and finally the relations of the precursor to his time.

Simultaneous knowledge of self, of the time and of the writer who reciprocally condition one another or form a system.

For example, the reestablishment of the sense of *atheism* in [the] contemporaries of Rabelais distinguishes the sense of the word in the sixteenth century from ours. But [that] marks nevertheless a divergence, an alterity between Rabelais and those who use the word. This is in reality a difference between dialectical thought and syllogistic thought in the Christian horizon, Febvre says.—Yes, but this difference can make Christianity shine forth in perspective. If the Christian horizon is only a psychological horizon, its reestablishment does not prove that Rabelais is no different from his contemporaries. We have to show that this is an ontological horizon. That is, [it] implies a coherent conception of Christianity. The psychological horizon, this would be to define Rabelais by what he thought and believed.

Jokes about priests prove that the same jokes were innocent and are today impious. Of course. Nevertheless, [they] prove perhaps our purism—but also the non-purism of the sixteenth century, perhaps that Christianity is too instituted in the sixteenth century in order to be [lived], perhaps that authentic Christianity presupposes non-institution, relative unbelief, something that is not obvious.

Febvre's idea is that the historical fabric is relatively loose, [82] (59*) there is a certain "tolerance" of all ideology, its existence in history is not that of a pure "opinion." The productions eventually crystallize upon a given structure of the world. Every historical "intention" is heavy. Only at certain moments do we have a decision, a choice, an option, not at every instant. There would be something false in demanding absolute ideological purity (cf. communism today) which exists only for the others.[34]

Consequently, there is no insularity of the Christian and the non-Christian, of the communist and the non-communist.

That does not mean at the same time that there are no breaks, no change, no deviations. Simply they are not always the most professed. These are dialectical mutations, shifts, changes to be appreciated in context. There is the weight of the whole which is there, tacitly accepted, congealed by language, the mental tool. But that does not prevent the fact that there is a breakthrough which prepares the changes of the tool: the "dam" of language, but thereby preparing an active mass. The fact that a certain word is missing is not decisive. There is what is between them.

Alterity, like identity, has to be appreciated by the *Nachvollzug* of the time, entering into its horizons, by going below the opinions, our and theirs, going all the way down to the soil. Communication by coexistence and not inaccessible or centrifugal *Sinngebung*.[35] It is in the imaginary, seen from the outside, by means of notions, that the cultures exclude one another or are unknowable. But besides this false for others, there is a true for others which does not exclude understanding, by the labor of the one against the other.

II. However this [is] a relatively privileged case.

Is there not a wholly other transcendence of institutions if we take them farther?

For example, our free marriage, with the prohibition of incest—how does it make us understand that marriage is arranged with a maternal cross-cousin and not arranged with a paternal cross-cousin or the reverse?[36] Apparent absurdity of marriage prohibited with parallel cousins.[37]

There are other structures of alliance, which are to be deciphered as [83] (60) such.[38]

Direct exchange:[39] bilateral marriage [is] connected to social structure; the social structure has to be disharmonic,[40] i.e., residence and filiation have to follow the lineage of the father and the lineage of the mother.[41] Existence of matrimonial classes. Short cycle [that procures] safety by means of the reciprocity of exchange, spirit of "security."[42]

Indirect or generalized exchange,[43] matrilateral marriage[44] with the daughter of the maternal uncle; harmonic regimes (residence and lineage go together)—greater, organic solidarity by means of the dependence of each in regard to the whole; decisive importance of the degree of kinship. Open cycle. Spirit of sociological "adventure."

This [is] obtained by [the] reading of the facts. [We elaborate the] theoretical construction on the basis of the facts, as in physics, but this *Sinngebung* is maintained in a close relation to lived experience because it is produced from the viewpoint of the constitution of the social connection, which is always started anew in each and intersects with what the primitives *say* (cf. Margaret Mead's indigenous people saying, when we insist, marrying his sister would be not to want to have a brother-in-law);[45] evidence of the social for others which is obvious. Sense of the incest prohibition: exchange.

However, this identification of sociology with lived experience, this "understanding" is, for Lévi-Strauss, only an order *quoad nos*. In itself, if the knowledge of the social and of social being is united, it is not the case that they have a relation of mutual implication (cf. the discussion of Febvre above). Social knowledge is a product or a reflection of social being.

Inductively, we come to [a] simple schema of the possibility of exchange, to three elementary possibilities: bilateral, matrilateral, and patrilateral marriage.[46] On the basis of these possibilities, systems constructed by these principles are derived [as] consequences. [Therefore], social essences, [and] mathematical expression of these essences. Existing societies undergo this logic.

The complex forms result from "development"[47] or [are] reactions to the consequences of the essences. Dialectical [process] because 1) there are reactions (for example, the transition to free marriage);[48] 2) in [a] given society, there is always bipolarity. For example, the *risk* of generalized exchange always gives rise to the obsession with direct or restricted exchange (hence the prescription at times of incestuous marriage = crisis).[49]

But dialectic understood in Engels's sense: dialectic of nature.[50]

Hence, realism of social essences which *are* the same ones in existing historical systems.

Where is this system of generalized exchange? Sometimes it is [84] (61) thought by someone ("planned sociology" of the Australian aborigines).[51] But the majority of the time not. Then the system is to be recognized in the social structure as a fact.[52]

Hence, systematic sociology which is independent of history, and whose laws therefore are not situated at the level of historical facts and are not the simple expression of modalities of existence, but a priori in relation to them.[53]

Hence, absolute knowledge and absolute relativism. If one is inside one sees order, if one is outside, not. [Therefore] relativism. Lived experience [is] irreplaceable, necessary. But by means of lived experience, we rediscover [the] functioning of structures that are in itself. Sociology is inside and outside because it reaches these structures. Phenomenology [is only] metaphors ("spirit of adventure," "spirit of security"), unconscious presentiment of laws that function without us, as in physics [the] atom does not need to know [the] laws in order to follow them.

This is the problem already posed by *Gestalttheorie*. It would be necessary to wonder what social "gravitation" means not outside of all thought but outside of all life.[54]

Problem that is analogous to that of Einstein. [For] Einstein, [there is a] plurality of times. By placing himself in Peter's location, and noting that Paul's time is interconnected with his system of reference, Einstein says that his time is dilated or contracted. But this "relativism" presupposes that one projects into Paul the image that Peter has of his time and that Paul does not have. [In other words] Einstein the physicist, interconnected with Peter, thinks that he is the universal spectator. A more radical relativism would teach him that Paul senses his time as Peter senses his own and would reestablish universal time not by comparison and coincidence of the two times that are in effect incomparable, but because for each his time is universal and each can know nothing of a time that would not be universal. For example, one cannot object that my present is future for an observer who is contemporaneous but situated elsewhere, for hypothetically he is not contemporaneous and one cannot crystallize my present [as being] his future. Paradoxes as soon as we want to interpret relativism in terms **[85] (62)** of the realist theory of knowledge (Einstein).

The same holds for Lévi-Strauss. His radical relativism (the insularity of cultures) is interconnected with an idea of absolute knowledge or coincidence with social being or sociology which contradicts the relativism and which is necessary to the relativism.

It is necessary to be more Einsteinian than Einstein and reestablish the world of perception with its "simultaneities"—likewise it is necessary to be more relativist than Lévi-Strauss and put knowledge back in the historical world of perception with its operations of "understanding."[55]

The field of social "gravitation," the field of structures, social being [is not] the access to the underside of the whole social, [is not] the understanding of Leibniz's God.

This dialectical milieu [is not] real. This milieu in which crises, problems, solutions, reversals, transformations are produced is not an in-itself. Difficulty of an in-itself that assures a sort of "finality" (for us), that gives rise to answers, etc.

For example, difficulty of understanding in this way [the] transition to the complex forms which are produced as a [?] solution to the crisis of generalized exchange. Emergence of something else.

[One must] take the social and sociology as an idealization of the social perception, [a] society, [a] matrimonial system as a symbolical system or social thing, i.e., as a principle of order according to a perceptual style, not according to an essence. Cf. Lévi-Strauss [speaking of the] orientation of the social perception of generalized exchange. Take that literally. Certainly there is a problem with the appearance of significant cores. Why are we able to think the social? There is a problem of the perceptual order. But [this order] is changing and sociology is [an] expression of it, [sociology is not] coincidence with the perceptual order. History is [its?] reality, history moreover which is not events, but right away intersubjectivity (transcendental history).

By means of this perceptual foundation (= Lévi-Strauss's unconscious), we would turn back upon the nature-culture distinction, or to the kinship-alliance distinction. We would discover [an] effective foundation [by means of the] utilization of psychoanalysis (and not only of *Totem and Taboo*)[56] and [by understanding the] sexual signification of nomenclature and classifications. The universal is there under this aspect.

[86] (63) Problem: is there a field of world history or universal history? Is there an intended accomplishment? A closure on itself? A *true* society?

The question is still, as in the history of knowledge, interrogation of history.

But [what is at issue is an] existential, not conceptual, universal, which is inserted by this very interrogation. There is, if not a true society (none of the existing societies is the true one, but even in principle no society can assert this), at least societies which ask themselves the question of the true society, "open societies" in a sense that is different from Bergson's: [conceiving the] idea of a recuperation of history by means of history. And there are other societies that we can call relatively false in relation to those who pose the question of the true society. This does not mean that in certain relations they are not more beautiful. But they do not play the mysterious game which consists in putting all humans into the game, in attempting to make the intermingling truly universal. They follow the letter of institution but not its spirit, which consists in not being limited, prohibited, enclosed on an island of customs. The spirit of institution consists in setting an unlimited historical labor underway.

[87] (*Institution* **first** page of the conclusion)
Lévi-Strauss: there is a logic of all the systems, a logic in itself and of their succession which is "development."

This logic [is] accessible provided that we happen to construct the system of possible relations—for example, restricted exchange (patrilateral marriage), generalized exchange (matrilateral marriage), bilateral marriage.

The logic determines and circumscribes the social existence of others, the passage through others (and through others who are unknown), which is the motor of the incest prohibition, the positive side of these prohibitions.

This logic [is] accessible to the understanding of the sociologist who constructs [a] systematic sociology that is constrained not to contradict the historical facts, but not constrained to give an account of them. [Distinction between] systematic order and historico-geographical order.

HISTORICAL INSTITUTION

The mathematical expression and the theory translate therefore a real or dialectical logic of nature.

Realism: we reach the social essences, which are the same ones as in the existing, historical systems, and which do not have to be justified inductively.

Identity of thought and being: the Australian aborigines are sociologists, in the sense that they are moved about by essences and they do not know the essence in their truth, they have an unconscious knowledge of them which surely directs them.

Difficulties:

But *where is* this truth of societies? The truth is not in the individuals, it is not in the sum of the individuals—it is in the field of social gravitation. This field is capable of posing and resolving "problems." It is the real seat of the dialectic. Philosophy of the *Gestalt*.

[88] (**second** page of the conclusion) Hence, the possibility of a phenomenological reading of the structures—which, however, does not turn them into *noemata;* they are the social real.

As for the historical viewpoint, systematic sociology is neutral in this regard. Historically, different structures coexist in one selfsame empirical system (for example, restricted exchange as the obsession of generalized exchange; for example, the homogeneity of the "archaic" and the "modern").

This means that Lévi-Strauss provides himself with an absolute observer, Cosmotheoros, with which he identifies himself, and over and against whom the social is an object. Lévi-Strauss, he is not in it. His knowledge is reflection or notation, is not taken into the social. Cf. Einstein: plurality of times which comes from the fact that, while having put himself in Peter's place, Einstein attributes to Paul the dilated or contracted time which is that of Paul seen from Peter's viewpoint. Therefore we have the paradox of multiple times and the simultaneity of my present with the future of another observer. This is possible only if we suppose "born at the same moment as me," which is hypothetically impossible. If we really abide by the hypothesis, [it is] impossible to assert a plurality of times. There is one sole existential time, i.e., the differently situated observers can do nothing but universalize their time. In fact, the times of different subjects are never comparable, and this is why we can call the times neither many nor single. The unique time of which we are speaking is presumptive time. In Einstein, [there is the] coexistence of a rationalism and paradoxes, paradoxes which are inevitable when the rationalism is at the same time realist.

The dialectic becomes a paradox when it is realized in this way. There is no dialectic of nature.

Hence, Lévi-Strauss's difficult position. [He] asserts absolute knowledge and at the same time absolute relativism. These two contradictory positions are sustained. It is necessary that the dialectic embrace subjectivity and the object, the social. Lévi-Strauss often asserts that lived experience cannot be penetrated, **[89]** (conclusion page **three**) or in any case that there is no substitute for it. But that leads in no way to [a] phenomenological sociology. Each time that he speaks the language of lived experience, Lévi-Strauss adds that these are only metaphors. Reality is of the same type as physical laws.[57]

Solution: the system would be based, not on [a] divine understanding which would be "the real" (for Lévi-Strauss as for Engels), not on [a] "teleology" of essences working behind our backs, but on [the] social configuration which would be the symbolic apparatus of this intersubjectivity. Take literally what Lévi-Strauss takes as a metaphor: perceptual orientation of the social space. Just as the perceptual thing is the lived principle of cohesion without being an essence, the symbolic system, the *pattern*, would be a social thing. A society [is] perceived just as a thing is—and, just like a thing, is never "pure." The *idea* that we form of it is historical and event-based, it is a becoming of sense, it is a dialectic in the Marxist and even in the Engelian sense. Logic, mathematics, phenomenology (in the sense of the being of essences) develop the implications, the "kernels." But that is the expression of . . . or the idealization which has an ontological sense that is different from the thing expressed.

In particular, [the] perceptual foundation of the system [is discovered] in sexuality. The system as the variation of a sexual being in the world who is a polymorph. [It is true that] the very notion of exchange supposes that women are only intermediaries between one man and another man (like food, goods). In fact, this is so. But isn't this still a historical fact?[58] And in order to think the social fully, wouldn't we have to have a notion that is more general than *exchange*, coexistence, more general than the social existence of others, intersubjectivity? Certainly, coexistence and intersubjectivity appear only in concrete societies, in historical situations, but there they are a foundation of interunderstanding.

Weakness of Lévi-Strauss's analysis when he makes the transition to complex forms **[90]** (conclusion page **four**): free marriage, except for some negative prescriptions, cannot pass for the development of the elementary forms of generalized exchange. There is a crisis here, but on the basis of this crisis, emergence of something else.

The system is always artificial. The essences of kinship are styles of existence. Impossible to understand exactly an emergence as emergence of something else unless one puts the kinship of different sectors into contact.

Thus, this is a problem of knowing whether there is a history that involves a field, that accomplishes an aim, is closed upon itself. And even in a relative sense as in [the] history of knowledge, a *true* society. There are at least, in a sense different from Bergson's, open societies and closed societies, societies which form the idea of a recuperation of history by means of history and other societies who do not do this (cf. China abandoning a part of its system of writing), and we can call the latter *false* societies even if we do not call the first ones *true*. This does not mean that in certain relations they are not more beautiful. But these societies do not play the mysterious game which consists in putting all humans in the balance. They are not faithful to the a priori of institution or to its spirit, and they clench upon the letter of it. They do not intend the *Miteinander* or the *Füreinander*, the universal intermingling.

SUMMARY FOR THURSDAY'S COURSE

Institution in Personal and Public History

In the concept of institution we are seeking a solution to the difficulties found in the philosophy of consciousness. Over and against consciousness, there are only the objects constituted by consciousness. Even if we grant that certain of the objects are "never completely" constituted (Husserl), they are at each moment the exact reflection of the acts and powers of consciousness. There is nothing in these constituted objects that is able to throw consciousness back into other perspectives. There is, from consciousness to the object, no exchange, no movement. When consciousness considers its own past, all that it knows is that there has been back in the past this other, which is mysteriously called me, but which has nothing in common with me except for an absolutely universal ipseity which I share as well with every "other" of whom I can form a concept. By means of a continuous series of explosions, my past has given way to my present. Finally, when consciousness considers others, their own existence is for consciousness only its pure negation; it does not know that they see it, it knows merely that it is seen. Diverse times and diverse temporalities are incompossible and form only a system of reciprocal exclusions.

If the subject were instituting, and not constituting, we would understand in contrast that the subject is not instantaneous and that the other person is not merely the negative of myself. What I have begun at certain decisive moments would be neither distant, in the past, as an objective memory, nor would it be actual as a memory assumed. Rather, what I have begun would be truly in the "between," as the field of my becoming during this period. And my relation to another person would not be reduced to an alternative. An instituting subject is able to coexist with another because the instituted is not the immediate reflection of the activity of the former and can be taken up by himself or by others without a total re-creation being at issue. Thus the instituted exists between others and myself, between me and myself, like a hinge, the consequence and the guarantee of our belonging to one selfsame world.

SUMMARY FOR THURSDAY'S COURSE

Therefore by institution, we were intending here those events in an experience which endow the experience with durable dimensions, in relation to which a whole series of other experiences will make sense, will form a thinkable sequel or a history—or again the events which deposit a sense in me, not just as something surviving or as a residue, but as the call to follow, the demand of a future.

The concept of institution has been approached through four different levels of phenomena, of which the first three deal with personal or intersubjective history and the last with public history.

There is something like an institution even in animality (there is an impregnation of the animal by the living beings which surround it at the beginning of its life)—and even in human functions which used to be considered purely "biological" (puberty presents the rhythm of preservation—the resumption and the surpassing of earlier events—here the Oedipal conflict—which is characteristic of institution). However, in the human the past is able not only to orient the future or to furnish the terms of the problems of the adult person, but also to give way to *investigation,* in Kafka's sense, or to an indefinite elaboration. Conservation and surpassing are more profound, so that it becomes impossible to explain behavior by means of its past, anymore than by means of its future. The analysis of love in Proust presents this "simultaneity," this crystallization upon each other of the past and the future, of subject and "object," of the positive and the negative. In a first approximation, the feeling is an illusion and the institution a habit, since a way of loving learned elsewhere or in childhood is being transferred, since the love bears only ever on the interior image of the "object." For such a love to be true and to reach the other person herself, it would be necessary that the love had never been lived by anyone. However, once it has been recognized that pure love is impossible and that it would be a pure negation, we still have to observe that this negation is a fact and that this impossibility has happened. Proust catches a glimpse of a *via negativa* of love, manifest beyond any question in the experience of a broken heart, though having a broken heart is the reality of separation and jealousy. At the highest point of alienation, jealousy becomes disinterestedness. It is quite impossible to claim that the present love is nothing but an echo of the past. On the contrary, the past takes on the outline of a preparation or premeditation of a present that exceeds it in meaning although it recognizes itself in it.

The institution of a painter's work, or of a style in the history of painting, reveals the same subterranean logic. A painter learns to paint otherwise by imitating his predecessors. Each of his works announces those to follow—and establishes the fact that these followers cannot be the same as him. Everything hangs together, and yet it would not be possible to say where it is going. Likewise, in the history of painting, the problems (the problem of perspective, for example) are rarely resolved directly. The investigation stops at an impasse, other investigations seem to create a diversion, but the new impulse allows the obstacle to be overcome from another direction. Thus, rather than a *problem*, there is an "interrogation" of painting, which is enough to give a common meaning to all its endeavors and which is enough to turn them into a history, but this common meaning never allows us to anticipate the history by means of concepts.

Is this true only for the pre-objective domain of personal life and art? Does the development of knowledge obey a manifest logic? If the development must have in it one truth, is it not necessary that the truths be connected in a system which only gradually reveals itself, but whose entirety resides in itself outside of time? In order to be more agile and apparently more deliberate, the movement of knowledge presents nevertheless this internal circulation between the past and the present which we have noticed in the other institutions. The series of "idealizations" which makes the whole number appear as a special case of a more essential number does not set us up in an intelligible world from which it could be deduced. Rather, the series of "idealizations" takes the evidence proper to the whole number, which remains implicit. The historicity of knowledge is not an "apparent" characteristic of knowledge which would leave us free to define truth "in itself" analytically. Even in the order of exact knowledge we must tend toward a "structural" conception of truth (Wertheimer). There is truth in the sense of a field common to the diverse enterprises of knowledge.

If theoretical consciousness, in its most assured forms, were not foreign to historicity, one might think that in return history would benefit from a rapprochement with theory and, with the preceding restrictions concerning the notion of system, allow itself to be dominated by thought. This would be to forget that thought has access to another historical horizon, to another "mental toolbox" (L. Febvre) only through the self-criticism of its categories, through a lateral penetration and not by a sort of ubiquity in principle. There occurs a simultaneous decentering and recentering of the elements of our own life, a movement by us toward the past and of the past reanimated toward us. And this working of the past against the present does not result in a closed universal history or in a complete system of all possible human combinations with respect to such an institution as, for example, kinship. Rather, it results in a picture of diverse, complex probabilities, which are always connected to local circumstances, burdened with a coefficient of facticity, and such that we can never say of one that it is more true than another, although we can say that one is more false, more artificial, and has less openness to a future which is less rich.

These fragmentary analyses are intended as a revision of Hegelianism, which is the discovery of phenomenology, of the living, real, and original relation between the elements of the world. But Hegelianism situates this relation in the past in order to subordinate it to the systematic vision of the philosopher. Either phenomenology is only an introduction to true knowledge, which remains estranged from the adventures of experience, or phenomenology dwells entirely within philosophy. Phenomenology cannot conclude with the pre-dialectical formula that "Being is," and it has to take into account the mediation of being. It is this development of phenomenology into the metaphysics of history that we wished to prepare here.

ENDNOTES FOR THE COURSE ON INSTITUTION

[INTRODUCTION]

1. *Hyle* may be rendered in English as "matter" and *Auffassung als* as "apprehension as."
2. *Abschattungen*, "profiles."
3. In a way that occurs quite frequently and was probably done while rereading the notes, Merleau-Ponty underlines the text that he has at first written. This is done so often that it cannot function as emphasis. However, certain words are underlined twice. Here they are transcribed in italics.
4. *Zeitpunkt*, "point of time."
5. *Urempfindung*, "originary sensation."
6. Merleau-Ponty, in the margin: "in relation to me, because I am, in relation to myself, instituted-instituting."
7. Merleau-Ponty, in the margin: "'mad' conception of fiat (Malraux's Being and doing)."
8. *Sache*, "thing."
9. Merleau-Ponty, in the margin: "that which is and demands to be; it has to become what it is."
10. Daniel Guérin, *Class Struggle in the First French Republic*, trans. Ian Patterson (London: Pluto, 1977; orig. pub. 1946).
11. See the critical analysis of Guérin's theses in Maurice Merleau-Ponty, *The Adventures of the Dialectic*, trans. Joseph Bien (Evanston, Ill.: Northwestern University Press, 1973), 211.
12. Merleau-Ponty, in the margin: "The sense of the contract consists in recognizing the other only insofar as he is defined by the very terms of the contract. Juridical opposition of the notions of contract and institution: pronounced nullification of the contracts in the name of institution."
13. Merleau-Ponty, in the margin: "Artificial to separate the pure time (of consciousness) and measured time. The way in which the measuring is attached to time, resists it, indicates that time is included in its very substance, and not merely participated: it is the granule of sugar that makes me wait, it is necessary therefore that I put a duration in it (Bergson in *Time and Free Will* [trans. F. L. Pogson (New York: Harper and Row, 1960)])."
14. Merleau-Ponty, in the margin: "Someone will say: but the baby, the sleepwalker, 'go out' only for others. In themselves, they are objects. No: there is change of tensions with the surroundings, and the voluntary mobility is the sublimation of the anchoring points, not 'objective' consciousness."
15. *Sinngebung*, "donation of sense."
16. *Stiftung* is the German term for "institution."
17. Merleau-Ponty, in the margin: "In animals the imprint is also reserved: fixation to man reappearing at puberty. But this mark possesses no indefinite productivity. Has no value of a symbolic matrix."

ENDNOTES FOR THE COURSE ON INSTITUTION

18. See also [19] (15).
19. Merleau-Ponty, in the margin: "Love: neither fated nor manufactured: instituted."
20. Merleau-Ponty, in the margin: "he did not want to love because he loved."
21. Merleau-Ponty, in the margin: "and to doubt the experience of mourning, this would still be to continue the game of jealousy."
22. Merleau-Ponty, in the margin: "Reality of love as institution, even when it does not appear before critical consciousness. Nexus. Hinge me-other. Common terrain."
23. Merleau-Ponty, in the margin: "The action on others would moreover already be public life."
24. Merleau-Ponty, in the margin: "Reactivation is not only the making explicit of what was implicit, but awakening of the total, originary intention of which it was only a partial expression. Contemporaneity of all the truths or of all the histories. Husserl rediscovers here one of the senses of Permanent Revolution: the anticipation of the future in the total past and in its non-clarified horizons. Each epoch anticipates and is late for itself. Through their horizons, the epochs hold fast. Continuous revolution, but because it has begun. But in order to found this against a revolutionary conception, it is necessary to show in what sense the future is *gestiftet* in the founding intention, in what sense it continues it as much as it changes it, for that is what conditions the discussion of Sartre's thesis: abrupt *Sinngebung*, which makes the absolutely new come forth, the prospective illusion—and my position: I admit revolution, but relativized."
25. *Gestiftet*, "instituted."
26. Max Wertheimer, *Experimentelle Studien über das Sehen von Bewegung* (Leipzig: J.A. Barth, 1912).
27. Merleau-Ponty, in the margin: "Manifest and latent institution. This is where the mystification of institution comes from: as knowledge, it is necessary that institution is also ignorance, as ignorance (of its actual functioning) institution is also the knowledge of it (since it is in history as use value)."
28. Cf. Claude Lévi-Strauss, "Race and History," in *Structural Anthropology*, vol. 2., trans. Monique Layton (Chicago: University of Chicago Press, 1976), 323-62.
29. See Lévi-Strauss, "Race and History," 355. Cf. the section "Chance and Civilization": "The problem of the relative rarity (for each system of references) of 'more cumulative' cultures ... is reduced to the well-known problem of the theory of probability" (353).
30. Ibid., 41.
31. Ibid., 40.
32. Merleau-Ponty, in the margin: "Or that it turns out capable of understanding them better than they understand themselves. Lévi-Strauss does not take into account this relation of envelopment: the Australians are great mathematicians because their kinship relations can be expressed rigorously only by math[ematics]. There is therefore in them operative math[ematics], but who

knows this? Lévi-Strauss: there is a kind of event to the second power. That of the West, which 'includes' the other kinds of events."

33. See Lévi-Strauss, *Race and History*, 30. In the margin, Merleau-Ponty writes: "relativism, insofar as professed, denies itself, because, by doing justice to other cultures, it attests the universality of the culture that does justice to the others."

34. See Max Weber, *The Protestant Ethic and the "Spirit" of Capitalism* (New York: Penguin Classics, 2002). Merleau-Ponty discusses Weber in *The Adventures of the Dialectic*, chapter 1.

35. *Rationalisierung* may be rendered in English as "rationalization" and *Wahlverwandschaft* as "elective affinity." But one should be aware that Merleau-Ponty renders *Wahlverwandschaft* as "parenté de choix," which literally means a kinship relation among the choices made in a historical epoch.

36. Lucian Febvre, *The Problem of Unbelief in the Sixteenth Century: The Religion of Rabelais*, trans. Beatrice Gottlieb (Cambridge, Mass.: Harvard University Press, 1982; orig. pub. 1942).

37. Merleau-Ponty, in the margin: "The Marxist revolution is institution in itself. But there is a big change when it becomes institution for itself."

38. Merleau-Ponty, in the margin: "Marx said that himself: the end of the prehistory. But if we take this word literally, it has to be the case that the revolution is a negativity that finally descends into things. Therefore, and in a refined form, the Revolution institutes nevertheless an absolute *other* state.

39. Merleau-Ponty, in the margin: "Woman as social institution: that means the pure subject (S. de Beauvoir). Show that there is between the objective-social and the biological institution or the consciousness a [situation?] of 'psyche.'" Cf. Simone de Beauvoir, *The Second Sex*, trans. H. M. Parshley (New York: Knopf, 1952).

40. Note that Merleau-Ponty continues at the bottom of page (11) and on the back of the same sheet; that is, the back of the sheet numbered [12] by the Bibliothèque nationale: "Not by virtue of causal dependence of the subject in regard to history (which determines it only by offering to it a symbolic system in which he remains 'free'), not by virtue of the dependence of history in regard to the subject (or at least [by virtue of the] a-causality of the subject)—there is no dependence of this kind: we are entirely enclosed in our time and institutions, we can fight against it only with it, indirectly, from the inside, by 'understanding' it. Ex. Simone's book on the second sex: 'woman' is made historical, a moment in [the] dynamic of masculine society. [Simone de Beauvoir] does not oppose to 'woman' another portrait of woman, but simply the fact that she is consciousness and not this or that, and therefore that she is oppressed. [There is] nothing between the objective real and the pure subject. Consequently she says merely: let's try, we'll see what woman can be. Some oppose 'facts' to it: but they are understood in the perspective of the woman who is oppressed by and docile in relation to the image that men make of her. No fact proves anything contrary. But at the limit no fact proves absolutely in favor: they say neither yes nor no, for one is able to understand them as 'exceptions' to the 'feminine nature.' Therefore at the limit conflict of two moral wills: the one: let's hold onto what has been done.

The other: we have to try something else. In the same way, Sartre and communism: [he] does not oppose the history of communism to capitalism, the discussion is open, the facts say neither yes nor no. Therefore a simple will not to stop the *Other*, a simple will *to try*. The proletariat and woman [are] justified in their action solely insofar as they are oppressed, others and rejection of this oppression. But in fact feminist or proletarian action is always *positing:* woman cannot make a claim against oppression without making a claim on herself in her difference (precisely because there is no crucial fact, the claim cannot be limited, cannot be based on the divergence of 'feminism'). Likewise the political apparatus of the proletariat cannot be instituted without making itself autonomous (taking up the arms of the bourgeoisie). Hence, impurity and violence, which is why Simone de Beauvoir and Sartre have only 'sympathy.' Therefore, the dependence of history in regard to the subject is, on the terrain of history, something other than what it wants to be. The dependence is understood (by those who approve of it as well as by those who criticize it) in [a] different sense than the one that it states for itself. This is the case because it is *immediate negation.* The immediate passage to the outside is a premature return to the positive.

"Our viewpoint: don't oppose the interpersonal to history, and try to [realize it there?] immediately, but, as they are united at the source (and not at the intentional endpoint, insofar as both are instituted and instituting), the criticism itself is relativized: it must be turned into a self-criticism, otherwise it fails—because the criticism is its opposite (the second sex is [historically?] 'feminism,' S[artre's] articles 'communism'), i.e., lateral criticism, and that cannot immediately motivate historical action. It is necessary that it invents its action, [rather? thus?] choosing between lateral action and revolutionary [action], the latter being the history that surpasses itself.

"Problem of the metaphysics of history: how is the mediation of personal relations through the things possible? Status of *Vernuft* in relation to 'Nature.'"

41. The Descartes quote comes from the "Replies" to the "Fifth Set of Objections." In English the full quote would be: "You next deny certain truths about the indetermination of the will; and although they are in themselves quite evident, I refuse to undertake to prove them before your eyes. For these matters are such that anyone ought to experience them in himself, rather than be convinced of them by ratiocination." See René Descartes, *The Philosophical Works of Descartes*, trans. Elizabeth S. Haldane and G.R.T. Ross (New York: Dover, 1955), 2:224–25. The Latin quotation can be found in *Oeuvres de Descartes*, ed. Charles Adam and Paul Tannery (Paris: Cerf, 1910), 7:377.

[INSTITUTION AND LIFE]

1. On pages (12)–(14) of the manuscript (BN [13–18]), Merleau-Ponty follows the text of Raymond Ruyer, "Les conceptions nouvelles de l'instinct," *Les Temps Modernes*, November 1953, 824–60. Merleau-Ponty's references to Ruyer, which are extremely precise, make sense only through some rather long quotations that we have reproduced in the endnotes below. It is possible to compare

this development with those that the *Nature* course devotes to animality and life in the years 1957–58 and 1959–60. See Maurice Merleau-Ponty, *Nature: Course Notes from the Collège de France*, trans. Robert Vallier (Evanston, Ill.: Northwestern University Press, 2003). The pages numbered by Merleau-Ponty from (12) to (14) (BN [13–15]) constitute a first version of the notes, which, with few changes, are taken up next in the handwritten pages bearing the page numbers (BN [16–18]). Moreover, Merleau-Ponty does his enumeration again (we have indicated this with asterisks). In order to avoid this repetition, we have therefore preserved from this first version only two sections (here presented in eleven-point font): the introductory passage and the final passage in which Merleau-Ponty compares those "fruitful moments" in the human experience of artistic creation where "genius" is born to the role of "imprints" in animal learning. (One can find again (cf. [21–17]) an allusion to this theme.)

2. Ruyer, "Les conceptions nouvelles," 825: "Certainly, instinct no longer appears as a sort of magic and marvelous gift of the individual animal. It shows itself to be able to be fragmented into thematic behaviors, which are triggered by and adjusted to signaling-stimuli multiples, or 'gnoses,' and dependent upon the level of an internal sensibility."

3. Cf. preceding note.

4. Ruyer, "Les conceptions nouvelles," 833.

5. Ibid., 854: "The finality of life is never pure, but it ends up providing a sense even to the fortuitous and to the accidental which upends it."

6. Ibid., 853: "The primary consciousness of the embryo or of the instinctive animal must be conceived, in many regards, as similar to dream consciousness in humans. In the dream, the mnemonic themes are called forth by resonance and are captured mutually by semi-causal, semi-logical influences. A lot of instinctual laws can be stated in the vocabulary of the psychoanalysis of dreams: condensation, overdetermination, displacement, etc."

7. Merleau-Ponty is referring to the course contained in the second part of this volume, *The Problem of Passivity: Sleep, the Unconscious, Memory*, which was given the same year on Mondays.

8. Ruyer, "Les conceptions nouvelles," 835.

9. Cf. the course from 1957–58 on the concept of nature; see Merleau-Ponty, *Nature*, 147: "If we graft tissue onto the embryo, the resulting organ depends on three factors: the genes present in the graft, the point of application of the graft, and the moment of the growth during which the graft takes place (chronogenic localization). The same thing happens in all creative behavior; there are always three elements on which something depends for the moment." Here Merleau-Ponty is basing what he is saying on Gesell. See A. Gesell and C. S. Amatruda, *The Embryology of Behavior: The Beginnings of the Human Mind* (Westport, Conn: Greenwood, 1971). This work was originally published in 1945. Merleau-Ponty is consulting the French translation: *L'embryologie du comportement* (Paris: Presses Universitaires de France, 1953).

10. Ruyer, "Les conceptions nouvelles," 825–26: "The parallelism between the laws of organic development and those of behavior are striking. Or rather, organic development, the development of bodily structures, and the development

of structures of behavior are unified. We can say that embryonic development is a behavior and that behavior develops by way of organic sketches. This entails the complete identification of the principle of development with the instinct."

11. Ibid., 826: "'Structure and function,' 'structure and behavior' are not at all like 'machine and function,' with the structure being the sufficient cause of the function. They develop together, nearly in step, the one at times anticipating a bit of the other, and calling forth the other according to the needs of the living being. The structure's massive anticipation of the function, represented by the fact that the embryo *in utero* forms the organs of free, breathing life, is more apparent than real. The embryo, floating freely, probably itself contributes to its equilibrium, the semicircular canals being very precocious in their growth.... Even the respiratory movements are outlined *in utero*, the embryo absorbing and expelling amniotic liquid." (Here Ruyer is referring to Gesell.)

12. Gesell's experiment cited by Ruyer, "Les conceptions nouvelles," 829.

13. Ruyer, "Les conceptions nouvelles," 831: "Organic maturation ... is indiscernible from a maturation of behavior. In relation to behavior, organic maturation is a genuine learning. That is, in order to unfold normally, it must discover in the internal environment, which a primary maturation has moreover already contributed to constitute, the 'reactions' or signal-stimuli that are indispensable for the pursuit of its own melody. And it must discover them at the right time."

14. Ibid., 846–47: "Automatic machines function like calculating machines, the only difference being that, by means of feedback, the effect of the function or rather the difference between the effect obtained and the 'ideal' effect imposed on the machine controls the later function. But everything happens in space and is actual. The organisms in contrast are regulated by trans-spatial feedbacks, with a non-materialized ideal."

15. Ibid., 834: "Young geese follow their parents soon after hatching, but if they are hatching in an artificial shelter, not only do they attach themselves to the first creature that they encounter, but also once they adopted the false-parents, they do not accept individuals of their own species, including their own parents: 'this mode of conditioning or "impregnation" (Lorenz says, *Prägung* [imprinting]) takes no more than a minute and the effects of it appear to be irrevocable.'" (Ruyer cites here Niko Tinbergen, *L'étude de l'instinct* [Paris: Payot, 1953].)

16. We are inserting into the body of the text the remark in the next paragraph which is marked with an asterisk*. It was discovered in the first version of the notes Merleau-Ponty made. Without having been able to take into account the speculations that Ruyer associates with it, Merleau-Ponty could not fail to notice the oxymoronic notion of "experimental Platonism," which echoes the thought of institution, since institution is concerned to surpass the opposition of fact and essence.

17. Ruyer, "Les conceptions nouvelles," 837: "Is the efficacious stimulus the *cause* of the behavior? It is obviously only the triggering signal of the behavior. But what sort of triggering is at issue? Is it possible to imagine, in the nervous system of the animal, an innate mechanism, a kind of lock that can be opened by the key which would be the efficacious gnosis? Certainly not. The stimulus is not

only 'configurational,' but it also cannot be defined independently of a 'sense,' of a general 'type' of situation, which cannot be translated completely into the terminology of geometry and the mechanical. The triggering is thematic: what triggers is 'expressive,' if not 'significant,' for the animal (the animal being sensitive to a 'speed' that is sometimes impossible to specify) whose gnoses are only signaletic specializations." Here Ruyer refers to Tinbergen again.

18. Ibid., 838–39: "The supra-normal stimulus accentuates an expressive character of the normal stimulus by means of laws that are analogous to those which, for example, make an image in memory evolve towards the 'most typical' (in the sense that we would say of the term intentionally that it is 'Platonistic').... The existence of supra-normal stimuli is an important argument against the mechanistic interpretation of the action of normal stimuli. The argument supports the thesis that the stimulus is really a 'gnosis,' an expressive signal for the consciousness of the animal. The supra-normal is efficacious because it presents the sense that is inherent in the signal, in the most pure state.... The method of simulacra, the study of supra-normal stimuli, allows us then to speak of an experimental Platonism, by means of which, beyond the organic type, the type in the philosophical sense of the word is revealed—beyond Lamarckian and utilitarian adaptation, the 'adaptation' to a world of essences. The efficaciousness of the supra-normal triggers, especially the social triggers, explains very probably the effects that people attribute to sexual or intra-species selection."

19. "Falling in love" is in English in the original.

20. The last phrase is in English. Merleau-Ponty says, "Pays et payse; sweet heart et sweet home."

21. Here we are reproducing the final passage from the suppressed first version.

22. Ruyer, "Les conceptions nouvelles," 855: "The mania to compare human societies to termite nests ... is only a 'commonplace.' ... In contrast, a bunch of human habits or customs truly manifest the presence of the same instinctive background that we find in a lot of other mammals and in birds.... A woman who 'makes the baby' in front of a man, and who begs for small symbolic gifts as proof of his power, meets up with a theme that is already well constituted in birds who 'demand symbolic nourishment.'" This passage is cited by Merleau-Ponty on p. [18] (14*).

23. "Falling in love" is in English.

24. Ruyer, "Les conceptions nouvelles," 835: "In light of these facts, we cannot stop ourselves from interpreting a lot of human experiences. Man knows also, especially in his youth, localized conditionings, fleeting moments of 'geniality,' of biological 'determination,' during which these acts or these impressions are as if carried over, or made deeper, by means of a subterranean organic potency. There is a time when 'the mind turns to girls,' a time to fall in love, or a time to enter into a marriage, the moment for a marriage that will always involve something more than a marriage of convenience, more than the kind of marriage that is accomplished too late with a woman who will never be, as Ecclesiastes says, 'the girl of his youth.' A lot of artists, probably most of them, live from such moments, not moments of enthusiastic inspiration but of 'accelerated condition-

ENDNOTES FOR THE COURSE ON INSTITUTION

ing' or of 'impregnation.' In his *Confessions d'un auteur dramatique*..., H. R. Lenormand spontaneously uses the same word as Lorenz in order to describe this experience. 'There is therefore, for the work that is coming into being, not only a prenatal life but also an unconscious impregnation.... The extreme brevity of these conceptual periods has always surprised me. I remained but three hours in the Mzab valley of Algeria. When Joseph Conrad tells me that the duration of his command in the archipelago of the West Indies was no more than a few weeks, I shuddered with a joy that he could not understand.'" Ruyer is referring to H. R. Lenormand, *Confessions d'un auteur dramatique* (Paris: Michel, 1949).

25. Ruyer, "Les conceptions nouvelles," 840–41 (commenting on Gesell): "Is an adult, for example, able to say 'I am breathing'?... 'Unnoticed' respiration is not, however, a pure physiological function. Its automatism is guided by consciousnesses that are halfway foreign to the 'I.' These consciousnesses, or respiratory themes, are multiple, as the analysis of the stages of respiratory behaviors in mammalian fetuses shows (Sir J. Bancroft). Each stage develops and is added onto the former rather than replacing it, just as voluntary respiration is added onto involuntary respiration."

26. Franz Kafka, "Recherche d'un chien," in *La muraille de Chine et autres écrits*, trans. J. Carrive and A. Vilatte (Paris: Gallimard, 1950). For the original German, see Franz Kafka, "Forschungen eines Hundes," in *Franz Kafka, Gesammelte Schriften*, vol. 5 (New York: Schocken Books, 1946), 233–78. For English, see Franz Kafka, *The Trial, America, In the Penal Settlement, Metamorphosis, The Castle, The Great Wall of China, Investigations of a Dog, The Diaries 1910–23: Complete and Unabridged* (London: Secher and Warburg, 1976). One should note that the French term *recherches* is being used to render the German *Forschungen*, which is usually rendered in English as "research" or, taking into account the plural but still more awkwardly in English, as "researches." We are rendering it as "investigation" in order to be consistent with the accepted English translation of Kafka's title. But it is important to keep in mind the link that *recherche* makes to Proust's *À la recherche du temps perdu*, a title that can be rendered in English as "In Search of Lost Time."

27. Ruyer provides the example of "displacement" following the passage cited in endnote 6 above ("Les conceptions nouvelles," 853).

28. Ibid., 855.

29. There are two unreadable words here.

30. Merleau-Ponty is using the first English translation of "The Passing of the Oedipus Complex," which appeared in October 1924 in the *International Journal of Psycho-Analysis* 5 (1924): 419–24; the translation employed the terms "schedule" for *Programm* and "cathexis" for *Besetzung* (which is usually translated into French as *investissement*).

31. Ibid., 419–20.

32. Ibid., 419.

33. Ibid., 420.

34. "Passing" is in English.

35. Merleau-Ponty adds between the lines: "at every age and reorganization of everything during puberty."

36. *Deckung:* the usual French translation of this Husserl term is *recouvrement;* the English is "coincidence."

37. In the margin, Merleau-Ponty writes: "where the way of posing the question already implies an answer (Bergson, Sartre)."

38. The abbreviation "B.P.S." means "Biology, Psychoanalysis, Sociology."

39. Merleau-Ponty, in the margin: "The 'understanding' of parental concerns is carried by the identification, i.e., by pre-maturation and absolute love."

40. "Urstiftung" is rendered into English as "originary institution" and "Endstiftung" as "final institution."

41. *Selbstaufhebung,* "self-sublation."

[INSTITUTION OF A FEELING]

1. We have not included some very elliptical notes at the bottom of page [28] (22) and at the top of page [29]. These notes are entirely taken up later, which Merleau-Ponty's pagination confirms when he starts with number [22].

2. Marcel Proust, *Swann's Way,* in vol. 1 of *Remembrance of Things Past,* trans. C. K. Scott Moncrieff and Terence Kilmartin, 3 vols. (New York: Random House, 1981), 214: "But at the time of life, tinged already with disenchantment, which Swann was approaching."

3. Proust, *Swann's Way,* 1:292–93: "One day when reflections of this sort had brought him back to the memory of the time when someone had spoken to him of Odette as of a 'kept woman,' and he was amusing himself once again with contrasting that strange personification, the 'kept woman'—an iridescent mixture of unknown and diabolical qualities embroidered, as in some fantasy of Gustave Moreau, with poison-dripping flowers interwoven with precious jewels—with the Odette on whose face he had seen the same expressions of pity for a sufferer, revolt against an act of injustice, gratitude for an act of kindness, which he had seen in earlier days on his own mother's face and on the faces of his friends . . . it happened that the thought of the banker reminded him that he must call on him shortly to draw some money. . . . And then, suddenly, he wondered whether that was not precisely what was implied by 'keeping a woman' . . . and whether it might not be possible to apply it to Odette, since he had known her (for he never suspected for a moment that she could ever have taken money from anyone before him), that title, which he had believed so wholly inapplicable to her, of 'kept woman.' He could not explore the idea further, for a sudden access of that mental lethargy which was, with him, congenial, intermittent and providential, happened at that moment to extinguish every particle of light in his brain."

4. In order to prepare for this part of the course devoted to the "Institution of a Feeling," Merleau-Ponty had written out several pages of citations and commentaries on *Remembrance of Things Past* (*À la recherche du temps perdu*). To the ones that Merleau-Ponty made, we have added other citations that we have chosen in order to clarify the more allusive but very precise references to Proust's text. As stated in note 2 above, our citations refer to Marcel Proust, *Remembrance*

of Things Past, trans. C. K. Scott Moncrieff and Terence Kilmartin (New York: Random House, 1981), in three volumes. Merleau-Ponty himself referred to the Gallimard edition of *À la recherche du temps perdu*, in the "Collection blanche" from 1926. We have indicated the passages that Merleau-Ponty himself copied out by placing an (MP) at the beginning of the citation.

5. (MP). "The purely subjective nature of the phenomenon that we call love, or how it creates, so to speak, a supplementary person, distinct from the person whom the world knows by the same name, a person most of whose constituent elements are derived from ourselves. And so there are very few who can regard as natural the enormous proportions that a person comes to assume in our eyes who is not the same as the person that they see" (Proust, *Within a Budding Grove*, in vol. 1 of *Remembrance of Things Past*, 505). Merleau-Ponty referred to "Swann in Love," but apparently the quotation he had in mind comes from *Within a Budding Grove*.

6. Proust, *Swann's Way*, 1:250: "pretexts, that is to say, which would enable him to prolong for the time being, and to renew for one day more, the disappointment and the torture engendered by the vain presence of this woman whom he pursued yet never dared embrace."

7. Ibid., 1:252: "Among all the methods by which love is brought into being, among all the agents which disseminate that blessed bane, there are few so efficacious as this gust of feverish agitation that sweeps over us from time to time. For then the die is cast, the person whose company we enjoy at that moment is the person we shall henceforward love. It is not even necessary for that person to have attracted us, up till then, more than or even as much as others. All that was needed was that our predilection should become exclusive. And that condition is fulfilled when—in this moment of deprivation—the quest for the pleasures we enjoyed in his or her company is suddenly replaced by an anxious, torturing need, whose object is the person alone, an absurd, irrational need which the laws of this world make it impossible to satisfy and difficult to assuage—the insensate, agonizing need to possess exclusively."

8. (MP). "He would gaze upon her searchingly, trying to recapture the charm which he had once seen in her, and no longer finding it. And yet the knowledge that within this new chrysalis it was still Odette who lurked, still the same fleeting, elusive will, was enough to keep Swann seeking as passionately as ever to capture her" (ibid., 1:318). Merleau-Ponty comments: "identity of the person as absence, and her history is only the repetition of an absence."

9. (MP). Merleau-Ponty comments first: "And yet, at that moment, instead of pitying himself," and then there is the citation: "Since he was in love with Odette, since he was in the habit of turning all his thoughts towards her, the pity with which he might have been inspired for himself he felt for her instead, and he murmured: 'Poor darling!'" (ibid., 1:307). Merleau-Ponty's commentary continues: "Here irrecusable love."

10. (MP). "'She'—he tried to ask himself what that meant; for it is a point of resemblance between love and death, far more striking than those which are usually pointed out, that they make us probe deeper, in the fear that its reality may elude us, into the mystery of personality. And this malady which Swann's

love had become had so proliferated, was so closely interwoven with all his habits, with all his actions, with his thoughts, his health, his sleep, his life, even with what he hoped for after his death, was so utterly inseparable from him, that it would have been impossible to eradicate it without almost destroying him; as surgeons say, his love is no longer operable" (ibid., 1:336).

11. (MP). "The actual charm of Odette was now in comparison with the fearsome terror which extended it like a cloudy halo all around her, the immense anxiety of not knowing at every hour of the day and night what she had been doing, of not possessing her wholly, always and everywhere!" (ibid., 1:376).

12. (MP). Merleau-Ponty comments: "Having left her tired and returning home, he says to himself that perhaps she deceives him and returns under her window. At this moment, what moves him is." And then we have the quotation from "Swann in Love": "a truth which, too, was interposed between himself and his mistress, receiving its light from her alone, an entirely individual truth"—"in this strange phase of love the personality of another person becomes so enlarged, so deepened, that the curiosity which he now felt stirring inside him with regard to the smallest details of a woman's daily life, was the same thirst for knowledge with which he had once studied history.... He felt a voluptuous pleasure in learning the truth which he passionately sought in the unique, ephemeral and precious transcript, on that translucent page, so warm, so beautiful" (ibid., 1:298–99). Merleau-Ponty's commentary continues: "truth = sexuality = reaching being itself = jealousy = universal concrete homosexuality, poly-sexuality. Love makes us interested in all kinds of tastes which existed before it, this is only at first sight, in reality, it is love which re-creates them." There is more commentary: "There is a truth of love since love is the love of truth."

13. Ibid., 1:379: "When it was the little phrase that spoke to him of the vanity of his sufferings, Swann found a solace in that very wisdom which, but a little while back, had seemed to him intolerable when he fancied he could read it on the faces of indifferent strangers who regarded his love as an insignificant aberration. For the little phrase, unlike them, whatever opinion it might hold on the transience of these states of the soul, saw in them something not, as all these people did, less serious than the events of everyday life, but, on the contrary, so far superior to it as to be alone worth while expressing. It was the charms of an intimate sadness that it sought to imitate, to re-create, and their very essence, for all that it consists in being incommunicable and in appearing trivial to everyone save him who experiences them, had been captured and made visible by the little phrase."

14. Proust, *Within a Budding Grove*, 1:853–54: "And indeed, the pleasure I derived from the little band, as noble as if it had been composed of Hellenic virgins, arose from the fact that it had something of the fleetingness of passing figures on the road. The evanescence of persons who are not known to us ... urges us into that state of pursuit in which there is no longer anything to stem the tide of imagination. To strip our pleasures of imagination is to reduce them to their own dimensions, that is to say, to nothing.... We need imagination, awakened by the uncertainty of being unable to attain its object, to create a goal which hides the other goal from us, and by substituting for sensual pleasures

the idea of penetrating another life, prevents us from recognizing that pleasure, from tasting its true savor, from restricting it to its own range."

15. (MP). "And in becoming a friend of one of them I should have penetrated—like a cultivated pagan or a meticulous Christian going among barbarians—a youthful society in which thoughtlessness, health, sensual pleasure, cruelty, un-intellectuality and joy held sway" (ibid., 1:888).

16. (MP). Ibid., 1:852–54. Merleau-Ponty comments: "What is loved is her whole life insofar as it is cruel, inaccessible, cunning. Happiness would be to exist for her, for 'her obscure and incessant will.' Not so much sensual pleasure as 'the idea of penetrating into a life,' not so much pleasure as imagining."

17. (MP). Ibid., 1:903. Merleau-Ponty comments: "He had taken them for 'mistresses of racing cyclists or prize-fighters.' They were the daughters of merchants."

18. Ibid., 1:935: "I might, for that matter, have guessed as much in advance, since the girl on the beach was a fabrication of my own. In spite of which, since I had, in my conversations with Elstir, identified her with Albertine, I felt myself in honor bound to fulfill to the real the promises of love made to the imagined Albertine. We betroth ourselves by proxy, and feel obliged to marry the intermediary."

19. Marcel Proust, *The Guermantes Way*, in vol. 2 of *Remembrance of Things Past*, 367: "Certainly I was not in the least in love with Albertine; daughter of the mists of the outside, she could satisfy the imaginary desire of which the change of weather had awakened in me."

20. Marcel Proust, *Cities of the Plain*, in vol. 2 of *Remembrance of Things Past*, 826: "Once again, my whole body was stirred by the painful longing to know what she could have been doing, by the latent love which we always carry within us; I almost thought for a moment that it was going to bind me to Albertine, but it confined itself to a stationary throbbing, the last echo of which died away without the machine's having been set in motion." Translators: "Sodome et Gomorrhe" is the French title of the two middle books in the *Recherche du temps perdu*. While Moncrieff and Kilmartin render this title in English as "Cities of the Plain," a literal translation would be "Sodom and Gomorrah."

21. (MP). Proust, *Cities of the Plain*, 2:826: "Sometimes, during these nights of waiting, our anxiety is due to a drug which we have taken. The sufferer, misinterpreting his own symptoms, thinks that he is anxious about the woman who fails to appear. Love is engendered in these cases, as are certain nervous ailments, by the inaccurate interpretation of a painful discomfort. An interpretation which it is useless to correct, at any rate so far as the love is concerned, it being a feeling which (whatever its cause) is invariably erroneous."

22. Ibid., 2:823–24: "'There now, look,' he went on, pointing to Albertine and Andrée who were waltzing slowly, tightly clasped together, 'I've left my glasses behind and I can't see very well, but they are certainly keenly aroused. It's not sufficiently known that women derive most excitement through their breasts. And theirs, as you see, are touching completely.'"

23. Ibid., 2:857: "As it happened, in thus underlining to Albertine these protestations of coldness towards her, I was merely—because of a particular cir-

cumstance and with a particular object in view—making more perceptible, accentuating more markedly, that binary rhythm which love adopts in all those who have too little confidence in themselves to believe that a woman can ever fall in love with them, and also that they themselves can genuinely fall in love with her."

24. (MP). Ibid., 2:864: "in a love that is not shared." Merleau-Ponty comments: "too lucid in order to believe that he is in love, therefore in order to believe that he is loved, therefore in order to have a love that is shared."

25. Ibid., 2:1048: "I was perhaps in love with Albertine, but I did not dare to let her see my love, so that, if it existed in me, it could only be like an abstract truth, of no value until it had been tested by experience; as it was, it seemed to me unrealizable and outside of the plane of life."

26. Ibid., 2:1051.

27. (MP). Ibid., 2:1154: "and anyone who wished to make a fresh drawing of things as they really were would now have had to place Albertine, not at a certain distance from me, but inside me."

28. Ibid., 2:1156.

29. Merleau-Ponty, in the margin: "the profanation."

30. Proust, *Cities of the Plain*, 2:857–58: "They know themselves well enough to have observed that in the presence of the most divergent types of woman they felt the same hopes, the same agonies, invented the same romances, . . . to have deduced therefore that their feelings, their actions bear no close and necessary relation to the woman they love, . . . and their sense of their own instability increases still further their misgivings that this woman, by whom they so long to be loved, does not love them." This citation follows the one found in endnote 23 above.

31. Ibid., 2:864.

32. Ibid., 2:778.

33. Ibid., 2:1154.

34. Ibid., 2:1156: "She was offering to me, in fact—and she alone could offer me—the sole remedy for the poison that was consuming me, a remedy homogeneous with it indeed, for although one was sweet and the other bitter, both were alike derived from Albertine."

35. Marcel Proust, *The Captive*, in vol. 3 of *Remembrance of Things Past*, 16.

36. Proust, *Cities of the Plain*, 2:1048.

37. Proust, *The Captive*, 3:92–93: "It is not so much to a person that we sacrifice our life as to everything of ours that may have been attached to that person, all those hours and days . . . in reality we create obligations (even if, by an apparent contradiction, they should lead to suicide) towards ourselves alone. If I was not in love with Albertine (and of this I could not be sure) then there was nothing extraordinary in the place that she occupied in my life: we live only with what we do not love, with what we have brought to live with us only in order to kill the intolerable love."

38. Ibid., 3:253–54: "and I began to realize that if, in the body of this septet, different elements presented themselves one after another to combine at the close, so also Vinteuil's sonata and, as I later discovered, his other works as

well, had been no more than timid essays, exquisite but very slight, beside the triumphal and consummate masterpiece now being revealed to me. And I could not help recalling by comparison that, in the same way too, I had thought of the other worlds that Vinteuil had created as being self-enclosed as each of my loves had been; whereas in reality I was obliged to admit that just as, within the context of the last of these—my love for Albertine—my first faint stirrings of love for her (at Balbec at the very beginning, then after the game of ferret, then on the night when she slept at the hotel, then in Paris on the foggy afternoon, then on the night of the Guermantes party, then at Balbec again, and finally in Paris where my life was now closely linked to hers) had been, so, if I now considered not my love for Albertine but my whole life, my other loves too had been no more than slight and timid essays that were paving the way, appeals that were unconsciously clamoring, for this vaster love: my love for Albertine."

39. Ibid., 3:254.

40. Marcel Proust, *The Fugitive*, in vol. 3 of *Remembrance of Things Past*, 426: "I had believed that I knew the state of my own heart. But our intelligence, however lucid, cannot perceive the elements that compose it and remain unsuspected so long as, from the volatile state in which they generally exist, a phenomenon capable of isolating them has not subjected them to the first stages of solidification."

41. Ibid., 3:510.

42. Ibid., 3:511.

43. Ibid., 3:512: "The example of Gilberte would have as little enabled me to form an idea of Albertine and guess that I should fall in love with her, as the memory of Vinteuil's sonata would have enabled me to imagine his septet."

44. Ibid., 3:516.

45. The text cited by Merleau-Ponty has variants in the French editions of Proust. For the equivalent passages in English, see *The Fugitive*, 3:517–18: "And yet how often we had expressed them, those painful, those ineluctable truths which dominated us and to which we were blind, the truth of our feelings, the truth of our destiny, how often we had expressed them without knowing it, without meaning it, in words which doubtless we ourselves thought mendacious but the prophetic force of which had been established by subsequent events. I remembered many words that each of us had uttered without knowing at the time the truth they contained, which indeed we had said thinking that we were play-acting and yet the falseness of which was very slight, very uninteresting, wholly confined within our pitiable insincerity, compared with what they contained unbeknownst to us—lies and errors falling short of the profound reality which neither of us perceived, truth extending beyond it, the truth of our natures, the essential laws of which escape us and require time before they reveal themselves, the truth of our destinies also. I had believed myself to be lying when I said to her at Balbec: 'The more I see you, the more I shall love you' (and yet it was that constant intimacy which, through the medium of jealousy, had attached me so strongly to her), 'I feel that I could be of use to you intellectually'; and in Paris: 'Do be careful. Remember that if you meet with an accident, it would break my heart' (and she: 'But I may meet with an accident'); in Paris too, on the evening when I had

pretended that I wished to leave her: 'Let me look at you again, and it will be for ever!' and she, when that same evening she had looked round the room: 'To think that I shall never see this room again, those books, that pianola, the whole house, I cannot believe it and yet it's true.' In her last letters again, when she had written (probably saying to herself that it was eye-wash): 'I leave you the best of myself' (and was it not now indeed to the fidelity, to the strength—also too frail, alas—of my memory that her intelligence, her kindness, her beauty were entrusted?) and: 'That doubly crepuscular moment, since night was falling and we were about to part, will be effaced from my thoughts only when darkness is complete' (that sentence written on the eve of the day when her mind had indeed been plunged into complete darkness, and when, in those last brief glimmers which the anguish of the moment subdivides ad infinitum, she had indeed perhaps recalled our last drive together and in the instant when everything forsakes us and we create a faith for ourselves, as atheists turn Christian on the battlefield, she had perhaps summoned to her aid the friend whom she had so often cursed but had so deeply respected, who himself—for all religions are alike—was cruel enough to hope that she had also had time to see herself as she was, to give her last thought to him, to confess her sins at length to him, to die in him). But to what purpose, since even if, at that moment, she had had time to see herself as she was, we had both of us understood where our happiness lay, what we ought to do, only when, only because, that happiness was no longer possible, when and because we could no longer realize it."

46. Ibid., 3:536.

47. Merleau-Ponty, in the margin: "endopsychical perception of the other."

48. Merleau-Ponty, in the margin: "Platonism of existence: ideas which are not 'from the mind.' Quotation to be read."

49. Marcel Proust, *Time Regained*, in vol. 3 of *Remembrance of Things Past*, 902–15.

50. Merleau-Ponty, in the margin: "the love for Albertine is as different from the ones preceding it just as the septet was from the sonata."

51. Between brackets, Merleau-Ponty writes: "[jealousy = homosexuality, i.e., identification with the beloved, captive love, will to be pleasing to the rivals immediate, not intentional (not oblative) love] [latent homosexuality = jealousy: the homosexual can conceive heterosexuality only as research of the same sex by way of the other, because the other is woman. He does not love Albertine, he loves those that she could love]." Apparently Merleau-Ponty is referring to a distinction made by Lagache. See D. Lagache, *La jalousie amoureuse* (Paris: Presses Universitaires de France, 1947). In short, Lagache identifies two fundamental dimensions in a love relation: one called "captative" implies the desire to have and possess the object, to assimilate it and identify it with oneself; the other dimension, called "oblative," implies the desire to give oneself and lose oneself in the love object, to identify with it. For more on this distinction, see Carlo Magginie, Eva Lundgren, and Emanuela Leuic, "Jealous Love and Morbid Jealousy," *Acta Biomed* 77 (2006): 137–46; online at: www.actabiomedica.it/data/2006/3_2006/maggini.pdf.

52. Merleau-Ponty, in the margin: "pure fact."

ENDNOTES FOR THE COURSE ON INSTITUTION

[THE INSTITUTION OF A WORK OF ART]

1. Merleau-Ponty bases his reflections on Erwin Panofsky, *Perspective as Symbolic Form*, trans. Christopher S. Wood (New York: Urzone, 1991).

2. Ibid., 40: "If perspective is not a factor of artistic value, at least it is a factor of style." *Stilmoment* may be rendered in English as "moment of style" and *Wertmoment* as "moment of value."

3. Merleau-Ponty, in the margin: "the wholly made connection of a *Bedeutungsinhalt* [content of meaning] to a sign of such a form, the circulating of a symbolic form."

4. Panofsky, *Perspective as Symbolic Form*, 35: "And perhaps it is more than mere accident that in Renaissance paraphrases of Euclid, indeed even in translations, precisely this Eighth Theorem was either entirely suppressed or 'emended' until it lost its original meaning. Evidently, the contradiction was felt between Euclid's *perspectiva naturalis* or *communis*, which sought simply to formulate mathematically the laws of natural vision (and so linked apparent size to the visual angle), and the *perspectiva artificialis* developed in the meantime, which on the contrary tried to provide a serviceable method for constructing images on two-dimensional surfaces. Clearly, this contradiction could be resolved only by abandoning the angle axiom; to recognize the axiom is to expose the creation of a perspectival image as, strictly speaking, an impossible task, for a sphere obviously cannot be unrolled on a surface."

5. Ibid., 38: "The extensions of the orthogonals do not merge at a single point, but rather only weakly converge, and thus meet in pairs at several points along a common axis. For when the circle is rolled out, the arcs break apart, so to speak, at the tips. This creates a 'fishbone' effect."

6. Ibid., 40: "But this mode of representing space suffers, in comparison to the modern mode, from a peculiar instability and internal inconsistency. For the modern vanishing-point construction distorts all widths, depths, and heights in proportion, and thus defines unequivocally the apparent size of any object, the size corresponding to its actual magnitude and its position with respect to the eye."

7. *Eindeutig festgelegt*, "established without equivocation."

8. "The *Körper-Nichtkörper* difference," i.e., "the difference between body and nonbody."

9. "*Übereinander* and the *Hintereinander*" may be rendered in English as "what is above them (bodies) and in their intervals."

10. Panofsky, *Perspective as Symbolic Form*, 41: "Yet even Hellenistic artistic imagination remained attached to individual objects, to such an extent that space was still perceived not as something that could embrace and dissolve the opposition between bodies and nonbodies, but only as what remains, so to speak, between the bodies.... Even where Greco-Roman art advanced to the representation of real interiors or real landscapes, this enriched and expanded world was still by no means a perfectly unified world, a world where bodies and the gaps between them were only differentiations or modifications of a continuum of a higher order."

11. *Aggregatraum*, "aggregative space."

12. Panofsky, *Perspective as Symbolic Form*, 42: "Magnitudes generally diminish as they recede, but this diminution is by no means constant. . . . The style of these paintings has been held up as a precursor of, or even parallel to, modern Impressionism; and yet they never achieve unified 'lighting.' Even when the notion of perspective as 'seeing through' is taken seriously. . . , the represented space remains an aggregate space; it never becomes that which modernity demands and realizes, a systematic space."

13. Ibid., 42–43: "Precisely here it becomes clear that antique 'impressionism' was only quasi-impressionism. For the modern movement to which we give this name always presupposes that higher unity, over and above empty space and bodies; as a result its observations automatically acquire direction and unity. This is how Impressionism can so persistently devalue and dissolve solid forms without even jeopardizing the stability of the space and the solidity of the individual objects; on the contrary, it conceals that stability and solidity. Antiquity, on the other hand, lacking that domineering unity, must, so to speak, purchase every spatial gain with a loss of corporeality, so that space really seems to consume objects. This explains the almost paradoxical phenomenon that . . . as soon as space in included in the representation, above all in landscape painting, that world becomes curiously unreal and inconsistent, like a dream or a mirage."

14. Ibid., 43–44: "As various as antique theories of space were, none of them succeeded in defining space as a system of simple relationships between height, width and depth. [Panofsky cites Cassirer.] In that case, in the guise of a 'coordinate system,' the difference between 'front' and 'back,' 'here' and 'there,' 'body' and 'nonbody' would have resolved into the higher and more abstract concept of three-dimensional extension, or even, as Arnold Geulincx puts it, the concept of a 'corpus generaliter sumptum' ('body taken in a general sense')."

15. Ibid., 43: "That feeling for space which was seeking expression in the plastic arts simply did not demand a systematic space. Systematic space was as unthinkable for antique philosophers as it was unimaginable for antique artists."

16. *Rückschlag*, "recoil."

17. Panofsky, *Perspective as Symbolic Form*, 47: "When work on certain artistic problems has advanced so far that further work in the same direction, proceeding from the same premises, appears unlikely to bear fruit, the result is often a great recoil, or perhaps better, a reversal of direction. Such reversals . . . create the possibility of erecting a new edifice out of the rubble of the old; they do this precisely by abandoning what has already been achieved, that is, by turning back to apparently more 'primitive' modes of representation."

18. Ibid., 48: "At the close of Antiquity, and in conjunction with the increase of Eastern influences (whose appearance here, to be sure, is less a cause than a symptom and instrument of the new development), the freely extended landscape and the closed interior space begin to disintegrate. The apparent succession of forms into depth gives way again to superposition and juxtaposition. The individual pictorial elements . . . are transmuted into forms which, if not completely leveled, are at least entirely oriented toward the plane. These forms

ENDNOTES FOR THE COURSE ON INSTITUTION

stand in relief against a gold or neutral ground and are arrayed without respect to any previous compositional logic."

19. Ibid., 48–49: "It can hardly be expressed more clearly than the principle of a space merely excised by the picture's edge is now beginning to give way to the principle of the surface bounded by the picture's edge, a surface that expects not to be seen through but rather filled. The 'foreshortenings' of Greco-Roman art, finally, lose their original representational meaning—that of creating space—and yet retain their fixed linear forms; they thus undergo the most curious, but often uncommonly expressive, reinterpretations: the former vista or 'looking through' begins to close up."

20. Ibid., 49: "At the same time it can be seen how precisely here the individual pictorial elements . . . could be joined in a new and, in a certain sense, more intimate relationship: in an immaterial but unbroken tissue, as it were, within which the rhythmic exchange of color and gold or, in relief sculpture, of light and dark, restores a kind of unity, even if only a coloristic or luminous unity. The particular form of this unity once again finds its theoretical analogue in the view of space of contemporary philosophy: in the metaphysics of light of pagan and Christian neo-Platonism. 'Space is nothing other than the finest light,' according to Proclus; here, just as in art, the world is conceived for the first time as a continuum. . . . Space has been transformed into a homogeneous and, so to speak, homogenizing fluid, immeasurable and indeed dimensionless."

21. Ibid., 50: "Now line is merely line, that is, graphic means of expression *sui generis* which finds its meaning in the delimitation and ornamentation of surfaces. Surface, meanwhile, is now merely surface, that is, no longer even the vague suggestion of an immaterial space, but rather the unconditionally two-dimensional surface of a material picture support." P. 51: "With this radical transformation, so it would appear, all spatial illusionism was abandoned, once and for all. And yet this transformation was precisely the precondition for the emergence of the truly modern view of space. For if Romanesque painting reduced bodies and space to surface, in the same way and with the same decisiveness, by these very means it also managed for the first time to confirm and establish the homogeneity of bodies and space. . . . From now on, bodies and space are bound to each other, for better or for worse. Subsequently, if a body is to liberate itself from its attachment to the surface, it cannot grow unless space grows with it at the same rate."

22. *Unendlichkeit des Bildes*, "infinity of the image."

23. *Wirklichkeitausschnitt*, "portion of reality."

24. Panofsky, *Perspective as Symbolic Form*, 55–56: "For the representation of a closed interior space . . . signifies a revolution in the formal assessment of the representation surface. This surface . . . is once again the transparent plane through which we are meant to believe that we are looking into a space, even if that space is still bounded on all sides. We may already define this surface as a 'picture plane' in the precise sense of the term. The view that had been blocked since antiquity, the vista or 'looking through,' has begun to open again; and we sense the possibility that the painted picture will once again become a section cut from an infinite space." Pp. 60–61: "The picture plane [of Van Eyck's *Virgin*

in the Church] cuts through the middle of the space. Space thus seems to extend forward across the picture plane.... The picture has become a mere 'slice' of reality, to the extent and in the sense that *imagined* space now reaches out in all directions beyond *represented* space, that precisely the finiteness of the picture makes perceptible the infiniteness and continuity of the space."

25. Ibid., 63: Alberti's definition was "to remain fundamental for all succeeding generations: 'The picture is a planar section of the visual pyramid.'"

26. Ibid., 66: "And yet this view of space ... is the same view that will later be rationalized by Cartesianism and formalized by Kantianism.... For not only did it elevate art to a 'science,' ... the subjective visual impression was indeed so far rationalized that this very impression could itself become the foundation for a solidly grounded and yet, in an entirely modern sense, 'infinite' experiential world. One could even compare the function of Renaissance perspective with that of critical philosophy, and the function of Greco-Roman perspective with that of skepticism. The result was a translation of psycho-physiological space into mathematical space; in other words, an objectification of the subjective."

27. Ibid., 67: "For perspective is by nature a two-edged sword.... Perspective creates distance between human beings and things ... but then in turn it abolishes this distance by, in a sense, drawing this world of things, an autonomous world confronting the individual, into the eye. Perspective subjects the artistic phenomenon to stable and even mathematically exact rules, but on the other hand, makes the phenomenon contingent upon human beings ... for these rules refer to the psychological and physical conditions of the visual impression.... Thus the history of perspective may be understood with equal justice as a triumph of the distancing and objectifying sense of the real, and as a triumph of the distance-denying human struggle for control." Pp. 68–69: "It thus stands to reason that the Renaissance would interpret the meaning of perspective entirely differently from the Baroque, and Italy entirely differently from the North: in the former cases, speaking quite generally, its objective significance was felt to be more essential, in the latter case its subjective significance." P. 72: "The great phantasmagorias of the Baroque—which in the final analysis were prepared by Raphael's *Sistine Madonna*, Dürer's *Apocalypse*, Grünewald's *Isenheim Altar*— ... would not have been possible without the perspectival view of space. Perspective, in transforming the *ousia* (reality) into *phainomenon* (appearance), seems to reduce the divine to a mere subject matter for human consciousness; but for that very reason, conversely, it expands human consciousness into a receptacle for the divine."

28. *Bildebene* may be rendered in English as "picture plane" and "Durchsehung" as "transversing view." "Perspectiva is an Italian word meaning traversing vision. It is in these terms that Dürer has sought to circumscribe the concept of perspective" (ibid., 27).

29. Ibid., p. 66.

30. *Weltgefühl*, "feeling of the world."

31. *Bedeutungsinhalt*, "content of meaning."

32. Panofsky, *Perspective as Symbolic Form*, 40–41: "But if perspective is not a factor of value, it is surely a factor of style. Indeed, it may even be characterized

as (to extend Ernst Cassirer's felicitous term to the history of art) one of those 'symbolic forms' in which 'spiritual meaning is attached to a concrete, material sign and intrinsically given to this sign.'"

33. Merleau-Ponty is referring to Pierre Francastel, *Peinture et société* (Lyon: Audin, 1951).

34. These are Merleau-Ponty's brackets. In the phrase "Italian painting," Merleau-Ponty had written only the letter "p."

35. *Schrägensicht,* "oblique view."

36. Panofsky, *Perspective as Symbolic Form,* 68: "And whether and to what extent an oblique view of the entire space seems admissible. In all of these questions, the 'claim' of the object (to use a modern term) confronts the ambition of the subject. The object intends to remain distanced from the spectator (precisely as something 'objective'); it wants to bring to bear, unimpeded, its own formal lawfulness (its symmetry, for example, or its frontality). It does not want to be referred to an eccentric vanishing point, nor certainly, as in the oblique view, governed by a coordinate system whose axes no longer even appear objective in the work, but rather exist only in the imagination of the beholder."

37. Cf. Maurice Merleau-Ponty, *The Prose of the World,* trans. John O'Neill (Evanston, Ill.: Northwestern University Press, 1973), 44: "[A] camera has registered the work of Matisse in slow motion...."

38. Merleau-Ponty has stated that he will take Cézanne as an example. All he does is set down on paper some brief comments about what he will call the "investigation" of a painter. His guide is Liliane Guerry, who wrote *Cézanne et l'expression de l'espace* (Paris: Flammarion, 1950); her name is mentioned only once. There is no doubt that Merleau-Ponty is explicitly referring to this work. Such as they are, his notes are elliptical to the point of being unintelligible. It therefore seems to be indispensable to clarify them by presenting some passages from Guerry's book, passages which refer precisely to the distinction among Cézanne's periods, or passages which refer to a concept, an example, an allusion to the difficulties of the painter and to the solution that he gives to the Renaissance problem. These notes on Guerry's book were written up by Claude Lefort. 1. Chapter 2 of Guerry's book is called "Compromise Solution." She writes: "For Cézanne the problem is a lot more complex [than for Pissarro], since the issue is not only to reproduce a fleeting luminous agreement, but also to express within an abstract space a synthesis of all possible harmonies. In order not to be fragmented into the infinity of colors that agree, the spatial masses must therefore assert themselves with stability, since they alone are borrowed from what is real, the luminous combinations being, like the space within which they are elaborated, the fruit of an intellection reconstruction" (53). On p. 54 she writes: "The characters are volumes which express themselves in their plenitude and which the vibration of the spots of color 'does not impair.' But their gestures remain suspended as if they were suddenly frozen in time. We think we're looking at mannequins and not living beings." And later, Guerry shows that when he escapes from the danger of spatial fragmentation, Cézanne confronts an opposite problem: "The characters like trees are nothing but the vibration of an immense luminous palpation. But the bodies lose all contour, all

substance." Concerning flowers, she writes: "Cézanne's predilection for vases of flowers, which he had never painted before and which he paints rarely after, is explained easily by the fact that, researching the expression of an atmospheric unity, he feared that this unity might be compromised by a too violent opposition between the object and space.... The flowers connect imperceptibly the mineral and the aerial in relation to which the flowers are equally distanced, heavier than the air which blows through their branches, but how much more fragile than the glass vases in which they are placed" (70). 2. At the beginning of chapter 3 ("The Equilibrium of the Unstable"), Guerry notes that beginning in 1878–79 it seems that a third period of Cézanne's work begins, the one that we call "constructivist." Speaking of the problems that Cézanne encounters in relation to the portrait, Guerry writes: "Both dangers lie in wait for the painter. A too compact and too heavy space may immobilize the form, freeze the physiognomy.... Most often, an inorganic and indifferent background, which is no longer a support for the form, lets the volumes collapse, dissociates the face through the diverse mobility of the expression" (74). Guerry observes, in another place, that, by giving free rein to his imagination in the portrait and letting himself be attracted more to the complexity and mobility of the model, the painter finds a counterpart in the requirement to fully master the gesture, so that, "brought back to the essential," it becomes "necessary and determined by fate." Therefore, "when we evoke Renoir's portrait of young *Mademoiselle Legrand*, we do not recall immediately that she has her hands crossed on her apron, which is proof that the gesture is not the only thing necessary for the structure of the image, while it is absolutely necessary in the portrait of *Madame Cézanne au fauteuil jaune*, so much so that we cannot imagine her in another position" (105–6). Guerry also speaks of bathers: "The image respects the essential givens of the concrete, but the accidental is effaced then in order to leave to the symbol its generality. The idealized body becomes the nude in itself. The male bather is no longer distinguished from the female bather to such a point that the sketches of feminine nudes have been able to serve as the basis for the composition of the *Baigneurs en plein air*, and, inversely, it's soldiers bathing who become the models of the *Grandes baigneuses*. The body is nothing but a pretext for the ordering of a harmony, for the research into a rhythmic agreement between itself and space" (112–13). Between autumn 1894 and July 1896, "The Success" (this is the title of the fourth chapter) is situated, according to Guerry. "Never," she notes, "has Cézanne's touch been lighter, more sensitive, more immediate, obeying pure sensation, and yet, never has his vision been so completely synthetic" (120). This is what she says about the importance of the watercolors: "The strokes of color space themselves out, the matter becomes more and more fluid. Such a technique is probably influenced by the technique in the watercolors that Cézanne used starting in 1890" (129). Concerning crystallization, Guerry cites Roger Fry (*Cézanne: A Study of His Development* [New York: Noonday, 1958]): "We can compare the synthesis for which Cézanne was seeking to establish in his compositions to the phenomenon of crystallization that pervades a liquid solution. In the watercolors, he was marking, according to this comparison, the germs on the basis of which crystallization irradiates in all directions." Finally she writes about a solution to the problem of the Renaissance: "This invisible vibration which unifies the character to the background settings connects it as well to the other side of the background, that is, to the spectator's concrete space. The lower edge of the picture, henceforth, no longer constitutes the limit of the figurative, spatial construction. More exactly, there is no longer a figurative construction; the latter becomes a fragment, moreover, just as the portion of space in which the spectator moves becomes a fragment of a supreme construction that engulfs at once the world of the image and the world of the object. . . . The spatial container is the same, only the appearance of the content is varied. Cézanne arrives intuitively at this supreme unification of the space which the theoreticians of the Renaissance were trying to reach by means of geometrical construction" (148–49). Guerry continues: "Just when Cézanne, by means of a diametrically opposed path, reaches this spatial synthesis for which the Renaissance theoreticians were seeking, just when he becomes 'classical,' just when the internal laws of his own perspective, which is the fruit of a superior intuition, discover, by the most beautiful of encounters, the laws that Leonardo and Dürer, after so many years of experimentation, had codified, at this precise moment, Cézanne's works of such a complete construction half open like a curtain to be ripped in order to enlarge the possibilities of escape all the way to infinity" (153).

[INSTITUTION OF A DOMAIN OF KNOWLEDGE]

1. The bottom of this page is left blank. The following page, "Institution (41)," is missing according to a note inserted by the Bibliothèque Nationale. Page (42) is continuous with (41) since it starts with the words "this propriety," which is the end of the last sentence of the lost sheet; this phrase also introduces the first complete sentence of sheet (42).

2. Here and in the pages that follow, Merleau-Ponty's reflection on "the institution of true knowledge" is based on Husserl's late text *The Crisis of European Sciences and Transcendental Phenomenology*, and especially the fragment "The Origin of Geometry." See Edmund Husserl, *The Crisis of European Sciences and Transcendental Phenomenology*, trans. David Carr (Evanston, Ill.: Northwestern University Press, 1970). See also Maurice Merleau-Ponty, *Husserl at the Limits of Phenomenology*, trans. Leonard Lawlor with Bettina Bergo (Evanston, Ill.: Northwestern University Press, 2002). The analyses in *Husserl at the Limits of Phenomenology* are anticipated in these pages of the *Institution* course.

3. Cf. Henri Bergson, introduction to *The Creative Mind*, trans. Mabelle L. Andison (New York: Citadel, 1992).

4. *Fundierung* may be rendered in English as "foundation." Cf. Maurice Merleau-Ponty, "The Philosopher and His Shadow," in *Signs*, trans. Richard C. McCleary (Evanston, Ill.: Northwestern University Press, 1964), 173.

5. Cf. Husserl, "Origin of Geometry," in *Crisis of European Sciences*, 353: "Geometry is handed down to us ready-made."

6. Cf. Husserl, "Origin of Geometry," 356. Here David Carr renders *Ur-*

stiftung as "primal establishment." *Endstiftung* means "final institution" or "final establishment."

7. *Lebenswelt* may be rendered in English as "life-world." See the third part of Husserl's *Crisis of European Sciences*.

8. "Insight" is in English in the original.

9. "Insight" is in English again.

10. "The Philosopher and His Shadow" speaks of the "singular relationship of *Selbstvergessenheit* that Husserl already names in *Ideen II*, and that he was to take up again later in the theory of sedimentation" (Merleau-Ponty, *Signs*, 173). See Edmund Husserl, *Ideas Pertaining to a Pure Phenomenology and to a Phenomenological Philosophy, Second Book*, trans. Richard Rojcewicz and André Schuwer (Dordrecht: Kluwer, 1989).

11. *Sinnentleerung* may be rendered in English as "the emptying out of sense" or "the emptying out of meaning." Here "sense" and "meaning" render the German *Sinn* and the French *sens*. See Husserl, *Crisis of European Sciences*, section 9, subsection f, p. 44: "This arithmetization of geometry leads almost automatically, in a certain way, to the emptying of its meaning." See also Husserl, "Origin of Geometry," 368: "Thus mathematics, emptied of meaning."

12. *Einmalig*, "one time" or "unique."

13. "The proof itself has its structure" is in English in the original. Cf. the discussion of Wertheimer in Maurice Merleau-Ponty, *Phenomenology of Perception*, trans. Colin Smith, trans. rev. Forrest Williams (London: Routledge and Kegan Paul, 1981), 384.

14. "*Innere* structure," "internal structure."

15. Merleau-Ponty, in the margin: "discovery by means of the case of an invariant in the variation."

16. See Merleau-Ponty, "The Algorithm and the Mystery of Language," in *The Prose of the World*, 115–30; example cited by Max Wertheimer in *Productive Thinking* (New York: Harper and Row, 1959).

17. Cf. Husserl, *Crisis of European Sciences*, appendix 1, "Philosophy and the Crisis of European Humanity" (The Vienna Lecture), 289: "A new spirit . . . dominates humanity through and through, creating new, infinite tasks."

[The Field of Culture]

1. The manuscript includes (pages [62–65]) a first version of the themes that we will see later in the course; we have preserved only some of the passages from these pages in the notes.

2. The first version specifies: "Signification is not a concept. What is it then? Distinguish between the concept and the idea. The concept always results from *Sinnentleerung*. For example, in scientism and objectivism *Sinnentleerung* of the foundation of science, which is done by idealization (Galileo) and construction on the basis of the lived world. The idea was the telos of an infinite task of idealization. The idea is always an idea in the Kantian sense. Thus the idea of science, the idea of philosophy. It is essential to the idea of presumptive being,

ENDNOTES FOR THE COURSE ON INSTITUTION

which is not actual in an instant, i.e., to be accomplished only by means of a series of steps made at different moments by the same human or by different humans taking turns."

3. *Vergessenheit*, "forgetfulness." Cf. Merleau-Ponty, "The Philosopher and His Shadow," 173: "Logical objectivity derives from carnal intersubjectivity, and it is carnal subjectivity itself which produces forgetfulness by wending its way toward logical objectivity."

4. Merleau-Ponty crossed-out: "What's at issue is the moment when something is 'understood' without explanation, without reactivation being necessary, obvious." Cf. the first version: "Sedimentation is the passage to the obvious. Evidence as institution."

5. *Das Erlebnis der Wahrheit*, "the experience of truth."

6. *Wesen ist was gewesen ist* may be rendered in English as "essence is what has been." Cf. G. W. F. Hegel, "Doctrine of Essence," in *The Science of Logic*, trans. A. V. Miller (London: George Allen and Unwin, 1969), 389: "The German language has preserved essence in the past participle [*gewesen*] of the verb to be; for essence is past—but timelessly past—being."

7. Concerning the notions of traditionality, soil, and horizon, see Husserl, "Origin of Geometry," in particular 354–56, 368–69, and 371.

8. Cf. Husserl, "Origin of Geometry," 370: "The ruling dogma of the separation in principle between epistemological elucidation and historical . . . explanation, between epistemological and genetic origin, is fundamentally mistaken. . . . Or rather, what is fundamentally mistaken is the limitation through which precisely the deepest and most genuine problems of history are concealed. If one thinks over our expositions . . . what they make obvious is precisely that what we know—namely, that the presently vital configuration 'geometry' is a tradition and is still being handed down—is not knowledge concerning an external causality which effects the succession of historical configurations . . . rather, to understand geometry or any given cultural fact is to be conscious of its historicity, albeit 'implicitly.'"

9. *Nachvollzug*, "reactualization" or "reoperation."

10. First version: "Institution . . . is not the positing of a concept, but of a being, or openness of a field. I.e., 1) institution gives to the future what it does not have; 2) the future will receive from it only what it will bring. Thales opening the field of geometry: he institutes, in the sense that it sets underway, by creating symbols and by employing these symbols, a labor which, through recurrence, will not stop itself, which, in principle, cannot be accomplished by him: we find in what he has done [the] principle of a research that is other and the same. . . . Reciprocally: the future receives only what it brings. By means of the preceding research the creator senses the movement toward his research. Its creation is reactivation. Traditionality is the forgetfulness of origins and their possession."

11. *Selbstverständlichkeit* may be rendered in English as "self-understanding" or as "obviousness." Cf. the first version: "Not to stop with the observation: there is a plurality of consciousnesses with certain common significations. But to seek how this is possible? If we take that as given, *some* consciousnesses, we fall short of philosophy, of the problem of truth. We remain in the familiarity of the cogito,

with its intentional object, and the correlation cogito-*cogitatum*, and the *cogitatum* undergoes a psychological reduction: it is the in-itself, inseparable correlate of the for-itself."

12. *Wahrnehmungsbereit*, "ready to be perceived."

13. *Füreinander*, "for one another."

[HISTORICAL INSTITUTION: PARTICULARITY AND UNIVERSALITY]

1. Merleau-Ponty, in the margin: "Cf. investigations as different as those of Sartre and Lévi-Strauss (*Nature and Civilization*): the social is opaque, obscure and [super-significant]. Lévi-Strauss: rigorous exteriority of the universes of culture."

2. Merleau-Ponty has in mind Fernand Braudel, *The Mediterranean and the Mediterranean World in the Age of Philip II*, trans. Siân Reynolds, 2 vols. (New York: Harper and Row, 1966). Finally, Merleau-Ponty is going to leave this reference aside.

3. Lévi-Strauss, *Race and History*, 24: "Wherever we go, we are bound to carry this system of criteria with us, and external cultural phenomena can be observed only through the distorting glass it interposes, even when it does not prevent us from seeing anything at all." P. 25: "Whenever we are inclined to describe a human culture as stagnant or stationary, we should therefore ask ourselves whether its apparent immobility may not result from our ignorance of its true interests, whether conscious or unconscious."

4. Merleau-Ponty refers to Claude Lévi-Strauss, "Diogène couché," *Les Temps Modernes*, March 1955, 1187–1220. This text is a response to an article by Roger Caillois, "Illusion à rebours," in *Nouvelle Revue Française*, December 1954 and January 1955, which is itself a response to Lévi-Strauss's *Race and History*.

5. Merleau-Ponty, in the margin: "Reservations about Lévi-Strauss's solution: [not] 'objective,' which would lead back to absolute knowledge. There's only historical, bastard knowledge, of a becoming of sense, comparison of the two things seen."

6. Febvre, *Problem of Unbelief*, 5–6.

7. Ibid., 132. This is in fact a quote from Viret that Febvre has reproduced in his text.

8. Ibid., 143.

9. Ibid., 144: "Let us hear what Aubert says . . .: 'As for Servetus's actual doctrine, it seems to us today to have almost timorous orthodoxy. . . . But didn't Servetus try to prove the divinity of Christ and, on the subject of the Trinity, didn't he conclude the existence of a single God in three persons? . . . But Farel and Calvin did not reason as we do. They deduced a thousand possible consequences from Servetus's doctrine. . . . They saw Z in A because they had noted all the intermediate stages between A and Z, and they condemned A in the name of Z without any hesitation whatever."

10. See Georges Friedmann, *De la Sainte Russie à l'USSR* (Paris: Gallimard, 1938).

11. "No *quatenus*" means "no to the extent that."

12. Febvre cites Rabelais on the basis of Abel LeFranc's "Etude sur Pantagruel," in Rabelais, *Oeuvres*, III (Paris, 1922). Febvre says that his book seeks to be a response to the problem of unbelief as presented by LeFranc (p. 3). Rabelais says according to LeFranc that "he had sold more copies in two months than the Bible in nine years." "Following a sort of crescendo, Alcofribas," LeFranc writes, "intends immediately, as a sort of direct attack, the very testimony of the Evangelists: 'I speak of it as Saint John spoke of the Apocalypse: *quod vidimus, testamur.*'" "Alcofribas" is an anagram of François Rabelais. Febvre takes up this comment about Saint John: "With some apprehension we pick up our copy of Rabelais and open to *Pantagruel*. We start laughing and think no more of the 'crescendo' of impiety . . . : nothing secret, nothing terrible or sacrilegious in any of those unmalicious obscenities, off-color tall tales, or old, perfectly safe clerical jokes whose inventor was certainly not Rabelais" (154).

13. Febvre, *Problem of Unbelief*, 155: "Plattard clearly saw that Rabelais's jokes belonged to the clerical tradition and were no different from those that enliven the genre of sermons joyeux. . . . One can gather a rich crop of Gospel phrases there, parodied with greater or lesser degrees of coarseness. . . . One sermon took as its texts the very word of the institution of the Last Supper: 'Eat and drink.' This is much more daring than 'Consummatum est,' whether read by Panurge . . . and the drinker's 'Sitio' that Abel LeFranc found so shocking." Febvre cites Rabelais's works on pp. 155n5 and 155n6.

14. Ibid., 155n6.

15. Ibid., 159: "Let us not pretend we do not know . . . that in Rabelais's time the mass . . . was not what it became for Catholics in the time of Bérulle and after: the religious act par excellence."

16. Merleau-Ponty refers to this comment in Febvre, *Problem of Unbelief*, 169: "and no one would have been shocked if a whole pack of dogs had gone running through the aisles. . . . A few years later dogs would cause a scandal if they so much as entered the church."

17. Febvre, *Problem of Unbelief*, 199–200. Here Febvre contests LeFranc's interpretation of Gargantua's "wholly to die": "He knows very well that the spiritual part of his soul will not suffer the fate of his body. . . . But what makes him sorrowful . . . is the idea of . . . giving up his present attachments."

18. Ibid., 210n67.

19. Merleau-Ponty, in the margin: "Cf. Modernism and current repression."

20. Merleau-Ponty cites Febvre, *Problem of Unbelief*, 325: "Let it be understood that we are not about to make any literal or summary interpretations, without counterweights or correctives, of an extraordinarily rich mind. . . . We know very well that . . . any phrase is susceptible of different translations. 'Rest anta nihil est [Eucharistia] imo perniciosa, nisi adsit Spiritus.' How is this sentence to be translated so that the thought is not falsified? 'This Eucharist, which is of such great value, is nothing but a danger if the Spirit does not give it its efficacy.' Here the very idea of the sacrament has been done away with and destroyed. But suppose we say: 'Will this precious Eucharist produce all beneficial effects

we ought to expect and not cause any unfortunate ones if the ground is poorly prepared?' Here is respectable orthodoxy, since the Church teaches that the sacraments sanctify only those who receive them with a good attitude. There is not one phrase that Erasmus employs on these burning issues that is not susceptible of two interpretations thoroughly different in spirit. Which is to say that people find in Erasmus—and this was already true in his own time—what is in themselves. The orthodox found their orthodoxy, the Reformed found their Reformation, the skeptics their irony."

21. Merleau-Ponty cites Febvre, *Problem of Unbelief,* 336: "Today Christianity is one religion among many.... We are not entirely correct when we do so. For whether we like it or not, the climate of our Western societies is still a profoundly Christian one. In the past, in the sixteenth century, it was all the more so. Christianity was the very air one breathed.... Today we make a choice to be a Christian or not. There was no choice in the sixteenth century.... Whether one wanted to or not, whether one clearly understood or not, one found oneself immersed from birth in a bath of Christianity from which one did not emerge even at death. Death was of necessity Christian, Christian even in a social sense, because of the rituals that no one could escape."

22. "Religion's Domination of Life" is the title of chapter 9 in part 4 of Febvre's *Problem of Unbelief.*

23. Febvre, *Problem of Unbelief,* 347–48: "What about public life? Is it necessary to remind ourselves how saturated with Christianity the state still was—in nature, in spirit, and structure? ... Even—perhaps especially—those who ... seemed to display a determined spirit of innovation. In the Calvinist Christian state of Geneva everyone had to bow to the sovereign authority of God and Jesus Christ."

24. "A Possible Support for Irreligion" is the title of chapter 10 in part 4 of Febvre's *Problem of Unbelief.*

25. Febvre, *Problem of Unbelief,* 355. Febvre writes under the title "mental tools": "Let us state ... the problem of knowing what clarity, comprehension, and, finally, efficacy (in our estimation, of course) men's thought was capable of. Frenchmen engaged in speculation without as yet having at their disposal in their own language any of the usual words that automatically come from our pens as soon as we start to engage in philosophy. The absence of these words entails not only inconvenience but actual inadequacy or deficiency of thought." Under the title "missing words," Febvre mentions notably "absolute," "relative," "confused," "complex," "adequate," "insoluble," "intentional," "intrinsic," "inherent"; "causality," "regularity," "concept," "criterion," "condition," "analysis," "synthesis," "deduction," "induction"; "Rationalism," "Deism," "Materialism," "Naturalism"; and then finally, "tolerance," "orthodoxy," and "heterodoxy."

26. Ibid., 359 (under the title "Syntax and Perspective"): "And just as perspective—*che dolce cosa!*—little by little became a necessity and then an instinct for artists, just as their whole view of the world (*our* view of the world) found itself imperceptibly changed, so the more regular, more harmonious use of tenses progressively allowed writers to introduce order into their thoughts, and perspective—depth if you will—into their narratives."

27. Ibid., 363: "There are action and reaction. The state of language impedes the free play of ideas, but in spite of everything the pressure of ideas causes linguistic frameworks to crack; it breaks them, enlarges them. . . . Language has often acted like a barrier, if not a dam; whence, in intellectual history, all those quantities of backed-up water that one day suddenly break through and sweep everything away."

28. "Greek Philosophy and Christian Faith: An Interchange" is the title of a section of chapter 10 in part 4 of Febvre's *Problem of Unbelief.*

29. Febvre, *Problem of Unbelief,* 388. Here Febvre evokes, from *Pantagruel,* book 5, "the astonishing allegory of Hearsay, the misshapen old fellow who is blind and palsied but all covered with ears that are always wide open and supplied with seven tongues that move at once in his furnace-door mouth. Through all his ears he receives incongruous and crude information from books and newspapers. . . . For if the men of that time made compilations . . . it was because for conquering the world's secrets, for forcing nature out of her hiding places, they had nothing—no weapons, no tools, no general plan."

30. Febvre, *Problem of Unbelief,* 393: "Fluid Time, Stagnant Time: Let us apply these reflections to the measurement of time. People were often still content to approximate it as peasants do—estimating daytime according to the sun and nighttime, or rather the end of nighttime, by listening for the rooster's crow." P. 395: "Thus we find fancifulness, imprecision, inexactness everywhere, the doing of men who did not even know their ages precisely. . . . When was Erasmus born? He did not know, only that the event took place on the eve of Saints Simon and Jude." P. 398: "Are we therefore surprised that men of the past lacked a historical sense? . . . For many men of that time the historical was confused with the mythical."

31. *Urzeit,* "originary time."

32. Febvre, *Problem of Unbelief,* 422: "The men of the sixteenth century were bubbling with ideas, and their whole century along with them. But they were confused ideas that they did not know how to convey clearly, that they could not find the words to express distinctly; brief ideas that they did not know how to expand, extend, or orchestrate. Once in awhile, in a sudden burst, they emitted a flash of light. A spark pierced the night darkness and then went out. And the darkness seemed blacker than ever. The sixteenth century was a century of precursors—that is, of men without a posterity, men who produced nothing. Leonardo and Palissy, enticed by the mysteries of the globe that up to then had not seemed to present a single scientist with a single problem about its inmost structure, revived Greek ideas that had gone unnoticed for two thousand years. They provided a foretaste of what would someday be geology and paleontology. It was too early. Those ideas did not really revive and become productive until two hundred years later."

33. Pages [79–80] involve hardly any significant variants in relation to the second more successful version, which we present here.

34. Merleau-Ponty, in the margin: "They (the writers of the sixteenth century) are too casually assumed to have swung at will from aggressive unbelief to the most traditional kind of belief. Can it be that the problems about their

opinions that we have declared to be insoluble have been brought into being by ourselves and by us alone?" Merleau-Ponty is quoting Febvre, *Problem of Unbelief*, 11. Febvre continues: "Do we not substitute our thought for theirs, and give the words they used meanings that were not in their minds?"

35. In the first version, Merleau-Ponty writes: "The mutation remains within the horizon of the time. Therefore the institutional whole of a time can be reactivated, on the condition that we let ourselves be carried along, by means of the documents, to the *Nachvollzug*. Our (Bérullian) time and the time of instituted Christianity communicate, not on the basis of our opinions and options, but on the condition of going below, not on the basis of the beliefs of the sixteenth century, but on the condition of going below, all the way down to the 'soil.' Communication of an existential order and not notional order. Therefore, the institution of each time, taken concretely, as a horizon, is *also* the means of understanding the other times: in a sense, the first condition is to know also that they are not thoroughly *other*. . . , to place oneself on the terrain of instituted, operative reactions. . . . Concrete universal."

36. Claude Lévi-Strauss, *The Elementary Structures of Kinship*, trans. James Harle Bell and John Richard von Sturmer, with Rodney Needham, ed. (Boston: Beacon, 1969). Merleau-Ponty refers to the original 1947 edition; a new edition appeared in 1967, on which the English translation is based.

37. Ibid., 99: "Firstly, in light of our own ideas on prohibited degrees, the system of marriage between cross-cousins appears profoundly irrational. Why set up a barrier between cross-cousins descended from collaterals of the same sex, when in respect to proximity both cases are the same? Nevertheless, to pass from one to the other makes all the difference between clearly marked incest (parallel cousins being likened to brothers and sisters) and unions which are not only possible but even those which are enjoined upon everybody (since cross-cousins are designated by the term for potential spouses). The distinction is incompatible with our biological criterion for incest."

38. Ibid., 129: "The characteristic feature of cross-cousin marriage cannot merely be reduced to the existence of a social barrier between biologically identical degrees. . . . The antipathy shown to parallel cousins does not simply disappear in the presence of cross-cousins; it is transformed into its opposite, that is to say, into affinity. Consequently, it is not enough to give a separate explanation for the prohibition of parallel cousins, nor would it serve any useful purpose to give an interpretation ignoring the fact that cross-cousins are included among possible spouses. Positive and negative phenomena mean nothing by themselves, but form parts of a whole. If our general concept is correct, cross-cousins are recommended *for the same reason* that parallel cousins are excluded." P. 130: "[This difference] expresses the law that a man cannot receive a wife except from the group from which a woman can be claimed, because in the previous generation a sister or a daughter was lost, while a brother owes a sister (or a father, a daughter) to the outside world if a woman was gained in the previous generation." P. 131: "In the final analysis, therefore, cross-cousin marriage simply expresses the fact that marriage must always be a giving and a receiving, but that one can receive only from him who is obliged to give, and that the giving must be to him

who has a right to receive, for the mutual gift between debtors leads to privilege, whereas the mutual gift between creditors leads inevitably to extinction."

39. Ibid., 177–78: "Let us consider three classical Australian systems, viz., moieties, sections and subsections. These systems have a basic structure.... Marriage always conforms to the rule that if a man of A can marry a woman of B, a man of B can marry a woman of A. Thus there is reciprocity between the sexes within the classes; or, if preferred, the marriage rules are indifferent to the sex of the spouses.... Systems exhibiting this characteristic, whatever the number of classes, are called systems of restricted exchange, meaning that the system can operate mechanisms of reciprocity only between two partners or between partners in multiples of two."

40. Ibid., 215–17: "A harmonic system is one in which the rule of residence is similar to the rule of descent, and a disharmonic regime is one in which they are opposed.... We have seen what happens under a disharmonic regime.... As we know, a matrilineal dichotomy leads to a division into four sections sanctioning marriage with the two unilateral cross-cousins, and with the bilateral cross-cousin. What happens under a harmonic regime?... The system will function as two dual systems juxtaposed. Instead of one, there will simply be two, and the degree of integration in the total system will remain unaltered.... Is the harmonic system then doomed to remain at that primitive stage of group integration which is represented by dual organization?... But another possibility remains open, namely that... of passing from a system of restricted exchange to a system of generalized exchange."

41. Merleau-Ponty, in the margin: "society formed from strong subdivisions."

42. Lévi-Strauss, *Elementary Structures*, 451: "Matrilateral marriage represents the most lucid and fruitful of the simple forms of reciprocity, whereas patrilateral marriage ... furnishes its poorest and most elementary application. But there is another side to the coin.... It is a risky venture. It is a long-term speculation which continually verges on bankruptcy, if the unanimity of the collaborations and the collective observance of the rules should ever come into default. The system of patrilateral marriage is a safer operation precisely because its aims are less ambitious. We might well say that it is the safest of marriage arrangements compatible with the incest prohibition. In relation to the formula of restricted exchange, which occupies a middle position, we must therefore oppose 'short cycle systems' and 'long cycle systems.' Patrilateral marriage ... permits the realization of the shorter cycle, but also, as regards its functional value, the more limited one; whereas matrilateral marriage offers a formula of inexhaustible potentialities for the formation of more and more extensive cycles. At the same time, it can be seen that the length of the cycle is in inverse ratio to its security."

43. Ibid., 178: "But there is a second possibility satisfying at the same time the exigencies of class exogamy and those of division, formulated or unformulated, into moieties. This possibility can be expressed by the formula: if an A man marries a B woman, a B man marries a C woman.... We propose to call the systems using this formula, *systems of generalized exchange*, indicating thereby

that they can establish reciprocal relationships between any number of partners. These relationships, moreover, are *oriented relationships*. For example, if a B man depends for his marriage upon class C, placed after his own, a B woman depends upon class A, placed before."

44. Merleau-Ponty, in the margin: "A→B→C→D."

45. Lévi-Strauss, *Elementary Structures*, 484–85: "Native theory confirms our conception even more directly. Mead's Arapesh informants had difficulty at first in answering her questions on possible infringement of the marriage prohibitions. However, when they eventually did express a comment the source of the misunderstanding was clearly revealed: they do not conceive of the prohibition as such, i.e., in its negative aspect; the prohibition is merely the reverse or counterpart of a positive obligation, which alone is present and active in consciousness. . . . Informants had difficulty placing themselves in this situation, for it was scarcely conceivable: 'What, you would like to marry your sister! What is the matter with you anyway? Don't you want a brother-in-law? Don't you realize that if you marry another man's sister and another man marries your sister, you will have at least two brothers-in-law, while if you marry your own sister you will have none? With whom will you hunt, with whom will you garden, whom will you go to visit?'"

46. Ibid., 464–65: "The three elementary structures of exchange, viz., bilateral, matrilateral, and patrilateral, are always present to the human mind, at least in an unconscious form, and it cannot evoke one of them without thinking of this structure in opposition to—but also in correlation with—the two others. Matrilateral and patrilateral marriage represent two poles of generalized exchange, but they are opposed to each other as the shortest and the longest cycles of exchange, and both are opposed to bilateral marriage as the general to the particular—since mathematics confirms that, in all combinations with general partners, the game for two should be treated as a particular case of the game for three. At the same time, bilateral marriage has the characteristic of alternation in common with patrilateral marriage, whereas it resembles matrilateral marriage in that both allow a general solution, and not a collection of partial solutions, as is the case with patrilateral marriage. The three forms of exchange thus constitute four pairs of opposition."

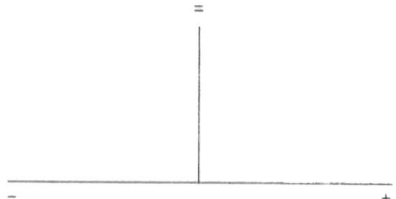

ENDNOTES FOR THE COURSE ON INSTITUTION

= Bilateral marriage; no cycle; formula: A↔B
− Patrilateral marriage; short cycle; formula: A→B
                                                                           A←B
+ Matrilateral marriage; long cycle; formula: A→B→C

47. Ibid., 465: "Does this logical priority correspond to an historical privilege? It is for the cultural historian to inquire into this. Confined as we are to a structural analysis, we need give only a brief justification of the proposition just advanced, and according to which complex kinship structures—i.e., not involving the positive determination of the type of preferred spouse—can be explained as the result of the development of combination of elementary structures."

48. Ibid., 476–77: "Its appearance [*swayamvara* marriage, or marriage of choice] would have been inconceivable but for the latent conflict between the ostensibly matrilateral orientation of systems of generalized exchange, and the patrilateral nostalgia which secretly undermines them, or, in other words, but for the unconscious belief in the security of short-cycle systems which is always found in societies engaged in the hazards of long-cycle systems."

49. Ibid., 454: "For if the matrilateral formula alone exerts a positive action, the patrilateral formula always exists, in a negative form, alongside it, as the second term of a correlative pair. It can be said that the two formulas are eternally coexistent. All the historical hypotheses imaginable will never succeed in providing anything more than the incomplete and approximate transfiguration of a dialectical process. Ghosts are never invoked with impunity. By clinging to the phantom of patrilateral marriage, systems of generalized exchange gain an assurance, but they are consequently exposed to a new risk, since patrilateral marriage is not only the counterpart of matrilateral marriage but also its negation. Within systems of reciprocity, marriage with the father's sister's daughter—short cycle—is to marriage with the mother's brother's daughter—long cycle—what incest is to the entirety of systems of reciprocity. To speak in mathematical terms, incest is the 'limit' of reciprocity, i.e., the point at which it cancels itself out. And what incest is to reciprocity in general, such is the lowest form of reciprocity (patrilateral marriage) in relation to the highest form (matrilateral marriage)." Pp. 474–75: "One conclusion immediately emerges from the study of simple forms of generalized exchange: that, kept in the simple state, they are not viable. Generalized exchange leads to hypergamy, i.e., the participants in the great cycle of exchange, gradually gaining differences in status from the very fact of the formula of exchange, can only receive spouses from partners occupying a superior or inferior position in the hierarchy. . . . There must be a solution to this problem. . . . Firstly, let us consider the case in which the contradiction inherent in the hypergamous rule in some way rigidifies the cycle of generalized exchange. The cycle is interrupted, the indefinite chain of prestations and counter-prestations seizes up. The partners mark time, and, placed in a position where it is impossible for them to fulfill their prestations, keep their daughters by marrying them to their sons, . . . changing hypergamy to endogamy. [Therefore] the Egyptian practice of consanguineal marriages."

50. Merleau-Ponty lists page numbers in the original edition of Claude

Lévi-Strauss, *Les structures élémentaires de la parenté* (Paris: Presses Universitaires de France, 1947), which correspond to Lévi-Strauss, *Elementary Structures,* 450–51: "For all these formulas express the same truth in various forms: a human group needs only proclaim the law of marriage with the mother's brother's daughter for a vast cycle of reciprocity between all generations and lineages to be organized, as harmonious and ineluctable as any physical or biological law. ... Biological laws have just been invoked above, and there would be a real piquancy in showing scorners of primitive logic that, by differentiating marriage relationships into 'types' with characteristic properties, primitive logic is proceeding no differently than does the biologist who classifies relationships between the sexes among the ciliates into from six to twenty-eight different formulas, or the geneticist, who differentiates between five and seven types of consanguineous marriage, according to the average rate of appearance of recessive characteristics in each type. Differentiations in no way inferior to primitive subtleties are then seen to appear between degrees of proximity which are customarily identified in popular thought: the results of union with the father's sister are not the same as those of union with the mother's sister; in genetics, the father's brother and the mother's brother receive different statuses, as also do cross- and parallel cousins. The empiricism of some contemporary sociologists merely repeats, on a different plane, the mistake of an outmoded idealism, and it must be answered in the same way: 'It is, therefore, from the history of nature and human society that the laws of dialectics are abstracted. For they are nothing but the most general laws of these two aspects of historical development, as well as of thought itself. ... [Hegel's] mistake lies in the fact that these laws are foisted on nature and history as laws of thought, and not deduced from them. ... The universe, willy-nilly, is made out to be arranged in accordance with a system of thought which itself is only the product of a definite stage of evolution of human thought. If we turn the thing around, then everything becomes simple, and the dialectical laws that look so extremely mysterious in idealist philosophy at once become simple and clear as noonday' [Friedrich Engels, *Dialectic of Nature* (New York: International, 1940), 26–27]." Lévi-Strauss concludes: "The laws of thought—primitive or civilized—are the same as those which are expressed in physical reality and in social reality, which is itself only one of its aspects."

51. Lévi-Strauss, *Elementary Structures,* 314: "The archaic nature of the material culture of the Australian aborigines has no correspondence in the field of social institutions. By contrast, their social institutions are the result of a long series of deliberate elaborations and systematic reforms. In short, the Australian sociology of the family is, as it were, a 'planned sociology.'"

52. Merleau-Ponty lists page numbers in the original edition of *Les structures élémentaires,* which correspond to Lévi-Strauss, *Elementary Structures,* 483: "No relationship can be arbitrarily isolated from all the other relationships. It is likewise impossible to remain on this or that side of the world of relationships. The social environment should not be conceived of as an empty framework within which beings and things can be linked, or simply juxtaposed. It is inseparable from the things which people it. Together they constitute a field of gravitation in which the weights and distances form a coordinated whole, and in which a

change in any element produces a change in the total equilibrium of the system." It is likely that Merleau-Ponty also has this passage in mind, Lévi-Strauss, *Elementary Structures*, 485: "There is thus no possible solution to the problem of incest within the biological family, even supposing this family to be already in a cultural context which imposes its specific demands upon it. The cultural context does not consist of a collection of abstract conditions. It results from a very simple fact which expresses it entirely, namely, that the biological family is no longer alone, and that it must ally itself with other families in order to endure."

53. Lévi-Strauss, *Elementary Structures*, 493: "The diversity of the historical and geographical modalities of the rules of kinship and marriage have appeared to us to exhaust all possible methods for ensuring the integration of biological families within the social group. We have thus established that superficially complicated and arbitrary rules may be reduced to a small number. There are only three possible elementary kinship structures; these three structures are constructed by means of two forms of exchange; and these two forms of exchange themselves depend upon a single differential characteristic, namely the harmonic or disharmonic character of the regime considered. Ultimately, the whole imposing apparatus of prescriptions and prohibitions could be reconstructed a priori from one question, and one alone: in the society concerned, what is the relationship between the rule of residence and the rule of descent?"

54. See ibid., 483.

55. Merleau-Ponty, in the margin: "In this regard, there is a lack of self-critique which makes Lévi-Strauss not see that the perspective taken on exchange is a construction based on the viewpoint of the Cosmotheoros, that his idea of truth in itself is a mode of the society to which he belongs: a postulate of interpretation by means of exchange [implies] masculinism. What psychoanalysis would have to say (against Freud) of this masculinism. This is perhaps adequate to existing societies but not to possible societies. 'Women,' 'men' [imply] a priori on the basis of Lévi-Strauss's schema—which psychoanalysis contests (postulate of nature)."

56. See Lévi-Strauss, *Elementary Structures*, 490–92, where Lévi-Strauss discusses Freud's *Totem and Taboo*.

57. Merleau-Ponty, in the margin: "Lévi-Strauss admits recently that this knowledge by laws could be brought into harmony with history and could result in a balance sheet for the relation between a society and all the laws."

58. Merleau-Ponty, in the margin: "Cosmotheoros is masculinist."

Part 2

The Problem of Passivity: Sleep, the Unconscious, Memory

Transcription by Stéphanie Ménasé. English translation by Heath Massey and Leonard Lawlor. Notes by Stéphanie Ménasé, Heath Massey, and Leonard Lawlor.

[Philosophy and the Phenomenon of Passivity]

[211] (1) No introduction: cf. other course.¹ [We set out the] passivity-activity problem; [it has an] *apparent* solution. [According to] Lachièze-Rey,² we constitute our passivity. [Thus], we recognize ourselves engaged, for example, in history, and all explanations through the external (psychoanalysis, Marxism) [are] true (since they are others' views of us). But the solution consists in transforming the dependence undergone into conscious and willed dependence, involuntary history into voluntary history, by making it. For example, I know my prehistoric connections with my native environment, I take them into account, but I re-create them, and I re-create from them through decision. I know my ties with the existing society and its defects, I take them into account, and the "gaze of the least favored,"³ which qualifies my philosophical solitude as complicity; but I can adopt an attitude that takes them into account and, nevertheless, saves consciousness, by adopting as a rule never to go *against* the disfavored in the social struggle. Why is this only an apparent solution?⁴

I. *Concerning the Psychoanalytic Past*

If I say that I am completely conscious of this past, not enveloped by it, I reject from it what is essential: its efficiency concerning my present. I do not see that precisely this attitude of omni-consciousness and of omni-judgment concerning the past is an attitude *toward it*, i.e., *rests on it*, disarms it, but, in doing so, is a reactive formation which does not allow itself to be separated from it. **[211 verso]** Is repression—or resistance. Even [the] radical freedom of da Vinci (natural child)⁵ and [that] of Valéry (naked consciousness) are within their history. Dialectic, which turns freedom into its opposite unless freedom truly embraces its opposite, does not live it abstractly, and surpasses it precisely by being it. Actualism and decisionism are neither actualism nor decisionism (Sartre saying that it is not even a matter of choice: pre-empirical choice); consciousness as immediate universal ends up being non-consciousness, for if I am conscious of everything, I am conscious of nothing. In order for there to be consciousness of *something*, there must not be consciousness of everything. A universal consciousness [is] ultimately not actual becoming conscious, but consciousness *in principle*, i.e., there is nothing in me which is not "consciousness of. . .";⁶ and since in fact, I learn about myself, it is necessary either that becoming conscious is ready-made before its time (= unconscious), or that there is nothing to know about me before the *Sinngebung*,⁷ i.e., no personal history, adversity, ambiguity, chaos that says neither yes nor no. But in the first case the thesis destroys itself and leaves it to us to think passivity,—in the second case of the omnipotence of doing as *Sinngebung*, one has not succeeded in integrating the personal past; one denies it since it has no probable sense in itself, since it has a sense only as object for me.

But in order to get out of these difficulties, it is not enough to reverse the positions and say, "I am what my past makes me." It is not enough **[212] (2)** to accept the past in order to surpass it, for by that means we can also be imprisoned in it, and far more directly. Example: Psychoanalysis as *fashion* implies "technical" attitude toward oneself, delight of passivity, self-interpretation that passivizes us—again, dialectic which causes this ostensible acceptance of the past is, in reality, a present that one manufactures. How to accept the past other than through a present decision that *encloses* us in it? In general, this passivism is helped by a passivity concerning the analyst. Transference: is there a true transference, i.e., recovery of a blocked history that finds its overcoming in the analysis? Or is there a transference in the sense of a passivity concerning the prestigious man (letters that one receives from one's audience— the passivism of young people)? What grounds Lévi-Strauss's interpretation is the psychoanalyst as conjurer, sorcerer; the manufacturing of a quasi-adventure that has just *displaced* the previous traumas.⁸ Singular value of the cause and the group: attempt to pass beyond this egotism. Freud's value: the true analysis does not turn the patient into an object, but ultimately a new subject, who is not carried by the driving force of the master's prestige. We can only catch a glimpse of this true dialectic; we are always carried forward by means of "impregnations," which are the constant themes of the genius and of each of us. Nevertheless, criterion of liberation: that this is full and not hollow, i.e., that the patient no longer needs his analyst, and even that he is capable **[212 verso]** of thinking beyond his analyst, or thinking *against* his analyst without this being aggressive. The analyst and the analysand [are] both *in the truth*, not as possessed truth or dogma, but as *aletheia*, unconcealment, and *Offenheit*.⁹ Extreme value of this attitude lies in it excluding the neurotic developments around psychoanalysis, which justify the hostility, e.g., of the Marxists, due to the passivism that results from it.

Thus, a) passivity, b) without passivism—

a) Against self-analysis, others are necessary (and not merely, as Moreno¹⁰ believes, the other of life that has become a spectacle or *drame en clair* thanks to auxiliary egos and to the deployment of the other such as I carry him in me). We need an other who knows without saying, or at least who is ready to know, taking into account counter-transference, who marks the place of truth which is not in the *struggle,* but in the co-presence. We need others toward whom I am not vitally situated, which would transform the analysis into narcissism and reduce the analysis to one of life's adventures, life itself being, conversely, a perpetual but non-thetic analysis. There is a self-knowledge that is not knowledge and not self-consciousness; there is a presence of the past that is not its presence as ob-ject; there is a sense of the past that is not in fact given in it, but also not what I will in the instant; and there is a doing that is not the *fiat* of a closed signification.

b) But it is necessary **[213] (3)** that all this not lead to passivism or past-ism, which would be actualism that is unaware of itself, actualism of bad faith. *Precisely if* we want to surpass decisionism, the narcissism of freedom—the "up to you to choose," which is really a disguised "do what I tell you"—if we want freedom to stop being an "ideology" or a fashion, i.e., a form of passivity, it is also necessary to surpass the affirmation of [the] omnipotence of the past, for despite appearances, it is the same thing. Cf. Sartre saying that the explanation through the outside is *entirely true as well as the cogito* and articulating the one upon the other through "consciousness of. . . ." A true theory of passivity is as remote from "my past explains me entirely" as it is from "I create the sense of my past ex nihilo." The solution through self-positing is an apparent solution; it is a sketch of a dialectic that attempts to absorb the thesis (passivity) in the antithesis (positing of receptivity), which fundamentally identifies them in a skeptical way, mashes one of the opposites onto the other. [The] binary dialectic [is] madness: madness of activism, madness of passivism. The ternary dialectic is itself madness and is reduced to the binary if one realizes the third term in one of the first two. (Proudhon: the synthesis is governmental; it is a matter of a pseudo-synthesis.) The true ternary dialectic does not realize the **[213 verso]** synthesis, not even in the future; it only accepts "permanent" realizations, not a realization that would be death ("mortal" freedom, Sartre wrote). But one must not return, nevertheless, to a continuous, binary dialectic; the dialectic is not binary because there truly are developments—Dialectic: the ternary dialectic becomes a binary dialectic (but authoritarian, which wills itself absolute), and the binary dialectic (of the thesis and the opposition) is, under certain conditions, the true ternary dialectic.

II. *Concerning the Historical Past*[11] *or, in General, the Historical Other*

Same attitude of consciousness: the *explanations* are true, and what consciousness sees is also true. Alienation by the For-Others and certainty of the For-Itself [are] both grounded, and solution by resumption of the For-Others in the For-Itself, creation by the For-Itself of a For-Others justifiable in the eyes of the Others. Self-positing-Doing: it is, in effect, the only solution. But in order for there to be a solution, it must not be 1) that the For-Itself concedes everything to the For-Others, nor 2) that it concede nothing to it.

Sartre's attitude is this:

1) Global concession of the For-Itself to the For-Others: the truth of a society is the gaze of the least favored, i.e., superimposition of a subjectivity in my own, because it has more moral rights than my own.[12]

2) But this concession, precisely because it is global, is nothing. For a) it only obligates one not to go against . . . the least favored; b) the concession does not subordinate me to a truth other than myself: it is still I who give this right to others; c) it does not see to it that *I accompany* the other: distance at the same time as connection. I give the other a duty at the same time as a right. Here there is a connection that is distance because it is created by me, where **[214] (4)** there needs to be distance that is a connection, a "respect" for the freedom of the other [which] is nonintervention of others in me, while it would be necessary to take responsibility for the other, not as infirm and impotent, but without rejecting from the other everything that one thinks. This is because one seeks *immmediate* unity of the For-Itself and the For-Others, which could only be double truth (alternation: others substituted for me, and me substituted for others; self-positing is: I substitute for myself another whom I probably made myself, or I am substituted for by others at the moment when I seem to be yielding to others). We would need not double truth, but truth of the double: that I am also others and that they are also me. The relation to conceive is like that of coupling, or like that of gestation, or like that of projection and introjection, or like that of speaking and hearing (Lagache, *Hallucinations verbales*),[13] or like that of writing and reading, the relation of "surpassing in my sense" or of "surpassing in his sense" of me by others or of others by me. And this presupposes that we stop conceiving both me and others as 1) absolute inherence in a hyletic flux, 2) absolute inherence in a universal for-itself.

These two notions are conjoined in Sartre; the Sartrean subject is absolute individuality and in this way immediately absolute universality. Hence, immediate unity of the For-itself and the For-others. It is necessary, in order to escape from this *equivocation* or *madness* (I am this *and* I am everything, *this* is *everything* and *everything* is *this*), that the individuality of the flux and its body, as well as the absolute universality of the subject, both be broken and give way to a dialectical movement, in order to give a true description of *my flux*. It is not absolutely individual springing forth in each of its instants and in this way absolutely universal; if it were that, I would not perceive [**214 verso**] a *world*. In order for me to perceive a world, it is necessary that along the absolutely individual flux there should be narrowings through space, where generalities can be precisely inscribed or encrusted, which is to say, things, qualities, ideas, conceived not as pure significations or relations, but as *Gestalten* linked to the individual. It is necessary that the dough of individuality rise and produce blisters or things (or "recollections"), (nuclei or ferments, neither spectacles in themselves nor consciousness of spectacle).[14] The Self-Others relation, or the bourgeois philosopher-proletarian relation, therefore, must not be a couple where sometimes one and sometimes the other dominates. Domination of the Other and it is respect for the Communist Party; domination of the Self and it is the Communist Party put to the side, on the outside, as an object of sympathy, not adherence. What is necessary is truly resumption, *Nachvollzug*[15] of external history, its passage in me and my passage in it. The Revolution was just that, but conceived as *real* passage of history in me and me in history (proletariat: *Selbstaufhebung*),[16] that is, inevitable anti-dialectic. The dialectic requires permanent revolution, that is, the self-contesting of power, which, therefore, should not be considered as an absolute and should be liberal—Ultraliberalism. The passivity-activity problem cannot be resolved through real absorption of one of the terms into the other; either ultra-subjectivism or ultra-objectivism of history, either irrational history (mythical, Sartre)[17] [**215**] (5) (the "things") or history receiving its pure sense from "humans"—Adversity and signification—There is a passivity of "humans" and an activity of "things" because there are symbolic systems and a record, at their levels, of everything that happens. This "record" is neither external causality, nor a reference to a meta-history *created* by the human will, but rather a reference to an imagination of history that is the truth of symbolic matrices. In short, our solution to the passivity-activity problem at the level of public history cannot be a mashing of one onto the other (Sartre), it cannot be a Hegelian or Marxist "synthesis" (which, as long as it is *possessed*, is no longer synthesis, but it, too, is the mashing of one term onto the other), but the fact that everything is offered up to a truth that is emergent and possessed by anyone. The delicate point is that this truth should be realized neither beyond the world, as it is by the *tala*,[18] nor on this side of it, as it is for the Marxists.

Direction of the analyses of sleep, dreams, the unconscious, the past: not to seek inductive and dispersed solutions to these problems one by one—there are no separate solutions, the solution is philosophical (no *psychology*)—but to reveal, with respect to these fragments of the philosophical whole, *the dimension* in which the solution can appear and the opening to the truth to be established. For example, sleep (or dreams, or the past, or the unconscious): what is its *theater,* which modalization of being does it realize?

To learn through these modalizations the notion of being at which we need to arrive. To loosen up the sedimentation that links us to *natural being* or *psychical being*, or encloses us in the **[215 verso]** dichotomy of *humans* and *things*.[19] Far from this being either reduction of philosophy to psychology or sociology, or superimposition of philosophical being on the ontology of these disciplines, [it is] an occasion to make philosophical being surge up as integral being at the intersection of these regions. (The "regions" in Sartre are simple specifications of a being that is defined from the outset as being in-itself [with its correlative, the For-Itself.] Cf. when he says that language poses *only* regional problems and conceives metaphysical problems as *beyond* these regional problems. For a truly phenomenological philosophy, the relationship of regional ontologies to philosophy is not the subsumption of the specific under the general, but the relationship of concentric circles.)

[216] (6) Solution sought to the problem of passivity in the perceived, i.e., pre-objective world, *Lebenswelt*,[20] thus without exogenous causality and with endogenous causality that is never pure activity of *Sinngebung*, the latter being carried by *Gestaltung* and, in particular, that of language.

One objects (Alquié)[21] that nothing is gained. Even once [the] phenomenal body and [the] pre-objective, perceived world are restored[22] and it is admitted that it is the phenomenal body which "acts" on the soul, what remains to be understood is [the] action of the objective body on the phenomenal body. It is only for me that my body is a phenomenal body; for others it remains an objective body, and an objective fact (severance of a nerve) provokes consequences in it that are forever unintelligible. It provokes them only *insofar as* the severance affects the phenomenal body. But after all, for an external witness and even for me, the severance has no meaning, and the action of the body on the soul remains just as problematic.

Reply: this is because one thinks that it is a matter, by recourse to the phenomenal body, of replacing the existing body with a body as object of thought, and of turning embodiment and the world into the correlatives of consciousness in the same Kantian-Cartesian sense. Then, in effect, one makes no progress.

But, by restoring the phenomenal body, we sought neither to show the ideality of the body, nor to reintegrate it with consciousness as one of its objects. We sought to show that it is a generalized subject, the invasion of natural and historical situations. The ideal body (in the Kantian sense), the "objective" body, and the whole world of "objective" science [are] considered as *constructa,* and the problem that Alquié poses [is] suppressed or transformed. One will be able to ask how we, being incarnate subjects, have the idea of science and absolute objectivity, but not how the universe of science intervenes in the universe of perception—Problem of "teleology," but not the problem of the union of objective-world and phenomenal-world.

Another objection (Lachièze-Rey) is then, if this is so, if **[216 verso]** the body is mediator of our relation to the world, and if you challenge the radical distinction, *res extensa, res cogitans,* it is finalism or vitalism. You admit that there is either preordination of the body to its field and to the "things" by means of a finality which transcends us, or presence of the whole in the parts by virtue of a quasi-*bodily soul*—Aristotelianism or pantheism: the form is with the matter. The structure of behavior, if it is not for a constituting consciousness, if this is in itself, it means that there is an intermediary between thing and signification, that in the reflex there is a "view" of the world. If the phenomenal body is not for a consciousness (and thus self-posited passivity), it has no ontological function—And if it does have one, this leads one to accept monadology or *physis.*[23]

Reply: the body is for someone; if there were not someone there who perceives it, it would not have the internal unity that I ascribe to it.[24] But this someone who perceives it (from the interior or the exterior) does not in that way turn it into [an] ideal unity because perception is not centrifugal *Sinngebung*—But, ultimately, does the sampled and grafted embryonic tissue (Ruyer), which develops according to the "competence" of the tissue to which it is added, *will* what it does or not? If not, you have gained nothing and it is in-itself. If so, you accept a vegetative soul and neo-finalism.[25] I say that the embryonic tissue, as grasped by methodical and organized perceptions (life science), necessarily appears as a *Gestalt,* i.e., as "dynamic knowing" of its parts by one another. But this does not mean Aristotelianism. This means that there is only the world that is perceived, i.e., not conceived as suprastructure of a human organism, which would amount to turning it into [a] particular region of objective being, but exactly that which is offered to my perception (with all its implications, i.e., also the perceived world of others and of those who lived before and who will live after) posited as being itself. This means a world to be rediscovered and a history to be rediscovered which surpass me and are there exactly where they have been, are, or have been seen.

[217] In sum, one attempts to pull me toward *idealism* or toward *monadology*, whereas my goal was to affirm the identity with being of the perceived world as such. In order to make this project—and therefore the surpassing of the activity (idealism)–passivity (finality) problem—understood, it is only necessary to enter once more into the elucidation of the world and the subject.

1) World side: do not limit oneself to the static image of the perceived world taken at an instant. Consider, not abstract perceptions in an isolating attitude, which I have done too much (hence, overestimation of sensing or of the quality as mute contact with an endpoint), but take up the analysis of the perceived world as being more than sensory. For example, my whole perception at each moment is only the relation of a human action, absolute plenitude is the result of isolating analysis. [The] sensible world [is] full of gaps, ellipses, allusions; objects are "physiognomies," "behaviors,"—[there is] anthropological space and physical space.

2) Subject side: do not consider only the "natural" body, consider everything that is sedimented above and describe the subject resolutely, not as consciousness, i.e., coincidence of being and knowledge, or pure negativity, but as the X to which fields (practical no less than sensory) are open. —In particular, it is necessary to introduce imaginary fields, ideological fields, mythical fields—linguistics and not only [the] repletion of sensing.

In this way, our subject matter this year is connected to our general problem of passivity. Sleep and the unconscious [are] to be understood not as degradations of consciousness by the absurd mechanism of the body—invasion of the third person into the first—but as internal possibility of what we call consciousness. This requires that this consciousness not be pure negativity, for then it would have no possibility of lying down [217 verso] in its body's place. This also presupposes, therefore, that sleep is not an object of consciousness (the idea of falling asleep keeps us from sleeping), that it is consciousness ensnared, stuck, and that it is not the combined operation of a second consciousness (the unconscious) and of a censor (the softened superego) resulting in a third consciousness—the ego and the dream, guardians of sleep—that it is a change of the subject's structure (indifferentiation, symbolic, affective matrix) such that the relation to being is radically changed and is no longer the conventional relation (i.e., instituted, obvious, objective). In this sense, the revelation of sleep: not that it shows me from where conscious life comes and to what it is due, but because it shows me 1) from where it has to spring forth and everything that the perceived world and perception have to do; 2) a layer of fantastic relations with the world, which is also constituted by them—anxiety not of freedom but of commitment. As for the problem of memory, it obliges us not only to pose the problem of mythical being, of the imaginary in the fabric of life, but also that of this imaginary which, moreover, has been, i.e., which cannot in any case be the simple correlate of negativity.

Thus, not psychology, but philosophy. Passing through these phenomena in order to redefine being, instead of presupposing an ontology of the In-itself and the For-itself.

My attempt at a solution [**218**] **(7)**
Return to this side of reflective consciousness in order to find a way out of its antinomies; [the] perceptual consciousness [is] introduced by the body from the world, which is not a world for me alone, but also for other bodies and in this way common history. No exogenous causality and no pure, endogenous causality or *Sinngebung*.

Objections: see notes, p. 6.[26] —Objections that don't follow the direction of the research: being is the perceived. Thus, develop this research. This year's subject.
[..][27]

[**118**] **(9)** Something fundamental to be rediscovered in what follows: in-itself implies for-itself, not only the for-itself of the spectator, but a kind of intimacy of self to itself, a kind of real unity of what exists. In fact, *for-itself* is often employed in this sense, which designates something. For example, when one says that economic phenomena exist or do not exist for-themselves, i.e., as distinct totality.

Hegel said *an sich oder für uns*,[28] wanting to bring the in-itself back to its condition. We are always implicit spectators. But there is also the idea there that an anonymous spectator is posited with each "in-itself" (the in-itself is for-itself: Ruyer). —Example: this colored surface holds itself together; it does not receive its unity from our representation or from a representation of its own.

However, does this tissue have an interior or not? And even this molecule: what is this *für sich Sein*?[29] With reason Ruyer speaks a language of signification with respect to the body. For example, grafted embryonic tissue developing according to the "competence" of the terrain where it is grafted. But where does this competence, these possibilities of the terrain, reside? Is this language to be taken literally? Ruyer: yes, but this does not mean that the tissue has a soul or a self-image; it is exactly as it appears to us with its spatiotemporal unity—no priority to the punctual or to the "substance." Behind the "structure" there is the "form"; the structure is only a "symptom" (ibid., p. 6). The form [is] a block of space and duration—realism of the form: the form as "in-itself." But if one does not think "substance," one cannot claim the notion of in-itself for the benefit of the form. If one abandons "punctualism," what one considers is not the existent insofar as it exists (for at the instant it is not complete and its future is not), but an existent surveyed from above, a spectacle or landscape. Bergson also said that the things are exactly as they appear to us, but he was not thinking them in themselves. In the instant in which one would arrive at the things themselves, there would be no in-itself; in the instant of the things, it would lack this hollow where their parts gather themselves. I do not accept form *in itself*. It remains for us to clarify this reality of the form as "image."

What I proposed [is] different from Ruyer; what Lachièze-Rey does not see is [the] ontological priority of the perceived world (and the phenomenal body), i.e., all being that has a meaning for us is to be conceived on the basis of the perceived world:

1) Ontological priority, i.e., it is not a matter of saying that the real is what appears in substruction in an organism endowed with perceptual apparatus or even in all of them. This would maintain the ontological priority of the "objective" world and would be absurd within the framework of this "objective" ontology (**[119] (10)** Desanti's reproach).[30] It is a matter of finding, in the world of which we have experience, [an]other being and [an]other sense, from which objective being is concealed, of which objective being is "idealization."

2) This priority of the perceived world does not mean that we accept punctualist or substantialist postulates and that we resort to the "psychical" or to "perception" in order to connect the discrete points of an in-itself (as the Kantian synthesis does), that we reduce being to the *perceptum*. It means that we take as real our experience with all its im-

plications (the others and their experiences, those who preceded us or will follow, and "nature," which is given as preceding us and underlying us), that in this experience the forms are an internal unity, their parts "dynamically know" one another, that there is no sense in affirming that they do not make it up, or that they do so, outside any perceived landscape, that the sole being of which we are able to speak is that of the perceived landscape. If one grants with Ruyer that to be in itself is already to be for itself, then one cannot differentiate between an organism and a subjectivity.[31] In the universe of perception we can differentiate, because they are evidenced in different ways.

[122 verso] (11) Is the phenomenal body, i.e., perceiving body, a vegetative soul, a finality?

Ruyer wants to reject the alternative: in itself or for itself; unity that is not that of the *percipere;* in-itself is for-itself, cohesion with-itself—cf. Köhler: [the] elements of a form "dynamically know" the others. But, ultimately, Ruyer founds this unity of the "true form" (interior of the structure) on the world of essences. Now, if this essences-existences relation is descending, from where do dystelies, contingency, and immersion in the causal order come? And if it is only ascending, one has only a reservoir of essences, and how would the causal order draw from it? The unity of cohesion of the true form is either for God, not in-itself, or unexplained. Return to the problem of being for-itself in the true form, which the finalist solution forgets.

The order of the phenomenal (phenomenal body, perceived world) [is] this order of the in-itself that is for itself. "View" of the reflex, "sensibility" of the body to significations, [it is not] a vegetative soul or monad, but the body such as it appears in my naive and scientific experience, in the *Einfühlung*[32] of the observer and what he observes; perceived body *is* body.

Let us clarify. This does not mean that my perception projects significations into it, finds preordination to consciousness in it (Kant, *Critique of Judgment*) which are not constitutive of it. In itself, it is not a grasping of significations, although it is for me. This means: refusal to distinguish between the body "in itself" and the body as it is perceived in human experience. It is exactly as it appears; perception is not a second projection that would leave its nature in itself intact. We do not bring its being back to its being perceived in the restrictive sense, for the reason that *percipere* is to be surpassed by . . . as much as to surpass, and thus *percipi* is to surpass as much as to be surpassed, not [a] *noema* enveloped by a *noesis*. By saying that the body is the perceived body, we mean the body such as it offers itself within the landscape of perception, not "thing"; but this perception is resumption, not constitution.

Ontological priority of the perceived: it is not a matter of reducing all being to a "sector" of this being—the "psychical"—by continuing to understand the former as a modality of "objective being." This would be anthropomorphism. **[123] (12)** It is not a matter of reducing all experience to its "lived" parts (in opposition to science, for example). It is a matter of becoming acquainted, through this lived or perceived, with [the] being that embraces both the perceived in the restricted sense and the being known which is called objective, i.e., idealized; science [is] challenged as dogmatic ontology of the in-itself, but integral to the universe of the perceived and true within that horizon. Simply put, the horizon is broader than science and reveals it as "idealization" in its classical procedures. The perceived [is] first, not as content of my consciousness, not as content of human consciousnesses, not as content of *Bewußtsein überhaupt*,[33] not as "human." There is something other than all that: the perceived yet mute (the human is precisely that which can see the inhuman). But this pre-human perceived:

1) Is defined only by relations, and the framework of a human experience: no being without "contours," "limits," "interior" and "exterior" situation and point of view. Science forgets the pre-human perceived, but it makes use of all this to give a physical sense to its operations.— And thus this relation, point of view, is not reducible to its objective universe.

2) Is accessible not only through a perceiving body, but also through human history: historicity of science; not reception of natural being, but historical elaboration. (Verification of theories: never true as representing the in-itself, but as provisional formulas within [a] horizon of the future. And this, not only in fact, but in principle: generalized relativity. Objectivity that shows through at the horizon, that is never a record of the in-itself. The ontological priority of the perceived [is] rediscovered by science in its very effort of objectification.) Therefore, a double relation between the "in-itself" and us, and not a unidirectional relation that would subject us to it. —"Natural" being presupposes us as spectator, authentically only *such* as it is offered within a field of perception.

Hence,

a) The world without humans or prior to humans: Laplace's nebulosity. We have said that the nebulosity is within the cultural world, not within "Nature," i.e., within the absolute in-itself; and in fact, if one placed it within the in-itself, it would be necessary to remove it from the in-itself through scientific progress, it would be necessary to make it non-historical. And how to understand birth within this in-itself of a human and a consciousness? The world prior to humans like the moon without inhabitants, i.e., spectacle for . . . X and for us. **(13)** The Marxist dialectic itself presupposes emergence. If there is emergence, this means that humans will never be able to think a nature without humans, and ultimately that the pure in-itself is a myth. Every cosmogony [is thought] in perceptual terms. Therefore, truth [is not] prior to us,—and not through us alone, either (cf. Brunschvicg, φ of consciousness)[34]—but the exchange between a world ready to be perceived and a perception that relies upon it. This exchange is what we were calling perception, and it is why perception is central in the ontology. The rationality of science is to [be conceived] as particular case of the logos of the perceptual world—Past truth, truth to come, truth of emergence.

b) The organism "in-itself": does the embryo have a "vegetative soul"? Life of parasites combined according to a plan of the world and infinite understanding? (Strange plan: why this abundance of finality?) If we do not believe this, it is not, for that matter, in order to pass to pure mechanism: creation of species imputed to chance (and simple elimination of what did not realize this arrangement).[35] Hegel's "cunning of Reason," but as philosophical myth: there is no absolute Reason behind the sequences. There is the fact that they are presented "as if" they were rational.—What there are, are totalities that 1) are not a fortuitous gathering of parts, 2) are not prior to all causal conditions. [The] totalities [are] exactly as perception offers them: imperfect and incomplete or less perfect totalities, dystelic or hypertelic.[36] There is exactly what we see: *Gestalten*. [The] cosmogony of the perceived world is prospective and retrospective: not finality, but "heavy" finality, trembling of the whole, "teleology" by means of the phenomena.

Husserl, *Umsturz der kopernikanischen Lehre: Die Erde als Ur-Arche bewegt sich nicht.*[37] Science: decentering. The earth is not the center, but the sun—which itself . . . [There is a] relativization of the perceived world, which is true within its order: it would be false to believe in the moving sun as naive perception does. This would be irrationalism. But there is, in the order of being and not of the beings, a truth of perception which remains. Objectivist ontology cannot be maintained. [The] relativization of theories prevents any of them from reflecting the beings and, even less so, being. Truth of perception: there is no objectivity without a point of view, in itself; i.e., an observer is necessary, with his "levels," his "soil," his "homeland," his perceptual "norms," in short, his "earth" (which is not fixed in the sense of the **[124] [14]** pre-Copernicans, but not simply a moving object within a system of relative movements). It is on the basis of this perceptual field that both pre-Copernican dogmatism and Copernican relativism are constructed. The "earth" is *archē*: [it] bears the possibility of all being above the nothingness, above the flood—seed of the threatened world, on the basis of which everything blooms again. It is "nature" in the sense of perceptual cosmogony, neither in itself nor for God, but our horizon. It is "in itself" and in a certain manner for itself (i.e., attached to itself, as its appearance in my experience proves) without which it would be in the sense of *percipere*, of synopsis: it is this "preparation for perception" that the Husserlian endpoint of teleology designates.

Why this effort has not been understood in its ontological sense (and has been reduced to either idealism or finality in the pantheistic or Aristotelian sense). It is because:

1) [The] analysis of the perceived begins in the common ontology. It surpasses itself from the interior. But the reader does not notice it: "psychological curiosities," "bodily representations," which do not make contact with being.

2) The author himself, in the grip of the common ontology, discovers in the perceived as residue, exception, resistance to this ontology, to knowledge, to intellectual consciousness; consequently, he privileges the aspects that contrast with relativizing knowledge: perception, mute contact with an endpoint, *Selbstgegebenheit*,[38] *leibhaftgegeben*[39] that is *Dingwahrnemung*.[40] This contracts the field of perception. The *Ding*[41] is absolute plenitude only in the face of isolating analysis, which reduces it to sensory components. Even so, it is moreover a hollow plenitude: presence, but absence. Its content is infinite, it is essential to it to present itself through *Abschattungen*,[42] therefore always to be beyond.

Thus,

1) One or several quale have the sense of a thing only through interior and exterior horizons. The horizon [is] what, behind the thing, enables it to be a thing: gaps, ellipses, allusions to the sensible world, divergence, variation, difference of the "world."

2) Consequently, we must describe, in the order of the perceived, not only *Dingwahrnemung*, but *Verhalten*,[43] of which it is a particular case; not only a sensory field, but **(15)** ideological, imaginary, mythical, praxical, and symbolic fields—historical surroundings and perception as reading of these surroundings. History, the horizon of my life, is to be rediscovered as much as the "perceptual" horizon, and like the perceptual horizon, it awaits its truth. This, perceived history with "its" sense—i.e., "traces," intuitions without consciousness and acts without agents—is re-

sumed by me like the perceived "thing" and only receives definitive sense thereby. But, as for the perceived thing, if there is no passivity toward it, there is probability of resumption, re-sumption of its unspecified *Sinngebung;* we surpass it in its sense—i.e., 1) private history, common life [is not] a construction of mine, 2) public history (channels of great communication) [is not] a construction of mine. In both cases, one has a symbolic ensemble of which the sense is presented as divergence and, consequently, not being a closed signification, requires a theory of the open consciousness. There is not the whole of being on one side, the whole of nothingness on the other, but no more are we specialized, conditioned nothingnesses. Consciousness [is not] the flux of *Erlebnisse*,[44] but consciousness of lacks, of open situations; consequently, in the movement that separates them there are narrowings, we live in intersubjectivity, even if, secondarily, this is interiorized as recollection. Me-others hinge, and not only incompatible perspectives that cancel each other out at a distance, like me-my body hinge, and not only apperception of myself, subject bound to a point of view.

The last problem is how this subject, relatively passive concerning its body and history, since it surpasses them only in their sense, nevertheless appears to itself as absolute. This subject is absolute in the sense that it can always interrupt. Is this subject absolute insofar as it does something? Insofar as its negativity is at work? Is doing this refusing the refusal, negation of the negation? No, it is carrying on with pressure that transforms. But the transformation comes as much from others and from things as from ourselves[45]—the possibility of refusal or death—the pure heart of hearts is not even for itself prior to being conscious of this or that. There are not perspectives alternating and bound only by the energy of each (world with several entrances, but each of which is absolutely alone), but this [and moreover] their common work that is recorded as history endowed with a certain truth.

This year's analyses move us closer to this true phenomenological ontology.

Is sleep and wakefulness, sleeping and wakeful consciousness, absence from the world and immediate presence to the world? Which is to say, consciousness of an absence and consciousness of a presence?

[Inserted page **125**].
Problem of a phenomenological ontology.[46]
Are sleep and wakefulness absence of the world, immediate presence to

the world? Is awakening birth? It is rebirth—The preservation of content—It cannot be "corporeal." Is it ideal? But what does this mean in the absence of idealizing consciousness? Thus, there is preservation of potentialities, *habitus*. Analogy with the problem of the body: the body becomes an indistinct being, and yet it can reconstitute itself. It is even the body that reawakens us. In a certain way, it stays awake (open sensory field—invasion and resuscitation of consciousness by *stimuli*). Memory of the body (Proust): it stays awake, not only as bearer of the relation to the world, but as bearer of the past. Therefore, sleep is not merely

    1) Modality of waking consciousness—sleep of consciousness is not consciousness of sleeping;

    2) Absence of waking consciousness—since consciousness remains at some distance. Sleep must preserve consciousness until its waking state. Its waking state must not be absolute self-presence, but itself motivable (by the *stimuli* of reawakening), without which it would never begin and never end (falling asleep).

    This is possible only

    1) If self-presence (consequently to others and the world) is neither nihilation nor, correlatively, the world and others pure articulations in front of me, and

    2) If *consciousness of . . . something* is always consciousness of a difference between terms that are not given positively,—and that appear as terms only through forgetfulness, interruption of analysis, *Vergessenheit*,[47] which is to say ultimately through the possibility of a clarity between two obscurities. Wakefulness [is] differentiation or diacritical system; sleep [is] dedifferentiation and passage not to absence of consciousness, not to consciousness of an indetermination, but to indetermination of consciousness—cf. vertigo or fulfillment by suppression of the levels. It is not the object that conceals itself from a subject who remains intact, nor a subject who sneaks away; it is a passage to the unarticulated object side and subject side at once. Reaction of the object on the subject: state of hypnosis through fixation on a shining point.

    Waking consciousness also a kind of average degree of articulations: we obtain the signification only on the condition of not seeking it directly.

[For an Ontology of the Perceived World]

[126] (14)¹ *Why* [is] phenomenological ontology *poorly understood? What to do in order to develop it?* For we are *caught up in objectivist ontology* and discover the perceived as *residue*.

Hence,
1) The restriction of the analysis of the perceived is reduced to what resists objectivist ontology: the *Dingwahrnemung* as mute contact with an endpoint: *Selbstgegebenheit, leibhaftgegeben,* presence. In reality, even at this level of Nature, it is the presence of an absence: infinite content, presentation by *Abschattungen*—Husserl does not want mutation of the thing or of the essence, but to gather in it that which is beyond. The problem is precisely not passive reception, not illusory construction, but sense at first sight which, with analysis, unmakes itself and, moreover, remakes itself. Cf. Pascal: language makes sense at first sight, which unmakes itself when we press it. To understand this birth and rebirth of sense: its birth in a Nature, its rebirth in a piece of knowledge. In order to understand this development, describe not only the *leibhaftgegeben,* but the perceptual universe with its gaps, ellipses, allusions, as "divergence," "variant" of the thesis of the world. This will enable us to understand that the "natural thing" appears as such only in a culture. There is a history of perception—cf. the perspective of the Renaissance.
2) The restriction of the analysis of the perceived to there being not only a history of perception, but also the perception of history, and there, too, a field to be rediscovered: perception of ideologies, of myths, of intellectual tools, of practical wholes. Here, too, the bi-directional genesis of the given to us, and also of us to the given (we only conceive history prior to us as a sector of our history). Or rather, not two opposed movements (the objective history we create, and our *Sinngebung* creating objective history, but even "objective" history lives only in our life, and even our *Sinngebung* are based on configuration of the past, are *urgestiftet* in it). What is given is their intersection, the articulation of these perspectives on each other. The "truth" of the past [to be conceived] neither in itself as if I surveyed it, nor for my present alone as if there were only one entrance to the system of the world, mine—the truth, as that which judges both the past lived by [127] (15) the human of the past and my undertaking: as their belonging to a single history. Thus to awaken wild history (beyond "objective" history, which does not concern

consciousnesses, and beyond history as an appendage of my personal adventure) as the debate of humans with the past "in itself" or the "true" past which they had to make, that is, the debate of humans with the past for me, and the debate within my own interpretation of the past with a "truth" of which I already have a sense, the gaze of other times on mine—In short, we never have closed significations; we, like the humans of the past, have only open significations and situations whose sense is in genesis. Consequently, consciousness [is neither] a flux of absolutely individual *Erlebnisse*, nor a place of eternal significations; there are, in the wall that separates consciouneesses, narrowings, but neither pure opacity, nor "windows."² We live in intersubjectivity, and the interiority of recollection is second; not alternating perspectives, incompossibles, which cancel each other out without making contact, at a distance, held together by adversity, resumed by "useless" heroism. We do not make contact with ourselves any more than we make contact with others. Thus, no absolute privilege of the I. [A] world with several compossible entrances; we are one for the others. Me-others hinge,³ which is common life, like me-my body hinge, which for me is not just weight, a curse, but also my flywheel. Accompany others, history, and not only endow it with sense by decision. Interpretation of history, which is never given with it, but which is nearer to or farther from it.

From this point of view, that of the open situation (which means not only open to decisionary *Sinngebung*, but also to what passes into others, within the past, and calls for their response), do not overestimate the problem of others and understand it through history, rather than understand the problem of history through the problem of others.

3) This expanded ontology leads to the last problem, which is truth and subjectivity, freedom. How does the perceptual and historical subject, which only surpasses the perceived and history in their sense, which is weighted by this ballast, which has a passivity (something that arises from an *Urstiftung*), appear as absolute beginning? It is nevertheless true that everything arises from me, I can make the lives related to mine disappear, criminal history, such that no truth will justify it or them.

We are all absolute insofar as we are able to suspend thought or action, to withdraw ourselves, to interrupt, and some absolutes [are] irreconcilable. Without me, nothing would be for me, thus nothing at all. And everyone can say it—But 1) the power not to do is all talk as long as it is not translated **[128] (16)** into action. 2) Now, to be translated into action, it must not be refusal of the refusal, not negation transformed immediately into relation, not play, but labor. "Doing" does not have to begin by crossing a margin of nothingness—Consequently, subjects are not alternating consciousnesses, but coexistence of subjects who are gathered together through truth as *a-letheia*. The *Vernunftproblem*:[4] this universal that shows through, the becoming true of the truth. Truth is never such that it can justify me absolutely against someone who rejects it, condemns it absolutely. There is always my fault—Truth is only ever perceptual, probability. The other truth, integral, complete, as soon as someone claims to attain it, is oppression, truth of someone. But reciprocally, the choice in the unknown, even generous, is dogmatism. Between the two, there is openness onto the truth, which makes intersubjectivity be as true as it can be, which is to say that no one claims to be absolutely in the right **[130] (17)** or absolutely wrong. [There is] common life and history which are also perceived, and which, at this level, have a preliminary sense which is not nothing. It is necessary to develop [this sense], to amplify it, to discuss, act, integrate what the others are saying. No probabilism in the sense in which probabilities are calculated, i.e., like the chances of an event, [but] probabilism in the sense of the maximum of truth at the moment. Perception as revelation of a new sense of truth, not of adequation, which suppresses the plurality of subjects and of perspectives, but as movement toward integration, openness.

4) Relationship of the course to these problems

In order for there to be truth (of history, of common life, in the very fabric of the perceived world: logos of the aesthetic world, of which the truth of adequation, of expression, is an idealization) in this sense, it is necessary 1) that the subject be that without which nothing has sense, and thereby absolute—the perspectives are not superimposable, each one is only itself; 2) but that this frontal relation of *Sinngebung* be composed with a lateral relation which retains it and ballasts it, relativizes its *Sinngebung* in advance; [that of each one] announces that of the others and inserts them in the same universe. Passivity is never frontal, as in realism, but always lateral, i.e., the subject recognizes itself as continuing a certain *Stiftung*, a certain perspective.

[135] (17)[5] Sleep, the unconscious, memory, instances of passivity.

1) Frontal passivity [is] impossible. Nothing can be the "cause" of a consciousness, nor the body of sleep, nor the unconscious of my actions, nor the past of our memories.

2) But passivity is necessary. Without it, we have *sleep* as one of the contents of the transcendental subject; the unconscious [becomes] refusal to assume something, *refusal to have consciousness* (regression), thus knowledge of something, thus bad faith; memory [becomes] conscious-

ness of the past, which is not content added to the present contents, but establishment of a dimension of the past. It is necessary to give access to the past to consciousness as posited by it, since the past cannot be in any trace, in any content—every trace or content being "*recordatione carens*."[6] Now, all this renders the fact of sleep incomprehensible (the sleep of consciousness is not simple consciousness of sleeping); the fact that my behaviors have intention or signification unknown to me, therefore operative unbeknownst to me, therefore not "intentional" in the psychological sense; finally, the fact of forgetting (of the non-surveyed).

3) Therefore, passivity is necessary, and passivity which does not render activity impossible—not confrontation of an act with a thing—but "softness in the dough" of consciousness, constitutional passivity, germ of sleep, disease, death present even within its acts, therefore, lateral passivity.

Conditions: that sense be neither pure non-being (Descartes: "I am not smoke,"[7] etc.) nor thought, self-possession (being whose entire essence is to think); that it be divergence between two or more perspectives (the sensible thing is this: not geometral, but that from which all the *Abschattungen* arise, and not only mine, but those of other perceiving bodies whom I know are perceiving due to their behavior within my sensible. The world is that upon which all these perspectives open, and I know that there is only one world, as the other perspectives insert themselves into mine). If sense is this, not positive, but an interval between . . . , then whether it is "natural" (from perception) **[136] (18)** or "cultural" (from thought), "passive" or "active," in any case it is never a pure act of the subject; [it is] inconceivable without the perspectives between which it is outlined, belonging to the things as much as to me, taken up but not created by me—Sense [is] like determinate negation, a certain divergence; it is incomplete in me, and it is determined in others. The thing, the sensible world, are only ever completed in others' perception, a fortiori the social world and history. My "social perception," with its vectors and its indexes of value, is only part of a whole which would integrate it into the social perceptions of everyone else. My significations end in others—and perhaps there is no positive, singular truth which gathers them together (for example, which gathers together the perspective of the artist with that of the proletarian). In any case, in me they are non-false rather than true, figures on a certain ground, divergence in relation to a certain falsity, and not internal adequation. We know what we want through what we do not want. If sense is no determinate being, the subject, as that for which there is sense, is noncoincidence with self without pure negation, nonpossession of self, but by definition that to which a perspectival divergence refers, and passivity is possible in it as an inferior degree of articulation. Not being an absolute survey, but a field, it is equally capable of wakefulness and sleep, consciousness and unconsciousness, memory and forgetfulness. Examine these phenomena, the field structure, the nature of sense as divergence or non-identity, truth as *aletheia*, which does not prevent error.

[SLEEP]

I. Sleep [137] (19)

What is it for a consciousness to sleep? How is sleep possible?

1) The first response is that it is a bodily fact. One can know it directly only through the objective body.
Physiological method: inversion of the elementary reflex (Babinski) inhibition in Pavlov's sense, dedifferentiation of the chronaxies.[1]
[Notion of] "center" of sleep sensitive to [an] electrical or chemical action.
In fact, as soon as we wish to elaborate, [the] questions [are posed]: how to understand the inversion of the elementary reflex? Is this liberation of an automatism? Is this new structuration? Is this inhibition in the passive sense (suppression of a function of staying awake) or inhibition in the active sense, i.e., attitude having a sense (according to Pavlov himself)?
Likewise, does the dedifferentiation of chronaxies mean that they are differentiated by [some] distribution centers according to a set schedule or according to the task? Thus, how to understand differentiation?
Centers: Is it a question of checkpoints for the phenomena, simple mechanisms of transmission? Or [is it a matter] of cause?
Biological method: Sleep would be a carbonic effect of autonarcosis, intoxication to be eliminated. But no parallelism between intoxication or exhaustion and sleep (children, the elderly).
[Instance of] sleep hindered or aided by circumstances and by habits. Why do dogs and cats sleep all the time—rodents and herbivores only a little? [Instance of] twins who share a single circulatory system, one sleeping and the other awake.
Example of evolution from [Henri] Piéron: He isolates the hypnotoxin, albuminoid substance [?] via alcohol, water soluble, destroyed by heat at 65° C, in [the] blood and cerebrospinal fluid of sleep-deprived dogs. Injected [138] (20) in normal dogs [it produces] somnolence. The cause of sleep is thought to be a bodily fact. But Piéron [discovers that] this substance acts not through direct intoxication, but by triggering inhibition of sensory and motor centers of the encephalomedullary axis. Sleep [is] not intoxication, but inhibitive, defensive reaction against in-

toxication. Hence sleep (in accordance with Piéron) [has] an active, "instructive" function, a defensive function. The need for sleep can precede exhaustion or even intoxication.[2]

Thus, it is necessary, in order to know sleep, to treat it as conduct, i.e., not only as [a] brute, bodily fact received by consciousness from the outside. There is an intention of sleep. Freud: "Just as by disrobing each night we plunge our body back into its primitive state, likewise by putting ourselves to sleep we undress our psyche, we deprive it of all acquisitions, and we return, not only by the nakedness of our body, but also by that of our mind, to the state of a newborn."[3] The memory of intrauterine life can be debated, but what is essential is not found there—for that would be to grasp the meaning of sleep as regressive conduct. Pavlov, in his experimental vision, runs up against the animal refusing conditioning. He calls this "reflex of freedom"—which is to say that there is a metareflexology—likewise, inhibition as active conduct—action in relation not only to positive realities, but to oneself—sleep as internal possibility of being and not as fact of the objective body.

2) Sleep as conduct—meaning to be found by examination of its intention.

Wakeful consciousness and sleepy consciousness to be compared—[to examine] sleepiness and awakening.

Sleepiness:
[Sartre:]

> So here I am, trunk bent, muscles relaxed, eyes closed, lying on my side; I feel myself paralysed by a kind of auto-suggestion; I can no longer follow my thoughts: they let themselves be absorbed by a mass of impressions that divert them and fascinate them, or else they stagnate or are repeated indefinitely.... The paralysis of my limbs and the fascination of my thoughts are but two aspects of a new structure: captive consciousness. **[139] (21)** The ground is prepared for hypnagogic images: I am in a special state, comparable to that of some psychaesthenics.... I can still reflect, which is to say produce consciousnesses of consciousnesses. But to maintain the integrity of the primary consciousnesses, the reflective consciousnesses must let themselves be fascinated in turn, must not posit the primary consciousnesses in order to observe and describe them. They must partake of their illusions, posit the objects they posit, follow them into captivity. To tell the truth, a certain indulgence is nec-

essary on my part. It remains in my power to shake this enchantment, to knock down these cardboard walls and to return to the wakeful world. This is why the transitory, unstable hypnagogic state is, in a sense, an artificial state. It is "the dream that cannot form itself." Consciousness does not want to congeal entirely, in the sense in which one says that cream does not want to congeal. . . . In a perfectly calm state one slides, without realizing it, from a state of simple fascination into a state of sleep.[4]

(Hypnagogic state = conscious fascination, usually resisted by the will to fall asleep, which hinders sleep.)

Autosuggestion: I no longer distinguish myself from my thoughts, I abandon myself to impressions. This fascination and immobility [are] the captive consciousness.—In order to grasp this captive consciousness, it is necessary that, like this consciousness, I stop observing and describing, that is, I stop opposing myself and verifying the form-matter relationship. However, I am not confused with these illusions, nor are they confused with their object. I can still return to the waking world. Sleep will be an abandonment of this possibility. Sartre describes it by describing [the] passage to dreams:

> The hypnagogic image was the abrupt persuasion into which consciousness suddenly fell; I was suddenly persuaded that such an entoptic spot *was* a fish as imaged. Now I am dreaming and this abrupt belief is enlarged and enriched: I am suddenly persuaded that this fish has a story, that it was caught in such a river, that it will appear on the table of the archbishop, etc. River, fish, archbishop are all equally imaginary, but they constitute a world. My consciousness is therefore consciousness of a world, I have projected all my knowledge, all my preoccupations, all my memories, and even that necessity of being-in-the-world that is imposed on being human, I have projected all this, but in the imaginary mode, on the image that I presently constitute. What has happened is **[140] (22)** that consciousness was entirely taken,[5] has entirely entered into the game and determined itself to produce syntheses in all their richness, but only in the imaginary mode. . . . Here attention no longer exists, nor the power to present its object as transcendent: consciousness is fascinated by a swarm of impressions, it grasps them *as* being this or that object as imaged, as *standing for* this or that, and then, suddenly, it is entirely in the game, it apprehends these shimmering impressions as *standing for* an object that is at the extreme point of a world whose contours are lost in the fog. So long as the dream endures, conscious-

ness cannot determine itself to reflect, it is carried along by its own decline and it continues indefinitely to grasp images. . . . It is because it is incapable of grasping what is real in the form of reality. . . .⁶

The imaginary world is given as a world without freedom: no more is it determined, it is the inverse of freedom, it is fatal. . . .⁷

The only means that disposes the sleeper to come out of a dream is the reflective observation: I am dreaming. And in order to make this observation, nothing is needed except to produce a reflective consciousness. Only, this reflective consciousness is almost impossible to produce, since the types of motivations that ordinarily solicit it are precisely those that the "enchanted" consciousness of the sleeper is no longer allowed to conceive.⁸

· Dream interrupted by either external stimulus or its immanent end (I am killed)—no *afterwards*—whence the hesitation that motivates reflection and reawakening—

> We can conclude that the dream is not given—contrary to what Descartes believed—as the apprehension of reality. On the contrary, it would lose all its sense, all its own nature, if it could be posited as real for a moment. It is above all a *story* and we take the kind of passionate interest in it that the naive reader takes when reading a novel. It is lived as fiction, and it is only in considering it as fiction that is given as such that we can understand the kind of reaction that it provokes in the sleeper. Only, it is a "spellbinding" fiction: consciousness . . . is tied up. And what it lives, at the same time as the fiction is apprehended as fiction, is the impossibility of leaving the fiction. Just as King Midas transformed everything he touched into gold, consciousness itself is determined to transform everything that it grasps into the imaginary: hence the fatal character of the dream. It is the grasp of this fatality **[141] (23)** that has often been confused for an apprehension of the dream world as reality.⁹

[Thus] sleep (with dreams, Sartre studies it only through this angle, but perhaps he is not able to conceive of others) [is] the moment when I unify myself with fascinating givens, because I leave reference to the observable behind and place it entirely at the service of unobservable imagining consciousness, i.e., consciousness which no longer articulates sense on adequate material, but which aims at some arbitrary emptiness through something arbitrary.

[. . . . .]¹⁰

[143] (23)[11] [It is necessary] to grasp what it is *to sleep*—falling asleep—in a sense an *act*, expressed by a verb—When I lie down I do something, I not only await sleep, I *lend myself to sleep*—indulgence. But I do not cause sleep; the will to sleep prevents sleep. The sleep of consciousness is not consciousness of sleep; sleep is the opposite of consciousness. Even in the case of tricks for falling asleep: for example, I avoid being conscious of anything, I try to remain between two thoughts. Still, this is only preparation. When sleep comes, it is something other than this consciousness which divides itself. It is a status (in the sense of a *grâce d'état* or *devoir d'état*). I call upon sleep, but it is sleep which comes. It has a motivation, it forms part of our life. [Thus, it is not a matter of] frontal passivity (only in limit cases: falling asleep as a crowd), but [of a] passivity nevertheless: one abandons oneself. Cf. sexual "passivity," even in the man, in the "active" seducer: he is "inspired" to act. Even the conduct by which the sexual partner is either turned into flesh or fascinated, numbed, this conduct is only convincing, only achieves its effect, if he is fascinated himself, if he is taken hold of as entirely as he takes hold. Strange activity which comes from beneath our decisions, carries us as much as we carry it.

To avert misunderstanding: there is no determinism here, submission to a foreign power; the event often only occurs after decision (to sleep, to seduce). But the event is not caused by it, only permitted by it, such that it is not what was decided that occurs. This is also applicable to the production of a work of art, perhaps to any action or undertaking as it is truly lived or done.

Relation to time, thus: "project" not in the ordinary sense of anticipated future, positioned at a distance, chosen from non-being; but rather being rising up toward, balancing itself on what is not yet—The present [is] the cradle of a future.

Projection is also introjection or conception. **[144] (24)**
Sartre's attempt to analyze this:
A. First, "captive consciousness": paralysis of limbs, fascination of thoughts.
1) Not true paralysis: I can shake myself, "knock down these cardboard walls." But I do not feel like doing it: "our consciousness comes to adhere to a relaxed muscle and, instead of purely and simply noting the hypotonicity, it lets itself be *charmed* in the proper sense by it, which is to say it does not observe it, but *accepts* it."[12] Vertigo of inertia, less and less probable that I move. Not having moved becomes the reason for not

moving; [the] present [ceases to be] proof or temptation of a future, immobility [is] self-caused—immobility that is no longer a variety of behavior, in possible alternation with movement, i.e., in relation of tension with milieu, situation, but an absolute of immobility. For Sartre, this is not to be understood in terms of motricity, of "I can," as modifications of our "bearing," but in terms of "consciousness," as an aspect of the "captive consciousness."

2) Thus the "fascination of thoughts" [is] more revealing than the "paralysis," [it] consists in this: autosuggestion. I.e., we are fascinated, not by submitting merely to an external force, but by considering as an external force that which comes from ourselves. There is no longer consciousness of what we do, of our significations, on the one hand, and of what the surroundings bring, on the other hand, but rather a confrontation of both, either determinism, or freedom. There is an alliance or complicity of our significations and these givens. We are at the mercy of (vague) suppositions, of the swarming impressions, and they are at the mercy of what we attempt to make them say. Thus, more than face-to-face subject-object, more than observable object, full, without gaps, of an infinite richness, and correlatively, more than subject on which we can reflect, for **[145]** (25) we are not faithful to these *noesis* except on the condition of not asking them of which *noema* they are *noesis*,[13] of taking their word. We no longer know either what we saw or if we saw; in the instant, we are persuaded that this entoptic spot is a fish. Perception is imagining consciousness, i.e., consciousness that aims at something arbitrary through an arbitrary *analogon* and does not need to see, i.e., [there is] signification-*hylé* adequation.[14] Fascination is immediate certainty, hollow consciousness, not full, [?], not actual, empty intention.

B. Then, passage to sleep.

Difference from the hypnagogic state: the latter is "artificial," i.e., unstable, "transitory," without equilibrium, between waking—i.e., accurate consciousness, which proves to be the adequation of intention and *Erfüllung*,[15] and which, consequently, can be consciousness of consciousness, since reflecting consciousness need not be complicit with reflected consciousness and follow it into captivity—and sleep, i.e., illusory consciousness, which cannot reflect in the absence of an object where it is captivated. Sleep will be this hollow consciousness, when it has lost the notion of the full to such an extent that it does not apperceive itself from its nothingness, and that, in the absence of a ground of being, it considers nothingness valuable. This very world, this being-in-the-world, which was the definition of consciousness, having completely disappeared, consciousness is free to utilize its form without being confronted by anything. The dream [is] imagining consciousness which believes that its phantasm is "the extreme point of a world," which has lost any notion of control by the real, which is thus "entirely at play."[16] Consciousness "congeals" or "is taken hold of," it decides to consider itself immediately and without reserve; i.e., it is outside the dilemma of freedom and determinism, in order to live in the indistinction of desire and reality, at once in the arbitrary and the fated. This ultra-objectivist and ultra-subjectivist structure, which is opposed to the mediation of the waking (freedom and determinism), is the narcissistic consciousness, without stepping back in relation to oneself, attached to oneself.

Thus, solidity of the state of sleep, different in nature from waking: consciousness can no longer posit itself in the face of things and in the face of itself, it is "dragged away by the fall," i.e., abundance of the imaginary; i.e., nothingness valued as being. An atom of being would be enough for it to be disclosed, an atom of reflection, of perception would be enough, then consciousness would stop being irrealized in imaginary consciousness. But how would a trace of being introduce itself? The fiction is "spellbinding," consciousness "enchanted," "tied up," "entirely at play," it seeks only to tell stories. Thus,

1) Nothing whatsoever is apprehended as "reality"; **[146] (26)** the dream is not even reality for the dreamer.

2) But, for this very reason, and because there is no distance from him to the dream, nor from him to his dreaming, there is no benchmark that contests its "persuasion"; sleep is a pseudo-world.

Problem of passivity: Sartre does not oppose sleep to waking as passivity to activity. These notions are separated. There are both passivity and activity in waking, and passivity and activity in sleep.

1) Waking: passivity in the sense that there are obstacles, and one observes, one awaits the response of the sensible givens in question; there are distance and tension between intention and *Erfüllung*; there is "articulated causality." And thereby, there is even the possibility of freedom, i.e., in this solid, faithful milieu, which is what it is, one can act precisely by virtue of its connections.

2) Sleep: passivity in the sense that there is no distance from self to things and from self to self, and that thus the impressions acquire sense without possible observation—passivity not in the sense of obstacle or barrier, but in the opposite sense of indistinction, fusion of things-myself, i.e., fate. Fate that is arbitrary and capricious as well: one sees what one wants; for lack of barrier, every intention to see is at once sight. Consciousness "has determined itself to produce hypotheses in all their

richness, but only in the imaginary mode. . ."; "consciousness itself is determined to transform everything that it grasps into the imaginary." The activity of oneiric consciousness [is] false activity, in bad faith, mad, [consisting in] making up what one wants, seeing at one's discretion, without barrier. . . .

[Perceptual Consciousness and Imagining Consciousness]

[Difference between perceptual and imagining consciousness][1]

[207] (1) Is this the difference? Perceptual consciousness and imagining consciousness? Consciousness of being and consciousness of nothingness? Adequation and bad faith?

1. "Fiction which is given as such" —Surely it is not truly given as nothingness, as fiction; in order to do that, it would have to be upon a background being, of perception, but precisely the background is lacking. A spellbinding fiction, a nothingness which no longer knows itself as nothingness, it is not emptiness.

2. Moreover, if this were truly emptiness, the pure "omnipotent" signification, there would never be reawakening. In that case, from where would the level of the world arrive for the dreamer? The "place" of the world has to remain marked within him. Dreams, sleep, are themselves confirmed, are carried along by its own decline.

From where does reawakening come? 1) External stimulus, says Sartre. But, having reduced the eloquence of the imaginary to the absence of the world, how could Sartre conceive that a consciousness capable of being bent to this point opens to the world that the oneiric structure closed to it? 2) Immanent impossibility of continuing the dream—I die: no *afterwards;* hence, the self-sufficiency of nothingness compromised for an instant, then hesitation, reflection, and reawakening.[2] But this reflection will be resumed from the attitude of waking, of distance from myself. And what will provide the benchmark of this distance, if not the structure of rigid consciousness? However, if consciousness can be trusted on this point, how would it remain capable of perceiving? Thus imagining consciousness has to keep the link with perceptual consciousness in two ways, and sleep must not be factual absence of waking and of the world. [The] *motivated* presence of the world [is] dismissed by Sartre.

3. Moreover, if the "solidity" of dreams or sleep were only absence of reference to the perceived world, the persuasion would have to be

complete. If the imaginary is emptiness, it can only pass for full on the condition of being completely empty. However, there are convincing, impressive dreams which coexist with consciousness of dreaming and even remain impressive after reawakening.

4. Waking and sleep less heterogeneous than Sartre says.

The distinction between perceptual and imagining consciousness is clear as far as a sensible object or a (2) living body is concerned: observable—non-observable. But neither the dream nor the waking world is made up of that. They are made up of behaviors, events, anecdotes. And here the distinction between the observable and the non-observable is certainly not applicable, for even in wakefulness one does not *observe* an interlocutor prior to understanding what he says and prior to responding to him, one does not await this signification nor the *Erfüllung* to believe in him. Our real life, inasmuch as it is addressed to beings, is already imaginary. There is neither verification nor *Erfüllung* for the impression that someone gives us in an encounter. Thus, there is an oneirism of wakefulness and, conversely, a quasi-perceptual character of dreams—the mythical.[3]

[208] (3) The "perceived world" is not adequation, nor is the "imaginary world," thus bad faith. There is no bad faith except by contrast with adequation. If there is no adequation anywhere, there is no bad faith anywhere. The properly perceptual level has its "beliefs" (Proust) which are impressionable, likewise those of dreams. The idea of adequation and of the "real" makes no sense as soon as we want to apply it to the human world. For example, nothing can make me consider as "*alter egos*" people that, from atop the towers of Notre Dame, I see as being no bigger than ants, or that I imagine as being confined in their houses as in termite mounds. I can do that no more than I can see the immobile sun. There is, then, a situation of solitude or solipsism—Conversely, nothing can make me see a person nearby as an automaton. The "beliefs" are due to the action of our body as "focusing" on things or others, and the certainty that this focusing carries is due not to an exact *Deckung*[4] of intention-*Erfüllung*, but to a structuration which is by no means without gaps (without gaps means nothing).

The oneiric experience of such a structuration also gives rise to a "belief" which is not belief in the dreamed thing as object for all, but as object for me, and which is not fundamentally other than that of the perceived. All perception of others is as much bad faith as the imaginary in the sense that it is projection and introjection, that it offers me a picture of myself as much as of the other, and that here, too, I mostly see what

I want. All this, not in order to deny the distinction made by Sartre, but to restore it.

5. (**2** continued) Sartre attributes [a] difference in nature to sleep and waking, imagining and perceptual consciousness. But at the same time, this difference in nature leaves them fundamentally homogeneous. To sleep, just as to be awake, is to be conscious of something, with a simple difference in hyletic structuration: adequation in one case, inadequation in the other. They are less homogeneous than Sartre says. Sleep [is] an activity of distancing the world.[5]

But is to sleep simply to work in the imaginary? Are dreams even sleep? [For] Freud, dreams are the protectors of sleep, [keep] even the connection with the world, in reality, from which sleep, on the contrary, turns away; hence, [if] a nightmare wakes me up, it has some relation to the anxieties of my life, to my dramas, and it is not arbitrary, simple disintegration, as Sartre describes it. And sleep, on the contrary, does not simply turn away from life, as Sartre believes, by passing to a life of the arbitrary, to the omnipotence of desire, but rather by keeping it at a distance, by pushing itself toward death. To sleep is neither immediate presence to the world nor pure absence. It is being *in the divergence.*

Thus the body, as perceptual focusing in general, as relation to dramatic situations, is the subject of dreams rather than the "imagining consciousness." Sleep is not the same thing as dreams, but the return to the dedifferentiated body. Symbolism, compromise between active body and dedifferentiated body, is not simply collapse of the intention-*Erfüllung* structure, absence of the real world.

[208] (**3** continued) It is a matter not of hyletic distinction, empty consciousness and full consciousness, the same consciousness,—but of structural distinction. (Moreover, from the moment that there is *analogon*, and this *analogon* is apprehended as "evoking" the real being of the absent object, imagining consciousness is not empty.) "Full" consciousness [means] not "observation," but "focusing," i.e., spectacle presenting itself as going toward an optimum, and summoning a certain positioning of the sensory apparatus toward it, i.e., the body-spectacle relation [is] unknown.[6] (**4**) Relation of the two variables, but as means-end relation, *Abschattungen*—The thing itself, i.e., insertion of the given in a "field"— And I know that I have seen because this animal of flesh has been fulfilled, or at least has believed it. Not transparency of the "I think," but its obstruction— "Empty" consciousness maintains this reference of field to the world, but distances it; I become my body not as openness to an effective space, "I can," power of a certain *bearing,* but as closedness to all

that (which is a modality of the fields, all the same). It is not truly nothingness of the world: 1) the world continues to exist—in the divergence; 2) the body becomes heavy, I lie there, I am its place, it marks my place; 3) though immobile, the body is not nothing; predominance of my respiration, I am its breathing; 4) finally, my situation in the world remains, and I give the body satisfaction through dreams which allow me to avoid *truly* taking a position. It is relative and provisional nothingness—by de-differentiation of the discriminating systems: a-praxis, a-phasia—loss of *contours*, levels.[7] But, ultimately, there are other beings, another science, on this side of space, not because the oneiric content is nothing and the something is forgotten, but because it is a *private object*. So the oneiric something becomes most of all projection of the individual drama where it is from, with all its roots.

The symbolism, says Sartre, is primarily an incapacity of *Deckung*, i.e., of "direct" or conventional consciousness. [The] symbolism reduces to negation; it is *inadequate* thought. For Freud, on the contrary, the inadequation is voluntary, deliberate. For me, the interrupted dream frees a mode of thought, not hollow, as Sartre believes, not lying, as Freud believes, but impressional. The notion of oneiric symbolism is the touchstone of a theory of passivity.

[209] (5) What do we mean when we say "it is the body which sleeps"? We mean, just as when we say "it is the body which perceives," sleep is not an act of *Sinngebung*. Sartre, because it is his subject, but also because it is the sole possibility for him, studies dreams above all. However, dreams are not sleep; they are a compromise between sleep and waking. Dreams [are] evidently reckless *Sinngebung*, fulfillment of the *Sinngebung*. But this, then, is not sleep (and consequently it is no longer truly the dream as cut from the cloth of sleep). The symbolism is going to appear as sliding of sense upon the materials. To understand it well, it is necessary to take stock of an alteration of sense itself, which consists in 1) [the] lowering of the barrier of the official personality, predominance of immediate desire through distancing of the world; 2) however, [the] control of this desire which, if it were overtly manifested, would provoke anxiety and reawakening. Thus semi-repression—semi-barrier. The disguise of symbolism, for Freud himself, is not uniquely due to repression. The renunciation of direct, adequate expression, *Erfüllung*, is a consequence of the fact that one sleeps, i.e., that one distances the discriminating apparatus and that one goes toward undifferentiation, aphasia, apraxia (cf. Freud showing that one does not truly speak in dreams, that there is no expression of logical relations in dreams).[8] But this does not mean limitless freedom of an arbitrary *Sinngebung*. This means employment of certain phenomena as *analogon* of certain others according to

connections which are, on the contrary, preestablished, in their general features. This means that here is a field of dreams as there is a field of *Sinnendaten*.[9] **(6)** Where is the dream for the dreamer? The question is of the same kind as this one: what is the "location" of pre-spatial sensory fields? The visual, the tactile, and the auditory do not fully coincide as soon as we leave the object itself and we consider them as an apparatus for sensing. What dreams in us is our existential field insofar as it distances the barrier from the situation and lets itself function without an absolute control.

Dreams dissolve in waking life just as monocular images ("phantoms") do in binocular perception. They reside, as monocular images do, in the pre-spatial—but not in nothingness. Sleep is the body and the existential field withdrawing from the world (and being permitted variations that the world no longer controls, in order to prevent the drama from being reborn), and coming back to their facticity. The description of oneiric consciousness as nihilation (Sartre) omits that there is not only omnipotence here, but also impotence, return to the archaeology of birth [which is] to be elaborated by analysis of symbolism. It is not intention to disguise, as Sartre says; it is powerlessness to repress proliferation of significations. There is a third hypothesis, and in Freud himself, namely return to the pre-objective organization of the world, of which the subject is the body in the *general* sense of apparatus for living, possession of *imaginings*.[10] [Thus, do not oppose] adequate consciousness and empty consciousness, but [conceive the] body as focusing on the world and situations, and [the] body as elaboration of *imaginings*.

Sartre's description is fascinated by the idea of a natural delusion of consciousness, of a solidity of dreams, which is self-presence, of a masquerade of the imaginary world which is nothing (nothing "real") and nevertheless counts as a world. But, putting that aside,[11] [if it is] expressed in terms of consciousness, as if the same consciousness, only emptied, presided over sleep and over perception, **[210] (7)** as if, therefore, unarticulated consciousness were consciousness of inarticulation, then [that] deforms the "nothingness" characteristic of the imaginary.[12] The passage to the dream is not passage to the absolute nothingness of pure signification. It is *partial* functioning of the signifying machine, the apparatus for living, furthermore reduced above all to interpersonal relations. Confusion in Sartre between nothingness of consciousness and consciousness of nothingness, and this is the case because his notion of consciousness does not allow him to accept into itself and on the side of the subject a principle of weakness, which gives to it the most and the least.

Thus, against Sartre's activism: "consciousness determines itself to. . ."; [oppose] theory of symbolism as touchstone—cf. Freud.

[SYMBOLISM]

[157] (33 continued)[1] Symbolism as touchstone
The intermediary dream is sleep and the world, absence and presence of the world. Dreams are symbolism. Something signifies a completely different thing, and not, as in waking, "itself." By examining this symbolic function we will examine the manner in which the sleeper is taken into it in order to absent himself, without absenting himself. Exact relation between the "imaginary" and the "real."[2]

[For] Sartre, [the] symbolism [is a] congenital powerlessness of fascinated consciousness to take something for what it is—It cannot stop the proliferation of significations: inadequate thought and hollow omnipotence—Immediate presence to the world (or freedom) has become absence of the world and arbitrariness.

Is it that? The symbolism is not indifferent functioning of consciousness in connection with present "*stimuli.*" It is at the service of existentialia, i.e., 1) of recent events, 2) insofar as they echo former events. It delimits a functioning which is not "consciousness of something" (simple, general function, *Erkenntnistheoretisch*),[3] but development of a "world-for-me" (oneirism of wakefulness, quasi-"reality" of dreams)—What is the subject of this "world-for-me" (world which is relations with others above all)? The [158] (34) "interior monologue" [is] an extremely approximate account of this oneirism (Blanchot).

[Inserted page 156].
Interior monologue
Maurice Blanchot, "Death of the Last Writer" (p. 491).[4]

> There is also chatter and what has been called interior monologue, which does not in the least, as we well know, reproduce what a man says to himself, for man does not speak to himself, and the deepest part of man is not silent but most often mute, reduced to a few scattered signs. Interior monologue is a coarse imitation, and one that imitates only the apparent traits of the uninterrupted and incessant flow of unspeaking speech. Let us recall that the strength of this speech is in its weakness; it is not heard, which is why we don't stop hearing it; it is as close as possible to silence, which is why it destroys silence completely. Finally, interior monologue has a center, the "I" that brings everything back to

itself, while that other speech has no center; it is essentially wandering and always outside.

(What I call the oneirism of wakefulness, the deployment of perceptual "beliefs," the flux and reflux which bear our acts and our abstentions, our speech and our silence, is not in fact conveyed by the interior monologue.)

(**34** continued) The "unspeaking speech" [is] the formation of my relations with others and their relations among themselves. Where does it operate? Who utters it? Who dreams? Dreams to be considered here as a modalization of life; thus, who lives? The symbolism of both dreams and life, common subject of the two (but not consciousness).

This does not mean that the two symbolisms are identical. But precisely, as symbolisms, they can be homogeneous without being confused. [The] imaginary-real relation is not [between] empty and full, unobservable and observable, two incomparable universes (and no more weak state and strong state of the same "sensible"), but entirely different species of structuration. Is the "visual" thing (the reflection) "real"? Is the "phantom" which only exists for one sense "real"? Is the "pre-spatial field" of touching as touching real? They are not, however, "imaginary." Is the monocular image "real"? It is not irreal. It simply disappears into the binocular image as if into its true place. Likewise, fantastic symbolism disappears in wakeful consciousness of this symbolism, but it does not contain consciousness, it did not have its truth in itself, and its prestige was not of simple irreflection, its capacity to represent another thing with itself was not simply impotence.

Freud discovered this positive symbolism; this meaning beyond the meaning has a double sense. One usually retains only the two separate meanings from it: manifest meaning and latent meaning. The latter [would be] reinstitution of an original meaning which was then repressed, buried in memory, by censorship. Unconscious and censor, two partners, two texts,—condensation, displacement—two meanings which have the same structure: "consciousness of. . . ." Freud himself presented things in this way. However, that is not his discovery. If the latent content were truly buried, dreams would not provide any relief from the desire. It is necessary that the latent content be accessible to him in some manner, that the one who dreams and the one who sees to the bottom of the dream are the same, and that there are not truly two persons (the unconscious and the censor, the id and the ego), but communication between them. The censor **[159]** (**35**) presupposes a pre-notion of what is censored. But this pre-notion is not a notion.

So, what is constitutive of the "phantasmic" milieu that resembles the world (the "theater of the dream," the world-for-me), and which is no more the world than the *Sinnending* is the *Ding*?[5] In what sense does the dreamer have access to the latent content? In what sense not? Is dreaming thinking the latent content such as it has been revealed to me by the "second account" and the analysis, and on the other hand, repressing this thought and substituting a compromise for it? To dream, is this to think? Is it necessary to imagine that the truth of my symbolism is 1) in the dream itself as a fiction which is given as fiction (Sartre), capricious *Auffassung*[6] which is known as such? 2) Completely outside the dream, result of which I ignore the genesis, of which the genesis is transcendent to me? (Freud taken literally)—The common postulate is that to dream is to think, it is to have consciousness of . . . , it is *cogitare*. The symbolism, either secondary (Freud) or negative (Sartre) [is] simply inexactitude or inattention. And if it were primitive? The second account is not simply restoration of latent content, but its translation into wakeful language, which precisely the dream does not speak. "Postulate of the priority of conventional thought." To restore the proper language of dreams—or rather, its constitutive symbolism (Politzer).[7]

Now, Freud has touched on this, the structure of oneiric thought. In Sartre, this structure [is] inaccuracy of the imaginary *and* bad faith. But if there is no good faith with regard to oneself, how are we able to call forth this Evil genius who hides me from myself? It is symbolism. In Politzer, there is no affirmation of the totality of consciousness (negation of the unconscious [is not] affirmation of the totality of consciousness), but there is a will to reduce repression [to] the "first person," [to] the moment of my "drama," i.e., "that which I do not want to assume." However, he himself rejected the idea of the priority of conventional thought. My contact with **[160] (36)** the truth of dreams is no more a "refusal" in the conventional sense than "bad faith." It is symbolic contact. In short, the examination of the structure of oneiric thought must not be carried out against repression, in order to dispense with repression. Two errors: to believe that the symbolism comes only from repression, and to believe that repression is reduced to the symbolic or oneiric state simply as privation, that it is pure falsehood in relation to always possible wakeful consciousness. These two errors presuppose the priority of conventional thought by identity. The second tendency is that of Sartre and even Politzer. The first is perhaps that of Freud in certain writings.

More precisely, Freud did not affirm the unconscious as satisfactory concept (cf. *On Dreams*).[8] At the very moment when he says there are "two creative functions of thought," he adds that this makes a "sort of demonology," "like a subordinate who would like to put his two cents into a superior's speech,"—he adds "psychological theory frustrated again"

THE PROBLEM OF PASSIVITY

and hopes that we will know one day what the unconscious is[9]—It is an operational concept.

Freud did not seek to reduce symbolism to repression (as he never reduced the constitutional to the acquired; on the contrary, without constitutional traits, he said, traumatisms would not be neuroses)—He wanted us not to limit research through considerations of structure (as Sartre and Politzer do).

But he does not deny the existence of an oneiric structure which is responsible for part of the way dreams look; he began the examination of it. He began with the exploration of "unconventional thought"—cf. *The Interpretation of Dreams*.[10] It is here that we seek the picture of primordial symbolism.

[161] (37) 1) We do not truly speak in dreams, we do not truly think in dreams. 2) Use of language (wordplay) in dreams, echoes, several centers. 3) No expression of logical relationships: whether alternatives, negations, etc. *The Interpretation of Dreams*, pp. 311–12.[11] The dream absurd negation of . . . , dreams in which we do not manage to do anything. 4) Feelings are not masked. Representations are subjected to censorship, not feelings; hence dreams in which feelings are not adapted to the content.

This indicates that 1) in the dream itself, there is imminence of the latent meaning (in the dream not reduced to the first report); 2) what prevents the latent meaning from being stated openly is that the very idea of *openly* or of *exactitude* makes no sense here, not simply because we are in the imaginary (formal reason), but because the unity is undivided. This sex is not sex because it is everything—ignored as sex because it is everything.

Method proper to the understanding of dreams: reverie over dreams, hermeneutical reverie. Because it is not something said, but an echo through totality. It is this system of echoes which also constitutes the oneirism of wakefulness (cf. Blanchot's unspeaking speech).

Notes for continuation[12] **[162 verso]**

The "science" of the world and the "science" of dreams. Being and oneirism. Investment and disinvestment (commitment)—It is under this form that we pose the problem of the imaginary and the real.

I.e., it cannot be a question:

1) Of distinguishing them absolutely (our "real" life is oneiric for all that which touches others) (all investment is at the same time counter-investment and hyper-investment, i.e., ambiguous);[13]

SYMBOLISM

2) Nor, of course, of confusing them: narcissism, egoism of the dream, or regression of the dream. Retreat before "the test of reality."

All that counts for us is drawn from the order of the "real" or the "event-based" (all traumas). And it is not a question of subordinating waking life to oneiric life. It is simply necessary to understand that they communicate. The fundamental function is desire and the fecundity of desire (cf. *Gradiva*).[14] Choice conceived as demonstrated and not as "vain" passion. It is necessary to conceive all of what Freud has described (domination of the past and childhood, domination of oneself over the other) and Proust (if one is open to oneself then one is closed to others and, inversely, if one is open to others then one is closed to oneself) not as the dogmatic explication of the human (there are forces of sublimation) but as hermeneutical reverie, introducing [some] unknown but not exclusive factors.

In particular, with regard to the imaginary-real distinction in the limited sense Sartre gave it, it is necessary to take up again:

1) The idea that the masquerading of the imaginary consists especially in the absence of the "real": theory of hallucination to be made first in relation to negative hallucination (non-recognition, paramnesia, imperception, i.e., ultimately recognition by the unconcious), and not in an equivalence between the imaginary and the sensory. Hallucination as function of the "heart" in Pascal's sense. Simply, Sartre is mistaken by means of his rigorous distinction between the "sensory" and the "non-sensory."

2) The idea that dreams are topical regression, not equivalent of sensoriality. Rather, they are regression to mythical consciousness.

3) The idea that symbolism is the imaginary, that the unconscious (or symbolic consciousness) is not to be connected back to a causal order. Rather, it consists in embodiment and the relation with others; projection and introjection are not operations of a "consciousness." Describe, outside any *Erkenntnis theoretisch* abstraction, the sedimentation, the relation with the world and others as relation not with ob-jects, but with what I have been, with "agencies." Here the rule is indistinctness and the exception, differentiation.

[DREAMS]

§. *Dream, rebus, not drawing* [166] (35)

Not (linguistic, pictorial) signs offering equivalent of signification, [but] *Bild*,[1] imaginary surface through which appears, transposed into the order of the expressed, being ... it expresses by bringing back concretions of the expressed.[2] Cf. *The Scoundrel*,[3] Noel Coward, drowned, reappears in his office, but with a piece of seaweed in his hand, which is a concretion of the sea. It expresses by condensation. Condensation is not only a procedure for masking from the eyes of the censor. It is the distinctive procedure of the dream, required by oneiric consciousness. Because oneiric consciousness [means] cores of existence, *imaginings*, sense instituted by events, talking seaweed; however, all this is from a general self and dominates a content which is unlimited.

1) What sense does it make to say that dreams contain or do not contain this or that?
Dreams are condensed, they subsume under *imaginings*. And it is in this way that a dream expresses—Freud: all the content of the associations was not in the dream-thought; we retrace the path from the latent to the manifest in the opposite direction, but we do not retrace it such as it was formed (Reading Notes, *The Interpretation of Dreams*).[4] In particular, his interpretation seems based on convoluted plays on words, but this covers up simple thoughts; [the] interpretation seems based on arbitrary associations, but there are no arbitrary associations (Reading Notes, pp. [21–22]).[5] There is an intentionality of dreams to be rediscovered, very special, not an intentionality of acts, positing objects, but an exhibition of concretions which "carpet" our life, its content neither individual nor conceptual. Apparent "clarity" (i.e., evidence) of certain dreams which, upon reawakening, appear lacunar, [but] this is due to [the] energy of condensation; [the] mode of oneiric consciousness is this condensation (Notes p. [12])[6]—The ambivalence of dreams is constitutive of them (Notes, pp. [8], [5], [13]). Overinterpretation [imposes itself] (bisexuality, Notes, p. [14]; refusal of a sexual "explanation" of all dreams, p. [14]—not that there was ever a complete absence of sexuality, but because regressive and infantile sexuality is not sexuality, p. [6]). Senseless to take an exhaustive inventory of the contents, cf. senseless

to take inventory of a vocabulary, because dreams are made from events that are formative of symbolic matrices, and consequently we cannot say that this or that is excluded from them. Thus, the elements are not traversed by rays of categorial thought: [the] "radiance" [exudes] from "several centers"—neighborhood of *Gegensinn*,[7] not positing on a plane of the object (Notes, p. [9]). [The notions of] richness and poverty of **[170] (36)** dreams signify absolutely nothing. It is rich because it is poor, because it provides articulation. What Sartre calls the false richness of the imaginary, considered as a true lack of reference point, nothingness which imposes upon it the form of being, is in reality the indestructibility of the childhood unconscious and of the traumatic past, i.e., the inherence in the world as absolute.

2) Dreams are not temporally circumscribed acts. Thus, the ubiquity of dreams thanks to our symbolic matrices—And also, they are transtemporal. Waking consciousness: time of consciousness and time of its object—Oneiric consciousness: it touches all times and does not incorporate this cleavage. The question arises, with respect to dreams, of knowing whether it makes sense to say that it began at such and such moment, and ended at such and such moment—(Notes, pp. [25–26])[8]—Dreams [are] initiated by that in us which receives events and classifies them in relation to our acquired intersubjective dimensions. Oneirism just beneath the surface of all waking life—"This 'shadow,' this germinative production, this 'active sedimentation' of my psychical life, this necessary implication of my acts of consciousness, this automatism which stirs within me, it is the *Unconscious*, the unconscious under its triple aspect: —underlying implication of psychical life not entirely engaged in the present action—imaginary focal point—and lyrical core of humanity" (H. Ey, *Études psychiatriques*, I, p. 242)[9]—"If life is a dream, the dream is a life" (E. d'Ors, on Calderon[10]).[11] Do not represent the "I live" by simple continuation of the *I dream*. It also includes the "I think," and we will have to reconstitute it in its entirety. But it is necessary to begin by describing the "I dream."

The "I dream"—On what is this condensation, this subjective universal, founded? On the fact that here consciousness does not constitute a world by exhibition of concepts in an intuition. It is side by side with its dream. Cf. the painter incapable of making his intention appear in the body, [hence the use of] banners.[12] Oneiric consciousness, likewise, does not make certain relationships appear, such as: when, because, just like, although, this or that. Is this therefore chaos? No, [there are] oneiric equivalents through another configuration: causal relation ([expressed by] introductory dream and main dream), negation (expressed by absurd dream, or by powerlessness to . . .). And above all, substitution of the "just like" for every relation: there are no true *lily* branches which are also red camellias, which are also cherry blossoms with an exotic look. [But] we must not say that the dreamer sees nothing. It is not determinate because it is everything; vertiginous proximity of the world, in our fields. Logical **[171] (37)** and temporal regression which is topical regression, i.e., in the absence of the current which goes from the world to our responses, our fields invested by our past. There is no "true doing" in the dream, there is only a "seeing doing": narcissism of the dream, dictatorship of the visible, prerogative of seeing. Thus dreaming [is not] consciousness of something with an element of distance, but all things [are] linked by their participation in my life as ambivalent. We wallow in being without taking leave, we exploit bodily presence in the world in order to make a pseudo-world where subject and object are indistinct. [There is a] subject-object solidarity which is not that of *noesis* and *noema*, but that of the body and perceived world, i.e., here the "categories" are always certain "variants" or "divergences" in relation to an initial situation toward others.

What can the world of the *lekton*[13] become at this level? This world spontaneously granted to [the] Kantian consciousness, [such that the] categorial attitude goes with the true denomination. Here language is havoc—words "pass for things" (Notes, pp. [8–9]) and they are no longer primarily for accessing things. Norekdal (p. [9])[14]—No actual speech in the dream, nor actual calculation, which presupposes subsumption and not coexistence. Speech utilized as wordplay, utilization of a ready-made symbolics, echoes in language (violet and *to violate*),[15] which appears very artificial to wakeful interpreting, but this is what is necessary in order to be placed back in [the] tide of oneiric consciousness, where words are things. This is why [the] discourse of the dream is to cut into pieces—A different signification, intentionality.

§. *Tendency of these descriptions*

The description of the oneiric structure (impossibility of expressing, dictatorship of figuration, condensation as sole means of expression) would attribute the disguise of latent thoughts as much to the condition of the dream as to [the] censor-repressed struggle—Consequently, latent content not to be represented as thought in the depth of ourselves in the mode of conventional thought, as an absolute observer would represent it. The unconsciousness of the unconscious [is the] unknown; but not known by someone in the depth of ourselves. The unconscious [is the] abandonment of the norms of wakeful expression, i.e., of the symbolic as symbolic of self, direct language, which presupposes distance and participation in the category. But this unconscious is not distant; it is quite near, as ambivalence. The "affective content" is not even unconscious or repressed[16] (Notes, p. [3]), i.e., the unconscious as pulsation of desire is not behind our back—In this direction, read note p. [28].[17] [The] unconscious [is the] implex, **[172] (38)** [the] animal, not only of words,[18] but of events, of symbolic emblems. [The] unconscious [is] unknown acting and organizing dream and life, principle of crystallization (*rameau de Salzbourg*),[19] not behind us, fully within our field, but pre-objective, like the principle of segregation of "things."[20]

This is not Freud's formulation. [He] accepts side by side the role of oneiric structure and the role of censorship and repression; displacement, recentering (Notes, p. [9])—Manufacturing of a veritable enigma which is comparable to those of newspapers which disguise a sentence in dialect as an inscription by mixing it with Latin—cf. *Leonardo da Vinci and a Memory of His Childhood*;[21] cf. *Gradiva*.[22] "in the sun," meaning to the Sun Hotel; cf. "framework" which is "turned about" by the first elaboration of the dream (pp. [9–10]). Realist theory of interpretation.

The "true" meaning [would be] not only different, but still known by a second self, clearly, in non-symbolic language, [thus] absolute knowledge; the unconscious [would be] "first," primary form of the "psychical"—What to think of this formulation of Freud's? It is inadequate for Freud himself; he speaks out against the spatialization of the agencies, and rightly so. The unconscious is not someone in me who clearly thinks a life of which I have only the appearance. By definition it is not an other. It is what I resist, of which I know that it is me, in relation to whom I organize my imperceptions. Consciousness and unconsciousness make but one divided being. Dialectic of Freudianism: by insisting on the symbolic power of consciousness, he discovers content which is latent, unconscious, but he is also prohibited from realizing it in conventional consciousness, in symbolism which would be symbolic of oneself.

Thus, to follow the distinction thought a moment ago: unconscious as pre-objective, function of the symbolic cores that drive and generalize an entire history. Elaborate on this conception.

In particular, distinguish it from [that of] "non-thetic consciousness." Non-thetic consciousness always has the truth at its disposal (freedom without degrees, truth to infinity and immanent). Perceptual consciousness is imperception qua perception. I see "things" on the condition of not constituting them. If perceptual consciousness does not *posit*, it is not because it has refrained from considering a constituting dynamic which would be there. It is because by nature it is sedimented consciousness, which does not actually constitute, which has never constituted; it is "openness to. . . ," always between sensing and the thing itself, never [is there some] resting correlative, always uprooted from oneself or from the world, [effecting] symbolic projections and introjections. Thematization, the call to a symbolism that would be symbolism of oneself, to verbalized knowledge, is a true transformation. That which is prior to it is truly other and not only implicit. The interpretation is not simply an explicit double of the given. It is its conversion into available "objective" significations, and it was never known as such. Hence the difficulty; the task is less of giving a sexual key, a sexual transcription into conventional thought that causes the over-signification of the sexual in pre-objective life to be found. The unconscious **[173]** **(39)** as perceptual consciousness is the solution sought by Freud, for it is necessary that the truth is there for us, and that it is not possessed.

Perceptual consciousness, while offering a seed of truth, an "idea of the truth" (Pascal), offers it only on the horizon, and hides the truth because it shows it. In the perceived, there can be duality of signification which is not the positing of a duality (ambiguous figures, Leonardo's vulture),[23] which is impossible in the pure signified. The perceived saves and it alone saves our duality, the duality to which Freud holds and which he thinks is saved by the idea of the unconscious (thinks wrongly, [for] the unconscious-consciousness dualism would suppress the duality by making the unconscious explicit) (by having two subjects). It saves "what the human soul keeps untamed and indestructible" (indestructible: allusion to the presence of the whole past, non-centrifugal memory)—cf. the "demonic power."[24] To live [is not] to be conscious—cf. paleontology, fossils, disclosure of recollections in the course of analysis. That of which we are conscious always turns its back more or less on what happens to us. I perceive myself in others, I perceive others in myself, I am in contact with my entire past, I have no temporal location, and my entire past is maintained only as the horizon of this present, sedimented.

To deepen this notion of the unconscious as sedimentation of the perceptual life (originary sedimentation: fields; secondary sedimentation: symbolic matrices), [the] adherence to a "private world" through which, however, there is a common world, the sedimentation that is forgotten and possibility of reactivation, it is not enough to examine dreams, i.e., the unconscious compromise—vital drama and variations around the vital drama sparked by events of the day, fortuitous crystallization. One has to see the unconscious at work against the [tenor?] of the real, making it leap or, on the contrary, mastered and "surpassed" by means of interpretation: [the] passage from dreams to delusions, [the] thrust of the repressed [and the] passage from unconscious conflict to neurosis, or to the cure.

See in these cases what the unconscious consists of, if our notion is enough—and [the] passivity-activity relationship. Here we will truly see that oneirism is not non-being of the imagining consciousness, but just beneath the surface of perceptual consciousness; that it is not the lie constitutive of [the] imagining consciousness qua imagining, "joyous" lie, but truly a struggle of oneself against oneself, repression, censorship consisting in the refusal of our passivity and its great supplier: sexuality. The body as metaphysical being (Unconsciousness as negative hallucination: Gradiva; Unconsciousness as promiscuity: Dora).

This will lead to [considering the] liberation of the unconscious and true memory, to [asking ourselves how] to conceive it correctly on the basis of the analysis.

[THE FREUDIAN UNCONSCIOUS]

True nature of the Freudian unconscious **[174] (40)**

I. *Simple examples*
The perception of the passer-by serving as pivot or hinge to the "thought transference" between husband and wife at the restaurant.[1]

The repressed perception of people encountered in the street serving as pivot to premonition. Premonition: manner of expressing that one already knew; and it is true—but through unrecognized perception.

[The] encroachment of one consciousness on the other, of a consciousness on the future, poetry of intersubjectivity and subjectivity based on unrecognized perception.

[The case of] Dora[2] [and the] analysand-analyst relationship. Agreement of the analysand with the analyst who discloses, based on a preliminary possession of the disclosed, a knowing that says neither yes or no, and at the level from which the non-knowing was already knowing:

> When I told Dora that I could not avoid supposing that her affection for her father must at a very early moment have amounted to her being completely in love with him, she of course gave me her usual reply: "I don't remember that." But she immediately went on to tell me something analagous about a seven-year-old girl who was her cousin . . . and in whom she often thought she saw a kind of reflection of her own childhood. This little girl had (not for the first time) been the witness of a heated dispute between her parents, and, when Dora happened to come in on a visit soon afterwards, whispered in her ear: "You can't think how I hate that person!" (pointing to her mother), "and when she's dead I shall marry Daddy." I am in the habit of regarding associations such as this, which bring forward something that agrees with the content of an assertion of mine, as confirmation from the unconscious of what I have said. No other kind of "Yes" can be extracted from the unconscious; there is no such thing at all as an unconscious "No."[3]

> (Footnote added 1923): "There is another very remarkable and entirely trustworthy form of confirmation from the unconscious, which I had

not recognized at the time this was written: namely, an exclamation on the part of the patient of 'I didn't think that' or 'I didn't think of that.' This can be translated point-blank into: 'Yes, I was unconscious of that.'"[4]

"Didn't think" [means] you are right, I did not know it, but I see that it was true, it was ready to become true. **[175] (41)** Here, as above, the unconscious, not being able to say "yes," strictly speaking (but merely to allow to do, to yield, to provide concordant associations), and not being able to say "no" at all, is not a knowledge, another subject, a second consciousness. And nevertheless, when it is revealed to itself, it is apperceived as having been there already. The problem is that of this *Wahrnehmungstbereitschaft*.[5]

Freud's tendency to translate it into terms of an unconscious perception, i.e., a knowing prior to knowledge. Example in "Dora," [where he interprets] Dora's dream in which there is a jewel box: "Perhaps you do not know that 'jewel-case' [*Schmuckkästen*] is a favourite expression for the same thing that you alluded to not long ago by means of the reticule you were wearing—for the female genitals, I mean.' 'I knew you would say that.' (Note: A very common way of putting aside a piece of knowledge that emerges from the repressed.) 'That is to say, you knew that it *was* so.'"[6] One would have to say: "you were not ignorant of it." But "you knew it" is too much. Dora knew that Freud was going to say that because she was accustomed to his type of interpretation. In his presence, conversing with him, she sees herself in this light and senses ahead of time his response at the end of what she is saying. That does not mean that in facing up to herself she knew, in the strict sense, what the "jewel box" is. There is a me-others system which causes me to have endopsychical perception of what the other will think of what I am saying. And, certainly, that enriches my idea of myself, for I perceive the other as my witness, and his perception of me becomes a component of my truth; but it remains attributable to him as well, to the side he has taken, and his perception reveals him to me as much as it reveals me to myself. My truth is a function composed of what is attributable to the other and to myself in his views of me. We also cannot say that foreseeing what he will say, spanning his consciousness and his freedom, I thereby recognize his opinion of me as true. However, I feel myself exposed to this interpretation; I recognize that something gives it a hold on my behavior. We cannot say that I always knew it nor regard this presentiment as a confession. The problem is indeed to elaborate a theory of the *Wahrnehmungstbereitschaft*. Making her cousin her mirror, etc., Dora was ready to know that her feeling for her father was love. But the very use **[176]** **(42)** that she made of her cousin was not named, was pre-objective, and thus also her knowing. She was ready to know, she did not know. How is that possible?

The first examples, very simple, indicate it: it is because it is a matter of perception. Perceiving her father as a love object is something different from classifying him with other men under the category of love objects. And precisely because it is he whom she loves, she cannot make this classification, and when she begins to fall in love with others, she will not recognize in this feeling the same feeling that she had for her father; and it will not be the same, in reality, due to the fact that it will come later. Their kinship will only be revealed in the conflict, the rivalry, the passage to hatred of the father, the rending. There was a perception of the father as love object, but there was no knowledge of this love.

One will ask, what is a perception that is not knowledge? How could we love, desire, without thinking that we love, that we desire? Freud, like Sartre, would say that there has to be a thought there. Freud placing it in another subject, Sartre making love begin with the conscious apprehension.

We are not bound to these attitudes if we have recourse to the perceptual order. The contact with the perceived is not ignorance and is not knowledge. Proof: the perception of a lack (Scheler) in a room or, more precisely, on a wall, we see that something is lacking without knowing how to say what.[7] Example that may clarify the nature of all perception: Dora's father so beloved to her insofar as he is that in relation to which the world has value, all others [appearing as] his reflections, different manners of not being her father, and, if, on the contrary, they have value for him, they also have value for Dora. But to know all that, Dora would need to have had the experience of a world where her father was not. As long as he is there, she loves through him everything that he loves, and consequently she does not know that it is he whom she loves. This dialectic, which ensures that primordial love is ignorance of love, is not peculiar to love; it is the dialectic of the primordial, of perception—To perceive is to have something before our eyes, for example; but **[177]** **(43)** the perceived is not reduced to this visible carapace which would be nothing [if there were no] interior and exterior horizon. The carapace [would be conceived] as the concretion of a much ampler visible (all the internal aspects, all the external perspectives), a certain impact on my visual, tactile, auditory fields, which separate most of the others from it, and finally a conviction of the world as unity of this spectacle and all the other concordant spectacles possible from other points of view and through which it offers transition. Thus, the duplicity of the perceived is there, gathered upon itself, it is now, at this instant, and it is everywhere. Cf. dialectic of "*this*" in Hegel: when I make the gesture, already the spectacle has changed, and it is a "this" in general to which I point. Thus, each perception is a vibration of the world, it touches well beyond what it touches, it awakens echoes in all my being in the world, it is super-significant—As particular, it would not be knowing, existing; its particularity is only what is lacking in order to be everything in the world. Cf. the case of the perception of an absence: the particular presence of the perceived is lack of a lack, possibility and not realization of its lack, repletion of the world. The perception of an identifiable "*this*" flees, therefore, and leads toward the whole, though it is gathered upon itself and precisely because it is a "*this*," for I never have the world in front of me, and I go to the world only by the concordant sequence of horizons which connect the thing to its inside and its outside. Perception is not, therefore, categorial subsumption, *Sinngebung*, experience of a *Zussamenstimmung* between a signification and an exterior, which would always require a mediator, and ultimately would end in the idea of constitution. Contact with the perceived, therefore, is not an exhaustion, a cognition, and by no means excludes non-knowledge.

Now, in reality, resulting from the order of perception, not only "sensible things," but also 1) my relationship with others as perceived, presented through the sensible, [for] the promiscuity of things in the sensible world will be extended into a promiscuity of others between them and with me, this time as subject of a *praxis* and not only subject of perception; 2) my relationship with my own past, [for] insofar as it has been perceived, it could not, in recollection, become something different from what it was in the present. And the **[178]** **(144)** spatial promiscuity will be a temporal promiscuity, that is to say, familiarity and ignorance. The theory of the unconscious, of memory, should be renewed through this reference to the perceptual order, i.e., to the order of coexistence in the world and in others—Cohesion of a life, a life always other, interpretation without cutting apart; existential eternity—

Let us apply this principle of interpretation to some new examples from Freud—First, a simple example.

II. *Premonitory dreams and the unconscious as "cohesion of a life"*

Recount the story of Frau B and give Freud's interpretation (notes on *Premonitory Dreams*, pp. 1–2).[8]

[Editor's note: We have included below the text to which Merleau-Ponty refers. It is located in the *Passivity* file in the archives.]

[245] Freud, *Premonitory Dreams* (1899) (cf. *Ges. Werke*, 17, 19–23)

Frau B. claims to have dreamed that she encountered Dr. K. [on] Kärortnerstrasse in front of a certain store, and she actually encountered him the next morning in that location. No proof (report, notes) that she remembered this dream before the encounter. She thought of this dream afterwards. At a young age, she married a wealthy, older man, who died some years later after having lost his money and contracted tuberculosis. She supported the household by giving piano lessons. Dr. K., the family physician, helped by looking after her husband and finding her first students for her. Another Dr. K., a lawyer, puts her husband's affairs in order and falls in love with her. But she is not happy on account of certain misgivings.[9] She recounts that one time, during this period, there was an extraordinary coincidence: she was home, thinking intensely about the lawyer, and in he walked. Coincidence which is nothing striking, since she thought of him often and he often came around—But which is probably the true content of her dream and the basis of her conviction that her dream came true.

Twenty-five years passed between this scene and the dream. In the meantime, she was widowed by a second husband, who left her a child and a fortune. All the while she felt affection for the lawyer, who became the administrator of her estate. We may suppose that she had awaited his visit in the preceding days. Hence, a nostalgic dream of the old days when he came around. Dreams of this kind are probably frequent: belated perception of the cruelty of her youth. But these dreams, which reawaken thoughts that she had repressed during her second marriage, she usually represses them. Thus she goes out, encounters the other Dr. K., who was linked to this whole happy-unhappy period of her love, and furthermore was a suitor. In these thoughts and in her dream, the latter is the screen figure which hides the other doctor K. Encountering the family physician Dr. K. reminded her of her dream. But the dream that is evoked can only come back in disguise: she inserts the indifferent K. in place of the important K.: "The contents of the dream—the rendezvous—were transferred to the belief that she had dreamed of this place in particular, for a rendezvous consists in two people coming to the same place at the same moment. And if she had the impression then that a dream had come true, this impression only explains her recollection of the scene in which she had wished desperately that he come and her wish had been fulfilled."

Thus the creation of a dream after the event is nothing other than a form of censorship which makes the return of the dream to consciousness possible.

(**44** continued) Truth of this interpretation:

1) the idea of the premonitory dream comes after the fact, after the encounter with K2;
2) this alleged premonition of the event represents a slightly different wish: to encounter K1, in connection with the past love. The wish plays the role of the pivot perception in the other dreams. It opened the way to the impression of telepathy or premonition. The eternitary impression of destiny is at bottom the consciousness of an indestructible wish, of the "omnipotence of the wish."

All of this is valid—but troubling. Is it a matter of a veritable disguising of unconscious wishes? It is necessary to suppose arbitrarily:
1) Waiting for K1's visit and dreams relating explicitly to him. She goes out in order to repress these dreams.
2) Unconsciousness of the true contents, the wish to see K., and functioning of K2 as screen figure or cover: insertion in the "premonitory" dream of K2 in order to disavow K1—the construction of the premonitory dream would be work of the censor. The dream (supposed by Freud) from the preceding nights (rendezvous with K1) is transformed by the censor into a premonitory dream of an encounter in such a place, respectable form of the notion of "rendezvous."
3) The impression "a dream has come true," which she has upon seeing K2, simply reproduces her happiness when K1 had showed up in the past, and quite naturally so, since K2 is K1. Oneirism (eternitary state: I knew that I would meet you) is thus a lie created in order to hide [179] (**45**) the univocal truth.
We would like to interpret differently. There is no deceptive work. It is not necessary to realize the *Deutung* in the form of an unconscious state, and oneirism is not falsehood, mode of appearance of the unconscious, but phenomenon. In fact, we begin from the fact that she has certainly believed in the premonition of the encounter with K2—Thus, this premonition which is indeed surely after the fact, and thus is not a precise account of what happened to her, must not be a lie; the possibility of this self-delusion must be founded, and founded on the dialectic of perceptual consciousness. The truth is perceived by her, not known.
Freud gives to her less access to the truth than is necessary (according to Freud, she doesn't know that K2 is "in reality" K1; in my view,

she perceives it)—and more knowledge of the truth than is necessary (for Freud, "her unconscious" knows that K1 is K2, that the premonition of the encounter is a rendezvous, that all this is the repetition of a past scene). Freud distinguishes a consciousness which is knowledge of a false version from an unconscious which is knowledge *of the* truth. Consequently, he can connect them in the same person only by means of [the thesis of a] deliberate falsification (censor that knows what she represses). For me, even at the level of the "conscious," I [would place?] contact with the truth and, consequently, this truth would not be repressed out of any grasp into an unconscious, but it would be a matter of a perceptual contact which is not knowledge.

Here we have:

1) Replacement of K1 by K2. K2 as cover or screen-persona. It is not a matter of camouflage (especially since K2 is not imagined, but actually encountered). If she transfers her desire to encounter K1 onto her encounter with K2, if K2 is a substitute, it is because a) K2 is linked to the entire period of love for K1. The recollection of someone is the recollection of an entire epoch of life, of a past self, of a drama or event. K2, whom she encounters, revives this drama. b) Deeper still: K2 was also a suitor, his role is parallel to that of K1, and she was not absolutely insensitive to it; it is the same heart which serves for all (Proust) and it establishes kinship between all those whom we love. There is neither mechanical association between K1 and K2 nor synthesis **[180] (46)** through a second consciousness and substitution of one for the other; there is the drama of this period of her life, which is a symbolic matrix, ordering all the perceptions, and in which K1 and K2 are implicated, which subsists in her under the form of a *generality, of a sensitive zone,* and as sensitive to walk-ons as to the principal actor.

2) Replacement of the rendezvous with K1 by the supposed premonitory dream. This displacement is not substitution of a more respectable version for a univocal truth (the dream of K1, the wish for the encounter). She sees K2 in the street. There is an impression of preexistence, that the encounter had been foreseen, anticipated. Must we say that this impression hides a wish to rendezvous with K1 as in the old days? She does not hide this unconscious recollection, she expresses all too well the essence of *desired encounter.* There is some blurring in this expression. The desired encounter will be presented as imagination of a premonitory dream. But this blurring is based on the generality of the drama, the style of life which abides. The day when KI arrived at the designated point, while she waited in her solitude, she had the experience of a kind of miracle. Reality answers her wish, this

life which appears external, committed elsewhere, and which answers her most secret vow, a *rendezvous* all the more moving that it was not expressed in words, that it is the rendezvous of desire with desire. It is this perfect encounter with the other which abides in her as *Stiftung* and causes her, upon seeing K2, who is nearly K1, to sense the same miracle reborn a little, to undergo an impression of telepathy (which is desire-reality encounter), i.e., it cannot possibly be by chance, it was inscribed in the secret structure of the world, it was written, thus visible, thus I dreamed it.

[181] (47) We do not alter the psychological interpretation. But the philosophical interpretation [becomes] not a second consciousness that knows the truth and that we censor, but the perception of K2 which happens to flip a switch and awakens echoes in perception. Perceptions of sensible things [are] correlatives of a corporeal schema. For example, I sense the horizontal and the vertical of the place through compromise between visual and sensorial structuration and structuration of my body and its norms.[10] The second element [is] brought to light when I press my hand and my arm against my heart and my free hand raises itself without the positing of a perceptual goal. My corporeal schema is displaced by the desire; its norm is elsewhere, and my empirical body joins up with it without explicit perception. The norm of the perceived is under the partial appearances. Not only is there a corporeal schema co-constituting spatial dimensions, there is a practical schema that produces the dimensions of intersubjectivity, as the first gives me distances transformed into shillings and pence, the second gives me others transformed into what they are worth or signify for my "machine for living." Frau B's practical schema is organized around the drama of K1. This drama was deposited in her as a classifying principle of everything that she perceives. The events crystallize on these lines of force—modify the implex and are modified by it—are "understood" by it, without explicit thought, just as distance is understood by the body which moves itself without explicit estimation of the distance. The unconscious is the symbolic matrix left behind by the event. The return to the event, analysis, the *Deutung*, unravel this fabric, but these are only effective if that which generates the event is truly recovered such as it was lived, not abstractly formulated. The unconscious is existential eternity, the cohesion of a life, the fecundity of the event.

However, is the pressure of the unconscious sufficiently explained by this persistence of the symbolic matrices?[11]

[182] (48) Is there not a true causality of the past, return of the repressed? For example, in the case of delusions?

[DELUSIONS: GRADIVA]

III. *Delusions* [Gradiva]

Norbert Hanold in Jensen's *Gradiva*—Publication of this book.[1]
Delusions are first seen from the interior, an atmosphere of fate, appearance of a premonition. It seems that reality is fashioned according to [a] wish by supernatural principle; poetry of delusion, dream-reality encounter. Then the delusion shatters. [Its] explanation is prosaic. If everything that happens serves the anticipation of the wish, it is because this wish itself was born from recollections of the same person. The future obeys the present only because it is the reawakening of a past, the return of the repressed.

1. Subjective account (cf. Notes, *Gradiva*, pp. 1-2-3).[2]
2. Beginning with p. 3—disintegration of the delusion, active intervention of *Gradiva*, and prosaic explanation (3-4).
3. Hence reinterpretation—Add note "A" on symptoms to the reinterpretation by Freud.

[Editors' note: The pages to which Merleau-Ponty refers—**[261] (1)** to **[263] (6)**—have been inserted below in smaller print.]

1. Lyrical account **[261] (1)**
In Rouen, Norbert Hanold finds a bas-relief of which he obtains a copy.
To give a poetic account (delusional): appearance of "premonition," creation of the real according to the heart of the wish, and a real account: real, prosaic account. What, exactly, is the mode of operation of the "unconscious"? Is the "tide" the action of recollections in the third person? Are the recollections there? Does the *Deutung* rediscover a "real"? Or is the prosaic explanation an appearance? And the reality: an assemblage of stilts which would order the perceptual unrolling, which simply was not identified for what it was.
"Gradiva," "the one who walks,"[3] which was taken as a "slice of life"; [Hanold] locates her in Pompeii, on these recently exhumed steppingstones. Seeks whether this gait is real—Studies the feet of women and girls to whom, until then, he paid no attention.
Dream of Pompeii: witness to the burial of the city. It is of Pompeii. And he sees Gradiva there, who "was living in her native town, and, *without his having suspected it, living as his contemporary.*"[4] He tries to warn her. She looks back, but

continues her walk and sits down on a step of the temple where the rain of ashes buries her.

Awakened, great certainty that she is from Pompeii. Goes to the window. Hears caged canary on the window across the way. Not completely awake, senses something: believes he has found Gradiva's gait—Goes out in the street undressed—jeers—returns—Hears canary again—Compares it to himself. (2) He, too, is in a cage.

Then, the decision forms in him to make a spring journey to Italy—"the impulse . . . had arisen from a feeling he could not name."[5] Neither goal nor object of the journey was fixed: agitation propels him from Rome to Naples and beyond.

Irritated by the honeymooners (at Rome), by marriage and the honeymooners in Italy—Goes to Pompeii because they go to Capri. In Pompeii, he is bothered by the peddlers, who also have to say, "my dear August," "my dear Grete"—Senses in Pompeii that he is especially discontented with himself: bad mood, he lacks something—Arriving in Pompeii, doesn't recall his dream.

At midday (the hour of specters, according to the ancients) goes alone to the ruins, "then . . . the dead wakened and Pompeii began to live once more"[6]—Sees a woman who walks like Gradiva. Then remembers his dream of Pompeii and understands that he came to Italy in order to go to Pompeii.

This is not a specter. Once [a] lizard is driven away by Gradiva's foot. Enters the house into which she had gone, finds her with something white on her knees, believes that this is the phantom of Gradiva buried in the year 79—He speaks Greek, Latin to her. She replies in German. He says, "I knew your voice sounded like that."[7]

He asks her to lie down on the steps of the temple as in his dream. She rises and goes away, after a butterfly (messenger of Hades) had fluttered around her. She calls to him to return the next day.

Goes into the hotels to drink some wine (searching for her) without finding her. The next day, goes to Pompeii by another route. Picks a stalk of asphodel, which seems to him to be "a message from beyond." Catches a glimpse of Gradiva [and exclaims] "Oh! if only you still existed and lived!"[8] Gradiva has a curious, intrigued air—asks him for an explanation: how was he near her when she fell asleep? He recounts his dream of the disappearance of Gradiva [and of] Pompeii. (Is Gradiva seen from the point of view of the archaeologist? Not completely, as she says things that he cannot understand, for example, what a pity that you did not find Gradiva's gait in the street, you would have been saved a long journey.)

Gradiva enters into his delusion. It is necessary to resign oneself to that which one cannot change, and "I have long grown used to being dead."[9] She asks him for the stalk of asphodel: "to those who are more fortunate people give roses in the spring; but to me it is right that you should give the flower of forgetfulness."[10]

"It would be a strange coincidence . . . if the treatment of the delusion were to coincide with its investigation and if the explanation of its origin were to be revealed precisely while it was being dissected."[11]

[262] (3) After Gradiva's departure, cheerful call of a bird from the ruins. He finds a "papyrus," a white object which is a sketchbook and which she left, a pledge to return. Wonders, what is the corporeal essence of Zoe-Gradiva?

While going for a walk, encounters an old scientist who catches a lizard with a grass snare ("Eimer" procedure)—wonders how one can take so long a journey for such foolish purposes.[12] Vaguely recognizes the man. Hanold discovers by chance the *Albergo del Sole*. The landlord tells him about the lovers exhumed at Pompeii, sells him a green metal clasp, which he buys without discriminating. Upon leaving, sees a tuft of asphodel, which appears to him to confirm the clasp's authenticity.

Jealousy: Wasn't Gradiva, when he encountered her, going to meet up with a dead person like the lovers?

At the hotel, two new guests, brother and sister (?) on account of their resemblance. She has a red Sorrento rose. Dreams that Gradiva sits in the grass, captures a lizard, saying to it, my colleague's procedure is truly good. With a short squawk, a bird catches the lizard and carries it away. Awakens refreshed—Picks Sorrento roses and goes to the rendezvous while wondering if Gradiva could not be visible apart from the hour of midday. Catches sight of the "brother" and the "sister," who kiss each other and, for the first time, is not annoyed by it. "The delirious old man crumbles away," he goes to the rendezvous, admits to her that he identifies her with the dead young woman—gives her the clasp. She says, did you find it in the sun? She offers him half of a roll and says to him, it seems to me that we shared a meal once before, two thousand years ago.

Hits a fly on her hand and notices that she is real. She, surprised: "you are obviously mad, Norbert Hanold." The amorous couple shows up and the woman says to Gradiva, you here, too, and on a honeymoon, as well. H. flees.

2. Dissection and prosaic explanation

Zoe converses with her friends and shows that she is a living being, wants to cure H., says that she is the daughter of a zoologist. She searches for H., who goes for a walk, wondering how to resolve the problem, which is that Gradiva is a living being—and yet this same Gradiva of whom he dreamed—H. wishes to flee—But less and less—"to avoid the realm of madness"—Encounters Gradiva. She reveals to him that she lives in the house with the canary, that she is a childhood friend. This appears to be the "simplest explanation." But something makes it "deep." It is the manner in which this past has "returned"; the strike on the hand: the prods of childhood. The entire delusion is constructed with childhood memories: Gradiva Bertgang (cf. her name Zoe, professor of zoology). When Hanold (4) turns away from her, she identifies him with her father: both confiscated, buried, both archaeopteryx, "her complaint applies with the same word to the man she loved and to her father."[13]

Hanold himself "forgot" it, from a special kind of forgetfulness, which is opposed to reactivation. [There is] repression, but the repressed is not destroyed, there are certain "psychical consequences . . . products of a modification of the forgotten memory . . ."[14]

Thus the return of the repressed [is distinguished by the] "remarkable *manner* of that return, which is accomplished by what seems like a piece of malicious treachery. It is precisely what was chosen as the instrument of repression . . . that becomes the vehicle for the return: in and behind the repressing force,[15] what is repressed proves itself victor in the end,"[16] "trivial similarities suffice for the repressed to emerge behind the repressing force and take effect by means of it,"[17] "how sensitive a human mind becomes in states of repression to any approach by what has been repressed."[18] It is primarily in the repressing archaeology that N. H. goes to find Gradiva. The delusion [creates an] "insufficient and deformed replica" of Zoe.

Gradiva = Bertgang.

The young girl: "the fact of someone having to die so as to come alive" is unique—"but no doubt that must be so for archaeologists."[19]

As soon as the dissection has begun, the sufferers themselves bring forward the solution to the final enigmas, as in an explosion.

H. confesses that he likes the young girl with the red rose, and thereby makes Zoe jealous (promiscuity)—She takes leave coldly, then he takes her hand again and kisses it, proposes to her a honeymoon in Italy with "her childhood friend who had . . . been dug out of the ruins."[20] Repression "by which something in the mind is at once made inaccessible and preserved."[21]

3. Reinterpretation

Dream of Pompeii and its burial. It means that Hanold has an "endopsychic perception" of repression.[22] The Pompeiian dream means that H. shares both place and time with the beloved. Through displacement, it is simply the real [that he senses?] in the imaginary. The theory of dream interpretation "[warns us] not to fall into the error of tracing the anxiety that may be felt in a dream to the content of the dream, and not to treat the content of the dream as though it were the content of an idea occurring in waking life."[23] "Dreams are, as one might say, the psychological delusions of normal people."[24] The Pompeiian dream and the decision to take the journey are, like every decision, surrounded by unconscious motives. The journey functions **[263] (5)** from the beginning "to serve his delusion" and to contribute to the "search" for Gradiva.[25] It is truly Zoe whom H. saw pass by in the street—it is her canary that he heard; he had "the gift of 'negative hallucination,' [and] possessed the art of not seeing and not recognizing people who were actually present . . ."[26] There was thus from the beginning "unconscious knowledge" of what we will learn about later. "The indications of Zoe's proximity (her appearance in the street and her bird's singing so near his window) intensified the effect of the dream, and in this position, so perilous for his resistance to his erotic feelings, he took to flight."[27] Victory of repression even though the pedestrian investigations were victory of the repressed. Yet this flight is also a compromise: "the journey to Pompeii, which was supposed to lead him away from the living Zoe, led him at least to her surrogate, to Gradiva."[28]

When he goes for a walk in Pompeii, he initially does not recall his Pompeiian dream. That is, the journey is not the direct result of the dream, but rebellion against it, rebellion which derives from a psychical force that wants to know nothing of the latent content.

H. goes to drink wine in the hotels before his first encounter with Gradiva. He doesn't think he is searching for her. However, that is what he is doing.

Interpretation of H.'s dream: Gradiva captures a lizard like the old man on a walk. Her "colleague" (Eimer) is the woman with the red Sorrento rose, "the sight of which reminded him of something as he looked across from his corner of the dining-room, but he could not think what."[29] What he dimly recalls here is Gradiva's remark that "to those who are more fortunate people give roses in the spring." This dream means that, for Hanold, Gradiva knows all too well that the other is catching a husband. The scene with the lizards is attributed to Gradiva since H. secretly recognized the professor. Moreover, the lizard is indicted by the observation that G. disappears through the gap in the wall.

H. confirmed in the authenticity of the clasp by the vision of the asphodel, that is, he recognizes the asphodel given to Gradiva, and he unconsciously knows that she lives there and that she is alive.

The delusion has an element of truth, and the true in the delusion "protects" the false.[30] "Somewhere in the sun Gradiva was sitting"[31] —this announces her relationship with the zoologist and her residence.

(6) The absurdity of the dream of Gradiva catching a lizard: "means of representation" of irony, of contempt, of the bitter contradiction—the dream means: she lives at the *Sole* with her father and teases me, wants to catch me. Zoe speaks with a double meaning: "It is a triumph of ingenuity and wit to be able to express the delusion and the truth in the same turn of words,"[32] ambiguity, "compromises between the conscious and the unconscious."[33] The translation of the delusion is ultimately: "look, all this only means that you love me."[34]

"The symptoms on account of which the treatment has been undertaken are nothing other than precipitates of earlier struggles connected with repression or the return of the repressed, and they can only be resolved and washed away by a fresh high tide of the same passions."[35]

The doctor observes the unconscious from outside, "the author no doubt proceeds differently. He directs his attention to the unconscious in his own mind, he listens to its possible developments and lends them artistic expression instead of suppressing them by conscious criticism."[36]

DELUSIONS: *GRADIVA*

[185] (48)[37] Problem of delusions: If the unconscious is only "implicit thought" (without second *I think* in me), how is there *delusion*, i.e., insurrection of the unconscious, of the repressed? Is this not causality of the unconscious in the third person? In relation to which we are *results*?

This is not Freud's thought:

1. [Freud] says that a theory of hallucination should begin with the negative hallucination. [Thus] the hallucination, apparently a causal production in the third person, would be an appearance; [thus] rather than a vision of the unseen, there would be actual vision unrecognized; [thus] the divergence of the subject in relation to the object would consist in the fact that the subject does not see it completely, not that the subject sees something other than that which is. Delusions are not "unconscious" in the sense of received from the outside by consciousness. They are based on perceptions (the bas-relief—the canary—the women in the street). The perceptions simply function as stimuli which are not grasped by the subject according to their "true" meaning (i.e., in the context of the repressed past). Cf. asphodel confirming the authenticity of the clasp (i.e., of [the] real presence of Gradiva); gesture of giving the asphodel. The unconscious [entails the] possibility of a development which has its logic (logic of the delusion—dialectic which causes the flight far from "danger," journey to Italy marches on toward Pompeii, and thus deepening of the delusion) which functions as substitute for the true, unperceived logic. Freud: two tracks with switches. The same perception has two senses, belongs to two contexts, functions openly following one logic and making use of another. But the real logic is not "hidden" and the "apparent" logic is not only given to the subject. Hanold knows, in a certain way, that Gradiva is a real woman who loves him, the threat of her love (cf. his dream when he identifies her with her father, the old scientist); he knows that he is defending himself against real love.

He simply knows it perceptually, as we know [186] (49) that such and such perceived structure announces such and such perceptual unwinding, not as evoking something possible, but crystallized in the appearance, contracted in it. Cf. when I walk and do what is necessary to overcome an obstacle, there is a correlation between movement and the perceived configuration without mediation by knowledge. This is because each relief appears as something "to get across," i.e., practical halo, i.e., divergence in relation to [a] norm. The unconscious [is] insertion of the perceived into my machine for acting (body, and secondary body of being in the world).

2. [Freud] says that the return of the repressed is effected by the repressing agency itself. Repression ". . .by which something in the mind is at once made inaccessible and preserved."[38] It is repression that produces the causality, the distinctive force of the repressed; it is the "no"

that produces the power of the affirmation of the unconscious. It is the "no" that is abandonment. How is this possible? That to which one says "no" must not be identical to that to which we are abandoned and which affirms itself. And in effect, that to which the "no" is applied is the repressed, sketched solely by its contours; it is the negative of the repressed, its hollowed-out trace; it is a systematic gap, efficacious emptiness. Such emptiness is not simple absence, but rather emptiness in the sense that the repressed past is represented before us not by its *type*, not in its unrolling as event, [but] is equipped with a force that overflows us, precisely insofar as it is not historically known, but only in its trace.

The productivity, the fecundity of the delusion, its aspect of destiny, this immense fabric born in one night like [a] mushroom, hollow fabric, false fabric and yet imposing, is the power of what we have desired, all the greater since we have also repressed it. Cf. Schilder's experiment: the inaccessible installs itself as a norm and **[187] (50)** *takes possession* of our body, it dictates the body's movements, precisely because it has been desired and repressed. In the same way, the past is "preserved" precisely by regressions, i.e., because it is not possessed. The unconscious = modality of embodiment, i.e., of repressed desire—Upheaval of the unconscious and erection of the body takes on the appearance of destiny, of subject, it autonomizes itself, precisely because we refuse it, by scotomization or autonomy. The negation, the *Verneinung*, is a mode of presence.

Thus [the] unconscious [is] perceptual logic[39]—position of an inaccessible (true transcendence) and consequently orientation toward it and access to it.

This clarifies the problem of memory, which is customarily posed as a dilemma between preservation and construction, passivity in the third person and atemporal activity. Neither of the two [is] satisfactory. It is necessary to understand that it is by positing the past as inaccessible that we maintain it intact, that there is negation which is position.

But before clarifying the relationship with our "unconscious" past, it is necessary to clarify the relationship with others—Before clarifying the "general" relationship (i.e., without thematization, i.e., with negative of the past) with our past, clarify the other generality which is that of the relationship with others. Here is, then, the generality that will make us understand what there is of the unconscious in our drama, in our relationship with others. Not that we have another "I think" who thinks—sexuality or homosexuality—while we think something else, but because this relationship with others is itself perceptual, i.e., because others form an articulated system there, a constellation, but are present there each and every one only as difference of the whole; and consequently they involve several readings: Dora.

[THE CASE OF DORA]

IV. *Dora*[1] [188] (51)

Observation of the patient—We do not interpret the symptoms ourselves.
First, second, third layers of significance—cf. notes, pp. (1–6) and p. (7).[2]

[Editors' note: Below, in smaller print, the notes on "Dora" (nine pages mentioned by Merleau-Ponty).]

Dora [252] (1)[3]
Father frequently ill: tuberculosis, retinal detachments, mental health problems (S).[4]
Age 8: respiratory trouble with fits.
Age 12: migraines and nervous coughs afterwards—lasting 3 to 5 weeks—aphonia during first half of an attack.
Especially close to her father.
Sick with fever (appendicitis?).
Depression and bad behavior.
Leaves letter announcing suicide.
After discussions with her father, disappears → amnesia—Freud sees her at age 16.
In the provinces at B., when her father is ill, intimate friendship with the K. couple. Frau K. had taken care of the father → gratitude.
K. goes for walks with Dora, gives her gifts. Dora looks after the two K. children. The father goes with Dora to see the K.'s as he was going to return to Vienna. Dora asks insistently not to stay, but to accompany him. Says to her mother that during one of their walks, K. had attempted to proposition her. K. responds to her father's reproaches with denials, and Frau K. says that Dora has nothing but sexual ideas in her head. She used to read Mantegazza's *Psychology of Love*.[5]
Dora, says the father, insists that he sever ties with Herr K., and especially with Frau K., whom she had previously admired. The father will not. K.'s aggression is invented, and he has a friendship with Frau K.
At age 14 had been embraced and kissed by Herr K. by surprise in [?]. Intense disgust (→ nervous symptoms, nausea)—Claims still to feel the pressure of

177

this embrace. Cannot walk by a man and a woman in affectionate conversation (erect member and displacement).

First layer of significance: her father and sexuality with Frau K.[6]
Not easy to make her speak about K., consciousness is completely turned toward her father. She cannot support his continuing relations with Frau K. **(2)** On this point, no gaps in her memory. The father used to say to Dora, I don't understand your animosity toward Frau K. He had wanted to commit suicide, Frau K. had prevented him from it, and he thinks that Dora should have been grateful. Dora does not believe this, [but rather she] thinks that they were on a rendezvous and that, surprised in the forest, they had given this pretext (thus plans her own pretend suicide).[7] Herr K. complains to Dora's mother.

Frau K., formerly ailing and nervous, is now full of life.

The father returns to B. from time to time under pretext of [needing] rest.

Later Dora's parents → Vienna, and the K.'s also.

Dora says that she feels as if she were handed over to Herr K., the ransom for his indulgence toward his wife and Dora's father. There is some truth. K. sends flowers, gives gifts [to Dora], and neither Dora's father nor Frau K. say anything.

That said, Dora asks, all that is true, what do you want to amend?

Second layer of signification: she loves K.

The analyst objects that these reproaches against someone else cover up remorse.

The reproaches against the father are "doubles" of other reproaches:

a) She, too, closed her eyes to her father's relations with Frau K. in order not to be troubled by these relations with Frau K. Her lucidity toward her father dates only from the story of the lake.

Despite warnings from her governess, Dora continues to be fond of Frau K. Dora has a falling-out with the governess when she understands that the governess's work is only for getting closer to her father, and that the governess is indifferent toward her. She only looks after Dora when **[253] (3)** the father is there.

This causes Dora to understand her own conduct toward Frau K.'s children: looking after them while their mother is with her father—But Herr K. is an affectionate father—Conclusion: during all these years, [Dora has been] in love with Herr K.

b) Another charge is that her father makes use of his illnesses as pretexts, cover-ups, likewise, her story. (Relationship of the notions: unconscious projection, layers of truth—the unconscious layer is the one that every feeling includes, from which every feeling is made, without which we would never feel this or that, and which produces at the same time a dialectic of feelings, scenarios, evolutions.)

Experiences stomach aches that "copy" her cousin, who, she says, has certain illnesses in order to attract attention. Copies love [of] Frau K. in that she was ill when her husband turned up. Precisely the opposite for Dora, since her bouts lasted for the duration of K.'s absence (aphonia).

"Somatic compliance" of hysteria—The bodily symptoms "express" [unconscious] contents.[8]

The goal of Dora's illness → divert her father from Frau K.

The "secondary function" of a symptom, which anchors it in the psyche.[9] It is like a man who makes a living from his disability.

Particularly keen anger against her father when he calls the scene of K.'s effrontery invented. Why? What other reproaches behind there? An unjustified reproach does not offend so much.[10]

"[A] single unconscious mental process or fantasy will scarcely ever suffice for the production of a symptom."[11] (Symptom, complex = unconscious = vortex)

(4) "If the occurrence of the symptom was to be made possible at all, it was essential that she should not be completely clear on the subject."[12]

The symptom has simultaneous and successive significations. A symptom remains and takes on another sense (cf. Society), vacillates—[image of a] wineskin refilled with new wine.[13]

Grievances against the father, "supervalent idea," which, therefore, is not founded on herself, but on something unconscious: "A normal train of thought, however intense it may be, can eventually be disposed of"[14]—Must be linked to contradictory thoughts. They are coupled, and the force of the first hides the second.

Dora's preoccupation with regard to her father's relations with Frau K. → she acts as her mother might act, substitutes herself for her mother, is jealous—Furthermore, identifies herself with Frau K. (penis-organ phantasm: her father is impotent), identifies herself with her father's two women—Is in love with her father.

But for a long time her love for her father did not prevent her from being friends with Frau K. If their friendship is no longer anything to her now, it is because this love has been reactivated; it is a reactionary formation in relation to . . . something else repressed.

The love for her father is reactivated in order to mask the love for K. since the episode at the lake. She calls the love for her father to the rescue in order for it to be understood that it is finished with K. . . . But overdetermination is the rule.[15]

Describe the body and "compliance," according to Freud, as treasury, sacrament.

---

[254] (5) *Third layer:* Frau K.

Falling-out with the governess when Dora becomes aware that she is not her friend, but wants only to get closer to her father.

She herself often mentions as enigmatic another estrangement: with her younger cousin (the one who was later to become engaged)[16]—Occurs when the cousin agrees to accompany Dora's father to B., Dora having refused.

Freud asks Dora how her relations with Frau K. were before the incident at the lake: much greater intimacy. Dora lived with the K.'s, shared Frau K.'s bedroom—confidante and adviser. Speaks with admiration of the whiteness of her body. Never a harsh word about Frau K. Only, says with melancholy that the gifts that her father gives her must have been chosen by Frau K., causing a complex. It seems that Dora has understood that Frau K. had betrayed her. When she had complained about Herr K., he had initially responded by professing his respect for her. Then, when he had encountered Dora's father afterwards, he had said, on the contrary, that it is impossible to respect a young woman who had read such books. . . . In short, Frau K. had betrayed the secrets of her intimate relationship with Dora—what she read, etc.—and Dora, as in the case of her governess, became aware that she had not been befriended for her own sake, and that Frau K. looked after her only in order to get closer to her father—

Perhaps this insult is itself fundamental; perhaps the insult of her father's sacrificing her in order to make his love for Frau K. possible is itself only covering for the insult given by Frau K.'s betraying her. Clue: her obstinate silence concerning the origin of her sexual knowledge and thus her attachment to Frau K.

(Historical problem of the mask: at a **(6)** certain point, doesn't the mask become the truth?)

Predominance of the grievances against her father. [This is] 1) means to repress her love for Herr K. 2) mask for her unconscious love for Frau K. —Says that she envies this woman's possession of her father—thinks that she envies her father's possession of this woman.

The revelatory words: "something might happen in the night so that it might be necessary to leave the room";[17] these words are like "switches" for the railroad. Placing them differently than in the contours of the dream, we reach the track of the unconscious thoughts (cf. should one have need to open the door in order to deliver coal . . .).[18]

The dream "stands . . . upon two legs":[19] one is a recent event, the other a childhood memory.

"When I set myself the task of bringing to light what human beings keep hidden within them, not by the compelling power of hypnosis, but by observing what they say and what they show, I thought the task was a harder one than it really is. He that has eyes to see and ears to hear may convince himself that no mortal can keep a secret. If his lips are silent, he chatters with his finger-tips; betrayal oozes out of him at every pore."[20]

Core of Dora's first dream: "The temptation is so strong. Dear Father, protect me as you used to in my childhood, and prevent my bed from being wetted."[21] (This is not the true version and the rest masks—The body as resonator, the unconscious as musical instrument, or what is lived, then, is not simple appearance.)

[255] (7) Need not to be disturbed, washing hands, etc., clues of masturbation.

Layers of signification of the symptomatic cough: "Grain of sand around which an oyster forms its pearl."[22]

"Here we are concerned with unconscious processes of thought which are twined around a pre-existing structure of organic connections, much as festoons of flowers are twined around a wire."[23] (For example, disgust at a man's embrace ← her father had venereal disease, and she assimilates this disease to her leukorrhea, i.e., renders the female organs horrible, wounding her self-esteem.)

Reasons for the falling-out with K.

(Displacement is the echo, the generality, the perceptual life.)

Dora recounts the scene at the lake. K., who said, "You know that my wife is nothing to me"—

In their final session, Dora says to Freud,[24] at the K.'s house there was a governess, and two days before the scene at the lake, the governess told me that K. had attempted to seduce her and had said, "you know that my wife is nothing to me." She had yielded, and a short time later, K. was no longer interested in her. It is because of these repeated words that Dora slaps K. (moreover, the father says the same thing about his wife).

Identification of Dora with this governess: she tells her parents what has happened, as the governess [wrote it] to her. Gives Freud two weeks' notice like a governess. Dora takes two weeks to tell her parents about the scene [at the lake].

In reality, after the scene at the lake, she waited, like the governess, for a new sign of affection.

Disappointment, then she accuses him in order to get revenge and (8) prompt his visit. He responds with denial and insult. If she is particularly hurt by the claim that she imagined everything, it is because that reminds her that she had imagined that Herr K.'s proposition might be serious.

Freud says that to her—She appears to be moved—And returns no more. (Revenge against Freud—and to give herself over to herself; Him: perhaps I could have held on to her with a more active attitude. But I respect freedom, and as for her, we never know what precisely is the nature of her resistance.)

Dora appears to be moved—Thus she recognizes that what Freud says is true—But is this the revelation of a truth about her love for K.? No, what Freud revealed to her is not the true version, but one of the elements of a connected and contradictory system (everything in the unconscious and in conscious life coexists, even through contradictories) in which she was always caught, but which depended on her to determine the final truth through the decision that she would make. Her orientation reveals that what Freud says *touches on the truth;* but by breaking with him, she displaces this truth by another. What is right about Sartre's idea is that our truth is deferred. But what is false is believing that we create it unconditioned—For Dora's decision remains within the framework of the system revealed by Freud, under the jurisdiction of the antecedent dialectic, and this dialectic manifests itself anew if she sinks deeper into the neurosis—Freud: perhaps K., by continuing to love her, would have overcome her repression,—perhaps there she would have found the means to get revenge again. Neurotics do not succeed in connecting their fantasy of love with love; they refuse that of which they dream when it is given to them in reality. The neurosis can be defeated by reality, and the doctor cannot foresee. Thus, not fate of the neurosis nor of love, but the decision which creates one or the other depends on intersubjectivity, **[256] (9)** on what will succeed in persuading the partner. What possesses malleable force over our life is not the decision, but the *Gestaltung* which surpasses the dialectical situation or not. *Gestaltung* [does not mean] process in the third person, others, but not *Sinngebung*—The Freudian *decision* is the movement in the constellation where Dora is set up, is perceptual decision, i.e., not imposed by the givens of the situation, but effective only if she takes them and reorders them not as a system of objects, but as a system of tensions attached to certain beings-things.

Clarify the relationship between this unconscious life and conscious life in the "normal." Sexuality as driving force of all symptoms (not = embodiment). "The symptoms of the disease are nothing else than *the patient's sexual activity.*"[25]

"[A] whole series of psychological experiences are revived, not as belonging to the past, but as applying to the person of the physician at the present moment."[26]

Dora transfers onto Freud, her father, Herr K.

Some months later, visited by Dora—she has gotten revenge on the K.'s by making K. acknowledge the scene at the lake and Frau K. her affair—Engages in her studies and doesn't want to marry.

Some years [later] she is married. The first moment announced a flight before life into the disease. The second that she would detach herself from her father and be reconquered by life.

(51 continued)

Examine 1) mode of "unconscious" relation with others; 2) thereby, unconscious, symbolism, "sexuality,"—childhood and present, somatic and "psychic"; 3) the indeterminism of "choice": it is not determined, but no sooner made than it is carried; it is thus never ex nihilo—The system of our relationships with others [offers?] this set of things which are possible.

1) From the superficial to the deep—The "conscious" is conscious precisely in order to hide the unconscious. The prevalent idea gets its strength from that which it disguises.

But that does not mean [going] from the apparent to the real, from the mask to the truth—For we also know that the repressing agency produces the strength of the repressed. It is by wishing to have her father's love to herself that Dora preserves love for Frau K. and makes it inaccessible.

Thus, the various layers of justifications have their truth, although there is a difference in "depth": ". . . thoughts in the unconscious live very comfortably side by side, and even contraries get on together without disputes—a state of things which persists often enough even in the conscious."[27] Freud says many times that "a complication of motives, an accumulation and conjunction of mental activities—in a word, overdetermination—is the rule."[28]

Not only is there a plurality of juxtaposed determinations, but this plurality is in principle, for Dora's father, Herr K., and Frau K. are not separate beings with a stance concerning *each one*. The stance toward one entails a stance toward the others, and sometimes, if the latter is intolerable, as a result the first stance is abandoned—love and identification [are] mixed in those with hysteria. Thus, to love her father [means] to love what he loves; to be in competition with him for Frau K., to love Frau K. Thus, love for Frau K. owes something to love for her father. Or even, to love her father [is] to identify with Frau K., to be loved by her father like Frau K. "After a part of her libido had once more turned **[189] (52)** towards her father, the symptom obtained what was perhaps its last meaning; it came to represent sexual intercourse with her father by means of Dora's identifying herself with Frau K."[29] Here [she] is in competition for her father with Frau K. The two circuits, one which posits the father as absolute, the other which posits Frau K. as absolute, do not exclude each other. There is even always something of one in the other, because to give and to receive, masculinity and femininity, are never absolutely distinct. Likewise, love for Herr K. [stands] in relation to identification with Frau K., and also entails [a] complicity with love for

Frau K. and for Dora's father. Love for Herr K. [is] cause and effect of the love for her father and for Frau K.

That is, there is no me-others relation—Dora-her father, Dora-Herr K., Dora-Frau K.—but relation to an interactive system. Cf. perception: there are accentuated sides and hidden sides, but that doesn't mean that one excludes the others, on the contrary. What is it that someone is? It is everything that he does, and Russian dolls—the problem is not me-others, but me-system of others, and consequently, it is not face-to-face of two [beings] for-itself. The other is not without the for-others of a third to whom it attaches itself, and without its for-others in them. Hence generality, not compression of two absolute fluxes—generality—There are fewer others than their relations, their differentiation. And consequently, there is also an insertion of myself in this chain. I am not more absolute than the other, I am part of all the sufferings which are between them. I suffer over there through identification. I am them. Thus, reproaches to father not only hide but even are reproaches to myself. Masks and illusions [are] founded on promiscuity and thus are not entirely masks and illusions. Substitutes: not substitutes so much as doubling, not screen personas so much as covering that *doubles, blurring.*

The plurality of interpretations, their infirmity covers over [the] simple reality which is [a] system of others and me (cf. Signorelli[30] → story of the Turk: "*signor,* when one no longer has that, it is better to die" → had learned in Athens of the suicide of a patient suffering from impotence—One must not suppose repression of this name by the agency who searches for it separately. But regional repression[31] of everything in which there was a trace of "*signor*" and thus of the linguistic coordination that would have outlined this word. . .).

Frau K., Herr K., represented in the dream by father and mother. This is not covering, dissimulation, but the same function of the parental couple and the K. couple in relation to Dora. Dora [is] ready to give to her father what her mother withholds from him, to Herr K. what Frau K. withholds from him. The relation of the father to the mother is the relation of Herr K. to Frau K. for Dora, as love offered; thus, pivot: the blaze, the love of the father and Frau K., and on this pivot **[190] (53)** unique imitation of Dora, who fears and summons this same fire and seeks a reflection of it by substituting herself for her mother, for Frau K., or for her father—to approach the blaze from many sides: the others substitutable because the self is perverse, polymorphic, imaginary.

Thus, 1) no absolutely deep and absolutely superficial—No absolutely conscious and absolutely unconscious—Because unique object with facets—the back of the object is not a zero of consciousness.

And for another reason: if these various commitments communicate, are a single system, it results from the fact that we can always pursue one or the other. For example, there is always [the] possibility of finding everything in the love of the father: first dream—Protect me from K.'s love, which threatens me only because you neglect me. Inversely, the possibility of finding the father's love in other projects[32] (the engineer—the second dream)—They communicate because they are rivals; they are the same in different modalities: past father, Frau K. impossible, Herr K. possible. According to Dora's orientation toward the past or future, → importance of such cathexis. But none is false or apparent. The reality of the future is no more contestable than that of the present or the past. No absolute difference between real and imaginary love, but not because all are imaginary, because all are real, i.e., cathexes.

In what sense do we speak of deep and superficial? There is the more hidden (not a word of reproach for Frau K., not a word about [her] sexual readings; already less hidden [the] love for Herr K. She takes a long time to acknowledge that she awaited new advances from him, that she was especially shocked by the fact that he spoke to her like a chambermaid) and the less hidden, more present, and more past. Hidden: strong and weak centered forms (labile, i.e., rigid and fragile)— But this difference is not absolute. Love for her father is in the process of becoming essentially love for Frau K., becoming that is not made of choice without return and can flow back upon itself, or even carry itself away beyond the whole (final solution where, with love for Frau K., love for her father is uprooted).

2) Symbolism, signifying and signified—Impossible to distribute the roles absolutely, to say that one of the relationships only signifies the other. It is a relationship to Eros which has many pairs of arms and clusters of faces. In particular, [it is] impossible to establish an exclusive relation to the past (father) and, beyond, somatic sexuality. Through childhood memories [the] current drama reawakens echoes of the childhood drama (dream on "two legs")[33] and reference to the most secret somatic sexuality where it is anchored. But this is neither cause nor effect; it is a *flywheel*, a grain of sand on which the oyster makes its pearl with time. Sexuality is a universal signified only because it is of a conscious being, i.e., which loves prematurely through its body—The most general formula is embodiment, i.e., incarnation of a freedom.[34]

Example: Key, room (Herr K. seeks to enter, Dora to close the door). Must we say: unconscious thinking reference to these symbols of **[191] (54)** sexual organs? Thus, another *I think*? No. These sexual images are translations in objective, i.e., super-perceptual, language, of a general body-exterior relation. Spatiality is from the start extension of my body, violation of my space, intrusion[35]—Thus, not a reference to sexuality as special function and symbolism as its dissimulation, but sexuality and embodiment in all the fabric of perception. One needs a second *I think* only if one ignores the carnal relation of the body to space, the body as mediator of being.

3) Truth and choice

Dora's truth is thus made of this system with all its facets. Becoming of the system: it teeters toward one of the centers of gravity; Dora hurls all the cathexes into this or that. Thus, the truth is not reduced to a final truth, i.e., to a final state of the system resulting from the choice. Dora's choice: choice of Herr K.; then, after disappointment by him and Frau K., she takes refuge in her childhood and in the neurosis. Then, orientation toward the future (the engineer). Finally, she liquidates the whole; she takes revenge on K. by making him acknowledge his proposition and Frau K. her affair, then applies herself to her studies and later gets married to an engineer.

These various choices are neither determined nor ex nihilo. Every time they are carried by something[36] (K.'s love accompanied by Frau K.'s presence—father's love and thus love of the K. couple) (General distinction by sadism and autonomy, which is thus not indifference).

Someone will say that if they are not determined, they are ex nihilo. Even carried, then, they are at least creatures of the instant. No: if it is never only a matter of transportation or transference or ambiguous carrying forward, even when there is a falling-out (sadism).[37] And what causes the choice, once it is made, to be confirmed, is not its omnipotence, which would change all the signs of the spiritual landscape in one stroke (freedom, like an eagle, changing all being in the world).

It is above all the logic of things done which forces the abandonment of the other choices, and the *grâce d'etat* of the commitment, i.e., ultimately our power of forgetting. Hence, the majority of important choices are scarcely uttered.[38] To choose is most often to put oneself in [a] situation such that one can no longer shrink back, and, in doing so, one always depends upon a previous situation which contained all because it was ambiguous. There is not **[192] (55)** a choice which is true in this sense, it is necessary to make the truth, without decisive reason, but it is because they are all true in some fashion, because of ambiguity, all prepared in previous ambiguity.[39] And consequently there is, if not a true choice, at least false choices or chosen fakes, those which are presented as absolute choice, which renounce the ambiguity from which they speak, try to silence it, to repress it, instead of acknowledging that they are becoming toward the truth, i.e., elimination of the impossible and the chosen fake, not without sacrifice.

[Editors' note: Below, in smaller print, follows a note (seven pages) inserted following the analysis of the case of Dora.]

Freud, *Dora*, p. 48[40] **[257] (1)**
Key, bedroom, symbols of male and female organs.
Does this mean that when Dora locks herself in and when Herr K.'s takes the key from her bedroom, these objects—key, bedroom—evoke in her unconscious the "positive" representation of the organs?
Certainly not; it means that Herr K.'s taking the key opens a path up to Dora and that Dora's locking herself in closes it again. There is no need for the unconscious evocation of (visual) images,[41] because the whole interpersonal perceptual field is a fabric of relations of embodiment, because all external spatiality presupposes the relationship between my body and the world, and thus that space is a projection of the corporeal *I can*.
The "unconscious" background which lines the key, the bedroom, is simply the pre-objective, oneiric background of all perception.
Conceive the dream images as the immediate manifestation of historical cores crystallized in Dora. For example, in the first dream she sees her father in place of Herr K. (actually seen in L. in the same attitude). One must not presuppose a force that will seek out the memory-image of her father and animate it before her. Her father, as a symbolic matrix of her life, is always immediately imaginable by her (here is the truth of Sartre's thesis: the image is non-vision, but not because consciousness is completely delivered over to **(2)** its power to signify, but because Dora's father is set up in her, like a spine in her body, like a permanent post on which she constantly holds herself up).
Correlatively, one must not imagine an unconscious thought: "This man pursues me . . . and if trouble befalls him, it will be Papa's fault," which would disguise itself under the form of I will dream that my father saves me from a fire.[42] No: the father, such as she carries him within her, is at the same time benefactor and malefactor; because she loves him, dreaming that he saves her is the same thing for her as dreaming that he does not save her but abandons her to K., for he can only appear in this way as the one who abandons because he is the one who would save. To say that dreams are the realization of a wish is to say that they substitute for the waking time of observation the optative time without which these observations could not be formulated; for the failure of my cathexes, these cathexes, themselves. [To say that] dreams are not observable is a manner of saying that they are not based on the science of reality, but that of desire. Sartre only reaches his conception of the imaginary as non-being because he interrogates it in the mode of contemplative consciousness, and, finding that the imaginary does not take part in it, he can only define it as non-being or delusion. But if we

interrogate dreams in the mode of practical consciousness, tied to the body, the world, and others, the alleged freedom and auto-fascination of consciousness is a relation to possible concepts. Sartre has at his disposal only the real and the possible as non-being. Dreams are the pressure of one on the other.

Yet, why does Dora want to ignore **[258] (3)** that her father abandons her, and why does she prefer to dream that he saves her? Why is everything here "turned into its opposite"?[43] Because the reproach to her father would be a reproach to herself, because the very position of someone who perceives others is such that he sees himself in them, believes it in itself, and knowing it, tries to flee this confusion in a pure others or a pure me, either all the good placed in others and the bad in me, or the reverse.[44] Consciousness inverted and, in this very inversion, knowing the ambiguous reality that it covers over. [One will seek to] save oneself from the equivocation in the positivity. Reduced into perceptual terms, the unconscious is not a proliferation of thoughts, hidden mechanisms, but an operation of perceptual links which are always equivocal links offering a univocal spectacle.

That the key, the bedroom symbolize this or that [does not mean that] there is an evocation of unconscious thoughts of this or that; but the key, the bedroom, in the perceptual field, are worth this or that, are stimuli, substitutes, triggering in us the same apparatus of being in the world that triggers this or that.[45]

The gift that one receives is a donation (K. gives her a gift; she had not been moved to give a gift in return).[46] The gift corporeally moves the same zone as the thing that one does. Passivity-activity—Femininity-masculinity—Here it is not a matter of a symbolism that covers over or masks sexuality. Sexuality itself is not a final explanation. A metaphysics of sexuality is necessary. It is necessary to understand why and how, in virtue of its own structure, it makes possible a *Leistung*[47] which interests the **(4)** whole of the individual's life. Sexuality itself, not being a "natural function," needs to be explicated. The problem that it poses (concern to resolve it) is to know how a life can enter into another life or how the latter [can] receive it. Physical love is the universal symbolized, is interested in every human operation, and makes its contribution, its weight, its flywheel, only because it is itself symbolic of the highest point of incarnation, embodiment, carnal relations with others. Psychoanalysis is, indeed, in the final analysis, existential psychoanalysis, but not in Sartre's sense, that is to say, as revelation of a position taken by "freedom," but as revelation of intercorporeality, of the ego-others assembly such as it is realized by each, of the symbolic system set up in our machine for living.

The dream stages Dora's father and mother, who cover over Herr K. and Frau K.; it simultaneously affirms that Dora is ready to give her father what her mother withholds from him, and to give to Herr K. what Frau K. withholds from him. The relation of symbolization comes from the generality of the relation which produces a pivot (fire). There is indistinctness rather than symbolization. And the pivot is ultimately Dora's life, inasmuch as she is this unique principle who seeks her happiness and her repose through the ballet of others. She "summon[s] up [her] old love for [her] father in order to protect [herself] against [her] love for Herr K."[48] What mediates this symbolization of K. by the father, of Frau K. by the mother, is also that, through her father's adventure with Frau K., Herr K. and Dora's mother are placed in the same situation, and that all four constitute a single system. The unconscious is this totality. The discursive description [259] (5) of these unconscious relations must, in Dora as in the analyst who "understands" her, boil down to the intuition of a single operation, both global and general.[49]

Freud, qua object for a transference in the imago of the father, himself intervenes in this constellation, but intervenes not in the context of "real" life—i.e., as a power as deadly as it is beneficent, as one of the elements of the ego-others "barrier"—but as a present-absent, revealer of this barrier. The unconscious, the gate (Moreno's "stereotypes")[50] are not behind the subject; they are the principle which selects what, for him, will be the thing or background, what, for him, will exist. The vision is in itself "unconscious"; its "intentions" always involve in their thickness a common thread of the unconscious, because the vision is vision, because it can see something only by giving up seeing all, by making the me-others relation emerge from its ambiguity.[51]

"A regularly formed dream stands, as it were, upon two legs, one of which is in contact with the main and current exciting cause, and the other with some momentous event in the years of childhood"[52] evokes the presence of the past which is not "preservation," which is on this side of preservation and non-preservation. [A] theory of memory [is] to be developed, like that of the thing and the perceptual survey. We will never be able to understand the thing or the recollection if we reduce the thing to the formula, the law of such and such materials: *what* is aimed at. Here the *what* is only the envelope of existence. And the affirmation of the past in its proper mode is confused with that of a memory of the world, of a place where all that has been cannot henceforth cease having been.

The childhood recollection: incontinence that (6) her father avoided by awakening her. Procession of episodes from childhood, where a spark lights up in each drive of life. Our highest thoughts are accompanied quietly by wretched worries, the agitation of the search gives us a stomach ache; we observe an incessant ritual toward our body: what does it matter? It is the fringe of generality which is inevitable because we were born.

The examination of a symptom requires an entire historical reconstitution. But the history sedimented there in the symptom is like a present institution and not like folded-up recollections.

There is a truth of delusions; there is a truth of the aspect that things have for the patient, a truth against which the "objective" and prosaic explanation does not absolutely prevail. Such an explanation is equal to the truth of the lived and the sedimentation only when the explanation really assumed by the transference becomes action, decision, in Freud's sense.

The final "layer of significance," the final "coating"[53] of the symptom of the cough, those which are in relation to Frau K. are not without relation to the first, i.e., the love for the father: "express by identification with Frau K. the sexual relations with the father." "Changes in . . . meaning."[54]

[260] (7) Example of existential decisions which have motives: why did I not kill myself during the first days after the scene at the lake?

Why, then, did I suddenly tell the thing to my parents?[55]

Modulations of existence: "where is the box?" said in life, becomes in the dream, "where is the station?" What the two have in common is the sexual-existential search. One is substitutable for the other because they are equivalents according to this schema. Box and station would signify the same research.[56] Likewise, contours of the dream analogous to those of scenes really lived with personas who are the doubles of the real love.[57] "Two hours in the Museum," [she] declines the offer of someone accompanying her, awaits the coming of [an] acquaintance to whom she must show Vienna.

The dream contains pieces of life subjected to its pressure because life is perceptual, crystallizes and projects on the things seen.[58]

[THE PROBLEM OF MEMORY]

The problem of memory [192] (55 continued)

The idea of another *I think* behind the *I think:* [it] comes from the supposition that there must be a synthetic operation that binds concordant significations, the present and childhood recollections, weaves the network of symbols, veils the sexual in the nonsexual, in short [there must be a synthetic orientation which] produced the operations that analysis will unravel.

For us, analysis does not pass back through routes already traveled, it is not implicit in the subject being analyzed, because he lived this past and did not think it, because this analysis transports the past into the mode of objective truth. In that, the analysis is expression, neither a copy (of a separate unconscious) nor pure creation (crushing of the past by the future), but elaboration of the truth (true surpassing), passage from the perceptual plane to a relatively "objective" plane.

A particularly important obstacle opposes this unconscious, someone will say. That is, there are no individual recollections in the depths of myself, connected and called up by another "I think," a second true life beneath my confused life. In all this history there are only sedimented practical schema—Nevertheless, there is revelation in the course of analysis, recollections that return, afflux of material. Thus, there [must] be an in-itself of memory, an unconscious containing recollections, which organizes them and brings them about at the right point.

If one wants to avoid that, then one must commit oneself to [the] theory of memory as construction, i.e., imposition of signification whose immanent plenitude provides every guarantee.

If [one accepts the image of] the unconscious as receptacle of recollections, then this revives the second "I think."

If memory is construction, then there is no longer a perceptual unconscious.[1]

[194] (55) (Last course) Passivity [is] not frontal, toward another *I*, but congenital to the *I*, insofar as something which happens to it, i.e., sparks redistribution of its landscape, of its cathexes, of the dimensions of its being in the world; i.e., introduces into a certain level, and affects in accordance with it certain values and significations, ends up by upsetting the level (Wertheimer's experiment)[2] and reorganizing it. Passivity [operates] in the assimilation or the resumption or the *Nachvollzug*. Ac-

cording to what? Not according to the sense given with the event. We can be crafty, maintain the operation of the old practical schema, repress [it]. But although there is no sense given, there are events whose historical inscription we can prevent only by refusing to see them, events that are unassimilable for our system, that refuse our *Sinngebung*. The choice to maintain the old system would then be pathological. Thus, the sense is never simply given to us, but it does not always allow itself to be constructed. When it does not allow itself to be constructed without division of the self from the self, our truth falls outside of us. Adversity is not always the same, it is different when there is relative plenitude and when there is hollow decision. Choice does not always consist in being made from scratch, i.e., in being placed in a situation such that one can no longer back up, in being made to attribute this or that. There is not *the* activity and *the* passivity, *the* choice and *the* non-choice (adversity), one clashing with the other, but choice that derives, for example, from the obviousness of the unacceptable (which does not mean that it accepts the alternative and bases affirmation on refusal)—There is passivity right there in activity. It is because such direction was given as "oblique" in the old level that by setting me up in it as "normal" I modify the sense of all the rest and establish a new level. The new level would be nothing definite without what preceded it, without my history. [And there is] activity right there in passivity. Outside certain limit cases where the event is not assimilable, I could always maintain my old level through regression.

But is this passivity here, before the event which interrogates or puts to the test my being in the world, sufficient to give an account of the **(56)** weight of my past?

If I choose to try to forget, to repress, the repressing agency, although it is completely active, is distantly the echo of another part of myself which continues to be polarized differently. It has no initiative, it is on the defensive.

Yet, is there not a passivity of the same kind outside of any regression or repression, in every case where a forgotten recollection comes back, and this time without our being able to subtend it by an operation [coming] from myself? Thus, is it not necessary for the past to have another reality, a power other than that which is based on our refusal?

Memory [and] preservation—It must be the case that what no longer is, *is* in order to act—Not being of the past and possibility of its return, [this leads to] being elsewhere, unconscious.

Difficulty: if [the] return [of the] past is the passage from a lesser being to being, by coming into being again, it becomes present again and no longer announces the past. The past "sense" can only be carried by that which *is not*, by consciousness insofar as it is trans-temporal.

THE PROBLEM OF MEMORY

Only consciousness can make nothingness come into the world. Hence, transcendental theory of memory—Memory is consciousness of the past, which we cannot derive from the present, nor even from "former presents" (unconscious recollections), which in principle must therefore belong to consciousness. Memory constructs or deploys the past.

Difficulty [with this response]: how can [consciousness] encounter obstacles in this deployment? If there are obstacles, this is because there is a *hyle* of the past, therefore because the past is not only that which I construct. The whole constituting apparatus is reconstruction, and there has to be another presence to me of the past on which the construction is measured. Construction is that without which there is no past for me, but not that through which the past is past for me.

The past is not a "real" fragment to be added to the present—*Nacheinander der Jetztpunkte*.[3] But **[195] (57)** it is no more an indifferent non-being (indifferent "significations"), and implied therefore in the general powers of consciousness as the place of non-being.

There must be a presence of the past which is absence; it is necessary that it be a certain absence. If it is signification in general, nothingness, or if it is preserved image, being, the consequence as far as it is concerned is not so different. In the two cases, it ceases to be past, a certain modalization of being, being which has been and is no longer, in order to become either being or non-being. It ceases to be torn from the present in order to be confused with it or absolutely opposed to it.

Such are the conditions to be fulfilled by a theory of the past. In summary, it is necessary that it not be in itself and that it not be solely for me, that it not be *Vorstellung*.[4]

[1.] It is necessary to do an analysis of the present again. Since the past is that which has been present, we cannot comprehend the modalization *has been*, the index of the past, if we conceive of the present badly. [Yet, we must] not conceive of the present as a picture (impressed in me or grasped by synopsis)—Especially insofar as what happens, the present, is not a picture. It is a variation of my grasp, a deviation of my anchorings. When it forms a picture, it is no longer. Perception of an event: the war, the love interest, as it is far from being a spectacle before me—it is a certain posture of my social body, my being for others, adopting a position through something in which it is found, as space is for me a certain polarization of my corporeal schema resuming on my account a part of external space. In the two gestures with their immanent sense **(58)**, in their quality, in their intention, there is a survey of the articulated situation. Survey, not synthesis, because sense is only difference in relation to the preceding level and always refers to a synthesis made once and for all, and which is my embodiment, openness to a field.

In particular, in order to exorcise the idea of the picture, revise our notion of the sensible as opacity which arrests the gaze and thus could "pass" only by becoming a weakened picture or equivalent signification. The sensible is not that, at least the sensible in the experience that we have of it—Not a point in the sensible which is of the nature of reflection rather than of the nature of the thing. The grain of color is already a certain manner of promising to the other senses their qualities; it is a certain relation of all our flesh to the bearer of the color (*Flächengarbe*), and even the surface color refers to an underside, that is, yet to many layers, and thus to a commerce of our body with it. We would reach the quale only by reaching the punctual. [There is] neither object-picture impressed in me, nor synthesis or composition, but a grasp of the gaze on the visible matter and reciprocally of the visible matter on the gaze (velvety, smooth, [rough?], pastel, etc.).

Thus, 1) do not reduce event-based perception, which is the vibration of our being in others, to that of sensible pictures; 2) do not reduce the sensible part itself to a picture.

A present is a certain unique position of the index of being in the world.

2. Yet when we have redefined presence in this way, its passage to the condition of past can be neither "effacement" or "weakening," the passage to a lesser being—nor passage to pure signification or essence or non-being.

[196] (59) First [the] weakening or [the] effacement of the picture does not work without the weakening or effacement of the one who perceives. Remembering something is remembering the manner in which we gained access to that something. And we have seen that it is through the body, thus remembering is a certain manner of being body.

However, how do we remember a former embodiment? We remember it as a possible of the actual body which, in principle, could not happen in the present (hence the difference from the possible of the future); it is eminently a possible, because it has been a real.

If the present is my thought about the world, by passing there can be no question that the thought becomes a picture before me, that the thought is "preserved" or grasped by "recognition" or centrifugal reminiscence. The thought can offer itself to me only as what has overtaken my actual thought from behind, steals its energy from it, makes itself recognized as its history.

THE PROBLEM OF MEMORY

The past of my body is present to it like its future, i.e., through a polarization of its power (Schilder's experiment), i.e., through a certain impassable absence or distance between this possible and the actual. It is a power of my body already employed.

Schilder's experiment should modify our idea not only of the presence of space, but also that of time. The presence of time is fleshly, as is that of space. It is always coupling, but here the power of surveying, not the power of grasping. "*Noli me tangere*"[5] is the word of the resurrection—

[The] past thus enclosed in the *I can* of my body, modalized in power without contact. Why do I speak of the body and not of consciousness? Because we cannot speak of consciousness, nothing to say about it, if it is truly nothing. One can only describe the phenomena of which it **(60)** is the mainspring, the invisible lining, and which, moreover, it animates only by closely wedding them: my body, language. Sartre turns his nothingness into another being, a productivity.

Cf. Proust's text[6] on the reference of the surroundings to the body which inhabits them and of the past body to the present: they are variations of one another and the surroundings are an explication of each. But of course, the body is substituted here for consciousness only as the place of our eruption into the world. As empirical body, it is no less determined than determining (it "turns" in the course of the search)—We consider it as a vinculum of the temporal and spatial distance, and transformer of space into time: *Erinnerung*.[7]

Commentary on the text [of Proust's]: "has in a circle around him . . ."[8]—i.e., he holds it through his body, which bears its norm. Proof: every deviation of his body in relation to the norm induces an interdependent entourage specifically from this difference. Memory of the body based on what is a type. It holds the past not as chronology, but across qualitative regions. Its attitude is existential (the "pattern of its tiredness"),[9] i.e., it seeks to complete itself through an adequate world,— it has an atmosphere of generality. If flavor, odor, touches, sounds of water running, movements of the trees, handling of boots, madeleines, cobblestones, [?] and ice cubes mediate authentic memory, it is because marginal, pre-objective, non-distant perceptions, which cover consciousness rather than being objects for it, express a fleshly, body-world nexus. Flavor by itself, for example, or odor, calls for a mode of existence, waits to have existed, and causes us to exist at once both in the past and now: [the] connection with the past [works] through a structural generality or alogical essence of fleshly perception. The problem of association: one rightly shows that it is never **[197] (61)** an objective link, in itself, from image to image; that the image is constructed, and the association filtered by a category. But this is not a category in the strict sense: a mode of affirmation, of attribution. It is a way of existing or being in the world through that situation. The foundation of the association is embodiment and, more generally, praxis.

"He has only to lift his arm to arrest the sun and turn it back in its course"[10]—The body [is] an apparatus not only for perceiving space, but also time. One of its postures signifies a certain thickness of elapsed time: "But if, while I slept, my eyes had not seen the time, my body had nevertheless contrived to calculate it, had measured the hours not on a dial superficially decorated with figures, but by the steadily growing weight of all my replenished forces which, like a powerful clock, it had allowed, notch by notch, to descend from my brain into the rest of my body where they now accumulated as far as the top of my knees the unimpaired abundance of their store."[11] Time is read in the corporeal schema, transformed into a certain redistribution of forces. Someone will say that this is, however, time only with reference to the time of consciousness, to the flux of absolute psychic individuals; these forces are only signs of time, the signification is elsewhere. No. Certainly, without a consciousness that lives this body, the body would not produce time, but it is not this consciousness that, by means of *Sinngebung*, begins with a time free of space and produces a measurement of time. The body is not an instrument, but an organ, i.e., time is incorporated, sedimented[12] in it through its generality, which causes it not to be solely a mass of *einmalig*[13] givens, but a spatiotemporal structure.

"Not knowing where I was, I could not even be sure at first who I was; I had only the most rudimentary sense of existence, such as may lurk and flicker in the depths of an animal's consciousness."[14] —Cf. "One fails to see what dictates the choice, or why, among the millions of human beings one might be, it is on the being one was the day before that unerringly one lays one's hand."[15] —The body is what answers the question "What time is it?" and "Where am I?" (Claudel).[16] And it answers the question, of course, thanks to the "information" of the senses that overlap, of the "recollections" that reappear, but this bearing is global, the details matter only by calling for a reorganization of the whole; in order to reappear, the things and tasks need **[198] (62)** only an allusion, and it is the body as link with a world and a past that "contains" these allusions.

3. This fleshly mediation being allowed, how are we to understand that it results in explicit recollections, that it "sets in motion" the memory, and where do we end up with respect to the problem of "preservation" or the "absolute survey"?

The problem is reversed. It is no longer the preservation of the image or a central capacity of retrospection linked to consciousness which causes there to be a past for us. We have *Selbstgegebenheit*[17] of the past when a recollection emerges from forgetfulness. For that, it is necessary for recollection to emerge from the past, but it is necessary for it to be there. It is forgetfulness that preserves, not absolute forgetting, as if the past had never been lived, but forgetfulness that still counts in consciousness as a soldier counts in the company: the forgetfulness which is disclosed as forgetfulness and thereby even as secret memory. Cf. Freud: it is by pushing back into forgetfulness that we make the past inaccessible, but also immutable. Freud himself indicates that not all forgetting is repression. Thus, the gesture of pushing back is not solely repression with a moral character, it is a more general gesture. [Therefore] Proust: "And as habit weakens everything, what best reminds us of a person is precisely what we had forgotten (because it was of no importance, and we therefore left it in full possession of its strength). That is why the better part of our memories exists outside us, in a blatter of rain, in the smell of an unaired room or of the first crackling brushwood fire in a cold grate: whatever, in short, we happen upon what our mind . . . had rejected. . . . It is thanks to this forgetfulness alone that we can from time to time recover the person that we were, place ourselves in relation to things as he was placed, suffer anew because we are no longer ourselves but he, and because he loved what now leaves us indifferent."[18] "We should never recapture it had not a few words (such as the 'head of the Ministry of Posts') been carefully locked away in forgetfulness, just as an author deposits in the National Library a copy of a book which might otherwise become unobtainable."[19] There is consciousness which possesses itself and its significations, since it can recuperate itself, and which fights greedily **[199]** **(63)** to maintain its coherence and its universality. But by doing that, consciousness creates another version of itself, an external pressure, and prepares one day to allow itself to be undone and redone through the repressed time of which it wants to know nothing or, rather, of which it claims to know everything. In reality, consciousness is not completely itself; the forgetfulness that it weaves thus places it in a secret relationship with the forgotten. Forgetfulness is not the opposite of preservation because it truly preserves. That being the case, the problem is reversed. It is not a matter of knowing how the apparently forgotten is preserved or how our power to survey goes beyond the evoked without being actualized. All evocation is in principle a drawing out, and the originary form of the consciousness of the past, which founds all, is not the series of temporal positions, but partial reliefs on a horizon which is accessible only gradually and in transition.

Indeed, the problem is reversed. We must not say the *present* is *real;*

how to add to this real a zone of past (whether by preservation of a true real which is effaced, or by ubiquity of a consciousness which is contemporaneous with everything)? Perhaps we must say that "reality is formed only in memory."[20] We mean the reality spectacle. The present is that which gluts the machine for living; we do not see it fully. It is the *Stiftung* of a field "to be developed" (like a cliché)—It is in the order of existence (of which knowledge is a development), the *Urerlebnis,* the position of a now that could no longer not have been. This seed remains to be developed. We can reflect in recollection. A recollection is like a marker planted for all time, all at once. Memory is completely active since it will be necessary to reflect. But this reflection is only ever coin from a treasure acquired at one time. Double current of memory: from us to the past, but to a past first instituted through its former presence. We must lose in order to have, but this possession of the developed past never consoles itself for not having arrived before the moment of the loss, and this is the presence that memory seeks.

Truth of the (realist) idea that the past is no longer: it is transcendent; we account for it in true memory. Truth of the idea that the past is entirely there: there is nothing of what I have touched which has not opened a field of re-memoration and does not stay near.

Forgetfulness that is memory, transcendence of the past that plants its arrow in me like a wound, for that which separates is also that which unites: dialectical philosophy. But dialectic which 1) is not definitive surpassing **[200] (64)** (unlike Hegelian dialectic); 2) is not, however, pure and simple alternative, since I test my kinship with contradictions. For example, in existential memory, through heartbreak. Thus, not a binary dialectic. Philosophy of ambiguity or perception is a third conception of the dialectic. To be clarified in next year's course, no longer with intuitive examples, but in philosophical clarity, situating dialectic and perception in relation to each other.[21]

APPENDIX

Three Notes on the Freudian Unconscious

[247] Pre-objective unconscious, organizing principle of appearances (this principle being able to be self-division, struggle against the "demonic") remains a genuine institution with its defenses. Would what renders it unconscious be precisely this sedimentation—or unconscious as second "I think" which escapes the first?

The theory of the second "I think" appears to be imposed by the extreme deformation of the unconscious in the manifest (for example, *signorelli* inhibited by *signor* which recalls something confided by a Turkish client about sexuality, which itself recalls the suicide of a client with a sexual problem)[1] through the "absurd" character of the manifestations of the unconscious. It seems that it would be a matter of two blind forces struggling, or even of a subordinate that attempts to chime in. The sophistication of these Freudian explanations would correspond to a stab in the dark. But the sophistication is only an appearance. It is a translation of the unconscious operation into the language of waking thought. It covers over simple intuition (which, however, is only accessible to a thought which "understands" the oneiric), and the "unconscious" that it symbolizes must itself be simple.

Essential remark: the forgetting or repression of Signorelli must be linked back to the regional repression of a whole category—this regional character is distinctive to the oneiric. The repression which suppresses this region is a simple act. The traumatizing event, insofar as it happens to me, deposits in me a category or an *existentiale*. What one translates by saying that one has lived something is precisely this learning, it is the event as fertile, as sedimenting a being in the world. Generality of the repressed, extraordinary subtlety of our perception, of its kinship with a whole series of givens. In fact, this is not subtle, it is massive. Cf. generality of our body, our hand, which is not an individual, concrete fragment, but power of a system of gestures, site of a set of equivalences founded by events which teach (acquisitions of habit)—Our relation to others [involves] such apparatuses. It is these apparatuses which play a part in repression and without any subtlety. I sense in Signorelli (or in the articulatory power Signorelli) an adherence to the category of

Signor which is cursed. It is this generality which is oneirism. There is no supposition here of an unconscious thought of the Signorelli-Signor relations and what follow. The traumatizing event created this relation not through thought but through establishment of a regional authority. What is distinctively oneiric and "unconscious" here is this signification of the whole *Signor* family, the constitution of a whole Signor block, or rather of a block of the failure (for the block of the acquired is, on the contrary, habitus with its generality).[2] The unconscious consists of having in the mode of not having (one has since one recognizes the "true" word at once when it returns, since one rejects the others), —this autonomy poses problems: How can one have what one does not have? What one does not have is the recollection of the trauma as event, such that the *Deutung* will reveal it (nor, moreover, the recollection of the *representation* "Signorelli"), and there is no discursive link here from one to the other through the "unconscious." What one does have is the event entered in the register, incorporated in our implex, i.e., currently represented by its general sense. What is this register? It is, in relation to the events of the human level, what the body is in relation to natural events, i.e., 1) a transmission-reception system, 2) a system of internal balancing in which each fragmented fact plays a part by virtue of its signification in the whole. All this produces a sedimented, thick configuration. What is essential to the unconscious is **[248]** that our life, precisely because it is not a consciousness of others, in indifferent balance, but a node of significations which are traces of events,[3] consisting of excrescences and gaps, forms a baroque system. Exactly as an adult or elderly body has its dynamic, its privileged positions, its style of gestures, and its syntax, an implex has its wrinkles and its own balancing processes, and the unconscious is our practical schema, where everything is inscribed in shillings and pence—This generality of the practical schema, which causes the empirical history that it resumes to be hidden by it rather than revealed (the passage from the event to its personal sense is nothing other than its impact on the system), is no more an illusion or an abstraction than my face and my language as distinct from some such instant of one or the other.

The application of this schema to present, individual situations [does not presuppose] categorial subsumption or knowledge, but dealings—This diaphragm being accepted, which is pre-objective, between *noesis* and *noema*,[4] it remains to be understood 1) what kind of center is the center to which all this happens, 2) what kind of freedom and "choice" it has, what relation it has with the organization of its duration—to conceive between it and its duration a relation of pressure. There is the choice (the neurosis or the cure), the yes or the no, but it does not suppress a certain pressure which comes from the "neurotic" character and can restore the "neurotic" (cf. Freud saying that Dora herself choosing Herr K. could have surpassed the neurosis, but also could have fallen back into it)—One can always say that if the choice were really choice, and not half-choice, the neurosis would not return, the doing would be to make oneself. But there is never choice which would truly be choice in a being which is situated, with a landscape of obstacles and pathways (and not constituted by that being as such actually, not all in the future)—The point at which all is in suspense, the center of indetermination, the immediate freedom never pierces history.

Another problem is the relationship of the practical schema to explicit memory, the sedimented, and reactivation. Is the efficiency of the practical schema sufficient to account for delusion? Is there not pressure here of the past as past, indestructible, preserved in itself? To produce a theory of preservation as perceptual survey. It is false to say that the past is preserved as the total of unconscious images. And it is false to say that the past is constructed on the basis of the present existential position. These are the alternatives of realism and idealism. The perceived world teaches us precisely an *Überschau*,[5] a survey that does not need to be a synthesis and construction, because it is a survey through the body, rendezvous given through the appearance to my body when it merely makes this movement and exercises its *I can*. Likewise, there is a survey of the past such as it has been, indestructible, which does not need to be a synthesis, nor, therefore, to be total knowledge because such recollection gives a rendezvous to my actual being-in-the-world in some such other "place" of the past if the implex merely renders itself to it. This is not a simple comparison. The implex and the body are not merely *analogues;* the body is our originary implex, and the implex our secondary body. To remember is to remember former embodiment, and to have a body is also to have a past of embodiment; there is a time of the body, a temporal structure of embodiment. Interlacing of the body and the implex—hence what Proust says about the body's memory.

The upheaval of "the unconscious," the affective and poetic charge of the canary's chirping,[6] the solemnity of a future which is at the same time past, and which springs from the depths of the past, the indestructible of what once has been (and which is *Gestiftet* as such by perception), the other sense that the unconscious gives to such present perception unbeknownst to us, its activity through which it seizes **[249]** what happens and fashions it, its power to organize our life, the sudden growth, the fecundity of delusion, like a mushroom which shoots up in a few hours, its enormous fabric, undifferentiated, its erection, these are particular cases of embodiment—This organization is not unconscious in the sense of an external fate, of another thinking and drifting in me. In the same way that lighting changes my perceptual field, lights here and there reflections of which I am not the author, my current existential position gives life to such a moment of my past over there which is ignited and again starts to drift in me. This position is tacit, perceptual, and thus the light that it throws on such facets of the past is also tacit. One sees such an element of the landscape lighting up in the twilight as if it were the past which "was coming." This is not its doing. Certainly it is for always, but everything is for always. If it again becomes the lining of my actual life, this is because it awaited but a gesture, which consisted only in my turning toward it; it is not a *Sinngebung*, it is a modulation of the implex, it is a fissure which was produced in it and, consequently, in which the emergence of this past becomes possible. Cf. the waves as we see them being formed (at night, for example): there is a crest of foam, next to it another is formed and widens, they approach, they will make only one wave, neither one nor the other knows it, but their very proximity prepares them for it, they confirm each other, they know each other dynamically. In this way, the present state of the implex's dynamic calls forth from the depths of the past or confirms what asks only to be put in words. The different "choices": either the past predominates and displaces the present (neurosis, withdrawal to the origins, lying play through which one replays them in the present), or the present predominates and succeeds in sweeping the past behind it, or it attempts to break with the past, but this is a new repression, and it is Sartrean choice. The noise of the sea, this activity of the state that is its own, this indefatigable thrust through every failure, this inextinguishable rumor, symbol within the distribution of our choices, of our freedom through every wave of our distant or recent life, symbol of our temporal ubiquity—of existential eternity—A tumult in the silence of the same kind.

Freud's error, however, is to conceive this thrust of the unconscious, of our life distributed in its whole field, past and present, nearby and distant, undivided, coherent, only as a lying thought. Frau B. thinks of K1, wishes to find him as in the past, and masks this thought, this wish, this premonition under the theme: I dreamt that I met K2, the dream erupted in her when she meets him. Certainly this dream is an invention—But not a lie, very nearly one—it expresses that the encounter with K2 appears with a halo of preexistence; the premonition is a retrospective consciousness that this present was prepared in the past; the "dream" expresses the encroachment of the past on the future, of the interior on the exterior, which, in reality, is called desire. And also the encroachment of one person on another. Certainly such a presentation of the desire and of the promiscuity distort them, but it does not presuppose that they are actually present in an unconscious; they are sedimented in Frau B.'s implex. It is this implex which gives to the perception of K2 the value of a moving event, and which turns him into the solemn symbol of K1—"Cover" persona, says Freud—This is not completely true. K1 differs from K2; they communicate in her. It is not that there is the appearance and the truth. Their relationship is of a part to the whole.[7] And the totality is already present in me, before the analysis, as promiscuity.

Cf. Dora: that it is not correct to say that the love for Frau K. is the truth and the rest is appearance.

It is the generality of repression and of living which explains the subtlety of the disguises.

[250] Freud reports two predictions (not realized) in which it seems that the subject to whom the prediction has been made has slipped into the terms of these predictions an unconscious content after the fact—(a woman, for example, attributes to fortune-tellers the prediction of two children at age thirty-two,—which is precisely her mother's fate)—Idea that we hear our unconscious in others—Perception of others and endopsychic perception → telepathy.

"*I am sorry to confess that I belong to that clan of unworthy individuals before whom the spirits cease their activities and the supernatural disappear.*"[8]

Freud, appointed professor, contemplates taking revenge on people who recently refused his treatment,—and at that very minute encounters them in the street. In reality, he had seen them, "*but this perception, following the model of negative hallucination, was set aside by certain emotionally accentuated motives and then asserted itself spontaneously as an emerging fantasy.*"

A husband and wife dining in a restaurant are surprised to see that they are thinking of the same person without anything having caused them to do so. In fact, they both had seen someone pass by who resembled that person without "consciously" noticing it, and the visual image had revived the association of the "double."

(If the unconscious is not a thinker in us who knows everything, and not the event-based genesis of our "symbolic matrices,"—nevertheless, we cannot reduce it to these symbolic matrices as tacit, as "general" forms, since analysis liberates concrete recollections which appear to be absolutely forgotten. Thus, it is necessary to examine the relationship of symbolic matrices to concrete events. The reappearance of forgotten recollections, nevertheless, should not be overestimated. It is above all the reappearance of a nexus, of a core of significations. Specify with an example *what* it is, the majority of the time, to remember: it is not an intuition—The perception itself, in its time, was not an intuition, but a vibration of the field—How would the recollection also be something other than differentiation, divergence, lack of. . . ?)

[251] The unconscious = Freudian poetry, the premonition of the future in the present, the pre-formation of the present in the past: the echo of others in me, of me in others, of the wish in the reality.

I. Example of the restaurant, etc.: the alleged hallucination (perception without object, telepathic perception at a distance). This perception not recognized but effective (negative hallucination). Relation to others and to the future: endopsychic[9] and based on the present—i.e., there it has an efficacity which does not depend on the sense that we give to it. It receives one, tacit, in its accordance with our wishes which are held in suspense. Efficacity: a perceived secretly makes itself recognized by us, and bears fruit according to this sense—There is a contact with the perceived that is not "unconsciousness," but that is not "official" consciousness. And perceptual consciousness is of this kind = proof: there is perception of a lack or a gap without our knowing what. Perception of a lack is not simple lack of perception → let us generalize. Perception of something is not simple presence of the concrete perceptual act. Here and there: regional consciousness, i.e., negative perception is coupled with a positive totality, in any case it is a gap or divergence in relation to a whole known from its style—Negative hallucination: that which is hallucination in it does not conform to the given, it is nonrecognition—Positive hallucination is a limit case of this fact; in reality, it is a perception, but not recognized for what it is. Negative hallucination is coupled with a perception in the true sense, its moving, poetic character, and its effectivity comes from what it has just touched in us more than what we officially know. It causes a super-signification to vibrate. Whether our past or others, it reawakens my link with my past, with others, or the links of others among themselves and with me—Ultimately, positive perception is the repletion of a certain lack, the thing as *Erfüllung* of a horizon— The tacit, silent character of the perceptual life is based on the fact that it is not a confrontation of a signification and an individual, for in order to recognize in this way, an intermediary would thus be necessary, and so on,—but it is based on the fact that all recognition involves first the contact with the thing itself as primitive, non-thetic fact, in the residence of a norm which is the perceptual horizon, and that this thesis of the world and all its potentialities is the secret of all partial perception, act-intentionality. This thesis, preceding any positive or negative perception, and in relation to which it is a modalization, divergence, has the result that in principle perception does not possess itself. It is *ek-stasis* or some such determinate obstacle to this *ek-stasis*. It is therefore essential to perception to be not a *Sinngebung, Zusammenstimmung*, of a signification and an exterior,[10] but example of a style, insertion into a field, not subsumption, but experience of a co-functioning in which we no longer know which gives and which receives, "response" of the bodily whole to what offers itself. Thus, perception is animated by an internal movement. It is always here and now, both partial and local event—and yet this hides and crystallizes a transcendent sense, which leads us beyond the thing itself. Recognition is not association of ideas and it is not construction; it is reinstitution of the entire world with respect to this given which it requires and which re-poses itself.

Perception taken in two contexts of significance: by definition it has more sense than it tells. Its dialectic: Hegel—while I point at this, the given changes and the sense of the gesture is generalized[12]—Promiscuity of perceptions: the horizontal structure expresses precisely that as soon as one specifies a perception, one is referred to the others.

SUMMARY FOR MONDAY'S COURSE

The Problem of Passivity: Sleep, the Unconscious, Memory

How to conceive that the subject never encounters obstacles? If the subject has posited them itself, then they are not obstacles. And if they truly resist the subject, then we are brought back to the difficulties of a philosophy which incorporates the subject in a cosmic order and treats the functioning of the mind as a particular case of natural finality.

It is this problem that every theory of perception runs up against; consequently the explication of perceptual experience must make us acquainted with a genus of being with regard to which the subject is not sovereign, without the subject being inserted in it.

This course has sought to extend the ontology of the perceived world beyond sensible nature. Whether it is a matter of understanding how consciousness can sleep, how it can be inspired by a past which apparently eludes it, or, finally, how access to that past is reopened, passivity is possible only on the condition that "to be conscious" is not "to donate a sense," which one holds in one's possession in a material of ungraspable knowledge. Rather, to be conscious is to realize a certain divergence, a certain variation in an already instituted existential field, which is always behind us and whose weight, like that of a flywheel, intervenes up into the actions by which we transform it. To live, for humans, is not merely to impose significations perpetually, but to continue a vortex of experience which is formed, with our birth, at the point of contact between the "outside" and the one who is called to live it.

To sleep is not, despite how it sounds, an act, an operation, the thought or consciousness of sleeping; it is a modality of perceptual progression—more precisely, it is the provisional involution or dedifferentiation of consciousness; it is the return to the unarticulated, the withdrawal to a global or pre-personal relation to the world. In sleep, the world is not truly absent, but rather distant, a distance in which the body marks our place and with which it continues to entertain a minimum of relations, which will render reawakening possible. A philosophy of consciousness translates—and distorts—this relation by positing that sleep-

SUMMARY FOR MONDAY'S COURSE

ing consists in being absent from the true world or present to an imaginary world without consistency. It is to treat the negative as positive in the absence of any landmarks or any controls. The negation of the world in sleep is also a manner of maintaining it. And sleeping consciousness is not therefore a recess of pure nothingness; it is encumbered with the debris of the past and present. It plays with them.

Dreams are not a simple variety of imagining consciousness such as it is in the waking state, namely, a pure power of intending something whatsoever by means of some such emblem. If the dream were just this limitless caprice, if it surrendered consciousness to its essential madness, which is based on the fact that it has no nature and is immediately what it invents of being or thinking that it is, then we would not see how sleeping consciousness could ever awaken or how it could ever take seriously the conditions that waking places on the affirmation of a reality. Nor would we see how our dreams could have for us the sort of weight that they owe to their relations with our past. The distinction between the real and the oneiric cannot be the simple distinction between a consciousness fulfilled by the senses and a consciousness given over to its own emptiness. The two modalities encroach upon one another. Our waking relations with things and, above all, with others, have in principle an oneiric character: others are present to us as dreams, as myths, and that is enough to contest the cleavage between the real and the imaginary.

The dream already raises the problem of the unconscious, the refuge of the dreaming subject, of what dreams in us, of the inexhaustible, indestructible ground from which our dreams are drawn. It is with good reason that Freud is reproached for having introduced, with the name "unconscious," a second thinking subject whose productions would simply be received by the first, and he himself admitted that this "demonology" was only a "crude psychological conception." But the discussion of the Freudian unconscious usually leads back to the monopoly of consciousness: the unconscious is reduced to what we decide not to accept, and, as this decision presupposes that we are in contact with the repressed, the unconscious is nothing more than a particular case of bad faith, a hesitation of the freedom which imagines. We thus lose sight of Freud's most interesting contribution—not the idea of a second "I think" which would know what we do not know about ourselves—but the idea of a symbolism which is primordial, originary, of a "nonconventional thought" (Politzer) enclosed in a "world for us," responsible for the dream and, more generally, the elaboration of our life. To dream is not to translate a latent content, which is clear to itself (or to the second thinking subject), into the also clear but deceptive language of manifest content; it is to live the latent content through a manifest content which is neither its "adequate" expression from the viewpoint of waking thought, nor, moreover, a deliberate disguise which *stands for* the latent content by virtue of certain equivalences, and modes of projection called forth by the primordial symbolism and the structure of oneiric consciousness. In Freud's *The Interpretation of Dreams* there is a complete description of oneiric consciousness—the consciousness which ignores the *no*, which only says *yes* tacitly, producing for the analyst the responses he expects from it, being incapable of speech, calculation, and actual thoughts, and thus reduced to the former elaborations of the subject, so that our dreams are not circumscribed at the moment we dream them and import wholesale into our present entire fragments of our earlier duration. These descriptions mean that the unconscious is a perceptual consciousness, it proceeds like perceptual consciousness by means of a logic of implication or promiscuity, it gradually follows a path whose total slope it does not know, and it intends objects and beings across the negative that the unconscious keeps from them, which is enough to regulate its steps without enabling it to designate them "by their name." Delusions, like dreams, are full of imminent truths and travel in a network of relations equivalent to true relations, which they do not possess, yet which they take into account. What is essential in Freudianism is not to have shown that beneath appearances there is another reality altogether, but that the analysis of a given behavior always finds in it several layers of signification, that they all have their truth, and that the plurality of possible interpretations is the discursive expression of a mixed life, where each choice always has several senses, without our being able to say that one of them alone is true.

The problem of memory is at a dead end as long as we hesitate between memory as preservation and memory as construction. We will always be able to show that consciousness finds in its "representations" only what it has put into them, that memory is thus construction—and that, however, behind the construction there must be another memory which evaluates the productions of the first, a past given gratuitously and in inverse ratio to our voluntary memory. The immanence and the transcendence of the past, the activity and the passivity of memory, can only be reconciled if we give up posing the problem in terms of representation. If, to begin with, the present is not a "representation" (*Vorstellung*), but a certain unique position of the index of being in the world; if our relations with the present when it slips into the past, like our relations with our spatial surroundings, were attributed to a postural schema which keeps in possession and designs a series of positions and temporal possibilities; and if the body is that which in every case answers the question "Where am I and what time is it?" then there would not be this alternative between preservation and construction. Memory would not be the opposite of forgetting, for we would see that true memory is found at the intersection of the two, at the instant in which the recollection that is forgotten and guarded by forgetfulness returns. We would see that explicit recollection and forgetting are two modes of our oblique relation with a past that is present to us only through the determinate emptiness that it leaves in us.

These descriptions, this phenomenology, are always something of a disappointment, because they limit themselves to detecting the negative in the positive and the positive in the negative. Reflection seems to demand supplementary clarifications. The description will have its full philosophical range only if we interrogate ourselves about the foundation of this demand itself, if we explain the reasons in principle by which the relations between the positive and the negative present themselves thus. This would be to lay the foundations of a dialectical philosophy.

[Reading Notes on Proust][1]
Proust—Memory

Proust, *Memory* **[237]**
Swann's Way[2]

It makes no sense to search for the equivalent of recollection in reality—(The recollection is neither the past that is reproduced or preserved nor a falsified past.)—Memory deforms reality, which nevertheless is formed as reality only in memory. And yet, there is a memory which gives the past "itself": that of, for example, provisionally forgotten recollections.[3]

[. . . . .]

Proust—Memory **[238] (1)**

". . . The contradiction is to seek in reality for the pictures that are stored in one's memory, which must inevitably lose the charm that comes to them from memory itself and from their not being apprehended by the senses. . . . The places we have known do not belong only to the world of space on which we map them for our own convenience."[4]

"But it is pre-eminently as the deepest layer of my mental soil, as the firm ground on which I still stand, that I regard the Méséglise and Guermantes ways. It is because I believed in things and in people while I walked along those paths that the things and the people they made known to me are the only ones that I still take seriously and that still bring me joy. Whether it is because the faith which creates has ceased to exist in me, or because reality takes shape in the memory alone, the flowers that people show me nowadays for the first time never seem to me to be true flowers."[5]

(There is faith only in the past—The indubitable and inaccessible real—distance and reality are unified—Mediation.)

"And as habit weakens everything, what best reminds us of a person is precisely what we had forgotten (because it was of no importance, and we therefore left it in full possession of its strength). That is why the better part of our memories exists outside us, in a blatter of rain, in the smell of an unaired room or of the first crackling brushwood fire in a cold grate: whatever, in short, we happen upon that our mind ... had rejected."[6]

"It is thanks to this forgetfulness alone that we can from time to time recover the person that we were, place ourselves in relation to things as he was placed, suffer anew because we are no longer ourselves but he, and because he loved what now leaves us indifferent."[7]

(Induction of a self by means of a modulation of the field: cf. the trees that ask to be said, that hollow out within themselves the place for speech. Likewise we have an odor that asks to be completed again by the self for whom it was the emblem. Cf. the past tangled in the bushes like wool—Problem of passivity—they can always say that these facts make sense only because I have endowed them with it—This is true. They would not have it *without me*, i.e., without my possession in principle of the whole past. But they do not have it *by means of me*, and this possession is the act common to me and to the odor. To me alone, I have only the universal possibility of memory.)

"Or rather we should never recapture it had not a few words (such as the 'head of the Ministry of Posts') been carefully locked away in forgetfulness, just as an author deposits in the National Library a copy of a book which might otherwise become unobtainable."[8]

[239] (2) (Forgetfulness: the recollection is saved precisely because it is inaccessible. Cf. Freud: at what point it is false to think that the survival of a recollection is "preservation." The past exists in the mode of forgetfulness.

(Paradoxically, it is in the order of the *for others* that there are "decisions," "choices," "commitments," a history made of projected significations. For myself, I am none of that, if I am frank. I know very well that I began or stopped thinking this or that in advance of saying it or of stopping to say it, and that what I have said has never been all of what I was thinking, at least when it was categorical and when I had a "position," closing my eyes to all of that, passing over it in silence. This is to adopt in principle a theory of the subject which is an external view on the subject. And it is to renounce that which, however, is the sole honorable goal that we can propose when we write: to live before others and before oneself in an undivided way.)

Memory of the body
"When a man is asleep, he has in a circle around him the chain

of the hours, the sequence of the years, the order of the heavenly host. Instinctively, when he awakes, he looks to these, and in an instant reads off his own position on the earth's surface and the time that has elapsed during his slumbers; but this order of procession is apt to grow confused, and to break its ranks. Suppose that, toward morning, after a night of insomnia, sleep descends upon him while he is reading, in quite a different position from that in which he normally goes to sleep, he has only to lift his arm to arrest the sun and turn it back in its course, and, at the moment of waking, he will have no idea of the time, but will conclude that he has just gone to bed. . . . For me it was enough if, in my bed, my sleep was so heavy as completely to relax my consciousness; for then I lost all sense of the place in which I had gone to sleep, and when I awoke in the middle of the night, not knowing where I was, I could not even be sure at first who I was; I had only the most rudimentary sense of existence, such as may lurk and flicker in the depths of an animal's consciousness; I was more destitute than the cave-dweller; but then my memory—not yet of the place in which I was, but of various other places where I had lived and might now very possibly be—would come like a rope let down from heaven to draw me up out of the abyss of not-being, from which I could never have escaped by myself. . . .

"Perhaps the immobility of the things that surround us is forced upon them by our conviction that they are themselves and not anything else, by the immobility of our conception of them. For it always happened that when I awoke like this, and my mind struggled **[240] (3)** in an unsuccessful attempt to discover where I was, everything revolved around me through the darkness: things, places, years. My body, still too heavy with sleep to move, would endeavor to construe from the pattern of its tiredness the position of its various limbs, in order to deduce therefore the direction of the wall, the location of the furniture, to piece together and give a name to the house in which it lay. Its memory, the composite memory of its ribs, its knees, its shoulder-blades, offered it a whole series of rooms in which it had at one time or another slept. . . ."[9]

[241] (4) (A man who sleeps is nowhere, in no span of time, possible everywhere and at all times. Upon reawakening, he has to find an index that designates to him the place and the hour where he is. Someone will say, but he remembers. No, what is at issue is not a portion of recollections—or the recollections are themselves conditioned by something else, by a global view, by a system in which they are set up.

(This system is the body—Proof: if the body remained in a posture which is not that of sleeping at night (insomnia, arm lifted), upon reawakening this posture has the following effect: an underestimation of the time that has elapsed—The posture works by means of its deviation or its divergence in relation to a normal posture—If the posture is even more distant from the normal one (in an armchair) the field is open more widely: magic armchair which makes possible multiple insertions into points of time and very distant places—Grasp of the body, according to modalities of its posture, on absolute points of space and time which are substitutable in regard to this modality.

(But even in a normal position, if sleep is really heavy, I "lost all sense of the place"—In light sleep, therefore, the body holds onto the place—And holding onto the place is also to hold onto personal identity. No longer knowing where I am, I no longer know who I am, I am in nothingness, irremediably. If I emerge from it, this is because something is brought to me by the body. I see as if in a rapid flashback[10] a whole series of civilizations, all of them coming up to my time and stopping there. The body is here what meshes with one of the things that are possible just like the tongue of the buckle fits into a notch on the belt.

(The body that we find upon reawakening is not a clearly articulated whole. It is a tiredness which merely has one form, at least as long as it is numb and immobile. As soon as it is ready to move, there is a place, in the form of its attitude, something which announces a time, a place (the body: general capacity to inhabit diverse situations), a house, thoughts about this house from before he had fallen asleep—The body as openness to total situations, to types of situations (for example, situations comparable for it, and equivalent for it by means of the multiple of space-time), cf. in these types, these totalities, the details are neither subordinated under a law nor grouped by a community of significations. They are assembled by a common style which, at the limit, is merely the style of an epoch. An attitude of the body signifies existentially all of what the epoch has contained, with **[242] (5)** even complementary perceptions (the light of the bedroom seen from the outside) which were not given to the one who sleeps during this epoch. A synthesis based on events, not an intellectual synthesis. We can understand it only by assuming that all these sectors of the past are present (but not represented) in the subject who sleeps so that he can, because of a brief beam of light, make appear such and such a detail in it, a detail in which the presence of the whole is attested. Here the body is the instrument of a presentification of the whole, a global sector of the past that I develop only once I am awake.

(Certainty happens when the body "had veered round for the last time" and the things are fixed in *their* place. This indicates that the body is not first sensed as having an absolute position in space, and that not only do the things turn around it (the wall in front of or behind my back). No, it has also pulled up its anchor just as the things have. The sole fixed point is its action of meshing with the things, which is specified by some kind of information that happens to me on the basis of the state of my body as I make my first attempts to move.

(This is an important point: the body not only as insertion in a physical space, but also in a space-time, i.e., in places of anthropological space which are situated differently following the moment of a duration to which they are related. What is important is that all of that comes to a conclusion not because of reasons but because of a sort of weight of the things that are possible, the weight of a metaphysical mechanism—Cf. Leibniz.)

"One fails to see what dictates the choice, or why, among the millions of human beings one might be, it is on the being one was the day before that unerringly one lays one's hand."[11] The resurrection in awakening is neither more nor less difficult to understand than any return of something forgotten.

(The body and its situation as "field," cf. the "field" of geometry.)

"It is in ourselves that we should rather seek to find those fixed places, contemporaneous with different years."[12]

For example, an overwhelming tiredness and its "organic dislocation" can place us back in a level of childhood tiredness and make us be children again.

"A memory in my arms"[13] makes him think that he is in Paris with Albertine when he is with Gilberte, asleep.

Recollections of a dream which come back only in the broad light of the afternoon when "the ray of a similar idea happens by chance to strike them."[14]

"But if, while I slept, my eyes had not seen the time, my body had nevertheless contrived to calculate it, had measured the hours not on a dial superficially decorated with figures, but by the steadily growing weight of all my replenished forces which, like a powerful clock, it had allowed, notch by notch, to descend from my brain into the rest of my body where they now accumulated as far as the top of my knees the unimpaired abundance of their store."[15]

(Corporeal schema and time: just as there is a grasp of space which founds space that is objectified or thought, it is necessary that there is a grasp of time which provides a temporal sense to measured time. And this grasp, this time which appears to us **[243]** **(6)** entirely counted, as in a taximeter where the trip is transformed into shillings and pence, this subjectivity, which prior to objectification, is still the perceiving body.)[16]

Recollection, "synthesis of survival and nothingness" (*Within a Bud-*

ding Grove), possible in the world of sleep, because the least dose of pain, when it is delivered, reverberates more assuredly in the machine for living and thinking than in this same machine when it is open to the world. In the waking world, where intelligence labors, there is only being, and the recollection of the one who is lost is reduced to the recollection of pacifying judgments that he has made about us. The true recollection is merely the recollection of the pain that we have caused others and therefore ourselves, and the double wake of death, which is traced in us like a lightning bolt, is truly continued in the recollection and its cruelties.

The odor and the flavors "await" and "hope" that we recognize them and enter the past through them (*Swann's Way*).

Even without speaking of the plurality of expressions ("the human face is truly . . . a whole bunch of faces that are juxtaposed at different levels that we do not see at once," *Within a Budding Grove*), there is an astonishment when we see someone again, an astonishment which is based on the fact that, at first glance, we had not remembered him well and had distorted him; rediscovering this aspect that he has in no way hidden from us, we are surprised and we remember at once—Finally, there is a surprise which comes from what the earlier glimpse had made us see and makes us expect, precisely because the glimpse was partial, and is always in contrast with what the new encounter shows to us (*Within a Budding Grove*).

(*Someone* is this recollection-forgetfulness which, however, is not destroyed and will make us say later, when we run into him again, I don't remember him like that, but in fact, it's really him, I can see it now, he is like that.)

These recollections are composed like events: views in another light, they make us jealous of a mistress who no longer exists (reflecting within the recollection) (*The Captive*).

The "recollections" are as arbitrary as the imagination, at a distance, of what we have not known. There is no reason for the real to resemble the recollections more than the imagination. The recollection is not inventive. "If, thanks to forgetfulness, the returning memory can throw no bridge, form no connecting link between itself and the present minute, if it remains in the context of its own place and date, if it keeps its distance, its isolation in the hollow of a valley or upon the highest peak of a mountain summit, for this very reason it causes us suddenly to breathe a new air, an air which is new precisely because we have breathed it in the past."[17]

[Reading Notes on Freud]
Freud—*The Interpretation of Dreams*[1]

[1] (1) The indifferent elements of dreams often represent either recently lived, important events, or an important event from inner life.

The freshness of an impression seems to confer on it "some kind of psychical value for purposes of dream-construction equivalent in some way to the value of emotionally coloured memories or trains of thought"[2] (cf. transference).

The indifferent appears in dreams only insofar as it is *recent*. The former indifferent appears only when, already in the past, it has taken on value through displacement. It is, therefore, not indifferent.

Thus, no indifferent sources of dreams, no insignificant dreams: "The apparently innocent dreams turn out to be quite the reverse when we take the trouble to analyze them. They are . . . wolves in sheep's clothing."[3]

Dream of the butcher and the vegetable grocer[4]

it is an event from the day (butcher shop closed);

but the butcher shop is open = way to express slovenliness in a man's dress

"not obtainable any longer":[5] Freud's expression in analysis indicating that one can no longer recover events from earliest childhood directly. She rejects the transference.

"I don't recognize that; I won't take it."[6] *I don't recognize that*, words said to the cook, but substituted in the dream for what she had added: "behave yourself properly" (which is rightly applied to a slovenly man).

The vegetable grocer gives asparagus and black radish **[2]** sexual themes.

Analysis shows that the grocer tells of a "continued history": provocative behavior on my part, defense on hers. This is a frequent accusation among sufferers of hysteria who have been assaulted. This was, in fact, the initial trauma.

Words heard (from the butcher, the analyst, the cook), incidents install themselves in a certain field. To dream [is not] to think or to know all this, nor to elaborate a "history" having a direction, as Sartre believes it does. To dream [is] to allow this whole affective field—the kinships, allusions, and correspondences that the provocation-defense relationship pose—to play out. To dream [is not] I think that. But it is thought according to significant nuclei, which are not present like objects. The aggression-defense relation is present, but only as projected in certain *examples*. It is essential to the relation for it not to appear in person, as a subjective mode of organization, but only in relations with others.

Passivity can be understood only on the basis of *event-based thought*. What is constitutive of it is that the signification is here, not by *Sinngebung* (neither by the analyst, nor above all by the patient), but welcoming to an event in a situation, situation and event themselves not *known*, but grasped through commitment, perceptually, as configuration, proof of reality, relief on . . . i.e., by existentialia and not categories. The fundamental fact is that there are certain structures, in themselves *not analyzed*, with the help of which we "understand" all the rest. This is because perception can make sense without its elements being composed in an adequate thought. [3] (2) This is because a sentence can be clear without the sense of the linguistic instruments which compose it being clear. Cf. in what sense the elements that the analysis will draw from the pictures of Van Gogh (insect's perspective) both are there and are not given there. The fundamental fact is that clarity, sense, and truth are in front of us, not within. We can direct ourselves in an experience according to styles, sure relations, yet without the organizational signification being possessed. And this is ultimately the case because the life of consciousness is not *Sinngebung* in the constituting sense, but the fact that something *happens* to someone.

Proof of the elements of infantile origin:

A subject who returns after twenty years to his native land dreams the night before that he is with an unknown person in an unknown land. But on the spot he realizes that he had dreamed of a place near his hometown and a friend of his father.

Physician in his thirties, having dreamed of a yellow lion, one day discovers the lion from his dream. It is a porcelain trinket laid aside long ago; his mother tells him that it was his favorite toy in his childhood.[7]

Not only recollections of childhood in dreams, but rebirth of the child:

F. dreams that he mistreats two of his Jewish colleagues—colleagues whom in fact he liked very much. Ambition: to be named professor, and not to fail like them. But he does not recognize in himself such great ambition. In any case, not to be a *professor extraordinarius*. This ambition is the one that he had as a child when he was told that an **[4]** old woman had prophesied to his mother that he would be a great man,—or when a beggar in the Prater[8] had prophesied to him that he would be a cabinet minister[9] → he studies law and medicine.

(What is this presence of the infantile ego in dreams? It is not the presence of event-based recollections; the event precisely has remained only through its trace, its *furrow* (Proust). Consciousness of event and consciousness of signification are two modalities of objective consciousness, and what is constitutive of oneiric fecundity is neither consciousness of a principle nor that of an event considered as *einmalig*, but an *emblem*, i.e., an event-framework.)

Series of dreams translating the wish to go to Rome. A wish whose realization Freud defers a long time for reasons of health, etc. "I discovered long since that it only needs a little courage to fulfill wishes which till then have been regarded as unattainable"[10]—fine description of dreams of Rome[11]—Showing the functioning of existentialia:

The "promised land"—the fantastic Rome is made of elements borrowed from another "capital" (Ravenna) and elements of Karlsbad. Karlsbad [linked to] Jewish stories of persecutions which keep one away from the capital. Ask the way to Zucker (→ sugar, diabetes, Karlsbad)— Conversation about diabetes planned with a friend in Prague. In the dreamed Rome, there are posters in German. Freud did not want to go to Prague (wishes that German were better known there—spoke Czech), but to Rome—Understands his wish to go to Rome through identification with Hannibal → his father's humiliation by a "Christian," Hamilcar-Hannibal opposition → Napoleon—In sum, layers of signification which are assembled in a fundamental relation to power and persecution. Karlsbad, Rome, crystallization of **[5]** (3) relations with others, these glimpsed through his father.

(This ≠ production around the infantile drama. But this is only a particular instance. Dreams express the current drama as well, the reaction to the present. Then they appear less faltering. It is necessary to understand that there is an oneirism (a regression) which allows the old existentialia to play a role, but also an oneirism which elaborates on the new.

(The feature common to both is that they live on what the events of the day before have created. It is the event-based which is *true*, and at the same time they contribute to the making of it, since our improvised behaviors toward others obviously utilize oneirism—Sartre's "I have decided to be conciliatory" = refusal to allow oneself to be carried by oneirism, but also the refusal of true, involuntary friendship.

(It would be necessary to examine an action which is not delusional, which is not a return of the repressed, and to show in it nevertheless the kinship with oneirism, even in the reasoning.)

"Dreams frequently seem to have more than one signification. Not only, as our examples have shown, may they include several wish-fulfillments one alongside the other; but a succession of meanings or wish-fulfillments may be superimposed on one another, the bottom one being the fulfillment of a wish dating from earliest childhood."[12]

Insensitivity in dreams in the face of the death of cherished ones. The significance of the dream is not the apparent significance. Not that one wishes for [6] the death of the one dreamed about, but because one wishes for the occasion to see such and such person again: ". . .the affect felt in the dream belongs to its latent content and not to its manifest content, . . . the dream's *affective* content has remained untouched by the distortion which has overtaken its *ideational* content."[13]

If the loved one is mourned in a dream, it does not mean that one actually wishes for his death, but that one wished it at some unspecified moment in the past. It is necessary to understand, moreover, that death and the wish for death do not have the same significance for a child as it does for us. An eight-year-old at the natural history museum says to his mother, "I'm so fond of you, Mummy: when you die I'll have you stuffed and I'll keep you in this room, so that I can see you *all* the time."[14]—Ten-year-old child: "I know father's dead, but what I can't understand is why he doesn't come home to supper."[15]

"Sexual wishes—if in their embryonic stage they deserve to be so described . . ."[16]

Exaggerated concern with respect to her mother: reactionary formation on the basis of hostility. "It is no longer hard to understand why hysterical girls are so often attached to their mothers . . ."[17]

Hamlet: unable to kill his father's murderer, in whom he recognizes himself; he is no better.

Macbeth: the subject is childlessness.[18]

[7] (4) "A dream is a picture-puzzle of this sort and our predecessors in the field of dream-interpretation have made the mistake of treating the rebus as a pictorial composition: and as such it has seemed to them nonsensical and worthless."[19]

"Suppose I have a picture-puzzle, a rebus, in front of me. It depicts a house with a boat on its roof, a single letter of the alphabet, the figure of a running man whose head has been conjured away, and so on. Now I might be misled into raising objections and declaring that the picture as a whole and its component parts are nonsensical. A boat has no business to be on the roof of a house, and a headless man cannot run. Moreover, the man is bigger than the house; and if the whole picture is intended to represent a landscape, letters of the alphabet are out of place in it since such objects do not occur in nature. But obviously we can only form a proper judgement of the rebus if we put aside criticisms such as these of the whole composition and its parts and if, instead, we try to replace each separate element by a syllable or word that can be represented by that element in some way or other. The words which are put together in this way are no longer nonsensical but may form a poetic phrase of the greatest beauty and significance."[20]

"The dream-thoughts and the dream-content are presented to us like two versions of the same subject-matter in two different languages. Or, more properly, the dream-content seems like a transcript of the dream-thoughts into another mode of expression, whose characters and syntactic laws it is our business to discover by comparing the original and the translation . . . a pictographic script, the characters of which have to be transposed individually into the language of the dream-thoughts."[21]

[8] (Freud's originality does not lie in the fact that he presupposes a *censorship* and makes the censor's symbolism available. The censorship is itself only a particular instance of noncoincidence, and Freudian symbolism is not to be conceived as a double text, but as wish and fear, i.e., transcendence, symbolism of projection, narcissistic or visual symbolism obtained by cathexis withdrawal and regression, in the service, not of a knowledge to be masked, but of a wish.)

Condensation:

Short dream, impoverished, cropped off. The analysis of it takes up six, eight, twelve times more space.

"It is in fact never possible to be sure that a dream has been completely interpreted. Even if the solution seems satisfactory and without gaps, the possibility always remains that the dream may have yet another meaning."[22]

Certain associations which are used in the interpretation are created during the analysis, but they would not have taken place unless they were made possible by the dream-thought. "Loop-lines . . . short-circuits, made possible by the existence of other and deeper-lying connecting paths."[23]

"Each of the elements of the dream's content turns out to have been 'overdetermined'—to have been represented in the dream-thoughts many times over."[24]

"It is true in general that words are treated in dreams as though they were concrete things, and for that reason they are apt to be combined [9] (5) in just the same way as presentations of concrete things."[25]

A colleague sends Freud an article in which he overestimates a physiological discovery in emphatic terms. Freud dreams the phrase, "*It's written in a positively norekdal style*"—formed from *Nora* + *Ekdal* (Ibsen). Freud had just read an article by the author on Ibsen shortly before.[26]

"Where spoken sentences occur in dreams and are expressly distinguished as such from thoughts, it is an invariable rule that the words spoken in the dream are derived from spoken words remembered in the dream-material."[27]

The elements which appear essential in the manifest content are often incidental in the latent content or dream-thought. "And, as a corollary, the converse of this assertion can be affirmed. What is clearly the essence of the dream-thoughts need not be represented in the dream at all. The dream is, as it were, *differently-centered* from the dream-thoughts—its contents have different elements as its central point."[28]

"They are not infrequently trains of thought starting out from more than one centre, though having points of contact"; ". . . almost invariably accompanied by its contradictory counterpart, linked with it by antithetical association."[29]

In this construction, the most varied logical relations: foreground, background, digressions, clarifications, conditions, demonstrations, oppositions.

What becomes of the *logical connections* "(which have [10] hitherto formed its framework) when the whole mass of these dream-thoughts is brought under the pressure of the dream-work, and its elements are turned about, broken into fragments and jammed together—almost like pack-ice . . ."?[30]

Whenever, because, just as, although, this or that, ". . .dreams have no means at their disposal for representing these logical relations between the dream-thoughts. For the most part dreams disregard all these conjunctions, and it is only the substantive content of dream-thoughts that they take over and manipulate. The restoration of the connections which the dream-work has destroyed is a task which has to be performed by the interpretive process."[31]

"The incapacity of dreams to express these things must lie in the nature of the psychical material out of which dreams are made. The plastic arts of painting and sculpture labor, indeed, under a similar limitation as compared with poetry, which can make use of speech—and here once again the reason for their incapacity lies in the nature of the material which these two forms of art manipulate in their effort to express something. Before painting became acquainted with the laws of expression by which it is governed, it made attempts to get over this handicap. In ancient paintings small labels were hung from the mouths of the persons represented, containing in written characters the speeches which the artist despaired of representing pictorially."[32]

There is no intellectual work in dreams. Intellectual operations, opinions, argumentations, etc., appear in the interpretation as *"material of the dream-thoughts and . . . not a representation of intellectual work performed during the dream itself.* What is reproduced by the ostensible thinking in the dream is the *subject-matter* of the dream-thoughts and not the *mutual relations between them,* the assertion of which constitutes thinking . . . all spoken sentences which occur in dreams and are specifically described as such are unmodified . . . reproductions [11] (6) of speeches which are also to be found among the recollections in the material of the dream-thoughts. A speech of this kind is often no more than an allusion to some event included among the dream-thoughts, and the meaning of the dream may be a totally different one."[33]

When there is a contradiction in the manifest content of a dream, it does not correspond directly to a contradiction between the dream-thoughts.

"But just as the art of painting eventually found a way of expressing, by means other than the floating labels, at least the *intention* of the words of the personages represented—affections, threats, warnings, and so on—so too there is a possible means by which dreams can take account of some of the logical relations between their dream-thoughts, by making an appropriate modification in the method of representation characteristic of dreams."[34]

READING NOTES ON FREUD

Logical relations translated by simultaneity; two elements joined by a dream always have a close relation.

Causal relations: introductory dream and main dream.[35]

There is no expression *in the dream* of either, or . . . when we say it, it is only because the dream is confused.

No expression of opposition or contradiction: dreams, like primitive languages, have only one term for two opposites in a series of qualities or actions. Dreams ignore the no. Example: flowers as symbols of innocence and guilt.[36]

By contrast, the dream abounds in "just as," identifications and composite formations. The "covering figure" who performs actions and also those of the persons whom it "covers."

[12] Sometimes this formation fails. Then we have an acting person, and "the other (and usually the more important one) appears as an attendant figure without any other function." " 'My mother was there as well' (Stekel). An element of this kind in the dream-content may be compared to the 'determinatives' used in hieroglyphic script, which are not meant to be pronounced but serve merely to elucidate other signs."[37]

Sometimes dreams indicate a trait common to two persons in order to express through it another which has been censored.

"Dreams are completely egoistic"[38] composition of objects: lilies which are camellias which are cherry blossoms with an exotic appearance.[39]

The relation " 'contrariwise' or 'just the reverse' "[40] is expressed in dreams through reversal of the temporal order or certain relations (of superiority, inferiority, etc.) in the content of the dream.

Elements of the dream all the more intense as they have been condensed.

Sometimes "the impression of clarity or indistinctness given by a dream has no connection at all with the make-up of the dream itself but arises from the material of the dream-thoughts and is a constituent of it."[41] Upon examination after awakening, this dream contains "the same gaps and flaws . . . as any other."[42]

Dream in which he is threatened with arrest and in which [the ability] to leave would be a sign of absolution. Yet he cannot, does not find his hat. "*Thus the 'not being able to do something' in this dream was a way of expressing a contradiction—a 'no.'* "[43]

Contamination of the two images as of the first verse by the second which, by mutual induction, conditions the first and is conditioned by it in such a way that we are unaware of searching for the rhyme.

[13] (7) ("A lady of my acquaintance had the following dream":)[44]

Performance at the opera, in which her sister hands the dreamer a burning lump of coal (the weather is cold) because, she says, "she had not known it *would be so long*. The dream did not specify *what* would be so long. If it were a story, we should say 'the performance'; but since it is a dream, we may take the phrase as an independent entity, decide that it was used ambiguously and add the words 'before she got married.' "[45]

Aptitude for visual figuration is a very important motive for adopting a mode of expression in dreams.

Witticisms, allusions—the daydreams of neurotics use these means to find figurations of the elements of the body in objects: symbolic architectonic of the body (pillars and columns = legs; doors = bodily orifices). Plant life and food are used to provide symbols. "The symptoms of hysteria could never be interpreted if we forgot that sexual symbolism can find its best hiding-place behind what is commonplace and inconspicuous."[46] Dreams utilize symbols "which are already present in unconscious thinking."[47]

The symbols of a dream "frequently have more than one or even several meanings, and, as with Chinese script, the correct interpretation can only be arrived at on each occasion from the context. This ambiguity of the symbols links up with the characteristic of dreams for admitting of 'over-interpretation'—for representing in a single piece of content thoughts and wishes which are often widely divergent in their nature."[48]

[14] Wordplay of a dream: *violet* employed by association with the English *to violate* in order to indicate rape.

"We can assert of many dreams, if they are carefully interpreted, that they are bisexual since they unquestionably admit of an 'over-interpretation' in which the dreamer's homosexual impulses are realized—impulses, that is, which are contrary to his normal sexual activities."[49] But, Freud against any monism of dreams: "dreams of hunger and thirst, dreams of convenience, etc."[50] "The assertion that all dreams require a sexual interpretation, against which critics rage so incessantly, occurs nowhere in my *Interpretation of Dreams*."[51]

The act of blinding oneself in the legend of Oedipus = castration.[52]

The ancients believe that dreams of relations with one's mother are signs of success and possession of the earth.

"I have found that people who know that they are preferred or favored by their mother give evidence in their lives of a peculiar self-reliance and an unshakable optimism which often seem like heroic attributes and bring actual success to their possessors."[53]

Importance of daydreams and unconscious thoughts about intrauterine life: anxiety of those who fear being buried alive.

[15] (8) "A man dreamt that *he was asked someone's name, but could not think of it*. He himself explained that what this meant was that 'he would never dream of such a thing.' "[54]

In the station, one moves the platform closer to the train: there is the expression of a reversal of the dream's content.[55]

Dream of numbers and Freud's ingenious interpretation.[56]

"The dream-work does not in fact carry out any calculations at all, whether correctly or incorrectly; it merely throws into the *form* of a calculation numbers which are present in the dream-thoughts and can serve as allusions to matter that cannot be represented in any other way."[57]

"However much speeches and conversations, whether reasonable or unreasonable in themselves, may figure in dreams, analysis invariably proves that all the dream has done is to extract from the dream-thoughts fragments of speeches which have really been made or heard. It deals with these fragments in the most arbitrary fashion. Not only does it drag them out of their context and cut them into pieces, incorporating some portions and rejecting others, but it often puts them together in a new order so that a speech which appears in the dream to be a connected whole turns out in analysis to be composed of three or four detached fragments."[58]

"Speeches in dreams have a structure similar to that of breccia, in which largish blocks of varous kinds of stone are cemented together by a binding medium."[59]

[16] It is not very surprising that the dead live and act in dreams. How many times are we led to say, " 'If my father were alive, what would he say to this?' Dreams are unable to express an 'if' of this kind except by representing the person concerned as present in some particular situation."[60]

"A dream is made absurd, then, if a judgment that something 'is absurd' is among the elements found in the dream-thoughts—that is to say, if any one of the dreamer's unconscious trains of thought has criticism or ridicule as its motive. *Absurdity* is accordingly one of the methods by which the dream-work represents a contradiction . . ."[61] "The dream-work is thus parodying the thought that has been presented to it as something ridiculous, by the method of creating something ridiculous in connection with that thought."[62]

Dreams of a dead father often absurd: is censored expression of the critique of the father's authority, such as it is constant in childhood.

Dream in which 1851 is regarded as indiscernible from 1856. Yet five years is the time that Freud deferred his marriage and made his fiancée wait; it is also the time that he assigns to the analysis in which he sees a patient the longest.[63] Hence he concludes that this indistinction means that "five years is nothing." (In reality, this is not a judgment; it is an arrangement of the perceptual world in which five functions as *nothing*.) The arrangement consists in the fact that five is annulled, not in that five is thought as null.

[17] "The ideational material has undergone displacements and substitutions, whereas the affects have remained unaltered."[64]

"In unconscious thinking itself, every train of thought is yoked with its contradictory opposite."[65]

The theory of "wish-fulfillment" does not at all exclude "punishment dreams" caused by masochism.[66]

"During the dream-work, sources of affect which are capable of producing the same affect come together in generating it."[67]

All of Freud's friends reincarnate more or less his childhood relationship with a nephew who was one year older than him. "They have been *revenants*."[68]

"'No one is irreplaceable!' 'There are nothing but *revenants:* all those we have lost come back . . . From here my thoughts went on to the subject of the names of my own children. I had insisted on their names being chosen, not according to the fashion of the moment, but in memory of people I have been fond of. Their names made the children into *revenants*."[69]

Freud: there is a secondary revision which tends to transform a dream into something like a daydream.

[18] There are likewise unconscious daydreams "stored up readymade . . . for many years and . . . aroused . . . at the moment . . . of the stimulus" (Maury's dream).[70] Hence, an apperception en bloc which can make a very brief dream very rich (blocks of *signification*).

"If I look around for something with which to compare the final form assumed by a dream as it appears after normal thought has made its contribution, I can think of nothing better than the enigmatic inscriptions with which *Fliegende Blätter* has for so long entertained its readers."[71] Sentence in dialect which one tries to make appear as a Latin inscription by carving up the words appropriately.

Dreams often represent the state instead of the object. For example, Silberer seeks to compare the Kantian and Schopenhauerian conceptions of time, dream = [vision of the dream?]: *"I was asking for information from a disobliging secretary who was bent over his writing-table and refused to put himself out at my insistent demand. He half straightened himself and gave me a disagreeable and uncomplying look."*[72] The dream-work "does not . . . judge . . .; it restricts itself to giving things a new form."[73]

Its obligation 1) obey the censor; 2) represent visually and auditorily.

[19] Lichtenberg: "...We live and perceive as well in dreams as in waking life, and the one is just as much a part of our existence as the other. It is one of the advantages of the human being that he dreams and knows it. The proper use has hardly been made of this. The dream is a life that, taken together with ours, becomes what we call human life. Dreams gradually blend into our waking life, and we cannot say where the one begins and the other leaves off."[74]

Hebbel: "Insane, crazy dreams, that nevertheless seem to us to be rational in the dream itself: the soul composes meaningless figures with an alphabet that it does not yet understand, like a child with the twenty-four letters; which is not at all to say, however, that this alphabet is itself meaningless."[75]

"Thus it was suggested that many apparently isolated dream symbols be grounded in folk psychology and, on the other hand, that meanings known from dreams be utilized to shed light on mythical traditions."[76]

When Freud does not understand a dream recounted by a patient, he makes the patient relate it again. The patient never retells it in the same words. And the passages recounted differently are those which could betray the dream.

[20] Surprising solidity of the dreams: Freud takes up dreams written down and half-interpreted a year or two before. He rediscovers the first interpretations,—with many other things which insist that he has overcome the resistances in the meantime. But the same interpretations are always there.[77] Moreover, patients often recounted childhood dreams with as much success as if they had been dreamed the day before.

Even when one has given coherent and complete interpretations: "... the same dream may perhaps have another interpretation as well, an 'over-interpretation...'"[78] Overinterpretation: "anagogic interpretation." For Freud, the case in which anagogic interpretation imposes itself is nevertheless rare.

"In the case of two consecutive dreams it can often be observed that one takes as its central point something that is only on the periphery of the other and *vice versa*, so that their interpretations too are mutually complementary. I have already given instances which show that different dreams dreamt on the same night are, as a quite general rule, to be treated in their interpretation as a single whole.

"There is often a passage in even the most thoroughly interpreted dream which has to be left obscure; this is because we become aware during the work of interpretation that at that point there is a tangle of dream-thoughts which cannot be unraveled and which moreover adds nothing to our knowledge of the content of the dream. This is the dream's navel, the spot where it reaches down into the unknown. The dream-thoughts to which we are led by interpretation cannot, from the nature of things, have any definite endings; they are bound to branch out in every direction into the intricate network of our world of thought. It is at some point where this meshwork is particularly close that the dream-wish **[21]** grows up, like a mushroom out of its mycelium."[79]

"Our procedure consists in abandoning all those purposive ideas which normally govern our reflections, in focusing our attention on a single element of the dream and in then taking note of whatever involuntary thoughts may occur to us in connection with it."[80] (A dream is the fulfillment of a wish,—but of a wish that has nothing to do with the purposes of wakeful activity—striking contrast between oneiric wish and wakeful wish, idea in Freud of a deep longing which is not at all our manifest longing.)

"It is demonstrably untrue that we are being carried along a purposeless stream of ideas when, in the process of interpreting a dream, we abandon reflection and allow involuntary ideas to emerge. It can be shown that all that we can ever get rid of are purposive ideas that are *known* to us; as soon as we have done this, *unknown*—or, as we accurately say, 'unconscious'—purposive ideas take charge and thereafter determine the course of the involuntary ideas. No influence that we can bring to bear upon our mental processes can ever enable us to think without purposive ideas; nor am I aware of any states of psychical confusion which can do so. . . . *Whenever one psychical element is linked with another by an objectionable or superficial association,* **[22]** *there is also a legitimate and deeper link between them which is subjected to the resistance of the censorship.*"[81] (The audience's smiles, the laborious aspect of Freud's interpretations, are based simply on the fact that the reader has not successfully placed himself back into the intentionality of the dream, at the crossroads; as soon as one is there, these convoluted relations appear quite simple. But also, it cannot be a matter of attributing such a subtlety to the dream-thoughts.)

"When I instruct a patient to abandon reflection of any kind and to tell me whatever comes into his head, I am relying firmly on the assumption that he will not be able to abandon the purposive ideas inherent in the treatment. . . . There is another purposive idea of which the patient has no suspicion—one relating to myself."[82]

"We follow a path which leads back from the elements of the dream to the dream-thoughts and . . . the dream-work followed one in the contrary direction. But it is highly improbable that these paths are passable in both ways. It appears, rather, that in the daytime we drive shafts which follow along fresh chains of thought and that these shafts make contact with the intermediate thoughts and the dream-thoughts now at one point and now at another. We can see how in this manner fresh daytime material inserts itself into the interpretive chains. It is probable, too, that the increase in resistance that has set in since the night makes new and more devious detours necessary. The number and **[23]** nature of the collaterals that we spin in this way during the day is of no psychological importance whatever, so long as they lead us to the dream-thoughts of which we are in search."[83]

"... *the scene of action of dreams is different from that of waking ideational life*. This is the only hypothesis that makes the special peculiarities of dream-life intelligible. What is presented to us in these words [by Fechner] is the idea of *psychical locality*."[84]

To reconstruct "the psychical apparatus"—no risk in this bold attempt "so long as we ... do not mistake the scaffolding for the building."[85] "Agencies" or "systems."

If in dreams there were only diminution of the resistance that closes the preconscious to the unconscious, we would have non-hallucinatory dreams made of our images from the day before. Hallucinatory dreams are only explained by saying that "the excitation moves in a backward direction."[86] The hallucinatory character of dreams is a limit case of the transference of the intensities that one calls condensation.

"In regression the fabric of the dream-thoughts is resolved into its raw material."[87]

During the day before, direct current of perception toward motility. This current is arrested at night, and nothing stands in the way of the regressive current.

[24] The only thoughts that become hallucinatory are those which are intimate relations with repressed or permanently unconscious recollections.[88] These recollections "lead to" the thought "through regression."[89]

"The transformation of thoughts into visual images may be in part the result of the attraction which memories couched in visual form and eager for revival bring to bear upon thoughts cut off from consciousness and struggling to find expression.... [A] dream might be described as a *substitute for an infantile scene modified by being transferred onto a recent experience*."[90]

A repressed thought is attracted by the unconscious at the same time as it is repressed by consciousness.

Three regressions: topical, temporal, and formal (principal modes of expression).

The three are united, for the one that is oldest "in psychical topography lies nearer to the perceptual end."[91]

Truly unconscious psychic acts are "indestructible."[92] Only they can trigger a dream: "in our unconscious, ever on the alert and, so to say, immortal," cf. "the Titans."[93]

For children "there is as yet no division or censorship between the preconscious and the unconscious."[94]

The unconscious: cf. ghosts of the underworld which come back to life if one gives them blood.[95]

A thought from the day can be the entrepreneur of a dream. But the unconscious alone supplies the capital.[96]

[25] The return of perception consists in reconstituting "the situation of the original satisfaction."[97] (Perception and wish) hallucination = wish.

A hysterical symptom: two opposing wishes, each arising from a different psychical system,[98] ... converge in a single expression.[99] "As in the case of dreams, there are no limits ... to the 'overdetermination' ..."[100] "*Throughout our whole sleeping state we know just as certainly that we are dreaming as we know that we are sleeping.*"[101] (Cf. imposing on oneself a condition of awakening. Sleep of wet nurses.)

Recollections constitute "residues of visual cathexes."[102]

"...the first portion of the dream-work has already begun during the day, under the control of the preconscious. Its second portion—the modification imposed by the censorship, the attraction exercised by unconscious scenes, and the forcing of its way to perception—no doubt proceeds all through the night; and in this respect we may perhaps always be right when we express a feeling of having been dreaming all night long, though we cannot say what. But it seems to me unnecessary to suppose that dream-processes really maintain, up to the moment of becoming conscious, the chronological order in which I have described them: that the first thing to appear is the transferred dream-wish, that distortion by the censorship follows, then the regressive change in direction, and so on. I have been obliged to adopt this order in my description; but what happens in reality is no doubt a simultaneous exploring of one path and another, a swinging of the excitation now this way and now that, until at last it accumulates in the direction that is most opportune and one particular grouping becomes the permanent one. Certain personal experiences of my own lead me to suspect that the dream-work often requires more than a day and a night in order to achieve its result; and if this is so, we need no longer feel any amazement at the extraordinary ingenuity shown in the construction of the dream.... It is like a firework, which takes hours to prepare but goes off in a moment."[103]

"In the unconscious, nothing can be brought to an end, nothing is past or forgotten."[104] "A humiliation that was experienced thirty years ago acts exactly like a fresh one throughout the thirty years, as soon as

READING NOTES ON FREUD

it has obtained access to the unconscious sources of emotion.... This is precisely the point at which psychotherapy has to intervene. Its task is to make it possible for the unconscious processes to be dealt with finally and to be forgotten."[105] The erasing of recollections is not the work of time. It is a secondary transformation, which requires hard labor. "What performs this work is the preconscious, and *psychotherapy can pursue no other course than to bring the unconscious under the domination of the preconscious.*"[106]

Dreams "represent and neutralize" unconscious excitations.

The concept "violence and struggling," under which a child arranges 1) recollection of a night when he heard the sexual struggling of his parents (and blood in the bed); 2) recollection of his violence toward his younger brother, whom he kicks, and his mother saying, "I'm afraid he'll be the death of him"; 3) recollection of an accident in which he cuts his hand with a hatchet, and of a man with a hatchet chasing his uncle (subsequent story of the uncle). All this produces a dream in which he is chased by a man with a hatchet [27] without being able to flee. The three elements are provided in the course of analysis. All this leads to a sadistic conception of the sexual act.[107]

The dream takes possession of "indifferent" elements from the day before in order to signify important but shocking elements.

Sensations of falling, floating, inhibition would be bodily elements which are always available, which are sometimes seized by dream-thought in order to make them carry its wishes.[108]

"The intensity of a whole train of thought may eventually be concentrated in a single ideational element. Here we have the fact of 'compression' or 'condensation'. . . mainly responsible for the bewildering impression made on us by dreams . . ."[109]

Condensations: cf. italics or bold print. Cf. primitive painters representing more important persons as larger in size.

"We have asserted that only a wish is able to set the apparatus in motion and that the course of the excitation in it is automatically regulated by feelings of pleasure and unpleasure."[110]

"The first wishing seems to have been a hallucinatory cathecting of the memory of satisfaction."[111]

The Freudian subject is the one which distributes the "cathexes," "sending out and withdrawing cathexes"[112] (investing itself). These cathexes sometimes result from an *attraction*.

Pleasure principle—tending toward perceptual identity. The principle of thought is different. [28] It is a "hyper-cathexis," work of consciousness[113]—Secondary system.

Freud himself corrects the notion that there could be spatiality in his schemas. There are not so much "two systems" as "two kinds of *processes of excitation* or *modes of its discharge.*"[114]

"Thus, we may speak of an unconscious thought seeking to convey itself into the preconscious so as to be able then to force its way through into consciousness. What we have in mind here is not the forming of a second thought situated in a new place, like a transcription which continues to exist alongside the original; and the notion of forcing a way through into consciousness must be kept carefully free from any idea of a change of locality. Again, we may speak of a preconscious thought being repressed or driven out and then taken over by the unconscious. These images, derived from a set of ideas relating to a struggle for a piece of ground, may tempt us to suppose that it is literally true that a mental grouping in one locality has been brought to an end and replaced by a fresh one in another locality. Let us replace these metaphors by something that seems to correspond better to the real state of affairs, and let us say instead that some particular mental grouping has had a cathexis of energy attached to it or withdrawn from it, so that the structure in question has come under the sway of a particular agency or been withdrawn from it."[115]

Such is the sense of "to repress" and "to penetrate," replacing the spatial with the dynamic.

The ancients [attributed] "the uncontrolled and indestructible forces in the human mind, to the 'daemonic' power which produces the dream-wish and which we find at work in our unconscious."[116] **[29]** "It is in any case instructive to get to know the much trampled soil from which our virtues proudly spring."[117]

"By picturing our wishes as fulfilled, dreams are after all leading us into the future. But this future, which the dreamer pictures as the present, has been molded by his indestructible wish into a perfect likeness of the past."[118]

ENDNOTES FOR THE COURSE ON PASSIVITY

[PHILOSOPHY AND THE PHENOMENON OF PASSIVITY]

1. Thursday's course of the same year, *Institution in Personal and Public History*. Merleau-Ponty is referring to the course contained in the first part of this volume.

2. See, for example, Pierre Lachièze-Rey, *L'idéalism kantien* (Paris: Alcan, 1932); and *Le moi, le monde, et Dieu* (Paris: Boisvin, 1950 [1938]).

3. Allusion to Jean-Paul Sartre, *The Communists and Peace*, trans. Martha Fletcher, John Kleinschmidt, and Philip Berk (New York: Braziller, 1968). Merleau-Ponty gives the exact citation in *Adventures of the Dialectic*, trans. Joseph J. Bien and Hugh J. Silverman (Evanston, Ill.: Northwestern University Press, 1973), 147: " 'To look at man and society *in their truth*, which is to say,' Sartre writes, 'with the eyes of the least favored.' "

4. This paragraph is particularly elliptical; the reference to P. Lachièze-Rey becomes clearer if we refer to a later version of the first part of the course, which we did not retain (cf. "Editors' Note to the French Edition"). Merleau-Ponty writes [109] (1): "Problem of passivity: posed by Kant in the period after the *Critiques*, *Opus postumum* (Lachièze-Rey).

"The 'Cosmotheoros' is also the 'inhabitant' of the world. Among other things, it sees itself conditioned by a personal and affective past. The philosopher knows himself to be historical. Solution according to Lachièze-Rey: he self-posits himself as receptivity; he passivizes himself. But if it is he who passivizes himself, he is not passivized—and if it is he whom he truly passivizes, it is not he who does it.

"The activity-passivity antinomy is not surmountable head-on, starting from these notions; and if we say that what is true is their pairing, my self-positing myself, then we adopt a third point of view, another ontology, and it is necessary to say which one."

5. Sigmund Freud, *Leonardo da Vinci and a Memory of His Childhood*, in vol. 11 of *The Standard Edition of the Complete Psychological Works of Sigmund Freud*, trans. and ed. James Strachey (London: Hogarth Press, 1961), 59–137.

6. Merleau-Ponty: "i.e., there is an absolute judge, a gaze without limit which I have to be. 'Ultra-objective' thought under the guise of ultra-subjectivity."

7. *Sinngebung* may be rendered in English as "donation of sense" or "meaning giving." This Husserlian term is a recurrent theme in Merleau-Ponty's criticisms of Sartre, whom he accuses of exaggerating the extent to which consciousness "gives meaning" to things and events. See, for example, Maurice Merleau-Ponty, *Phenomenology of Perception*, trans. Colin Smith (London: Routledge Classics, 2002), xii, 164, 498, 504ff.; *Adventures of the Dialectic*, 138n78, 198ff.; and *The Visible and the Invisible*, trans. Alphonso Lingis (Evanston, Ill.: Northwestern University Press, 1968), 181. See also "Course Summary," p. 206.

8. Cf. Claude Lévi-Strauss, "The Sorcerer and His Magic," in *Structural Anthropology*, trans. Claire Jacobson et al. (London: Allen Lane, 1949), 167–85.

9. *Offenheit* may be rendered in English as "openness." On the interpretation of truth as *aletheia* or "unconcealment," see Martin Heidegger, *Being and Time*, trans. John Macquarrie and Edward Robinson (New York: Harper and Row, 1962), 256ff. See also his "On the Essence of Truth," trans. John Sallis, in *Pathmarks*, ed. William O'Neill (Cambridge, Eng.: Cambridge University Press, 1998), 136–54; and "Plato's Doctrine of Truth," trans. Thomas Sheehan, in *Pathmarks*, 155–82.

10. Jacob Levy Moreno, *Psychodrama*, vol. 1 (New York: Beacon House, 1932).

11. Merleau-Ponty, in the margin: "We see connections between passivity, past, unconsciousness, memory."

12. Merleau-Ponty cites Sartre's phrase in *Adventures of the Dialectic*, 147: "'To look at man and society in their truth, that is to say, with the eyes of the least favored' (*The Communists and Peace*)."

13. D. Lagache, *The Works of Daniel Lagache: Selected Papers*, trans. Elisabeth Holder (London: Karnac Books, 1993). See Maurice Merleau-Ponty, *Consciousness and the Acquisition of Language*, trans. Hugh J. Silverman (Evanston, Ill.: Northwestern University Press, 1973), 64.

14. Merleau-Ponty: "Error of *The Imaginary:* to describe the imagining consciousness as nihilation: it is always a circumscribed nothingness, a nothingness of this or that, and this is why Sartre did not describe in *The Imaginary* [Jean-Paul Sartre, *The Imaginary*, trans. Jonathan Webber (New York: Routledge, 2004)] *what is imagined in the image:* he does not show why it is an imaginary presence or a quasi-presence—Examine in relation to the dream."

15. *Nachvollzug*, "reoperation."

16. *Selbstaufhebung*, "self-overcoming."

17. Merleau-Ponty: "Is the 'mythical,' which Sartre methodically introduces as constitutive of history, of the imaginary in Sartre's sense? If so, it is without rational control—If, on the contrary, it is of the imaginary in *my* sense of a 'historical imagination,' there is a *truth* of it."

18. *Tala:* expression employed by students at the École Normal Supérieur to designate "those who go to Mass": "von/t à la messe," hence "t/à la."

19. At the conclusion of "Sartre and Ultrabolshevism," Merleau-Ponty writes: "The question is to know whether, as Sartre says, there are only *humans* and *things* or whether there is also the interworld, which we call history, symbolism, truth-to-be-made" (*Adventures of the Dialectic*, 200).

20. *Lebenswelt*, "life-world." See Edmund Husserl, *The Crisis of European Sciences and Transcendental Philosophy*, trans. David Carr (Evanston, Ill.: Northwestern University Press, 1970).

21. F. Alquié, *La decouverte metaphysique de l'homme chez Descartes* (Paris: Presses Universitaires de France, 1987 [1950]).

22. Merleau-Ponty: "You return to activity."

23. *Physis*, "nature."

ENDNOTES FOR THE COURSE ON PASSIVITY

24. Merleau-Ponty: "This does not mean: in itself the body does not have internal unity, it only has it for me. This means: it only has perceived being."

25. R. Ruyer, "Les conceptions nouvelles de l'instinct" *Les Temps Modernes*, November 1953, 824–60. Cf. the reference to Ruyer above, p. 83.

26. Cf. pp. 122ff.

27. The pages [109] (1) to [118] (9)—beginning—have been replaced by another introduction to the same course: pages [211] (1) to [218] (7). Here we resume the main text at page (9), which lays the groundwork for the critique of Ruyer and the analysis of the relation between in-itself and for-itself.

28. *An sich oder für uns*, "in itself or for us."

29. *Für sich Sein*, "being for-itself."

30. Jean-Toussaint Desanti had not yet published the books that would bring him notoriety. See *La philosophie silencieuse* (Paris: Seuil, 1975); *Introduction à la phénoménologie* (Paris: Gallimard, 1994 [1976]); and *Les idéalités mathématiques* (Paris: Seuil, 2008 [1968]).

31. Merleau-Ponty: "Hormones 'know' what they are going to do."

32. *Einfühlung*, "empathy."

33. *Bewußtsein überhaupt*, "consciousness in general."

34. Merleau-Ponty's use of the Greek letter phi probably refers to the word "philosophy": "cf. Brunschvicg, philosophy of consciousness."

35. Merleau-Ponty: "That applicable to the parasites,—but not without a 'tendency' toward life in them—not applicable to the species themselves."

36. See Maurice Merleau-Ponty, *Nature: Course Notes from the Collège de France*, trans. Robert Vallier (Evanston, Ill.: Northwestern University Press, 2003), 250 and 255.

37. Unpublished text to which the author draws attention again in a note to *The Visible and the Invisible*, 259. See Edmund Husserl, "Foundational Investigations of the Phenomenological Origin of the Spatiality of Nature: The Originary Ark, the Earth, Does Not Move," trans. Fred Kersten, rev. Leonard Lawlor, in *Husserl at the Limits of Phenomenology*, ed. Leonard Lawlor with Bettina Bergo (Evanston, Ill.: Northwestern University Press, 2002), 117–31.

38. *Selbstgegebenheit*, "capacity to be given to oneself."

39. *Leibhaftgegeben*, "bodily given." See Edmund Husserl, *Ideas Pertaining to a Pure Phenomenology and to a Phenomenological Philosophy, Second Book: Studies in the Phenomenology of Constitution*, trans. Richard Rojcewicz and André Schuwer (Dordrecht: Kluwer Academic, 1989).

40. *Dingwahrnemung*, "perception of the thing."

41. *Ding*, "thing."

42. *Abschattungen*, "adumbrations."

43. *Verhalten*, "behavior."

44. *Erlebnisse*, "lived experiences."

45. Merleau-Ponty, in the margin: "How are others and myself absolute beings? Status of rationality? Of truth?"

46. It is likely that Merleau-Ponty composed this note separately and then inserted it after his numbered page (15) of notes for the course lectures; the

note echoes the question stated in the last two sentences of (15). Apparently he did this so that, when he decided to return to this question, he would have some idea of how to reformulate the argument developed starting on his numbered page (14). Because Merleau-Ponty himself did not number the page on which the note was written, the Bibliothèque Nationale gave it the number [125]. Because the note is inserted and looks to be not directly a lecture note, it is presented here in a smaller typeface.

47. *Vergessenheit*, "forgetfulness."

[FOR AN ONTOLOGY OF THE PERCEIVED WORLD]

1. Despite the numbering that signals a new draft of the pages preceding (14) and (15), it seemed advisable to preserve the first version.
2. See Edmund Husserl, *Cartesian Meditations: An Introduction to Phenomenology*, trans. Dorion Cairns (Dordrecht: Kluwer Academic, 1988).
3. See also the "Introduction" section of the *Institution* course, p. 6.
4. *Vernunftproblem*, "the problem of reason."
5. New draft of the arguments from pages [131] (18) to [134] (21).
6. "*Recordatione carens*" may be rendered in English as "lacking memory." In his *Theoria Motus Abstracti (Theory of Abstract Motion)*, Leibniz writes, "Omni enim corpus est mens momentanea, seu carens *recordatione*..." (Every body is an instantaneous mind or a mind lacking memory...). See Georg Wilhelm Leibniz, *Sämtliche Schriften und Briefe*, vol. 6, ed. Deutschen Akademie der Wissenschaften (Berlin: Akademie Verlag, 1966), 266.
7. "I am not a wind, a breath, a vapor." René Descartes, *The Philosophical Works of Descartes*, vol. 1, trans. Elizabeth S. Haldane and G. R. T. Ross (New York: Cambridge University Press, 1973), 152.

[SLEEP]

1. Maurice Merleau-Ponty, *The Structure of Behavior*, trans. Alden L. Fisher (Pittsburgh: Duquesne University Press, 1983 [1963]), 17–21 and 56–62; and Maurice Merleau-Ponty, *The Primacy of Perception*, ed. James M. Edie (Evanston, Ill.: Northwestern University Press, 1964), 76–78.
2. Merleau-Ponty is apparently referring to Henri Piéron's *Le problem physiologique du sommeil* (Paris: Masson, 1913).
3. Sigmund Freud, *Introduction à la psychanalyse*, trans. S. Jankelevitch (Paris: Payot, 1949). No page number is included in the citation, and the passage does not appear in the work cited exactly as quoted. Merleau-Ponty may be referring to the passage (pp. 100–101) in which Freud likens falling asleep to withdrawing into the womb and awakening to being reborn. However, neither here nor elsewhere in these lectures does Freud speak explicitly of sleep as an undressing of the psyche. See Sigmund Freud, *Introductory Lectures on Psycho-Analysis*, in vol. 15

of *The Standard Edition of the Complete Psychological Works of Sigmund Freud*, trans. James Strachey (London: Hogarth Press, 1961), 88–90.

4. Sartre, *The Imaginary*, 44–45.

5. "Consciousness is entirely *taken hold of*" in the sense of "*caught*" or "*gripped*" conveys the sense of Sartre's "conscience s'est prise tout entière." See Merleau-Ponty's analogy with seduction, p. 142 below. However, in light of the quotation on p. 140 above, "*congealed*" may also be appropriate.

6. Sartre, *The Imaginary*, 167–68.

7. Ibid., 169.

8. Ibid., 174.

9. Ibid., 175.

10. The argument from the end of the paragraph is resumed in the next draft.

11. Another sequence of writing resumed at page (23).

12. Sartre, *The Imaginary*, 41.

13. See Edmund Husserl, *Ideas Pertaining to a Pure Phenomenology and to a Phenomenological Philosophy, First Book: General Introduction to a Pure Phenomenology*, trans. F. Kersten (The Hague: Martinus Nijhoff, 1983). See also Sartre, *The Imaginary*.

14. *Hylé*, "matter."

15. *Erfüllung*, "fulfillment."

16. Merleau-Ponty: "i.e., the ostensible presence of an 'imaginary world' or a 'state of sleep' is only the absence of the 'real world' or of fulfilled consciousness, at a distance from the object and itself, or of the barrier between self and object, self and self."

[PERCEPTUAL CONSCIOUSNESS AND IMAGINING CONSCIOUSNESS]

1. The seven pages inserted here were obviously composed after the preceding sequence of writing. They constitute a precise summary of the argument against Sartre, and at the same time they announce the reflection on symbolism. They resume the set of arguments from pages [147] (27) to [157] (33).

2. Sartre, *The Imaginary*, 174–75: "or some external stimulus is imposed . . . The second motivation that can bring about the cessation of the dream is always found in the dream itself: it can be, in fact, that the dreamed story ends with an event that is itself given as something final, which is to say as something for which a succeeding event is inconceivable. For example, I often dream that I am about to be guillotined . . . Consciousness hesitates, this hesitation motivates a reflection, and this is the awakening."

3. Merleau-Ponty: "Perception of the child (from his drawing) which is not articulated perception. It is from this same fabric that sleep is made. Show that the vigilant structure of which Sartre speaks is, moreover, not *Deckung*, intention, *Erfüllung*, but openness of 'fields.'" We follow Merleau-Ponty's guidelines, which note in square brackets in the margin on page [208] (3): "transfer the text from page three to here."

4. *Deckung*, "coincidence."

5. Merleau-Ponty, in the margin: "To seek what is false and true in this analysis: the positivity of nothingness; to express it in my language (body)."

6. Merleau-Ponty, in the margin: "My thesis: the waking-sleep structures are structures of the knowing body—not presence to the world and absence to the world, but present-absent."

7. Merleau-Ponty: "The 'consciousness of something' [is] consciousness of a figure-and-ground configuration, even of a fold, of a divergence, not of a signification. Consequently, the oneiric consciousness of something [brings about the result that] fields function emptily. It is not unconsciousness of not having seen; it is field which is no longer inscribed on the world."

8. See p. 154 below.

9. *Sinnendaten*, "sensory data."

10. Merleau-Ponty: "*Imaginings* = types of situations and types of behaviors, favorite formation of the situations and the behaviors."

11. Merleau-Ponty: "But the natural delusion of consciousness is its embodiment, its birth."

12. Merleau-Ponty: "Nothingness, Sartre himself is obliged to fulfill it somewhat with the *analogon*, with the living imaginary as it is in the actor."

[Symbolism]

1. We resume the thread of the draft of the course notes. The seven preceding pages resume the synthetic mode of the argument from pages [147] (27) to [157] (33).

2. Cf. working notes, Merleau-Ponty, *The Visible and the Invisible*, 266 and 270–71.

3. *Erkenntnistheoretisch*, "theoretical knowledge."

4. Merleau-Ponty refers to "Mort du dernier écrivain," *Nouvelle Revue Française*, March 1955. The text can be found in Maurice Blanchot, *The Book to Come*, trans. Charlotte Mandell (Stanford, Calif.: Stanford University Press, 2003), 222–23. We have reproduced this English translation.

5. "*Sinnending* is the *Ding*": "meanings of the thing are the thing."

6. *Auffassung*, "apprehension."

7. See Merleau-Ponty, *Phenomenology of Perception*, 168; and Maurice Merleau-Ponty, "L'enfant vu par l'adulte," in *Merleau-Ponty à la Sorbonne: Resume de cours 1949–1952* (Paris: Cynara, 1988), 95; the reference is to Georges Politzer, *Critique of the Foundations of Psychology: The Psychology of Psychoanalyis*, trans. Maurice Apprey (Pittsburgh: Duquesne University Press, 1994 [1928]).

8. Sigmund Freud, *On Dreams*, in vol. 5 of *The Standard Edition of the Complete Psychological Works of Sigmund Freud*, trans. James Strachey (London: Hogarth Press, 1953), 629–86.

9. Freud, *On Dreams*, 676–77: "We have no reason to disguise the fact that in the hypothesis which we have set up in order to explain the dream-work a part

is played by what might be described as a 'daemonic' element. We have gathered an impression that the formation of obscure dreams occurs *as though* one person who was dependent upon a second person had to make a remark which was bound to be disagreeable in the ears of this second one; and it is on the basis of this simile that we have arrived at the concepts of dream-distortion and censorship, and have endeavoured to translate our impression into a psychological theory which is no doubt crude but is at least lucid. Whatever it may be with which a further investigation of the subject may enable us to identify our first and second agencies, we may safely expect to find a confirmation of some correlate of our hypothesis that the second agency controls access to consciousness and can bar the first agency from such access."

10. Sigmund Freud, *The Interpretation of Dreams*, in vols. 4–5 of *The Standard Edition of the Complete Psychological Works of Sigmund Freud*, trans. James Strachey (London: Hogarth Press, 1953), 5:397–99.

11. See Merleau-Ponty's "Reading Notes on Freud," pp. 221–23 below.

12. Title indicated in the margin by the author.

13. "*Investissement*" may also be rendered in English as "cathexis" and "*contreinvestissement*" as "counter-cathexis."

14. Sigmund Freud, *Delusions and Dreams in Jensen's "Gradiva,"* in vol. 9 of *The Standard Edition of the Complete Psychological Works of Sigmund Freud*, trans. James Strachey (London: Hogarth Press, 1959).

[DREAMS]

1. *Bild*, "image," "picture."
2. Merleau-Ponty: "Cf. Collages."
3. *The Scoundrel*, film by Ben Hecht and Charles MacArthur, 1934.
4. Merleau-Ponty returns to his reading notes on *The Interpretation of Dreams*, which are reproduced in this volume in the "Reading Notes on Freud." The text of Freud's to which Merleau-Ponty refers is this: "[It is true that in carrying out the interpretation in the waking state] we follow a path which leads back from the elements of the dream to the dream-thoughts and that the dream-work followed one in the contrary direction. But it is highly improbable that these paths are passable in both ways. It appears, rather, that in the daytime we drive shafts which follow along fresh chains of thought and that those shafts make contact with the intermediate thoughts and the dream-thoughts now at one point and now at another. We can see how in this manner fresh daytime material inserts itself into the interpretive chains. It is probable, too, that the increase in resistance that has set in since the night makes new and more devious detours necessary" (Freud, *Interpretation of Dreams*, 5:532). The introductory clause in brackets is elided by Merleau-Ponty. The passage quoted here is located in the "Reading Notes on Freud" at p. [22]. Mereleau-Ponty makes similar parenthetical references to various passages in the "Reading Notes on Freud" throughout this chapter, e.g., "(Notes p. [12])." The bracketed page numbers added by the editors

to these references refer to the (Bibliothèque Nationale) page numbers in the "Reading Notes on Freud."

5. Freud, *Interpretation of Dreams*, 5:528–30: "For it is demonstrably untrue that we are being carried along a purposeless stream of ideas when, in the process of interpreting a dream, we abandon reflection and allow involuntary ideas to emerge. It can be shown that all that we can ever get rid of are purposive ideas that are *known* to us; as soon as we have done this, *unknown*—or, as we accurately say, 'unconscious'—purposive ideas take charge and thereafter determine the course of the involuntary ideas. No influence that we can bring to bear upon our mental processes can ever enable us to think without purposive ideas; nor am I aware of any states of psychical confusion which can do so.... *Whenever one psychical element is linked with another by an objectionable or superficial association, there is also a legitimate and deeper link between them which is subjected to the resistance of the censorship.*"

6. Merleau-Ponty: "Cf. condensation is strangeness (notes, p. [27]). Condensation: italics" (*Intepretations of Dreams*).

7. *Gegensinn*, "counter-sense" or "absurdity."

8. Freud, *Interpretation of Dreams*, 5:575–76: "The first portion of the dream-work has already begun during the day, under the control of the preconscious. Its second portion—the modification imposed by the censorship, the attraction exercised by unconscious scenes, and the forcing of its way to perception—no doubt proceeds all through the night; and in this respect we may perhaps always be right when we express a feeling of having been dreaming all night long, though we cannot say what. But it seems to me unnecessary to suppose that dream-processes really maintain, up to the moment of becoming conscious, the chronological order in which I have described them: that the first thing to appear is the transferred dream-wish, that distortion by the censorship follows, then the regressive change in direction, and so on. I have been obliged to adopt this order in my description; but what happens in reality is no doubt a simultaneous exploring of one path and another, a swinging of the excitation now this way and now that, until at last it accumulates in the direction that is most opportune and one particular grouping becomes the permanent one. Certain personal experiences of my own lead me to suspect that the dream-work often requires more than a day and a night in order to achieve its result; and if this is so, we need no longer feel any amazement at the extraordinary ingenuity shown in the construction of the dream.... It is like a firework, which takes hours to prepare but goes off in a moment."

9. See Henri Ey, *Consciousness: A Phenomenological Study of Being Conscious and Becoming Conscious*, trans. John H. Flodstrom (Bloomington: Indiana University Press, 1978).

10. Eugenio d'Ors, "El sueño es vida" (prologue of 1940), in *Jardin Botanico* 2 (Barcelona: Maginales Tuquets Editors, 1982).

11. Merleau-Ponty: "Cf. Lichtenberg, cited by Freud." (The citation is actually that of Freud's colleague Otto Rank, whose "Dreams and Poetry" and "Dreams and Myth" were included at the end of chapter 7 in the fourth through seventh editions of *The Interpretation of Dreams* [see Strachey's "Editor's Introduc-

tion" to the *Standard Edition*, vol. 4, p. xiii]. See Otto Rank, "Dreams and Poetry," in Lydia Marinelli and Andreas Mayer, *Dreaming by the Book: Freud's "The Interpretation of Dreams" and the History of the Psychoanalytic Movement*, trans. Susan Fairfield [New York: Other, 2003], 194). See also "Reading Notes on Freud," p. [19].

12. Merleau-Ponty: "Notes, pp. [10]–[11]."

13. *Lekton*, "spoken" or "signified." *Lekton* is a Stoic term meaning something like a signification which is not bound to its factual event. Merleau-Ponty uses the term in *The Visible and the Invisible*, 88.

14. Freud, *Interpretation of Dreams*, 4:296: "I saw that the monstrosity was composed of the two names 'Nora' and 'Ekdal'—characters in two well-known plays of Ibsen's."

15. "*To violate*" is in English. "Violet" is associated with the English verb "violate" in order to represent rape.

16. Merleau-Ponty: "The dream's *affective* content has remained untouched by the distortion which has overtaken its *ideational* content" (Freud, *Interpretation of Dreams*, 4:249).

17. Freud, *Interpretation of Dreams*, 5:610: "Thus, we may speak of an unconscious thought seeking to convey itself into the preconscious so as to be able then to force its way through into consciousness. What we have in mind here is not the forming of a second thought situated in a new place, like a transcription which continues to exist alongside the original; and the notion of forcing a way through into consciousness must be kept carefully free from any idea of a change of locality. Again, we may speak of a preconscious thought being repressed or driven out and then taken over by the unconscious. These images, derived from a set of ideas relating to a struggle for a piece of ground, may tempt us to suppose that it is literally true that a mental grouping in one locality has been brought to an end and replaced by a fresh one in another locality. Let us replace these metaphors by something that seems to correspond better to the real state of affairs, and let us say instead that some particular mental grouping has had a cathexis of energy attached to it or withdrawn from it, so that the structure in question has come under the sway of a particular agency or been withdrawn from it."

18. Reference to Paul Valéry, who gives the names "implex" and "linguistic animal" to the constitution of a system of capacities from our relationship with the world and others. Merleau-Ponty describes this implex as "mixed" and as a "mongrel which guarantees, on this side of our willing, the connection between what we do and what we will." Maurice Merleau-Ponty, "L'usage litteraire du langage (cours de 1952–53)," in *Résumés de cours: Collège de France 1952–1960* (Paris: Gallimard, 1968), 27.

19. See Stendhal, *Love*, trans. Gilbert Sale and Suzanne Sale (New York: Penguin, 1975).

20. Merleau-Ponty: "This makes truth transcendent to the I think (desiring, thinking is not the thought of desiring [or] of seeing) without our being transformed into objects of an absolute thinker."

21. Sigmund Freud, *Leonardo da Vinci and a Memory of His Childhood*, trans. James Strachey (London: W. W. Norton, 1989).

22. Freud, *Delusions and Dreams*, 109.

23. Freud, *Leonardo da Vinci*, 82–84.

24. See Freud, *Interpretation of Dreams*, 5:614: "The respect paid to dreams in antiquity is, however, based upon correct psychological insight and is the homage paid to the uncontrolled and indestructible forces in the human mind, to the 'daemonic' power which produces the dream-wish and which we find at work in our unconscious."

[THE FREUDIAN UNCONSCIOUS]

1. See "Appendix: Three Notes on the Freudian Unconscious," p. 199.
2. Sigmund Freud, *Fragment of an Analysis of a Case of Hysteria*, in vol. 7 of *The Standard Edition of the Complete Psychological Works of Sigmund Freud*, trans. and ed. James Strachey (London: Hogarth Press, 1957).
3. Freud, *A Case of Hysteria*, 57.
4. Ibid., 57n2.
5. *Wahrnehmungsbereitschaft*, "readiness to perceive."
6. Freud, *A Case of Hysteria*, 69.
7. Max Scheler, "The Idols of Self-Knowledge," in *Selected Philosophical Essays*, trans. David R. Lachterman (Evanston, Ill.: Northwestern University Press, 1973), 73; Merleau-Ponty, *Phenomenology of Perception*, 67.
8. Reproduced in G. Devereux, *Psychoanalysis and the Occult* (New York: International University Press, 1953). Cf. the working note from April 1960 on telepathy and corporeity in Merleau-Ponty, *The Visible and the Invisible*, 244–45.
9. Merleau-Ponty: "And she does not surrender even though she loves him, because of her mindset and her education. It is her first and last passion."
10. Merleau-Ponty, in the margin: "We alter only the philosophical interpretation. Bergson: unconscious, lacuna of consciousness, and lacuna which is not only non-being, emptiness, but operative, active emptiness. Under this emptiness, Freud supposes unconscious thoughts of the same type as our conscious acts. I propose to consider that as *Deutung* in later objective language. Explication in terms of developed past. In the instant, there is only play in our dimensions such as they result from our history. Comparison: experience showing how effort displaces our vertical, so that after pressure of the hand on the heart, it will seek our vertical higher than before. No representation of the objective position or of the new position to reach. Suppression of a divergence, of a difference in direction. Thus Frau B. reacts to K2 as she would to K1. Love for K1 has set a norm or level. There is not a representation of K1, one of K2, and a disguising of the one under the other, but rather their non-differentiation. Schilder's analysis [Paul Schilder, *Das Körperschema* (Berlin: Springer, 1923), cited in Merleau-Ponty, *Phenomenology of Perception*, 77]: there has to be a corporeal schema which gives positions and distances in terms of *I can*. Likewise here a practical schema which establishes or reestablishes these norms by distributing valences to all that is presented. The unconscious means fecundity of the event, a kind of existential eternity: whatever one does, it will be this relation between sense and what was lived, since the lived is generalized in dimensions, cohesion of a life. But all that does

not need to be realized in unconscious thoughts. Yet, is there not a true pressure of the past, return of the repressed—Example: delusion."

11. See "Appendix: Three Notes on the Freudian Unconscious."

[DELUSIONS: GRADIVA]

1. Jensen's novella *Gradiva* was published in 1903, and Freud's essay on it appeared in 1907. Sigmund Freud, *Delusions and Dreams in Jensen's "Gradiva,"* in vol. 9 of *The Standard Edition of the Complete Psychological Works of Sigmund Freud*, trans. James Strachey (London: Hogarth Press, 1959), 1–95.
2. Merleau-Ponty returns to these reading notes on *Gradiva*.
3. In Strachey's English translation, Gradiva means "the girl who steps along." Freud, *Delusions and Dreams*, 11.
4. Freud, *Delusions and Dreams*, 12.
5. Ibid., 65.
6. Ibid., 16.
7. Ibid., 19.
8. Ibid., 20.
9. Ibid., 21.
10. Ibid.
11. Ibid., 22.
12. Ibid., 23.
13. Ibid., 33.
14. Ibid., 34.
15. In this passage, "force" refers to the "*Instanz*" or agency of repression. See "*l'instance*" in *Vocabulaire de la psychanalyse*, by Jean Laplanche and J.-B. Pontalis (Paris: Presses Universitaires de France, 1973), 202–3.
16. Freud, *Delusions and Dreams*, 35.
17. Ibid., 36.
18. Ibid., 35–36.
19. Ibid., 37.
20. Ibid., 39.
21. Ibid., 40.
22. Ibid., 51.
23. Ibid., 60.
24. Ibid., 62.
25. Ibid., 66.
26. Ibid., 67.
27. Ibid.
28. Ibid.
29. Ibid., 74–75.
30. Ibid., 80.
31. Ibid., 81.
32. Ibid., 84.
33. Ibid., 85.

34. Ibid., 88.

35. Ibid., 90.

36. Ibid., 92.

37. This page which is numbered again with 48 starts a new revision which is obviously to be substituted for note A, which was abandoned in the middle of the first sheet numbered 49.

38. Freud, *Delusions and Dreams*, 40.

39. Here and in the discussion that follows, Merleau-Ponty uses "position" in the sense of an act or process rather than a state or condition, particularly as the contrary of negation.

[THE CASE OF DORA]

1. Sigmund Freud, *Fragment of an Analysis of a Case of Hysteria*, in vol. 7 of *The Standard Edition of the Complete Psychological Works of Sigmund Freud*, trans. James Strachey (London: Hogarth Press, 1959), 1–122.

2. Merleau-Ponty refers to his notes on "Dora," which are reproduced in this volume.

3. This section refers in particular to Freud's *Fragment of an Analysis of a Case of Hysteria*, 15–32.

4. Merleau-Ponty: "We will examine neither the problem of hysteria nor the interpretation of the two dreams, but only the signification of the unconscious."

5. The actual title is *Fisiologia dell'amore* (1896). See Paola Mantegazza, *The Physiology of Love and Other Writings*, ed. Nicoletta Pireddu (Toronto: University of Toronto Press, 2007).

6. This section refers to Freud, *A Case of Hysteria*, 32–35.

7. Merleau-Ponty: "Which thus implies love."

8. Freud, *A Case of Hysteria*, 40–41.

9. Ibid., 43.

10. Merleau-Ponty, in the margin: "Give explanation p. (7)."

11. Freud, *A Case of Hysteria*, 47.

12. Ibid., 48.

13. Ibid., 53–54.

14. Ibid., 54.

15. Ibid., 60.

16. See ibid., 61.

17. Ibid., 65. Merleau-Ponty quotes the somewhat abbreviated French translation: "on peut avoir besoin de sortir la nuit."

18. In *A Case of Hysteria*, 65, we find at the bottom of the page this note by Freud: "I laid stress on these words because they took me aback. They seemed to have an ambiguous ring about them. Are not certain physical needs referred to in the same words? Now, in a line of associations ambiguous words (or, as we may call them, "switch-words") act like points at a junction. If the points are switched across from the position in which they appear to lie in the dream, then we find

ourselves on another set of rails; and along this second track run the thoughts which we are in search of but which still lie concealed behind the dream."

19. Ibid., 71: "A regularly formed dream stands, as it were, upon two legs, one of which is in contact with the main and current existing cause, and the other with some momentous event in the years of childhood."

20. Ibid., 77–78.

21. Ibid., 73n1.

22. Ibid., 83.

23. Ibid., 84–85.

24. Here Merleau-Ponty's notes skip to another part of Freud's text. See *A Case of Hysteria*, 105ff.

25. Merleau-Ponty [244]: "Freud, Dora = 'the symptoms of the disease are . . . the patient's sexual activity' (Freud, *A Case of Hysteria*, 115).

"Must we say sexual activity? As if 'normal' sexual activity was suppressed and transformed into a disease? This 'causality' is in reality obtained by probable reasoning: what would happen if the patient had had 'normal' sexual activity? He would not have been diseased (Max Weber). But this reasoning is perhaps fallacious since precisely his sexual activity, in advance, was not 'normal,' and since, for his sexual activity to have been normal, it must have been necessary that he is not himself. Causality, properly speaking, is only in play when atypical sexual activity dominates, totally explains the whole of life, i.e., reaches a vital impasse.

"Causality is the limit-case that we obtain when sublimation is absolutely lacking and the dialectic is reduced to 'dialectical mechanics,' perpetual reappearance of the same problem, powerlessness to live.

"That being the case, what 'sexual activity' means in this sentence of Freud's is that the disease, the relationship with oneself and others, are incontestably 'eroticized.' We sense in them (to a lesser degree than in the 'normal') that the vital dialectic is weighty, that it stirs up blocks of the past, of embodiment—that life is neither immanent nor pure." (Cf. Maurice Merleau-Ponty, "The Body in Its Sexual Being," in *Phenomenology of Perception*, 178–201.)

26. Freud, *A Case of Hysteria*, 116.

27. Ibid., 61.

28. Ibid., 60.

29. Ibid., 83.

30. This refers to an analysis of Freud's in which he links his failure to recall the name of the Italian painter "Signorelli" to the repression of thoughts about death and sexuality. See "Appendix: Three Notes on the Freudian Unconscious."

31. Merleau-Ponty: "Not subtlety, but generality and regional participations under alogical essences."

32. Merleau-Ponty: "'Transferring' itself because the father's love was already something other than itself."

33. See p. 180 above.

34. Merleau-Ponty: "In the case of hysteria, one has, it is true, a particular somatic compliance, i.e., expression through the particularly energetic and active body."

35. Merleau-Ponty: "And the proof that this dialectic does not have for its unique sense the dialectic of somatic sexuality is that the objective fulfillment of the latter does not necessarily cause the sexualization of life to stop: it must be a true fulfillment, which has effective, spiritual conditions. Thus, true formula: not objective body first, not consciousness first, but their nexus—Thus, no measurement of the sense by 'objective' sexuality."

36. Merleau-Ponty: "More precisely, by other motives. Where there is ambiguity, there can be neither determinism nor ex nihilo and 'free' choice."

37. Merleau-Ponty: "After the falling-out, Dora is by no means insensitive: new attack when Mr. K. is nearly run over before her eyes."

38. Merleau-Ponty: "The 'choice' is an appearance from the outside, summary, abridged from a becoming where there is more than the choice."

39. Merleau-Ponty: "All preserved in that which is adopted."

40. Freud, *A Case of Hysteria*, 66–67.

41. Merleau-Ponty, in the margin: "symbolism—sexuality."

42. Merleau-Ponty, in the margin: "symbolism, conscious and unconscious."

43. Freud, *A Case of Hysteria*, 69.

44. Ibid.

45. Merleau-Ponty, in the margin: "One needs a second *I think* only if one ignores the historical-carnal relation to the world."

46. Freud, *A Case of Hysteria*, 69.

47. *Leistung,* "achievement."

48. Citation omitted: Freud, *A Case of Hysteria*, 70.

49. Merleau-Ponty, in the margin: "generality (cf. Signorelli)."

50. Moreno, *Psychodrama*, vol. 1. See Merleau-Ponty, *Merleau-Ponty à la Sorbonne*, 155ff.

51. Merleau-Ponty, in the margin: "The unconscious: excess of the perceptual over the notional."

52. Freud, *A Case of Hysteria*, 71.

53. Ibid., 83.

54. Ibid. Merleau-Ponty, in the margin: "System."

55. Ibid., 95.

56. Ibid., 96. Merleau-Ponty, in the margin: "K. doubling, blurring and not dissimulation."

57. Ibid. Merleau-Ponty, in the margin: "I would say doubles rather than substitutes."

58. Ibid., 97–98.

[THE PROBLEM OF MEMORY]

1. Page [193] (56) is crossed out.

2. Max Wertheimer, *Experimentelle Studien über das Sehen von Bewegung* Leipzig: J. A. Barth, 1912; see Merleau-Ponty, *Phenomenology of Perception*, 289: "If we so contrive it that a subject sees the room in which he is only through a mir-

ror which reflects it at an angle at 45° to the vertical, the subject at first sees the room 'slantwise'. . . . After a few minutes a sudden change occurs . . ." [the vertical is reestablished].

3. *Nacheinander der Jetztpunkte*, "series of nows," expression borrowed from Heidegger to qualify the commonsense view. Cf. Merleau-Ponty, *Phenomenology of Perception*, 479.

4. *Vorstellung*, "representation."

5. "*Noli me tangere*," "do not touch me."

6. Merleau-Ponty: "Notes, p. 2." (Merleau-Ponty is referring to the "Reading Notes on Proust," p. [239].)

7. *Erinnerung*, "recollection."

8. Marcel Proust, *Swann's Way*, in vol. 1 of *Remembrance of Things Past*, trans. C. K. Scott Moncrieff and Terence Kilmartin, 3 vols. (New York: Random House, 1981), 5: "When a man is asleep, he has in a circle around him the chain of the hours, the sequence of the years, the order of the heavenly host. Instinctively, when he awakes, he looks to these, and in an instant reads off his own position on the earth's surface and the time that has elapsed during his slumbers; but this order of procession is apt to grow confused, and to break its ranks." (See the "Reading Notes on Proust," p. [239].)

9. Proust, *Swann's Way*, 1:6 ("Reading Notes on Proust," p. [240]).

10. Proust, *Swann's Way*, 1:5 ("Reading Notes on Proust," p. [239]).

11. Marcel Proust, *Within a Budding Grove*, in vol. 1 of *Remembrance of Things Past*, 879 ("Reading Notes on Proust," p. [242]).

12. Merleau-Ponty: "It is not a clock and does not count objective simultaneities: it counts coexistence."

13. *Einmalig*, "singular," "unique."

14. Proust, *Swann's Way*, 1:4 ("Reading Notes on Proust," p. [240]).

15. Marcel Proust, *The Guermantes Way*, in vol. 2 of *Remembrance of Things Past*, 86 ("Reading Notes on Proust," p. [242]).

16. P. Claudel, *Poetic Art*, trans. Renee Spodheim (New York: Philosophical Library, 1948), 4. Cf. Merleau-Ponty, *The Visible and the Invisible*, 103–4 and 121.

17. *Selbstgegebenheit*, "self-givenness."

18. Proust, *Within a Budding Grove*, 1:692 ("Reading Notes on Proust," p. [238]).

19. Proust, *Within a Budding Grove*, 1:692 ("Reading Notes on Proust," p. [238]).

20. Proust, *Swann's Way*, 1:201 ("Cf. Reading Notes on Proust," p. [238]).

21. Next year's course is called "Dialectical Philosophy."

[APPENDIX: THREE NOTES ON THE FREUDIAN UNCONSCIOUS]

1. Sigmund Freud, *Psychopathology of Everyday Life*, in vol. 11 of *The Standard Edition of the Complete Psychological Works of Sigmund Freud*, trans. James Strachey (London: Hogarth Press, 1960), chapter 1.

2. Merleau-Ponty: "Cf. problem of the hallucination of amputees and con-

versely of the anesthetized hysteric—It is not solely a matter of a disassociated consciousness or, on the contrary, of a subsistence of the total consciousness despite subtraction of the 'contents.'"

3. Merleau-Ponty: "And which delimit a historico-existential position."
4. Husserl, *Ideas I*.
5. *Überschau*, "overlook."
6. See p. 173 above, on *Gradiva*.
7. Merleau-Ponty, in the margin: "Describe the functioning of the perceptions which trigger the delusion in *Gradiva*."
8. Devereux, *Psychoanalysis and the Occult*, 53. This quote is in English, and so is the following quotation.
9. Merleau-Ponty: "Cf. When I have endopsychic perception of others, I have endopsychic perception of my past and of myself, and it is a witness for me of myself."
10. Merleau-Ponty: "Cf. ultimately creation or constitution."
11. See G. W. F. Hegel, "Sense-Certainty," in *Phenomenology of Spirit*, trans. A. V. Miller (Oxford: Oxford University Press, 1977), 58–66.

[READING NOTES ON PROUST]

1. The brackets and parentheses that one will find in the body of the text are those of Merleau-Ponty. They generally enclose his commentaries.
2. As in the *Institution* lectures, Merleau-Ponty cites the "Collection blanche" version of a *À la recherche du temps perdu*, which was published in 1926.
3. The break in the text refers to the omission of quotes from Proust which Merleau-Ponty has reproduced.
4. Proust, *Swann's Way*, 1:462.
5. Ibid., 201.
6. Proust, *Within a Budding Grove*, 1:692.
7. Ibid.
8. Ibid.
9. In Merleau-Ponty's notes, this quotation runs for another page, through [241] (4), ending with, "But . . . my memory had been set in motion; as a rule I did not attempt to go to sleep again at once, but used to spend the greater part of the night recalling our life in the old days." Proust, *Swann's Way*, 1:5–7.
10. "Flash back" appears in English in the original.
11. Proust, *The Guermantes Way*, 2:86.
12. Ibid., 2:89.
13. Proust, *Time Regained*, in vol. 3 of *Remembrance of Things Past*, 716.
14. Proust, *The Guermantes Way*, 2:85.
15. Proust, *Within a Budding Grove*, 1:879.
16. In the margin, Merleau-Ponty writes: "We can show (Piaget) that time is very incomplete before having been measured—But what would we measure, what would time be, if there were not first a perceptual intuition of time?"
17. Proust, *Time Regained*, 3:903.

[READING NOTES ON FREUD]

1. The citations below replace Merleau-Ponty's in-text citations and footnotes to *La science des rêves*. All citations are to Sigmund Freud, *The Interpretation of Dreams*, trans. James Strachey, in vols. 4 and 5 of *The Standard Edition of the Complete Psychological Works of Sigmund Freud* (London: Hogarth Press, 1953).
2. Freud, *Interpretation of Dreams*, 4:181.
3. Ibid., 4:182–83.
4. Ibid., 4:183–85.
5. Ibid., 4:184.
6. Ibid., 4:183.
7. Ibid., 4:190.
8. Ibid., 4:192. Merleau-Ponty: "Name of a café."
9. Ibid., 4:193.
10. Ibid., 4:194n1.
11. Ibid., 4:193–98.
12. Ibid., 4:219.
13. Ibid., 4:248–49.
14. Ibid., 4:254.
15. Ibid., 4:254n1.
16. Ibid., 4:257.
17. Ibid., 4:260.
18. Ibid., 4:266.
19. Ibid., 4:278.
20. Ibid., 4:277–78.
21. Ibid., 4:277.
22. Ibid., 4:279.
23. Ibid., 4:280.
24. Ibid., 4:283.
25. Ibid., 4:295–96. Here Strachey's English translation deviates significantly from the French translation cited by Merleau-Ponty, according to which the words featured in dreams "are subject to the same compositions, displacements, substitutions, and condensations as the images of objects [*sont sujets aux mêmes compositions, déplacements, substitutions et condensations que les images d'objets*]." See Sigmund Freud, *La science des rêves*, trans. Ignace Meyerson (Paris: Alcan, 1926), 222.
26. Freud, *Interpretation of Dreams*, 4: 296.
27. Ibid., 4:304.
28. Ibid., 4:305.
29. Ibid., 4:312. Here again, the English translation differs from the French, which reads, "nearly always a thought clearly aimed in a direction close to a thought with the opposite meaning [*presque toujours une pensée nettement dirigée dans un sens a près d'elle une pensée de sens opposé*]." Freud, *La science des rêves*, 232.
30. Freud, *Interpretation of Dreams*, 4:312. The phrase in brackets has been moved from its position at the end of the sentence in the English translation, which is a transposition of the French, in an effort to reproduce Merleau-Ponty's notes more exactly.

31. Ibid.
32. Ibid.
33. Ibid., 4:313.
34. Ibid., 4:313–14.
35. Ibid., 4:314–15. Cf. 347–48.
36. Ibid., 4:318–19.
37. Ibid., 4:321.
38. Ibid., 4:322.
39. Ibid., 4:325.
40. Ibid., 4:326.
41. Ibid., 4:331.
42. Ibid.
43. Ibid., 4:337. The French translation reads: "Not to succeed in doing what one wills [*Ne pas arriver à faire ce que l'on veut*] . . ." Freud, *La science des rêves*, 251.
44. Freud, *Interpretation of Dreams*, 5:342.
45. Ibid., 5:343.
46. Ibid., 5:346.
47. Ibid., 5:349.
48. Ibid., 5:353.
49. Ibid., 5:396.
50. Ibid.
51. Ibid., 5:397.
52. Ibid., 5:398.
53. Ibid., 5:398n1.
54. Ibid., 5:408.
55. Ibid.
56. Ibid., 5:415–16.
57. Ibid., 5:418.
58. Ibid.
59. Ibid., 5:419.
60. Ibid., 5:429.
61. Ibid., 5:434.
62. Ibid., 5:435n1.
63. Ibid., 5:438.
64. Ibid., 5:460. The French translation reads: "The representative contents [*Les contenus représentatifs*] . . ." Freud, *La science des rêves*, 342.
65. Freud, *Interpretation of Dreams*, 5:468.
66. Ibid., 5:475–76.
67. Ibid., 5:480.
68. Ibid., 5:483. "*Revenants*" is in French in Freud; the term means "ghosts."
69. Ibid., 5:486.
70. Ibid., 5:496. In the English translation, the full sentence reads: "Is it highly improbable that Maury's dream represents a phantasy which had been stored up ready-made in his memory for many years and which was aroused—or

I would rather say 'alluded to'—at the moment at which he became aware of the stimulus which woke him?"

71. Ibid., 5:500.

72. Ibid., 5:504. Freud is quoting from Herbert Silberer, "Bericht über eine Methode, gewisse symbolische Halluzinations-Erscheinungen hervorzurufen und zu beobachten," *Jahrbuch für psychoanalytische und psychopathologische Forschungen*, 1 (1909): 513.

73. Freud, *Interpretation of Dreams*, 507.

74. Quoted in Rank, "Dreams and Poetry," 194. Freud inserted Rank's essay in the fourth edition of *The Interpretation of Dreams* between chapters 6 and 7, and he removed it from the seventh edition. Consequently, the essay was included in the 1950 reprint of *La science des rêves* used here by Merleau-Ponty, but it does not appear in the *Standard Edition* of Freud's works.

75. Rank, "Dreams and Poetry," 200–201.

76. Otto Rank, "Dreams and Myth," in Marinelli and Mayer, *Dreaming by the Book*, 220.

77. Freud, *Interpretation of Dreams*, 5:521–22.

78. Ibid. 5:523.

79. Ibid., 5:525.

80. Ibid., 5:526–27.

81. Ibid., 5:528–30.

82. Ibid., 5:531–32.

83. Ibid., 5:532.

84. Ibid., 5:536. Shortly before this passage, Freud cites G. T. Fechner, *Elements der Psychophysik*, vol. 2 (Leipzig: Breitkopf und Härtel, 1860 [1889]), 520–21.

85. Freud, *Interpretation of Dreams*, 5:537.

86. Ibid., 5:542.

87. Ibid., 5:543.

88. Ibid., 5:544.

89. Ibid., 5:545–46. The passage referred to by Merleau-Ponty reads: "We must not overlook the influence of memories, mostly from childhood, which have been suppressed or have remained unconscious. The thoughts which are connected with a memory of this kind and which are forbidden expression by the censorship are, as it were, attracted by the memory into regression as being the form of representation in which the memory itself is couched."

90. Ibid., 5:546.

91. Ibid., 5:548.

92. Ibid., 5:553n1.

93. Ibid., 5:553.

94. Ibid.

95. Ibid., 5:553n1.

96. Ibid., 5:561.

97. Ibid., 5:566.

98. Merleau-Ponty: "Cf. Vomiting spells, which signify a desire to be preg-

nant and at the same time self-punishment, since they risk causing the sufferer to lose her physical beauty."

99. Freud, *Interpretation of Dreams*, 5:569.
100. Ibid.
101. Ibid., 5:571.
102. Ibid., 5:574.
103. Ibid., 5:575–76.
104. Ibid., 5:577.
105. Ibid., 5:578.
106. Ibid.
107. Ibid., 5:584–85.
108. Merleau-Ponty: "Freud writes: 'Sensations of falling, . . . or floating, or being inhibited . . . provide a material which is accessible at any time and of which the dream-work makes use, whenever it has need of it, for expressing the dream-thoughts.'" Freud, *Interpretation of Dreams*, 5:590.
109. Freud, *Interpretation of Dreams*, 5:595.
110. Ibid., 5:598.
111. Ibid., 5:598.
112. Ibid., 5:599.
113. Ibid., 5:602–3.
114. Ibid., 5:610.
115. Ibid.
116. Ibid., 5:614. According to the French translation, the ancients "rightly foresee the importance of what the human soul guards of the uncontrolled and the indestructible."
117. Ibid., 5:621.
118. Ibid., 5:621.

Bibliography of Texts Relevant to the Courses on Institution and Passivity

Alquié, Ferdinand. *La découverte métaphysique de l'homme chez Descartes.* Paris: Presses Universitaires de France, 1950, reissued in 1989.
Beauvoir, Simone de. *The Second Sex.* Translated by H. M. Parshley. New York: Knopf, 1952.
Bergson, Henri. *The Creative Mind.* Translated by Mabelle L. Andison. New York: Citadel, 1992.
———. *Time and Free Will.* Translated by F. L. Pogson. New York: Harper and Row, 1960.
Blanchot, Maurice. "The Death of the Last Writer." In *The Book to Come.* Translated by Charlotte Mandel. Stanford, Calif.: Stanford University Press, 2003.
Braudel, Fernand. *The Mediterranean and the Mediterranean World in the Age of Philip II.* Translated by Siân Reynolds. 2 vols. New York: Harper and Row, 1966.
Claudel, Paul. *Poetic Art.* Translated by Renee Spodheim. New York: Philosophical Library, 1948.
———. *The Satin Slipper.* Translated by John O'Connor. New York: Sheed and Ward, 1945.
Descartes, René. *The Philosophical Works of Descartes.* Translated by Elizabeth S. Haldane and G. R. T. Ross. 2 vols. New York: Dover, 1955.
Devereux, George. *Psychoanalysis and the Occult.* New York: International University Press, 1953.
Ey, Henri. *Études psychiatriques,* vol. 1. Paris: Desclée de Brouwer, 1948.
Febvre, Lucian. *The Problem of Unbelief in the Sixteenth Century: The Religion of Rabelais.* Translated by Beatrice Gottlieb. Cambridge, Mass.: Harvard University Press, 1982; orig. pub. 1942.
Francastel, Pierre. *Peinture et société.* Lyon: Audin, 1951.
Freud, Sigmund. "The Passing of the Oedipus Complex." In the *International Journal of Psycho-Analysis,* 5 (1924): 419–24.
———. *The Standard Edition of the Complete Psychological Works of Sigmund Freud.* Translated under the general editorship of James Strachey, in collaboration with Anna Freud, assisted by Alix Strachey and Alan Tyson. 24 vols. London: Hogarth Press, 1953–74.
Friedmann, Georges. *De la Sainte Russie à l'USSR.* Paris: Gallimard, 1938.

Guérin, Daniel. *Class Struggle in the First French Republic.* Translated by Ian Patterson. London: Pluto, 1977; orig. pub. 1946.
Guerry, Liliane. *Cézanne et l'expression de l'espace.* Paris: Flammarion, 1950.
Husserl, Edmund. *The Crisis of European Sciences and Transcendental Phenomenology.* Translated by David Carr. Evanston, Ill.: Northwestern University Press, 1970.
———. *Ideas Pertaining to a Pure Phenomenology and to a Phenomenological Philosophy, Second Book.* Translated by Richard Rojcewicz and André Schuwer. Dordrecht: Kluwer, 1989.
———. *The Phenomenology of Internal Time-Consciousness.* Translated by James Churchill. Bloomington: Indiana University Press, 1964.
Kant, Immanuel. *The Critique of Pure Reason.* Translated by Norman Kemp Smith. New York: St. Martin's, 1965.
Lachièze-Rey, Pierre. *Le moi, le monde, et Dieu.* Paris: Boivin, 1938.
———. *L'idealisme kantien.* Paris: Alcan, 1932.
———. "Réflexions sur l'activité spirituelle constituante." In *Recherches philosophiques, 1933–1934.* Paris: Boivin, 1934.
Lagache, Daniel. *The Works of Daniel Lagache: Selected Papers.* Translated by Elisabeth Holder. London: Karnac Books, 1993.
Lévi-Strauss, Claude. "Diogène couché." *Les Temps Modernes,* March 1955, 1187–1220.
———. *The Elementary Structures of Kinship.* Translated by James Harle Bell and John Richard von Sturmer, with Rodney Needham, editor. Boston: Beacon, 1969.
———. "Race and History." In *Structural Anthropology,* vol. 2. Translated by Monique Layton. Chicago: University of Chicago Press, 1976.
Moreno, Jacob Levy. *Psychodrama,* vol. 1. New York: Beacon House, 1932.
Ors, Eugenio d'. "El sueño es vida" (prologue from 1940), in *Jardin Botanico* 2. Barcelona: Maginales Tuquets Editors, 1982.
Panofsky, Erwin. *Perspective as Symbolic Form.* Translated by Christopher S. Wood. New York: Urzone, 1991.
Politizier, Georges. *Critique of the Foundations of Psychology.* Translated by Maurice Apprey. Pittsburgh: Duquesne University Press, 1994.
Proust, Marcel. *Remembrance of Things Past.* Translated by C. K. Scott Moncrieff and Terence Kilmartin. 3 vols. New York: Random House, 1981.
Ruyer, Raymond. *Éléments de psycho-biologie.* Paris: Presses Universitaires de France, 1946.
———. "Les conceptions nouvelles de l'instinct." *Les Temps Modernes,* November 1953, 824–60.
Sartre, Jean-Paul. *The Imaginary.* Translated by Jonathan Webber. London: Routledge, 2004.
Scheler, Max. *Selected Philosophical Essays.* Translated by David R. Lachterman. Evanston, Ill.: Northwestern University Press, 1973.
Schilder, Paul. *Das Körperschema.* Berlin: Springer, 1923.
———. *The Image and Appearance of the Human Body.* New York: International Universities Press, 1950.

BIBLIOGRAPHY OF TEXTS RELEVANT TO THE COURSES ON
INSTITUTION AND PASSIVITY

Valéry, Paul. *The Collected Works of Paul Valéry*. 15 vols. Princeton: Princeton University Press, 1956.
Weber, Max. *The Protestant Ethic and the "Spirit" of Capitalism*. New York: Penguin Classics, 2002.
Wertheimer, Max. *Experimentelle Studien über das Sehen von Bewegung*. Leipzig: J. A. Barth, 1912.
———. *Productive Thinking*. New York: Harper and Row, 1959.

Texts by Maurice Merleau-Ponty Relevant to the *Passivity* Course

Adventures of the Dialectic. Translated by Joseph Bien. Evanston, Ill.: Northwestern University Press, 1973.
Consciousness and the Acquisition of Language. Translated by Hugh J. Silverman. Evanston, Ill.: Northwestern University Press, 1973.
Husserl at the Limits of Phenomenology. Translated by Leonard Lawlor with Bettina Bergo. Evanston, Ill.: Northwestern University Press, 2002.
In Praise of Philosophy and Other Essays. Translated by John Wild, James M. Edie, and John O'Neill. Evanston, Ill.: Northwestern University Press, 1988. This volume contains the summaries of Merleau-Ponty's courses at the Collège de France.
Nature: Course Notes from the Collège de France. Translated by Robert Vallier. Evanston, Ill.: Northwestern University Press, 2003.
Phenomenology of Perception. Translated by Colin Smith, translation revised by Forrest Williams. London: Routledge and Kegan Paul, 1981.
The Primacy of Perception. Edited by James M. Edie. Evanston, Ill.: Northwestern University Press, 1964.
The Prose of the World. Translated by John O'Neill. Evanston, Ill.: Northwestern University Press, 1973.
Signs. Translated by Richard C. McCleary. Evanston, Ill.: Northwestern University Press, 1964.
Themes from the Lectures at the Collège de France, 1952–1960. Translated by John O'Neill. Evanston, Ill.: Northwestern University Press, 1970.
The Visible and the Invisible. Translated by Alphonso Lingis. Evanston, Ill.: Northwestern University Press, 1968.

Index

above-bodies (*Übereinander*), 95n. *See also* Übereinander
Abschattungen (profiles), 5, 80n2, 130, 133, 136, 148, 235n42. *See also* adumbrations, profiles
absence, 130, 133, 155, 176, 193, 195; and consciousness, 132, 143, 146; and Febvre, 106n25; and field, xxii, xxv, 158; and Freud, 20, 179; and love, 33, 35, 37, 39; and Proust, 29–30, 33–35, 37, 39, 89n8; and sexuality, 156; and world, 131–32, 146, 148, 151, 158, 165, 207, 237n16, 238n6
absurd, xxiv, 26, 89n7, 124, 126, 154, 158, 199, 225
absurdity (*Gegensinn*), 69, 174, 225, 240n7. *See also Gegensinn*
achievement (*Leistung*), 21, 64, 246n47. *See also Leistung*
activism: and passivism, xx, 119; and Sartre, 150
activity, 18, 234n22; and institution, xix, 6–7, 76, 201; and passivity, ix, xxii–xxiii, 7, 117, 121, 124, 136, 142, 144–45, 161, 176, 188, 192, 208, 233n4; and sexuality, 142, 182, 188, 245n25; and signification, 5, 121; and *Sinngebung*, 122, 188; and sleep, 142, 144–45, 148, 228; and the symbolic, 7, 121, 188, 202
adumbrations (*Abschattungen*), 235n42. *See also Abschattungen*, profiles
advent, xiii, xv, 6, 13, 22
adventure, 13, 79, 119, 134, 189; in *Adventures of the Dialectic*, xiii, 80n11, 82n34, 233n3, 233n7, 234n12, 234n19; as adventurous, xxix; quasi-, 118; spirit of, 69–70
aesthetic, 46, 51, 135

aggregative space (*Aggregatraum*), 45, 96n11–12. *See also Aggregatraum*
Aggregatraum (aggregative space), 43, 96n11. *See also* aggregative space
Alberti, Leon Battista, 44, 98n25
aletheia (unconcealment), 118, 135, 137, 234n9. *See also* unconcealment
Algeria, 87
Alquié, Ferdinand, xxi, 122–23, 234n21
alterity, xx, 34, 36, 65, 68
analogon, 142, 148–49. *See also* analogue, analogy
analogue, 97n20, 201, 238n12. *See also Analogon*, analogy
analogy, 132, 237n5. *See also Analogon*, analogue
analysand, 118, 162. *See also* analysis, analyst
analysis, 5, 42, 51, 74, 98n27, 119, 130, 132, 160, 188, 193, 217, 238n5, 242n10; and behavior, xxix, 87n25, 208; and dream, 153, 161, 220–21, 231; and Febvre, 106n25; and Freud, 118, 161, 169, 187, 203, 208, 216, 220–21, 225, 242n2, 244n1, 244n3, 245n30; and Heidegger, 248n2; and language, xvi; and memory, 191, 203; and Merleau-Ponty, xvi, xxiv, 80n11; and perception, 133; and Proust, xxix, 33, 38, 77; and Ruyer, xxi, 87n25, 235n27; and structural (Lévi-Strauss), 108n38, 111n47; and symbolism, 150; and thought, xvi; and world, xxi, 124. *See also* analysand, analyst
analyst, xx, xxvii, 118, 162, 178, 189, 208, 216, 217. *See also* analysand, analysis
animal: and behavior, xi, 18–19, 84n2, 85n17; as human, 18–20, 22, 54, 84n6,

257

148, 196, 212; and implex, 47, 159, 241n18; and impregnation, xi, 9, 77; and imprint, 9, 84n1; and institution, 9, 18–19, 52–54, 77; and life, 16; and Lorenz, xi; and Pavlov, 139; and stimuli, 86n18. *See also* animality
animality, xi, 16, 17, 18, 19, 20, 52, 77, 84. *See also* animal
an sich (in-itself), 125, 235n28. *See also* in-itself
anxiety, 23–24, 30–32, 36–37, 90n11, 91n21, 125, 149, 173, 224
appearance, xv, xxix, xxxiv, 18, 21, 36, 48, 54, 64, 71, 96, 98, 101n28, 111n48, 112n50, 119, 130, 159, 167–70, 175–76, 181, 199, 201, 203, 208, 223, 246n38, 254; as dis-, 10, 171; as re-, 203–4, 245
apprehension (*Auffassung*), 164, 210, 238n6. *See also Auffassung*
apprehension as (*Auffassung als*), xvii, xxvi, 61, 80n1, 140–41, 144, 148. *See also Auffassung als*
Aristotelianism, 123, 130
arithmetic, xvii, 55, 62; as arithmetical, 12, 52, 55; as arithmetization, 102. *See also* geometry, mathematics
art, xv, 39–43, 52, 78, 95n10, 96n15, 97n19–20, 98n26, 99n32, 142, 173, 222, 247n16
artist, 22, 40, 42, 86n24, 96n15, 106n26, 136, 222
Auffassung (apprehension), 153, 238n6. *See also* apprehension
Auffassung als (apprehension as), 5, 61, 80n1. *See also* apprehension as
Aufhebung (sublation), 26. *See also* overcoming, sublation, surpassing

Babinski, Joseph, 138
bad faith, xxvii, 29, 119, 135, 145–47, 153, 207
Bancroft, Sir J., 87n25
Bedeutungsinhalt (content of meaning), 45, 95n3, 98n31. *See also* content of meaning
behavior (*Verhalten*): and animal, xi, 18–19, 84n2, 87n25; as creative, 84n9; in Freud, 164, 177, 208, 216; as human, 19, 124; and institution, 22, 28; and organization, 16–17, 84n10; and perception, xxi, 124, 136; in Ruyer, 84n9–85n11, 85n13, 85n17, 87n25; in Sartre, 143, 147, 218; and signification, xxix, 208; as sleep, 136, 147; and *Stiftung*, 19; and structure, 85n11, 123; in *The Structure of Behavior*, xxiv, 236n1; and time, xvii, 77, 216; types of (*Imaginings*), xxvi, 238n10; and *Verhalten*, 235n43. *See also Verhalten*
being (*Sein*), xxi–xxii, 8, 61, 79, 87n24, 108n34, 122, 125, 158, 192, 215; absolute, 235n45; *as*, 140; atom of, 144; in Bergson, 242n10; of the body, 161, 186, 194; in "The Body as Sexual Being," 245n25; and consciousness, 6, 117, 125, 131, 146, 159, 207; in Descartes, 5, 136; in the dream, 207, 227; as essence, 103n6; and event, x; and expression, 156; in Ey's *A Phenomenological Study of Being Conscious and Becoming Conscious*, 193; for, 60–61; for-itself, 60, 125, 127, 184, 235n29; in Freud, xxiv; genus of, xix–xx, xxix, 8, 206; ground of, 143; in Hegel, 59, 103n6; in Heidegger's *Being and Time*, 234n9; human, xi, 227; in Husserl, 6; in-itself, 122, 125, 130; in-the-world, 140, 143, 165, 175, 186, 188, 191–92, 194, 196, 199, 201, 208; and institution, xv, 8; in Kant, 102n2, 126; and knowledge, xxi, 124, 128; in Malraux, 80n7; mathematical, 56; mythical, 125; natural, 122, 128, 130; non–, 5, 7–8, 136, 142, 161, 187–88, 193–94, 212, 242n10; and nothingness, xxiv, 130–31, 143–44, 146, 157, 193, 195; objective, 123, 126, 128; and oneirism, 154; and ontology, 122, 125, 128; order of, 129; and other, 126, 194; and perception, xxi, 55, 123–30, 146, 235n24; positive, 34; presumptive, 102n2; psychical, 122, 128; in Sartre, xxiv, 195; sexual, xxiv, 74, 90n12; social, 71; spoken, 55; and thought, 73; and time, ix–x, xxii, 103n6; trace of, 144; in Valéry, xxii. *See also* essence, ontology
Benedict XIV, 66
Bergson, Henri, 17, 54, 72, 75, 126, 242n10; and *The Creative Mind*, 101n3; and *Time and Free Will*, 80n13, 88n37

INDEX

Bérulle, Pierre de, 105n15
Besetzung (cathexis), 87n30. *See also* cathexis, *Investissement,* investment
Bewußtsein überhaupt (consciousness in general), 128, 235n33. *See also* consciousness
Bild (image), 156, 239n1. *See also* image, picture
Bildebene (picture plane), 44–45, 98n28. *See also* picture plane
birth, xx, 8, 18, 29, 106n21, 129, 206; and embodiment, 238n11; and institution, xix, 8–9; as love, 9–10, 33, 38; re-, 33, 38, 132–33, 217; in Sartre, 150; of sense, 133; and sleep, 132, 150, 217; in Valéry, xxii
Blanchot, Maurice, 154; and *The Book to Come*, 238n4; and "Death of the Last Writer," 151; and monologue, xxv, 151
Bocage, Madame du, 66
bodily given (*Leibhaftgegeben*), 235n39. *See also Leibhaftgegeben*
body, 10, 19, 194; active, 148, 245n34; adult, 200; animal, 54; in "The Body in Its Sexual Being," xxiv, 245n25; child's, 21; in Claudel, 196; and constitution, 8, 128, 132; de-differentiated, 148, 206; and desire, 30; expression of, 48, 238n5; and field, 123, 148–50, 214; in Freud, 139, 150, 161, 179–81, 185–89, 224; generality of the, 96n14, 199; of gestures, 5, 10, 199–200; as Geulinx's *corpus generaliter sumptum*, 96n14; as hinge, 131, 134; and I-can, xxv, 148–49, 187, 195, 201; ideal, 100n38, 123; and *imaginings,* 150; as implex, 201; and institution, 8, 10, 24, 30; in Kant, 123; in Lachièze-Rey, xxi, 123, 126; in Leibniz, 214, 236n6; living, 147, 150; love of the, 30, 33, 37, 185; as mediator, 123, 186; memory of, 201, 211–12; and movement, 120, 169, 176, 201; as natural, xxi, 124, 200; non-, 95n8, 96n14; objective, 122, 138–39, 150, 224, 246n35; the other's, 30, 188, 193; and painting, 157; and passivity, xx, 131, 135; perceiving, 127–28, 148–49, 158, 169, 175, 186, 195–96, 199, 201, 214, 235n24; as phenomenal, xxi, 122–23, 126–27; primitive, 139; in

Proust, 30, 33, 37, 39, 91n20, 92n38, 132, 195–96, 201, 209–14; and puberty, 22, 24; in Ruyer, 126; in Sartre, 147–49, 187–88; *schedule* of the, 21; in Schilder, 176, 195; sexual, 185–86, 246n35; and signification, 126–27, 185, 195, 200; and sleep, 124, 132, 135, 138–39, 147–50, 188, 196, 206, 211–13, 238n6; social, 193; and soul, 39, 105n17, 122; and space, 97n21, 100n38, 148, 150, 185–87, 196, 209, 213–14; spectacle, 148, 193; of the State, 12; structuration of, 169; survey, 201; and time, 195–96, 201, 209, 211, 213–14; in Valéry, xxii; and world, xxv, 123, 125, 148–50, 158, 175, 187–88, 195, 199, 201, 206, 238n6
bourgeoisie, 7, 13, 26, 83
Braudel, Fernand, 104n2
Brunschvicg, Léon, 53, 129, 235n34

Caillois, Roger, 104n4
Calderón de la Barca, Pedro, 157
Calvin, John, 65, 104n9
Calvinist, 106n23
capitalism, xiii, xvii, 13, 82n34, 83
Cardinal Domenico Silvio Passionei, 66
Cardinal Jacques Davy du Perron, 65
Cartesian, xxi, 8, 12, 15, 45, 52, 56, 98n26, 123, 236n2
Cassirer, Ernst, 44, 46, 96n14, 99n32
category, 159, 164, 196, 199; as categories, xvii–xviii, xxvi, 78, 158, 217, 247n2. *See also* existentialia
cathexis (*Besetzung*), 17, 185, 220, 232, 241n17; counter-, 239n13; and crystallization, 9, 28; hyper-, 231; and institution, 9; and Oedipus complex, 9, 87n30; and other, 18. *See also Besetzung,* crystallization, *investissement,* investment
causality, 9, 15, 17, 19, 82, 106, 122, 144, 169, 175, 245n25; as endogenous, 122, 125; as exogenous, 122, 125; as external, 103, 121
censorship, xxiii, xxviii, 125, 152, 154, 156, 158–59, 161, 166–69, 220, 223, 225–26, 228, 230, 239n9, 240n5, 240n8, 251n89
centering, 24, 49, 52; as re-, 25, 49, 78, 159

Cézanne, Paul, xvi, 44, 47, 99–101n38; in *Cézanne's Doubt*, xvi; in *Cézanne et l'expression de l'espace*, 48, 99n38; and Madame Cézanne, 48
Chauvin, Rémy, xi
childhood: and dream, 189, 214, 216–17, 219, 225–27; and Freud, 155, 159, 162, 172–73, 180–81, 183, 185–86, 189, 216–17, 219, 225–27, 233n5, 241n21, 245n19, 251n89; and institution, xi, 25, 77; and love, 77; and memory, 191, 214, 251n89; and Oedipal Complex, xi, 25, 185; and Proust, 214; and Sartre, 157
China, 75, 87
Christ, Jesus, 65, 104n9, 106n23. *See also* Christian, Christianity
Christian, 7, 43, 45, 66, 68, 91n15, 94n45, 97n20, 106n21, 106n23, 107n28, 218; anti-, 66
Christianity, xix, 66–68, 106n21, 106n23, 108n35
Claudel, Paul, 196, 247n16
cleavage, xxiv, xxviii, 157, 207
cogito, 15, 60, 103n11, 104n11, 119
coincidence (*Deckung*), xxi, 14–15, 71, 88n36, 124, 166, 172, 238n4; non-, x, 136, 220. *See also Deckung*
Colette, Sidonie-Gabrielle, 8
communication, xvii–xviii, xxiii, 108n35, 131; and intersubjectivity, 6, 28, 69; and the unconscious, 152; in Weber, xiii
condensation, xxvi, xxviii, xxxiii; and censorship, xxviii, 156, 158; and dream, xxvi, 84n6, 156–58, 220, 229, 231; in Freud, xxviii, 152, 240n6, 250n25; and painting, 231
configuration: as configurational, 86n17; in Husserl, 103n8; and language, 51; in Lévi-Strauss, 74; and oneiric, 157, 238n7; and perspective, 6, 133, 175, 217; and unconscious, 200, 238n7
Conrad, Joseph, 18, 22, 87
conscious: in Freud, xxvi, 168, 174, 240n8; in Lévi-Strauss, 104n3, 242n10; and passivity, 125, 206; in Politzer, xxvii; and unconscious, xxvi–xxvii, 117–18, 168, 174, 182–85, 240n8, 246n42. *See also* consciousness

consciousness, xxi, xxvii, 195, 238n11, 246n35; absolute, 14, 23, 26, 60, 98n27, 103n11, 117, 124, 129, 131, 135–37, 193; adequate, 150; in Alquié, xxi; animal, 84n6, 86n18, 196, 212; in Bergson, 242n10; in Brunschvicg, 129, 235n34; captive, 139–44, 151; Cartesian, 123; in *Consciousness and the Acquisition of Language*, xxxin19, 234n13; constituting, x, xiii, xvi, 9–10, 76, 123, 136, 160, 217–18; contemplative, 187; conventional, 149, 159; creative, 24, 58; critical, 46, 81n22; in de Beauvoir, 82n39–40; dream, 84n6, 125, 147, 153, 158, 166, 207, 229; empty, 148, 150, 207, 242n10; in Ey's *Consciousness: A Phenomenological Study of Being Conscious and Becoming Conscious*, 240n9; and freedom, 28; in Freud, 153, 156, 159–63, 166–69, 175, 178, 184, 187, 192, 202, 204, 207–8, 229, 231–32, 239n9, 241n17, 242n10, 248n2; fulfilled, 237n16; full, 148; in Hegel, 14; historical, 50, 60, 63, 119, 134; hollow, 143; in Husserl, 5–6, 20, 58–59, 76, 233n7; ideal, 132; illusory, 143; imaginary, 144–45; imagining, 141, 143, 146–48, 150, 161, 207, 234n14, 237; in general (*Bewußtein überhaupt*), 128, 235n33; and institution, 8–9, 12–13, 15, 23, 76, 82n39; intellectual, 130; intentional, 59; Kantian, 123, 127, 158; life of, 5; in Mead, 110n45; and memory, 195–98, 208; mythical, 155; naked, 117; narcissistic, 144; non-, 117; non-thetic, 159; objective, 80n14, 218; and Oedipus complex, 25; omni-, 117; oneiric, xxv, 145, 150, 156–58, 161, 167, 207–8, 218; open, 131; and passivity, 136, 200; perceptual, xxiv, xxviii, 125, 131, 143, 146–48, 159–61, 167, 204, 208, 237; philosophy of, xvi, xxix, 63, 76, 207, 235n34; in Politzer, xxvii–xxviii, 153; practical, 188; and preconscious, 232, 241n17; pure, 46; reflective, 125, 139–41, 143; regional, 204; in Ruyer, 87n25; in Sartre, xxiv, 119, 139–46, 149–51, 153, 155, 187–88, 233n7, 237n2, 237n5; sedimented, 160; self-, 119; and sleep, 124–25, 132, 135–42, 147, 206–7, 212; spectator, 6,

INDEX

10, 121; symbolic, 155, 159; theoretical, 78; and time, 7, 80n13, 157, 196; and tradition, 52, 58; and unconsciousness, 159–61, 167, 204, 207, 229, 232, 238n7, 242n10; universal, 117; in Valéry, 117; wakeful, xxvi, xxviii, 131–32, 139, 144, 147, 152–53, 155, 157. *See also Bewußtein überhaupt*
constitution: co-, 169; as constituting, x, xiii, xvi, 6, 9–10, 67, 123, 159, 193; as creation, 248n10; and dreams, 156–57; in Freud, 154–60, 189, 200–201, 230; in Husserl, 235n39; and institution, x, 8, 76, 157; and passivity, 117, 125–28, 136, 217; in Politzer, 153; as re-, xviii, xxvi, 132, 157, 189, 230; in Sartre, 140; and *Sinngebung,* 8, 69, 165, 217; and symbolism, 152–53; in Valéry, 241n18. *See also* sense donation, *Sinngebung*
contamination, 17, 223
content, xxxiv, 101; and *Abschattungen,* 130, 133; as affective, 159, 219, 241n16; and *Auffassung als,* 5; and body, 179; and consciousness, 5, 128, 136, 156, 158, 248n3; and dream, xxiv, xxvi–xxvii, 152–54, 156, 158, 166–67, 173–74, 207–8, 219–25, 227, 241n16; and form, 5, 95n3; and Freud, xxvi–xxvii, 152–54, 156, 159, 162, 166–67, 173–74, 179, 203, 207–8, 225, 241n16, 251n64; and horizon, 46, 128; as ideational, 219, 241n16; and institution, 7, 23; as latent, xxvi, 13, 152–53, 156, 158–59, 174, 207–8, 219, 221; as manifest, xxvi, 156, 207–8, 219, 221–22; as oneiric, 149, 156, 158; and sleep, 132, 135–36; and *Stiftung,* 13
content of meaning (*Bedeutungsinhalt*), 95n3, 98n31. *See also Bedeutungsinhalt*
Cosmotheoros, 64, 73, 113n55, 113n58, 233n4
creation: artistic, 41–42, 50, 78, 84n1, 95n4–5, 96n17, 97n19, 98n27; and behavior, 84n9; in Bergson, 101n3; and constitution, 9, 248n10; continuous, 58–59; and feeling, 28–40; and the for-itself, 120; in Freud, 153, 166–70, 173, 182, 218, 221, 225; in Husserl, 102n17; and institution, 14, 19, 41, 76, 103n10; intellectual, 53; and love, 29–36, 39,

89n5, 90n12, 93n38; and nature, 84n9, 129; and passivity, 117, 119–21; pure, 24, 26, 62–63, 191; as re-, 9, 41–42, 47, 62, 76, 90n12–13, 117; and *Sinngebung,* 133; and *Stiftung,* 51; and time, 54
crystallization, 48, 77, 100, 159, 160, 218; and cathexis, 9, 28. *See also* cathexis
culture, vii, xii, xv, xvii, xviii, 54, 58, 64, 69, 71, 81n29, 82n33, 102, 104n1, 104n3, 112n51, 133

Darmaillacq, Dominique, v, xi, xxxiii, 3
death: in Blanchot, xxxin20, 151; and dreams, 219, 231; in Febvre, 106n21; in Freud, 219, 231, 245n30; and passivity, 131, 136; in Proust, 31, 36–38, 89n10, 215; and refusal, 131; in Sartre, 119, 148
decentering, xviii, 52, 59, 78, 129
Deckung (coincidence), 22, 88n36, 147, 149, 237n3, 238n4. *See also* coincidence
Desanti, Jean-Toussaint, 126, 235n30
Descartes, René, 5, 83n41, 136, 141, 234n21, 236n7
Devereux, George, 242n8, 248n8
deviation, xxxv, 17, 47, 68, 193, 195, 212. *See also* divergence, variation
dialectic: in *Adventures of the Dialectic,* xiii, 80n11, 82n34, 233n3, 233n7, 234n12, 234n19; anti-, 121; binary, 119, 198; as dialectical, 21, 68, 70–71, 111n49, 121, 182, 245n25, 247n21; in Engels, 70, 74, 112n50; and freedom, 117, 119; in Freud, 21, 118, 159, 164, 167, 175, 179, 182, 226, 245n25, 246n35; in Hegel, xv, 62, 112n50, 165, 198, 205; in Lévi-Strauss, 74, 111n49, 112n50; in Marx, 62, 74, 129; of nature, 70, 73–74; in phenomenology, 79; philosophy of, 198, 209, 247n21; pre-, 79; in Sartre, 117, 119; ternary, 119
differentiation, 132, 138, 155, 184, 204; de-, xxv, 132, 138, 148–49, 206; in-, xxvi, 125; non-, 242n10; un-, 149, 201
dimension, 122, 242n10; and corporeal schema, 169; as dimensionless, 43, 97n20; and dream, 157; and experience, x, 8, 77; and field, xx, 13, 23; and geometry, 55; and institution, x, 8, 13, 25, 77; and intersubjectivity,

169; in Lagache, 94n51; and painting, xv, 43–45; and passivity, 191; and perspective, 43–45, 96n14, 97n21; and Proclus, 97n20; in Proust, 90n14; and *Stiftung*, 19; as three-dimensional, 43–45, 96n14; and time, xix; as two-dimensional, 95n4, 97n21

Ding (thing), 130, 153, 235n41, 238n5. *See also Dingwahrnemung, Sache, Sinnending*

Dingwahrnemung (perception of the thing), 130, 133, 235n40. *See also Ding, Sinnending*

displacement, xiii, 118, 202; and animality, 18–20; and dream, 84n6, 168, 173, 216, 249n25; as echo, 181; in Freud, xxviii, 18, 152, 159, 168–69, 173, 178, 181–82, 216, 226, 242n10, 249n25; in Lévi-Strauss, 118; in Lukács, xiii; and Oedipus complex, 22; in Ruyer, 87n27; and substitute, 19, 168, 226, 249n25

divergence, xxii, xxxv, 7, 11, 46, 51, 68, 83, 130–33, 136–37, 148–49, 158, 175, 204–6, 212, 238n7, 242n10. *See also* deviation, variation

domain of knowledge, xii, xiv–xv, xvii, 11, 50–51, 101. *See also Erkenntnistheoretisch*, theoretical knowledge

d'Ors i Rovira, Eugenio, 157, 240n10

dream, xxv, 16, 84n6, 121, 149, 153–58, 167, 232; and affective content, 219, 241n16; content, xxiv, xxvii, 156, 173, 220–27; and delusion, 160, 170, 173, 208; in d'Ors, 157; in Fechner, 229; and field, xxv, 150, 217, 220; in Freud, xxiii, xxv–xxix, xxxiv, 148–49, 152, 154, 156, 159, 163–75, 180–90, 202, 208, 216–31, 241n11; in Freud's *Delusions and Dreams in Jensen's "Gradiva,"* 239n14, 241n22, 243n1, 243n3–38; in Freud's *Interpretation of Dreams*, xxiv, xxvi, xxviii, 153–56, 208, 216, 224, 239n4, 239n10, 240n5–6, 240n8, 240n11, 241n14, 241n16–17, 242n24, 249n1–252n118; in Freud's *On Dreams*, 238n8–9; in Freud's *Premonitory Dreams*, 165–68; and ideational content, 219, 241n16; as imagining consciousness, 144, 148, 207; intentionality, 156, 158; interpretation, xxvi–xxvii, xxix, xxxiv, 160, 165, 173, 220, 222, 224, 227–28, 240n5; in Kant, 226; and latent content, xxvi–xxvii, 152–58, 207, 219, 221; in Lichtenberg, 227; and manifest content, xxvi–xxvii, 219–22; and the oneiric, xxv, xxvii, 146–47, 156–58, 207–8, 228; and painting, 96n13, 157; and passivity, xxii–xxiv, 149; in Politzer, 153, 207; in Proust, 214; in Rank, 240n11; and reality, 170, 182, 207; and rebus, 156; in Sartre, 140–41, 146–49, 153, 157, 234n14, 237n2; in Schopenhauer, 226; in Silberer, 226; and speech, 158, 208, 221–22; and unconscious, xii, xxvi, xxviii–xxix, 121–22, 125, 159–60, 173, 207, 224–25, 230–31, 244n4; wish, 228–32, 240n8, 242n24; work, xxviii, 222, 225–30, 239n4

Durchsehung (transversing view), 44–45, 98n28. *See also* transversing view

Dürer, Albrecht, 44–45, 48, 98n27–28, 101n38

earth, 44–45, 211, 224; in Husserl's *Umsturz*, 129–30, 235n37; in Proust, 247n8

echo, 15, 151, 236n46; and animality,18; and displacement, 181; and dream, 154, 158, 185; in Freud, 169, 181, 185, 192, 204; in Hegel, 165; and institution, 85n16; and love, 35, 77, 185; and the other, 28, 204; and perception, 169; in Proust, 35, 77, 91n20; and repression, 192

ego, 21, 23, 118, 125, 152, 218; alter-, 18, 147; centric, 35; ism, 155, 223; others, 188–89; super-, 20, 125; tism, 118

eindeutig festgelegt (established without equivocation), 43, 95n7

Einfühlung (empathy), 127, 235n32. *See also* empathy

einmalig (unique), 54, 102n12, 196, 218, 247n13. *See also* singular, unique

Einstein, Albert, 70–71, 73; as Einsteinian, 71

elective affinity (*Wahlverwandschaft*), xiii, 82n35. *See also Wahlverwandschaft*

empathy (*Einfühlung*), 235n32. *See also Einfühlung*

empirical, xiii, 21, 37, 55, 57, 59, 73, 117, 169, 195, 200

INDEX

empiricism, xxii, 5, 112
empiricist, 55
emptying out of sense (*Sinnentleerung*), xxiv, 102n11, 143, 147–48, 150, 152. *See also* Sinnentleerung
Endstiftung (final institution), 25, 52, 58, 61–62, 88n40, 102n6. *See also* institution, *Stiftung*
Engels, Friedrich, 70, 74, 112
epoch, xvii, xxi, 66–67, 81n24, 82n35, 168, 213
Erasmus, Desiderius, 66–67, 106–7
Erfüllung (fulfillment), 143–44, 147–49, 204, 237n3, 237n15; intention-, 147–48. *See also* fulfillment
Erinnerung (recollection), 195, 247n7. *See also* recollection
Erkenntnistheoretisch (theoretical knowledge), 151, 155, 238n3. *See also* domain of knowledge, theoretical knowledge
Erlebnis der Wahrheit (experience of truth), 59, 103n5
Erlebnisse (lived experiences), 131, 134, 235n44; ur-, 198
error, 137; in Freud, 153, 173, 202; in Husserl, 64; and love, 9, 36; in Proust, 9, 36–37, 93n45; in Sartre, 234n14
essence, 11–12, 36–38, 50–61, 70–74, 85n16, 86n18, 90n13, 103n6, 127, 133, 136, 168, 194–95, 221, 245n31; as what has been (*Wesen ist was gewesen ist*), 59, 103n6; in Freud, 172; in Heidegger's "On the Essence of Truth," 234n9; non-, 38; order of, 53. *See also* being, ontology
established without equivocation (*Eindeutig festgelegt*), 95n7. *See also* Eindeutig festgelegt
establishment (*Stiftung*), x, xiii–xviii, 8, 11, 25, 30, 37, 43, 50, 67, 77, 93n45, 97n21, 100n38, 110n43, 122, 136, 168, 185, 192, 200, 242n10; final (*End*), 102n6; pre-, 150; primal (*Ur*), 102n6; re (*Nach*), 68, 71, 242n10, 247n2. *See also* foundation, institution, *Stiftung*
Euclid, 42, 55, 95n4
Europe, 13
European, 43, 45; in Husserl's *The Crisis of European Sciences,* 101n2, 101n5, 102n7, 102n11, 102n17, 234n20

event, x–xix, xxiii–xxix, 6, 10, 13, 15, 17–18, 21–22, 50–51, 71, 77, 107n30, 135, 142, 147, 151, 156–60, 166, 213, 241n13; based, 14, 74, 155, 194, 203, 217–18; character, 14; framework, 218; in Freud, 167–69, 176, 180, 189, 192–94, 199–200, 203–5, 216–18, 222, 242n10, 245n19; in Lévi-Strauss, 82n32; matrixes, 13; ness, 13–14; in Proust, 90n13, 93n45, 215, 218; pure, 54; in Sartre, 233n7, 237n2
existence: field of, x; and institution, 23, 30, 37; order of, 53, 198; pre-, 168
existential, 49, 54, 59, 72–73, 165, 169, 195, 202, 242n10; as *existentiale,* 199; field, xxiv–xxvi, 150, 206; historico-, 248n3; memory, 198; order, 108n35; position, 201; psychoanalysis, 188; sexual, 190
existentialia, xxvi, 151, 217–18, 242n2. *See also* category
expression, xv, 70, 73–74, 86n17–18; as analysis, 191, 208, 216; of the body, 48, 179, 195, 238n5; in *Cézanne et l'expression de l'espace,* 48, 99n38; in Freud, 135–59, 163, 168–69, 174, 190, 202, 205, 208, 216, 218, 220, 222–25, 229–30, 240n8, 245n34, 252n89, 252n108; and institution, xvi; in Lévi-Strauss, 108n38, 109n43, 110n45, 112n50, 113n52; order of, 71, 156; and perspective, 42–47, 96n15, 97n19, 97n21; and *The Prose of the World,* xvi; and reactivation, 81n24; in "The Sensible World and the World of Expression," xvi; and *Sinngebung,* 53, 135, 149, 205; as symbolism, 149, 154–59, 163, 168–69, 174, 190, 202, 205, 208, 215–16, 218, 220, 222–25, 229, 230, 240n8, 252n89, 252n108; theory of, xvi
exterior, 165, 185, 205; as exteriority, xx, 59, 62, 67, 104n1; and interior, 58, 61–62, 64, 67, 123, 128, 130, 164, 202
Ey, Henri, 157, 240n9

faith, xii, 66–67, 94, 107, 153, 210; as faithful, xiii, 75, 143–44
Farel, Guillaume, 65, 104
Febvre, Lucien, xvii, xix, xxx, 64, 66–69; and *The Problem of Unbelief in the Six-*

teenth Century: The Religion of Rabelais, xviii, 82n36, 104n6–10, 105n12–18, 105n20–107n30, 107n32, 107n34; and Rabelais, 14; in *Sense and Nonsense*, xxxn13

Fechner, Gustav Theodor, 229, 251n84

feeling, xii, 64, 91n21, 92n30, 93n45, 96n15, 154, 164, 171, 174, 178–79, 230–31, 240n8; institution of, xii, xiv, xvii, xix, 9, 28–33, 36–37, 50, 77, 88, 88n4. *See also* feeling of the world, *Weltgefühl*

fiat, 6, 80n7; of signification, 5, 119

field, xvii, xx–xxii, xxxin16, 6, 11–12, 23, 53, 59, 76, 124, 137, 148–49, 158–60, 204–5, 211, 217, 238n7; of action, x; affective, 217; auditory, 164; of the body, 123, 150, 214; of culture, xviii, 58, 102; of dreams, 150, 220; of existence, x; existential, xxiv–xxvi, 150, 206; of geometry, 103n10, 214; of gravitation, 112n52; historical, 13, 72, 75; ideological, xxi, 58; imaginary, xxi, 124; and institution, ix, 60–64, 72, 112n51, 198, 206; of knowledge, x, 78; logical, 124; mythical, xxi, 124; oneiric, xxviii; open, 8, 13, 42, 44, 55, 57, 62, 103n10, 194, 198, 212, 237n3; of painting, 41, 47; of perception, 128–30, 133, 160, 187–88, 202; of presence, 7; sensible, xxvii, 130, 132, 150; social, 71, 73, 112n51; spatial, 152; symbolic, 6, 130, 160; temporal, xvii, xix; visual, 42; in Weber, xiii

finalism, xxi, 123

flesh, 142, 148, 194–96

forgetfulness (*Vergessenheit*), 22, 36–37, 51–52, 54, 58, 103n3, 103n10, 132, 136–37, 171, 173, 186, 197–99, 209, 211, 215, 236n47. *See also Vergessenheit*

for-itself (*für sich*), xxix, 104n11, 120, 122, 125–27, 184, 235n27, 235n29. *See also für sich*

for-one-another (*Füreinander*), 104n13. *See also Füreinander*

Forschungen (research), 87n26. *See also* investigation, research, search

foundation (*Fundierung*), x, xiv–xv, xix, 12–13, 17, 22, 29, 36, 52, 59–60, 81n24, 98n26, 101n4, 102n2, 106n20, 157, 209; as founded, 14, 29, 47, 58,

62; in Freud, 167, 171, 179, 184, 196–97, 199; perceptual, 71, 74; in Proust, 29, 32–33, 214; re-, 47; in Ruyer, 127. *See also* establishment, *Fundierung*, institution, *Stiftung*

Francastel, Pierre, 46, 99

freedom, 15, 28, 31, 117, 125, 134, 144, 149, 151, 159, 182, 185–86, 200–202, 207; Pavlov's "reflex of-," 139; in Sartre, xx, 119–20, 141, 143, 188

Freud, Sigmund, 211, 239n11; and *Delusions and Dreams in Jensen's "Gradiva,"* xix, xxix, xxxiv, 155, 159, 170, 175, 239n14, 241n22, 243n1, 243n3–244n38; and *Dora*, xxix, xxxiv, 162–64, 177–90, 201, 203, 244; and dream, xxiii, xxv–xxvii, xxxiv, 148–50, 153–54, 156, 159, 165–68, 187, 190, 202, 207, 216–28, 238n9, 239n4–240n5, 240n8, 241n16–17; and *Fragment of an Analysis of a Case of Hysteria*, 242n2–4, 242n6, 244n1, 244n3, 244n6–246n58; as Freudian, xxxv, 182, 199, 207, 220, 231; as Freudianism, xxix, 159, 208; and institution, xix, 20–21, 152; and *The Interpretation of Dreams*, xxiv, xxvi, xxviii, 154, 156, 208, 216, 224, 239n10, 239n4–240n6, 240n8, 240n11, 241n14, 241n16–17, 242n24, 249n1–252n118; and *Introductory Lectures on Psycho-Analysis*, 236n3; and *Leonardo da Vinci and a Memory of His Childhood*, 159, 233n5, 241n21, 242n23; and Lévi-Strauss, 113n55–56, 118; and Oedipus complex, 20, 224; and *On Dreams*, 153, 238n8–9; and *The Passing of the Oedipus Complex*, 20–21; and passivity, xix, xxiv, 149; and *Premonitory Dreams*, 165–68; and Proust, xxxn1, xxxiv, 155, 197; and psychoanalysis, xxiv, 113n55, 118; and *Psychopathology of Everyday Life*, 247n1; and repression, xxvi, xxviii, 149, 154, 159, 166, 175, 183, 197, 202–3; and Sartre, xxiv, xxxn1, 148–50, 153–54, 164, 187, 202; and symbolism, xxvi, 149–50, 152–54, 159–60, 187, 189, 208, 220; and *Totem and Taboo*, 113n56; and the unconscious, xxvi, xxviii–xxix, xxxiv, 152, 154, 159–60, 162–63, 167–68, 175, 183, 187, 189, 199, 204, 207,

INDEX

224–25, 241n17, 242, 242n1, 242n10, 243n11, 247
Friedmann, Georges, 65, 104n10
Fry, Roger, 100
fulfillment (*Erfüllung*), 48, 89n7, 132, 148, 193, 237n15–16, 246n35; in Freud, 166, 207, 218–19, 226, 228, 232; imaginary, 9; in Lévi-Strauss, 111n49; in Proust, 91n18; in Sartre, 238n12; and *Sinngebung*, 149; wish-, 219, 226, 228, 232. *See also Erfüllung*
Fundierung (foundation), 52, 55, 101n4. *See also* establishment, foundation, institution, *Stiftung*
füreinander (for-one-another), 61, 75, 104n13. *See also* for-one-another
für sich (for-itself), 126, 235n29. *See also* for-itself

Galileo Galilei, 102n2
Gauss, Carl Friedrich, 55
Gegensinn (absurdity), 157, 240n7. *See also* absurdity
Geneva, 67, 106n23
geometry, 49, 51–52, 55–56, 86n17; in Husserl's *The Origin of Geometry*, 101n2, 101n5–6, 102n11, 103n7–9, 214. *See also* arithmetic, mathematics
Gesell, Arnold, 17, 84n9, 85n11–12, 87n25
Gestalt, 123; as *Gestalten*, 121, 129; as *Gestalttheorie*, 70; as Gestaltist, 52; as *Gestaltung*, 122, 182; philosophy of, 73
gestiftet (instituted), 12, 81n24–25; *ur-*, 133, 201. *See also* institution, *Stiftung*
Geulincx, Arnold, 43, 45, 96
Gilson, Etienne, 66
Goethe, Johann Wolfgang, 6, 9
Grünewald, Matthias, 98n27
Guérin, Daniel, xiv, 7, 80n10–11
Guéroult, Martial, xvi
Guerry, Liliane, 48, 99–101n38

Hamlet, 219
Hannibal, 218
Hebbel, Christian Friedrich, 227
Hecht, Ben, 239n3
Hegel, G. W. F., xv, 59; and absolute, 59; and dialectic, 129, 165, 205; and history, 14, 63, 112n50; and in-itself, 125; and Marxism, 14, 62; and *Phenomenology of Spirit*, 248n5; and *The Science of Logic*, 103n6
Hegelian, xii, 79, 121, 198
Heidegger, Martin, 234n9, 247n3, 248n2
hinge, xxvi, 6, 60, 76, 81n22, 131, 134, 162. *See also* pivot
Hintereinander (in the intervals), 43, 45, 95n9. *See also* intervals
historicity, xii, xvii, xix, 13–14, 51–52, 58, 78, 103n8, 128
Hitler, Adolf, 65
horizon, xx, 34, 46, 55, 59–61, 63–65, 67–68, 78, 81n24, 103n7, 108n35, 128, 160, 164–65, 197, 204; and institution, 14; perceptual, 130, 205
Husserl, Edmund, xvi, 5, 59, 64, 81n24, 133; and animality, 20; and consciousness, 58, 76; and constitution, 76; and *The Crisis of the European Sciences and Transcendental Phenomenology*, 101n2, 101n5–102n7, 102n11, 102n17, 103n7–8, 234n20, 236n2; and *Deckung*, 88n36; and *Foundational Investigations of the Phenomenological Origin of the Spatiality of Nature: The Originary Ark, The Earth, Does Not Move*, 129, 235n37; and *Gestalt*, 52; and *Husserl at the Limits of Phenomenology*, 101n2, 235n37; and *Ideas I*, 237n13, 248n5; and *Ideas II*, 102n10, 235n39; and *Lebenswelt*, 53, 102n7, 234n20; and "The Origin of Geometry," 101n2, 101n5–6, 102n11, 103n7–8; and *Stiftung*, xv
Husserlian, 130, 233n7
hyle, 5, 80n1, 193, 237n14; hyletic, 120, 148; signification-, 143
hysteria, 179, 183, 216, 224, 244n4, 245n34; in *Fragment of an Analysis of a Case of Hysteria*, 242n2–3, 242n6, 244n1, 244n3, 244n6, 244n8, 244n11, 244n18, 245n24–26, 246n40, 246n43, 246n46, 246n48, 246n52; as hysteric, 248n3; as hysterical, 29, 219, 230

Ibsen, Henrik, 221, 241n14
"I can," xxv, 6, 58, 76, 143, 148, 187, 195, 201, 242n10
idealism, 5, 13–14, 112n50, 124, 130, 201, 233n2

INDEX

illusion, xiii–xiv, 28–35, 37–39, 50, 55–56, 58–59, 77, 81n24, 97n21, 104n4, 139–40, 184, 200
image (*Bild*), xi, xxi, xxiii–xxiv, xxvi–xxvii, 19–20, 35, 70, 77, 82, 86n18, 100n38, 124, 139–41, 150, 152, 179, 185, 187, 191, 193, 195, 197, 201, 203, 223, 229, 232, 241n17, 250n25; as *Bild*, 239n1; memory-, 187; and perspective, 42–46, 95n4; in Sartre's *The Imaginary*, 234n14; self-, 126. *See also Bild*, picture
imaginary, xxiv–xxv, 23, 25, 29, 32, 34–35, 37, 39, 69, 91n19, 125, 130, 140–41, 144–57, 173, 184–85, 187, 207, 238n12; field, xxi, 121; fulfillment, 9; non-fulfillment, 21; in Sartre's *The Imaginary*, 234n14, 234n17, 237n4–9, 237n12–13, 237n2; sexuality, 21; world, 237n16
imagination, 35, 90n14, 95n10, 99n36, 100n38, 121, 168, 215, 234n17
imagining consciousness, 141–48, 161, 207, 234n14, 237
imaginings (*imagines*), xxxv, 156, 238n10
immanence, 11–12, 21, 23–25, 54, 60, 141, 146, 159, 191, 193, 208, 245n25
implex, 47, 159, 169, 200–203, 241n18
impregnation, xi, 9, 77, 85n15, 87n24, 118. *See also* imprint, institution
imprint, xiii, 9, 17–18, 24, 80n17, 84n1, 85n15. *See also* impregnation, institution
infinity of the image (*Unendlichkeit des Bildes*), 97n22. *See also Unendlichkeit des Bildes*
in-itself (*an sich*), xxix, 7–8, 16, 24, 39, 46, 51, 53–54, 56, 61, 69–72, 78, 82n37, 100, 104n11, 113n55, 118, 122–23, 125–30, 133–34, 152, 188–89, 191, 193, 195, 201, 235n24, 235n27–28. *See also an sich*
innere structure (internal structure), 55, 102n14. *See also* internal structure
institution (*Stiftung*), xxxv, 69, 80n6, 80n12, 80n16, 81n25, 82n37–40, 85n16, 88n40, 102n6, 103n4, 125; and animality, 9, 16–22, 52–53, 77; anonymous, 15; of art; 40–49, 77, 95; of the body, 10, 19–24, 30–40; as capitalism, xvii, 14; in "Cezanne's Doubt," xvi; and Christianity, 68, 105n13, 108n35; and the cogito, 15; collective, 41; and consciousness, xxix, 8, 10, 12–15, 20, 23–24, 60, 76, 82n39; and constitution, x, 6, 8, 10, 28, 39, 53, 61, 76; and culture, 54, 58–61; and custom, xiv, 72; of a domain of knowledge, xiii–xv, xvii, 11, 50–53, 61–62, 81n27, 101, 101n1–2; of a feeling, xii–xiv, xvii, xix, 9, 28, 36, 50, 88, 88n4; and field, ix–x, 7, 13, 23, 47, 60–61, 64, 103n10, 206; and figuration, xxiii; final (*end*), 88n40, 102n6; in Freud, 19–20, 152, 156, 189, 199; of geometry, 50–51, 103n10; and Hegel, 14, 62–63; and history, ix–xiv, xvii, xix, 9, 12–15, 17, 23–26, 36, 41, 50–53, 60–78, 81n27, 104, 189, 198; and horizon, 14, 61, 63; human, 16–23; and Husserl, 64, 76; in *Institution in Personal and Public History*, ix–xix, xxxiii–xxxvi, 3, 76, 80, 233n1, 236n3, 248n2; and latency, 20–24, 81n27; in Lévi-Strauss, 63, 72–75, 112n51; and life, 16, 83; and love, xvii, xix, xxxv, 9–10, 22, 25–26, 30–40, 48, 77, 81n19, 81n22; of mathematics, xv, 12; of negativity, 62; non-, 21, 68; of Oedipus complex, 20–25, 77; originary (*ur*), 88n40; and painting, 10, 42–50, 61, 77–78; partial, 12; particularizing, 13–14, 62, 104; and passivity, xix; personal, 9, 11, 25, 36, 41, 61, 77; as perspective, 42–47; and philosophy, xix, xxix, 7, 14, 26, 51, 60, 64, 76; private, 15, 41, 48; in *The Prose of the World*, xv–xvi, xxxn6; in Proust, 30–40, 50, 77, 88n4; and puberty, 9, 11, 20–24, 77; public, 15, 41, 62–75, 77; re-, 11, 152, 205; and sexuality, 20–25; and subjectivity, 6–7, 9–10, 61, 76; and time, ix–xii, xix, 7–8, 14, 19–20, 24, 28, 58, 77–78, 108n35; of truth, 53, 61–63, 77–78; universalizing, 13, 62, 104; vital, 20; of a work, xii–xiv, xvii, 10–11, 40–50, 61, 77. *See also* establishment, foundation, impregnation, imprint, *Stiftung*
interior, xxv, xxxin20, 58–59, 77, 95n10, 96n18, 97n24, 123, 126–28, 130, 151–52, 164, 170, 202
interiority, x, 41, 59, 61–62, 64, 67, 134

INDEX

internal structure (*innere* structure), 16, 102n14. *See also innere* structure
intersubjectivity, xvi, xxiii, 6, 15, 60–62, 71, 74, 77, 103n3, 131, 134–35, 157, 162, 169, 182. *See also* subjectivity
intervals (*Hintereinander*), 95n9, 136. *See also Hintereinander*
introjection, xxv, 6, 120, 142, 147, 155, 160
investigation (*Forschungen*), x, xiii–xiv, xvi, xxix, 24, 33, 41, 46, 48, 78, 104n1, 239n9; in Freud, 172, 174; in Husserl, 235n37; in Kafka, xxxv, 19–20, 77, 87n26; of the painter, 99n38. *See also Forschungen*, research, search
investissement (cathexis), 87n30, 239n13. *See also Besetzung*, cathexis, investment
investment (*Besetzung*), 9, 154. *See also Besetzung*, cathexis, *Investissement*
invisible, xxii, 35, 37, 101n38, 195; in *The Visible and the Invisible*, xxii, xxxn16, xxxv, 233n7, 235n37, 238n2, 241n13, 242n8, 247n16
irreal, 152; as irreality, 10; as irrealized, 144

jealousy, 7, 9–10, 29–33, 38–39, 77, 81n21, 90n12, 93n45, 94n51, 172–73, 179, 215
Jensen, Wilhelm: and *Gradiva*, xix, 170, 239n14, 243n1. *See also* Freud
Jesus Christ. *See* Christ, Jesus
jewel-case (*Schmuckkästen*), 163. *See also Schmuckkästen*

Kafka, Franz: and investigation, xxxv, 19–20, 77, 87n26
Kant, Immanuel, xiii; and *The Critique of Judgment*, 127; and *Opus Postumum*, 233n4
Kantian, xxi, 98n26, 123, 158, 233n2; and body, 123; and constitution, x, xiii; and idea, xiii, 102n2; and synthesis, 126; and time, 226
Kantianism. *See* Kantian
Karlsbad, 218
Kierkegaard, Søren, 7
kinship, 7, 13, 20, 41, 63, 69, 71, 74–75, 78, 81n32, 82n35, 111n47, 113n53, 164, 168, 198–99, 217, 219; in Lévi-Strauss's *The Elementary Structures of Kinship*, 108n36, 109n42, 110n45, 112n50–113n56
Köhler, Wolfgang, 127
Körper-Nichtkörper difference (difference between body and non-body), 43, 95n8

Lachiéze-Rey, Pierre, xxi, 117, 123, 126, 233n2, 233n4–5
lack, xi, 21, 30, 34, 36, 113n55, 126, 131, 144, 157, 164–65, 171, 204
La Fontaine, Jean de, 20
Lagache, Daniel, 94n51, 120, 234n13
Lamarckian, 86
language, xv–xvi, xxii, xxv–xxvii, 10–11, 24–25, 42, 45–46, 51–54, 61, 67–68, 74, 103n6, 106n25, 107n27, 122, 126, 133, 153–54, 158–59, 185, 195, 199–200, 208, 220, 223, 238n5, 242n10; "The Algorithm and the Mystery of Language" in *The Prose of the World*, xv, 102n16; in *Consciousness and the Acquisition of Language*, xxxin19, 234n13; in "Indirect Language and the Voices of Silence," xiv, xxxn5
Laplace, Pierre-Simon, 128
Laplanche, Jean, 243n15
Lawlor, Leonard, v, ix, 3, 76, 115, 206
Lebenswelt (life-world), 53, 102n7, 122, 234n20. *See also* life-world
Lefort, Claude, v, vii, ix, xxxin16, xxxin20, xxxiii, 99n38
LeFranc, Abel, 65, 105n12–13, 105n17
Leibhaftgegeben (bodily given), 235n39. *See also* bodily given
Leibniz, G. W., 71, 214, 236n6
Leistung (achievement), 188, 246n47. *See also* achievement
lekton (signified), 51, 158, 241n13
Lenormand, H. R., 87
Leonardo da Vinci, 48, 117; in *Leonardo da Vinci and a Memory of His Childhood*, 159, 233n5, 241n21, 242n23
Leuic, Emanuela, 94n51
level, xx, xxv–xxvi, xxviii, 6, 46, 70, 77, 84n2, 121, 129, 132–33, 135, 146–47, 149, 158, 162, 168, 191–92, 194, 200, 214–15, 242n10
Lévi-Strauss, Claude, xiv, xvii–xviii, 13–14, 63, 69, 71–74, 81n28–82n33,

104n1, 104n3–5, 108n36–113n57, 118, 234n8
Lichtenberg, Georg Christoph, 227, 240n11
life-world (*Lebenswelt*), 102n7, 234n20. See also *Lebenswelt*
Lorenz, Konrad, xi, 17–18, 85, 87
love, 18–20, 22, 28–40, 50, 77, 81n20, 86n19, 86n23–24, 88n39, 89n5–94n51, 162, 164, 166–68, 172–75, 178–90, 193, 197, 203, 211, 219, 242n9–10, 244n7, 245n32; institution of, xii, xix, xxxv, 9–10, 25, 30, 48, 81n19, 81n22; in "Jealous Love and Morbid Jealousy," 94n51; as love affair, xiv, xvii, 9, 26, 29, 35; in Mantegazza's *The Physiology of Love and Other Writings,* 177, 244n5; non-, 34; in Stendhal's *Love,* 241n19; in *Swann in Love,* 9, 30–31, 89n5, 90n12
Lukács, Georg, xiii
Lundgren, Eva, 94n51
Luther, Martin, 65

MacArthur, Charles, 239n3
Macbeth, 220
Magginie, Carlo, 94n51
Malraux, André, 14, 47, 80n7
Mantegazza, Paolo, 177, 244n5
Marx, Karl, xiv, 7, 24, 62, 82
Marxism, xiii, 117
Marxist, xii, xiv, 7, 14, 74, 82, 118, 121, 129
mask, 26, 154, 156, 179–81, 183–84, 188, 202, 220
masochism, 29, 226
Massey, Heath, v, ix, 3, 76, 115, 206
mathematics, xii, xv, 12, 55, 74, 102n11, 110n46. See also arithmetic, geometry
Matisse, Henri, 47, 99n37
matrix, xiv, xxvi, 13, 18–20, 22, 47, 80n17, 121, 125, 157, 160, 168–69, 187, 203
Mead, Margaret, 69, 110
memory (*memoir*), xii, xxii, xxiv, xxxv, 11, 32, 37, 76, 86n18, 88n3, 93n43, 94n45, 115, 125, 132, 135–39, 152, 160–61, 165, 173, 176–80, 187–89, 191–98, 201, 206–15, 226, 231, 234n11, 236n6, 246, 248n9, 250n70, 251n89; in Freud's *Leonardo da Vinci and a Memory of His Childhood,* 159, 233n5, 241n21

Ménasé, Stéphanie, v, xxxiii, 115
Merleau-Ponty, Maurice, 80n6, 80n9, 80n11–12, 80n14, 80n17, 81n19–23, 81n27, 82n35, 86n20, 86n22, 87n35, 88n1, 88n39, 92n29, 94n47–48, 94n52, 95n3, 99n34, 102n15, 103n4, 105n19, 108n35, 109n41, 110n44, 114n58, 166, 170, 177, 233n6, 234n11, 234n22, 235n24, 235n31, 235n34–35, 235n45–46, 237n3, 237n16, 238n5–7, 238n10–11, 239n2, 241n12, 241n20, 242n9, 244n17, 244n39, 245n31–32, 245n34–246n39, 246n41–42, 246n45, 246n49–51, 246n54, 246n56–57, 247n12, 248n3–4, 248n1, 248n10–11; and *Adventures of the Dialectic,* xiii, 80n11, 233n3, 233n7, 234n12, 234n19; and Alquié, xxi; and Bergson, 80n13, 88n37, 242n10; and Blanchot, xxv, 238n4; and Braudel, 104n2; and Cézanne, xvi, 99n38; and "Cézanne's Doubt," xvi; and Chauvin, xi; and Claudel, 247n16; and *Consciousness and the Acquisition of Language,* xxxin18, 234n13; and de Beauvoir, 82n39–83n40; and Febvre, xvii–xix, xxx, xxxn1, xxxn13, 105n16, 105n20–21, 107n34; and Francastel, 99n33; and Freud, xix, xxiii–xxxn1, xxxiv–xxxv, 87n30, 113n55, 236n3, 239n11, 239n4, 240n6, 240n11, 241n16, 242n10, 243n2, 244n2, 244n4, 244n7, 244n10, 245n24–25, 248n8, 249n1, 249n8, 249n25, 250n30, 251n74, 251n89, 252n98, 252n108; and Gesell, 84n9; and Guérin, xiv, 80n11; and Guéroult, xvi; and Guerry, 99n38; and Hegel, xv; and Heidegger, 247n3; and *Humanism and Terror,* xvi; and Husserl, xv–xvi, 81n24, 101n2, 102n10, 223n7; and *In Praise of Philosophy and Other Essays,* xxxn2; and *Institution in Personal and Public History,* ix–xix, xxxiv–xxxv, 80n3, 101n2, 233n1, 248n2; and Kafka, xxxv; and Kant, xiii, 233n4; and Lachiéze-Rey, xxi, 223n4; and Lagache, 94n51, 234n13; and Lévi-Strauss, xiv, xviii, 81n32–82n33, 104n1, 104n4–5, 108n36, 111n50, 112n52, 113n55, 113n57;

INDEX

and Lukács, xiii; and Malraux, 80n7; and Marx, xiv, 82n38; and Marxism, xiii–xiv, 82n37; and *Material for a Philosophy of History,* xii–xiii; and Matisse, 99n37; and *Nature,* xi, 83–84n1, 84n9, 234n36; and "The Novel and Metaphysics," xvi; and *The Origin of Truth,* xvi; and Panofsky, 95n1; and *Phenomenology of Perception,* xxii, xxiv, xxxn15, xxxin18, 102n13, 233n7, 242n7, 242n10, 245n25, 246n2, 247n3; and Piaget, 249n16; and Piéron, 236n2; and Politzer, xxvii–xxviii, 238n7; and *The Primacy of Perception,* xxxin19, 236n1, 238n7; and *The Problem of Passivity,* ix, xix–xxix, xxxiv–xxxv, 84n7; and *The Prose of the World,* xiv–xv, xxxn4, xxxn6, 99n37, 102n16; and Proust, xvii, xxix–xxxn1, xxxv, 36, 88n4–89n5, 89n8–90n12, 91n15–17, 91n21, 92n24, 92n27, 93–94n45, 94n50–51, 247n6, 248n2–3, 248n9; and Ruyer, xi, xxi, 83n1, 85n16, 86n22; and Sartre, xx, xxiii–xxiv, xxxn1, xxxvi, 81n24, 88n37, 104n1, 233n3, 233n7, 234n12–13, 234n17, 234n19, 237n5, 238n12; and Scheler, 242n7; and Schilder, 242n10; and Seignobos, xii; and *Sense and Nonsense,* xii, xviii, xxxn3, xxxn13; and *Signs,* xxxn5, 101n4, 102n10, 103n3; and *The Structure of Behavior,* xxiv, 236n1; and Trotsky, xiv; and Valéry, 241n18; and *The Visible and the Invisible,* xxii, xxxn16, xxxv, 233n7, 238n2, 241n13, 242n8, 247n16; and Weber, xii–xiii, 82n34; and Wertheimer, 102n13, 102n16, 246n2
mirror, 22, 28, 33, 37, 163
Miteinander (with-one-another), 75
mobility, 43, 80n14, 100n38; as immobility, xxv, 104n3, 140, 143, 212
Moreau, Gustave, 88
Moreno, Jacob Levy, 118, 189, 234n10, 246n50
motility, 8, 229
myth, xiii, 67, 129, 133, 207, 240n11, 251n76; as mythical, xx–xxi, 107n30, 121, 124–25, 130, 147, 155, 227, 234n17; as mythological, 32–33

Nacheinander der Jetztpunkte (series of nows), 193, 247n3
Nachvollzug (reoperation), 59, 61, 68, 103n9, 108n35, 121, 191, 234n15. *See also* reactualization, reoperation
Naples, 171
Napoleon Bonaparte, 218
narcissism, 119, 155, 158; as narcissistic, 31–32, 144, 220
nature, xxix, 28, 30, 44, 46–47, 52, 56, 70–71, 73–74, 82n40, 83n40, 89n5, 93n45, 98n27, 106n23, 107n29, 112n50, 112n51, 113n55, 127–30, 133, 137, 141, 144, 148, 159, 162, 164, 182, 194, 206–7, 220, 222, 224, 228–29, 234n23; in *Dialectic of Nature,* 112n50; in "Foundational Investigations of the Phenomenological Origin of the Spatiality of Nature," 235n37; as natural, xi, xxi, 16, 35, 42, 56, 89n5, 95n4, 117, 122–24, 128, 133, 136, 150, 188, 200, 206, 219, 238n11; *naturalis,* 42, 95n4; as naturalism, 106n25; in *Nature and Civilization,* 104n1; in *Nature: Course Notes from the Collège de France,* xi, 84n1, 84n9, 235n36; as non-natural, xiv, 13; as supernatural, 170, 203; as unnatural, 17. *See also physis*
negation (*Verneinung*), 5–9, 33, 35, 39, 61–62, 76–77, 83n40, 111n49, 131, 134, 136, 149, 153–54, 158, 176, 207, 244n39. *See also Verneinung*
negativity, xiii, xxi, 15, 26, 62, 82n38, 124–25, 131
neurosis, 160, 182, 186, 200–202; as neuroses, 154
nihilation, 132, 150, 234n14
noema, 127, 143, 158, 200; as *noemata,* 73
noesis, 127, 143, 158, 200
nothingness, xxiv, 130–31, 134, 143–44, 146, 149–50, 157, 193, 195, 207, 213–14, 234n14, 238n5, 238n12
Notre Dame, 147

oblique view (*Schrägensicht*), 99n35. *See also Schrägensicht*
Oedipus complex, 9, 15, 20–25; in Freud's *The Passing of the Oedipus Complex,* 20, 87n30; as legend of Oedipus, 224; as Oedipal civilization, 15; as

Oedipal conflict, xii, 77; as Oedipal history, 25
Offenheit (openness), 118, 234n9. *See also* openness
oneirism, xxv, 147, 151–54, 157, 161, 167, 200, 218–19; as oneiric, xxv–xxviii, 43, 145–50, 153–59, 187, 199–200, 207–8, 218, 228, 238n7
ontology, ix, xix, xxi, xxix, 122, 125–26, 128–34, 206, 233n4, 236. *See also* being, essence
openness (*Offenheit*), xi, xix, 8, 12–13, 15, 25, 42, 54, 58, 79, 103n10, 135, 148, 160, 194, 213, 234n9, 237n3. *See also Offenheit*
originary time (*Urzeit*), 7, 107n31. *See also Urzeit*
overcoming (*Aufhebung*), xii–xiii, xvii, xix, xxii, xxxv, 5, 78, 118, 175, 182, 227. *See also Aufhebung*, sublation, surpassing
overdetermination, 84n6, 179, 183, 221, 230
overlook (*Überschau*), 248n6. *See also Überschau*

painting, xii, xv, 10, 31, 41–50, 61, 77–78, 96n12–13, 97n21, 99n34, 222
Palissy, Bernard, 107
Panofsky, Erwin, 42–43, 46; and *Perspective as Symbolic Form*, 95n1–2, 95n4–6, 96n12–15, 96n17–97n21, 97n24–98n28, 98n32, 99n36
Paris: in Febvre, 64; in Proust, 32–34, 93n38, 214
Pascal, Blaise, 51, 133, 155, 160
passivity, 137, 166; and activism, xx; and activity, ix, xxii–xxiii, 7, 117, 121–22, 124, 136, 144, 161, 176, 188, 192, 233; and body, xxii, xxv, 122–24, 131, 135, 149, 161; and delusion, xix, 170–77; as dream, xxii–xxv, 121, 144, 149; and event, 217; and freedom, xx, 117, 119–20, 188; and frontal, 135, 142, 191; and history, xx, 117, 119, 121, 124, 131, 133–34, 192, 233; and institution, ix–x, xvi, xix; and lateral, 135–36; as memory, xxii, xxiv, 135, 161, 176, 192, 208, 211, 234; and ontology (being), x, xix–xx, xxix, 123–24, 131, 133, 136, 161, 192, 208, 233; and passivism, xx, 118–19, 233; and past, 117–19, 136, 176, 192, 208, 211; and perception, xvi, xix–xx, xxii–xxvi, 122–24, 133, 136, 149; in *The Problem of Passivity*, ix, xix, xx, xxii, xxiv, xxix, xxxiv, 84n7, 115, 117, 133, 206, 233; as sexuality, 142, 161, 176, 188; and *Sinngebung* (sense-donation), xx, 118, 122, 131, 134–35, 149, 188, 192, 206, 217; as sleep, xxii–xxiii, xv, 121, 124, 131, 135, 138, 144, 149, 206; and subject, xvi, xix–xxv, xxix, 124, 131, 135–36; and (oneiric) symbolism, 149, 161, 188; and time, ix, xvi, xix, xxii–xxiii, 7, 118, 176; and unconscious, xxii, 118, 121, 124, 135, 161, 176, 234; and world, xvi, xx–xxvi, 123–24, 131, 133, 135–36, 149, 192, 208
Pavlov, Ivan, 138–39
perception, xvi, xix–xxvii, 31, 34, 55, 64, 71, 94n47, 123–30, 133, 135–36, 143–47, 150, 159, 162–69, 173, 175, 184–87, 193–95, 198–206, 213, 217, 229–30, 237n3, 240n8, 248n7, 248n9; as apperception, 131, 226; im-, 155, 159; in *Phenomenology of Perception*, xxii, xxiv, xxxn15, xxxin18, 102n13, 233n7, 238n7, 242n7, 242n10, 245n25, 246n2–247n3; in *The Primacy of Perception*, xxxin19, 236n1. *See also Dingwahrnemung*
perception of the thing (*Dingwahrnemung*), 235n40. *See also Dingwahrnemung*, perception
perspective, xx, 6–7, 44–48, 52, 58, 67–68, 76, 82n40, 101n38, 131–36, 164; ancient, 41–42; angular, 42; *artificialis*, 42, 95n4; *communis*, 95n4; as *Durchsehung*, 44–45, 98n28; in Febvre, 106n26; in Lévi-Strauss, 113n55; *naturalis*, 42, 95n4; in Panofsky's *Perspective as Symbolic Form*, 95n1–6, 95n10–98n29, 98n32, 99n36; philosophical, 14; planimetric, 42, 44–45; problem of, xii, 78; Renaissance, 41–42, 98n26, 133; temporal, 5; Van Gogh (of the insect), 46, 217
phenomenology, xxi, 70, 74, 209; in Desanti's *Introduction á la phénoménologie*, 235n30; in Hegel, 79; in Hegel's

INDEX

Phenomenology of Spirit, 248n12; in *Husserl at the Limits of Phenomenology,* 101n2, 235n37; in Husserl's *Cartesian Meditations: An Introduction to Phenomenology,* 236n2; in Husserl's *The Crisis of European Sciences and Transcendental Phenomenology,* 101n2; in Husserl's *Ideas Pertaining to a Pure Phenomenology and to a Phenomenological Philosophy, Second Book,* 102n10, 235n39, 237n13; in Merleau-Ponty, xvi, xx, xxi, xxiv; and perception, xvi, xx; in *Phenomenology and the Sciences of Man,* xxxin19; in *The Phenomenology of Perception,* xxii, xxiv, xxxn15, xxxin18, 102n13, 233n7, 238n7, 242n7, 242n10, 245n25, 246n2, 247n3
physis, 123, 234n23. *See also* nature
picture (*Bild*), xxvi, 5, 38, 44, 47–48, 78, 97n19, 97n21, 98n25, 101n38, 147, 154, 193–94, 210, 217, 220, 232, 239n1. *See also Bild,* image
picture plane (*Bildebene*), 97n24, 98n28. *See also Bildebene*
Piéron, Henri, 138–39, 236n2
Pissarro, Camille, 99
pivot, xxvi, 60–61, 162, 167, 184, 188–89. *See also* hinge
Platonism, 35, 86, 94n48; as experimental, 17, 85–86; as neo-, 43, 45, 97n20
Plattard, Jean, 105n13
point of time (*Zeitpunkt*), 80n4. *See also Zeitpunkt*
Politzer, Georges, xxvii–xxviii, 153–54, 207; and *Critique of the Foundations of Psychology,* xxvii, xxxin21, 238n7
Pompeii, 170–75
Pontalis, Jean-Bertrand, xxviii, xxxin22, 243n15
portion of reality (*Wirklichkeitausschnitt*), 97n23. *See also Wirklichkeitausschnitt*
Portmann, Adolf, xi
Prague, 218
praxis, 11, 62, 149, 165, 196
problem of reason (*Vernuftproblem*), 236n4. *See also Vernuftproblem*
Proclus, 43, 45, 97
profane, 35; as profanation, 35, 92n29
profiles (*Abschattungen*), 80n2. *See also Abschattungen,* adumbrations

Programm (schedule), 87n30. *See also* schedule
projection, xxv, 6, 120, 127, 142, 147, 149, 155, 160, 178, 187, 208, 220
proletariat, xiii, xx, 83n40, 121
Proudhon, Pierre-Joseph, 119
Proust, Marcel, xxxv, 44, 147, 247n6; and Albertine, xxix, 10, 32–39, 91n18–92n34, 93n43, 94n50, 214; and *The Captive,* 29, 32, 92n35, 92n37–93n39; and *Cities of the Plain,* 91n20–92n34, 92n36; and Freud, xxxn1, xxxiv, 155, 168, 197; and *The Fugitive,* 10, 32, 36–37, 93n40–94n48; and Gilberte, 35, 93n43, 214; and *The Guermantes Way,* 91n19, 247n15, 248n11–12, 248n14; and institution, xvii, 7, 36, 39, 50, 77, 248n2; and jealousy, 10, 29, 38–39, 77, 94n51; and love, xvii, 10, 29–39, 77, 89n5–90n13, 91n16, 91n18–94n51; and memory, 132, 155, 195, 197, 201, 210, 218; and Odette, xxix, 30–31, 88n3, 89n8–90n13; and passivity, xxxiv, 7; and *Remembrance of Things Past,* 87n26, 88n2, 88n4–89n5, 91n20, 94n49, 247n8, 247n11, 247n15, 248n2; and Sartre, xxxn1; and Swann, xxix, 9, 30–32, 88n2–3; and *Swann in Love,* 30–31, 89n5; and *Swann's Way,* 31, 87n26, 88n2–3, 89n6–90n13, 210, 247n8–10, 247n14, 247n20, 248n4–5, 248n9; and time, 7, 77, 88n2; and *Time Regained,* 38, 50, 94n49, 248n13, 248n17; and *Within a Budding Grove,* 32, 35, 89n5, 90n14–91n18, 247n11, 247n18–19, 248n6–8, 248n15
psychoanalysis, 72, 84n6, 87n30, 88n38, 113n55, 117–18, 188, 236n3, 242n8, 248n9, 253
psychology, xxiv, 50–51, 122, 125, 227; in *Critique of the Foundations of Psychology,* xxvii, xxxin21, 238n7; in *Review of Existential Psychology and Psychiatry,* xxxin22
puberty, xi, xiv, 9, 11, 19–26, 77, 80n17, 87n35

Rabelais, Francois, xix, 14, 65–68; in Febvre's *The Problem of Unbelief in the Sixteenth Century: The Religion of Rabelais,* xviii, 82n36, 105n12–18

INDEX

Rank, Otto, 240n11, 251n74–76
Raphael, 98
Rationalisierung (rationalization), 14, 82n35. *See also* rationalization
rationalization (*Rationalisierung*), 82n35. *See also Rationalisierung*
Ravenna, 218
reactivation, x, xii, 9, 12, 18, 22, 52, 59, 81n24, 103n4, 103n10, 160, 173, 201; as reactivate, 12, 22, 58, 67; as reactivated, xxiv, 23, 108n35, 179
reactualization (*Nachvollzug*), 103n9. *See also Nachvollzug*, reoperation
ready to be perceived (*Wahrnehmungsbereit*), 104n12, 129. *See also Wahrnehmungsbereit*
realism, xiv, 56, 70, 73, 126, 135, 201
realist, 30, 71, 73, 159, 198
reality, xiii, xxix, 10, 16, 25, 28–31, 34–39, 44–46, 56, 68, 71, 74, 77, 81n22, 89n10, 90n12, 92n37, 93n38, 93n45, 97n23, 98n24, 98n27, 112n50, 118, 126, 133, 139, 141, 144, 148, 151, 155, 157, 164–65, 167, 169–70, 181–82, 184–85, 187–88, 192, 197–98, 202–4, 207–8, 210, 217, 226, 230, 240n8, 245n25
reason (*Vernuft*), 44–46, 129, 154. *See also Vernuft*
Rebus, xxvi, 156, 220
recoil (*Rückschlag*), 38, 43, 45, 96n16–17. *See also Rückschlag*
recollection (*Erinnerung*), xxxv, 5, 121, 131, 134, 160, 165–70, 189–93, 196–204, 209–18, 222, 229–31, 247n7. *See also Erinnerung*
region, 122–23, 195, 199; as regional, xxi, 122, 184, 199–200, 204, 245n31
relativism, xxviii, 14, 63–64, 70–71, 74, 82n33, 130
Renoir, Pierre-Auguste, 48, 100
reoperation (*Nachvollzug*), 103n9, 234n15. *See also Nachvollzug*, reactualization
representation (*Vorstellung*), 5, 55, 95n10, 96n13, 96n17, 97n19, 97n24, 126, 130, 154, 174, 187, 200, 208, 222, 242n10, 247n4, 251n89. *See also Vorstellung*
repression, xxvi–xxviii, 105n19, 117, 149–54, 158–63, 166–70, 173–76, 179–80, 182–86, 192, 197, 199, 202–3,

207, 219, 229, 232, 241n17, 243n10, 243n15, 245n30
research (*Forschungen*), xxix–xxx, xxxv, 11, 20, 41, 87n26, 94n51, 100n38, 103n10, 125, 154, 190. *See also Forschungen*, investigation, search
residue, x, xxvi, 9, 13, 77, 130, 133, 230
Revolution, 11–13, 26–27, 83n40, 97n24; French, xiii, xvii; Industrial, 13; Marxist, 14, 82n37, 82n38, 121; permanent, xiv, 7, 14, 81n24, 121
Riviére, Jacques, 29
Rome, 171, 218
Rückschlag (recoil), 43, 96n16. *See also* recoil
Ruyer, Raymond, xxi, 16–17, 123, 126–27, 235n27; and "Les conceptions nouvelles de l'instinct," xi, 83n1, 84n2, 84n4, 84n8, 84n10–85n15, 85n17–86n18, 86n22, 86n24–87n25, 87n27–28, 235n25

Sache (thing), 7, 80n8. *See also Ding*
sadism, 29, 186
Saint Francis de Sales, 66
Saint John, 66, 105
Saint Jude, 107
Saint Paul, 65, 70–71, 73
Saint Simon, 107
Saint Thomas Aquinas, 66
sapphism, 32
Sartre, Jean-Paul, xx, xxvi, 81n24, 88n37, 104n1, 117, 119, 121–22, 146, 164, 182, 217–18, 237n5, 237n3; and communism, 83n40; and *The Communists and the Peace*, 233n3, 234n12; and de Beauvoir, 83n40; and for-itself, 120; and freedom, 117, 119, 188, 202; and the imaginary, 153, 155, 157, 187; and *The Imaginary*, 234n14, 237n2, 237n4, 237n6, 237n12–13; and Merleau-Ponty, xxiv, xxxn1; and the mythical, 121, 234n17; and nothingness, 146, 150, 157, 195, 238n12; and *Sinngebung*, 81, 233n7; and sleep, xxiii, 139–44, 147–51, 153; and symbolism, 149–51, 153–54, 188, 234n19, 237n1; and sympathy, 83n40
schedule (*Programm*), 21–22, 24, 26, 87n30, 138. *See also Programm*

INDEX

Scheler, Max, 164, 242n7
Schilder, Paul, 176, 195, 242n10
Schmuckkästen (jewel-case), 163. *See also* jewel-case
Schopenhauer, Arthur, 226
Schrägensicht (oblique view), 46, 99n35. *See also* oblique view
science, xvii, xviii, 6, 14, 54, 63, 98n26, 102n2, 123, 128–29, 149, 154, 187; in *The Crisis of European Sciences and Transcendental Phenomenology*, 101n2, 101n5, 102n7, 102n11, 102n17, 234n20; in *La science des rêves*, 249n1, 249n25, 249n29, 250n43, 250n64, 251n74; in "Phenomenology and the Sciences of Man," xxxin19; in *The Science of Logic*, 103n6
search (*Forschungen*), xxx, xxxv, 26, 41, 44, 173, 189–90, 195, 229, 245n18. *See also Forschungen*, investigation, research
Seignobos, Charles, xii
Selbstaufhebung (self-overcoming), 26, 88n41, 121, 234n16. *See also* self-overcoming, self-sublation
Selbstgegebenheit (self-givenness), 130, 133, 197, 235n38, 247n17. *See also* self-givenness
Selbstvergessenheit (self-forgetfulness), 102n10. *See also* self-forgetfulness
Selbstverständlichkeit (self-understanding), 60, 103n11. *See also* self-understanding
self-forgetfulness (*Selbstvergessenheit*), 102n10. *See also Selbstvergessenheit*
self-givenness (*Selbstgegebenheit*), 247n17. *See also Selbstgegebenheit*
self-overcoming (*Selbstaufhebung*), 31, 234n16. *See also Selbstaufhebung*, self-sublation
self-sublation (*Selbstaufhebung*), 88n41. *See also Selbstaufhebung*, self-overcoming
self-understanding (*Selbstverständlichkeit*), 103n11. *See also Selbstverständlichkeit*
sense donation (*Sinngebung*), xx, 39, 60, 80n15, 188, 206, 233n7. *See also Sinngebung*
sensory data (*Sinnendaten*), 238n9. *See also Sinnendaten*
Servetus, Michael, 65, 104n9
sexual, 86n18; being, 74, 156, 160, 177, 180, 182–83, 185, 190–91, 199, 216, 219, 224, 231, 245n25; bi-, 224; "The Body in Its Sexual Being" in *Phenomenology of Perception*, xxiv, 245n25; as hetero-, 38–39; as homo-, 38–39, 94n51, 224; non-, 191; passivity, 142; signification, 72
sexuality, 18, 20, 74, 90n12, 156, 161, 176–78, 182–88, 199, 245n30, 246n35, 246n41; bi-, 156; as hetero-, 39, 94n51; as homo-, 38–39, 90n12, 94n51, 176; imaginary, 21; as poly-, 39, 90n12
Signorelli, Luca, 184, 199–200, 245n30, 246n49
Silberer, Herbert, 226, 251n72
singular (*einmalig*), x, xv, xxii, 9, 102n10, 118, 136, 247n13. *See also einmalig*, unique
Sinn (sense), 102n11
Sinnendaten (sensory data), 150, 238n9. *See also* sensory data
Sinnending (sense of the thing), 153, 238n5. *See also Ding, Dingwahrnemung*
Sinnentleerung (emptying out of sense), 54, 58–59, 102n11, 102n2. *See also* emptying out of sense
Sinngebung (sense donation), 8, 39, 53, 56, 61, 69, 80n15, 81n24, 118, 122–23, 125, 131, 133–35, 149, 165, 182, 192, 196, 202, 205, 217, 233n7. *See also* sense donation
skepticism, xviii, 64, 67, 98n26
sleep, xxii–xxv, xxviii, 19, 34, 39, 44, 90n10, 121–25, 131–32, 135–51, 171, 206–7, 211–14, 230, 236, 236n3, 237n3, 237n16, 238n6, 247n8, 248n9; in *The Problem of Passivity: Sleep, the Unconscious, Memory*, 84n7, 115, 206; walker, 8, 80n14
Sodom and Gomorrah, 32, 91n20
space, xx–xxiii, 43–45, 48, 55, 58, 74, 85n14, 95n6, 95n10–98n27, 99n36, 121, 124, 126, 148–49, 185–87, 193, 195–96, 210, 213–14, 220; in *Cézanne et l'expression de l'espace*, 99n38. *See also* aggregative space, *Aggregatraum*
spectator, xviii, 6, 10, 63, 70, 99n36, 101n38, 125–26, 128
speech, xxv, 28, 42, 46, 51, 58, 158, 208, 211, 222, 225; in Blanchot, xxv, xxxin20, 151–54; in "The Problem of Speech," xvi

Stekel, Wilhelm, 223
Stendhal, 31, 241
stereotype, 24, 189
Stiftung (institution), xv, 9, 13, 19, 51, 59, 61, 80n16, 135, 169, 198; as *end-*, 25, 52, 58, 61–62, 88n40, 102n6; as *ur-*, 25, 52, 58, 61–62, 88n40, 101n6. *See also* establishment, foundation, institution
Stilmoment (moment of style), 42, 45, 95n2. *See also* style
Strachey, James, xxxv, 233n5, 237n3, 238n8, 239n10, 239n14, 240n11, 241n21, 242n2, 243n1, 243n3, 244n1, 247n1, 249n1, 249n25
structuration, 138, 147–48, 152, 169
structure, xi, xv, xviii, xxv, xxvi, xxvii, xxix, 6, 13, 16, 21, 46, 53–56, 60, 62, 68–71, 73, 84n10, 85n11, 100n38, 102n13–14, 106n23, 107n32, 109n39, 110n46, 111n47, 111n50, 113n53, 123, 125–27, 137, 139, 144, 146, 148, 152–54, 158–59, 169, 175, 181, 188, 196, 201, 205, 208, 217, 225, 232, 237n3, 238n6, 241n17; in *Elementary Structures of Kinship*, 108n36, 109n42, 110n45, 112n50–113n53, 113n56; as restructuring, xv; as structural, 52, 56, 78, 111n47, 148, 195; in *Structural Anthropology*, 81n28, 234n8; in *The Structure of Behavior*, xxiv, 236n1; as structuring, x, xvi, 52; as supra-, 123
style, 7, 42, 48, 71, 74, 77, 95n2, 96n12, 98n32, 168, 200, 204–5, 213, 217, 221; Romanesque, 43, 45. *See also Stilmoment*
subjectivity, 29–30, 34, 44–45, 61, 74, 103n3, 120, 127, 134, 162, 214; ultra-, 233n6. *See also* intersubjectivity
sublation (*Aufhebung*), 88n41. *See also Aufhebung*, overcoming, surpassing
sublimation, 51, 54, 80n14, 155, 245n25
substance, 7, 9, 47, 54, 80n13, 100n38, 126, 138
substitute, xi, 19, 25, 74, 108n34, 120, 168, 175, 179, 184, 187–88, 229, 246n57
substitution, 19, 39, 45, 158, 168, 226, 249n25
surpassing (*Aufhebung*), xxxv, 6, 12, 14, 20, 22–23, 26–27, 36, 40, 47, 50–55, 59, 64, 77, 83n40, 85n16, 117–20, 124, 127, 130–31, 134, 160, 182, 191, 198, 201. *See also Aufhebung*, overcoming, sublation
survey, 58, 137, 189, 193, 197, 201; as absolute, 196; as non-, 136; as surveyed, 126, 133; as surveying, 195
symbolic, 19, 86n22, 131, 151, 154, 158–60; accumulation, 15; activity, 7; apparatus, 59, 74; and body, 224; consciousness, 155, 159; field, 6, 130; form, 43–48, 95n3, 99n32; matrix, 13, 18–22, 47, 80n17, 121, 125, 157, 160, 168–69, 187, 203; non-, 159; order, xxvii; in Panofsky's *Perspective as Symbolic Form*, 95n1–99n36; systems, 15, 71, 74, 82n40, 121, 188. *See also* symbolism
symbolism, 54, 148–51, 153–55, 159–60, 185–89, 207, 220, 234n19, 237n1, 238, 246n42, 251n72; constitutive, 153; dream, xxvii, 151–52, 224, 227; Freudian, 220; oneiric, 149; positive, xxvi, 152; primordial, xxvi–xxvii, 154, 208; sexual, 224, 246n41; unconscious, 183. *See also* symbolic
symptom, 43, 91n21, 96n18, 126, 170, 174, 177, 179, 182–83, 189–90, 224, 230, 245n25; as symptomatic, 181
synthesis, 48, 62, 99n38–101n38, 106n25, 119, 121, 126, 168, 193–94, 201, 213–14

temporality, xxii, 8, 76; animal, 20; as atemporal, xvii, 176; human, 20, 54; as temporal, x, xvii, 5, 126, 157–58, 160, 165, 195–97, 201–2, 208, 214, 223, 229; trans-, 7, 154, 192
Thales, 59–60, 103n10
theoretical knowledge (*Erkenntnistheoretisch*), 238n3. *See also Erkenntnistheoretisch*
thickness, xxviii, 6–7, 61, 189, 196
Tinbergen, Nikolaas, 85–86
Tintoretto, 48
trace, x, xv–xvi, xxii, 5, 14, 25, 47, 50, 58, 67, 131, 136, 144, 176, 184, 200, 218
track(s), 17, 22, 24–25, 175, 180, 245n18
transcendence, 69, 176, 198, 208, 220; as transcended, 39; as transcendent, 10, 62, 140, 153, 198, 205, 241n20; as transcends, 123

INDEX

transcendental, xiii, 53, 59, 71, 135, 193; in *The Crisis of European Sciences and Transcendental Phenomenology*, 101n2, 101n5, 102n7, 102n11, 102n17, 234n20
transference, 118, 162, 186, 189–90, 216, 229; as counter-, 119
transversing view (*Durchsehung*), 98n28. *See also Durchsehung*
Trotsky, Leon, xiv, 7
type: of behaviors, xxvi, 238n10; of expression, 47; in Freud 141, 163, 176; as *Imaginings*, 238n10; of interpretation, 163; of kinship; 111n47, 112n50; in Lévi-Strauss, 111n47, 112n50; of memory, 195; of motivation, 141; organic, 86n18; philosophical sense of, 86n18; political, xx; of praxis, 11; in Proust, 92n30, 195; of reality, 74; of situation, 53, 86n17, 213, 238n10; as trace, 176; of women, 92n30. *See also* imaginings

Übereinander (above-bodies), 43, 45, 95n9. *See also* above-bodies
Überschau (overlook), 201, 248n5. *See also* overlook
Uexküll, Jacob von, xi
unconcealment, x, 118, 234n9. *See also aletheia*
unconscious, 121–22; and conscious, xxvi–xxvii, 117–18, 160, 174, 182–85, 246n42; in Freud, xxvi, xxviii–xxix, xxxiv, 152–93, 199–204, 207–8, 224–32, 240n5, 241n17, 242n1, 242n10, 242n24, 243n11, 244n4, 245n30, 246n51, 251n89; in Lévi-Strauss, 71, 104n3, 110n45–111n48; in Lorenz, 87n24; and passivity, xxii, 124–25, 135, 161; and phenomenology, 70; in Politzer, xxvii, 153; in Pontalis's "The Unconscious in Merleau-Ponty," xxxin22; and preconscious, 229–32, 240n8, 241n17; in *The Problem of Passivity: Sleep, Unconscious, Memory*, 84n7, 115, 206; and repression, xxviii; in Sartre, 157
Unendlichkeit des Bildes (infinity of the image), 44, 97n22. *See also* infinity of the image

unique (*einmalig*), 73, 90n12, 102n12, 173, 184, 189, 194, 208, 246n35, 247n13. *See also einmalig*, singular
Urempfindung (originary sensation), 6, 80n5
Urzeit (originary time), 67, 107n31. *See also* originary time

Valéry, Paul, xxii, 61, 117, 241n18
Van Eyck, Jan, 97
Van Gogh, Vincent, 46, 217
variation, 43, 74, 102n15, 130, 150, 160, 193, 195, 206. *See also* deviation, divergence
Vergessenheit (forgetfulness), 58, 103n3, 132, 236n47; as *selbst-* (self-), 102n10. *See also* forgetfulness
Verhalten (behavior), 130, 235n43. *See also* behavior
Verneinung (negation), 176. *See also* negation
Vernuft (reason), 83. *See also* reason
Vernunftproblem (problem of reason), 135, 236n4. *See also* problem of reason
Vienna, 177–78, 190; in Husserl's *Vienna Lecture*, 102n17
Viret, Pierre, 65, 104n7
visible, xxiii, xxxn1, 10, 12, 48, 52, 90n13, 101n38, 158, 164, 169, 172, 194; in *The Visible and the Invisible*, xxii, xxxn16, xxxv, 233n7, 235n37, 238n2, 241n13, 242n8, 247n16
vital, 20, 40, 103, 119, 160, 245n25
vitalism, xxi, 123
Vorstellung (representation), 193, 208, 247n4. *See also* representation

Wahlverwandschaft (elective affinity), 14, 82n35. *See also* elective affinity
Wahrnehmungsbereit (ready to be perceived), 60, 104n12; as *Wahrnehmungsbereitschaft*, 163, 242n5. *See also* ready to be perceived
waking, xxiii, xxviii, 143–44, 146–51, 155, 173, 187, 199, 207–8, 212, 215, 227, 229, 238n6, 239n4; consciousness, 132, 144, 157; world, 140, 147
Weber, Max, 245n25; and *The Adventures of the Dialectic*, 82n34; and capitalism, 13; and conceptual history, xii; and

elective affinity, xiii; and *The Protestant Ethic and the "Spirit" of Capitalism*, 82n34; and *Rationalisierung*, 14; and *Wahlverwandschaft*, 14

Weltgefühl (feeling of the world), 44, 46, 98n30. *See also* feeling

Wertheimer, Max, 12; and experiment, 25, 191; and *Experimentelle Studien über das Sehen von Bewegung*, 81n26, 246n2; and *Productive Thinking*, 102n16; and structural truth, 55, 57, 78, 102n13

Wertmoment (moment of value), 42, 45, 95n2

Wesen ist was gewesen ist (essence as what has been), 59, 103n6. *See also* essence

Wirklichkeitausschnitt (portion of reality), 44, 97n23. *See also* portion of reality

wish, xxxv, 34, 36, 41, 62, 79, 92n27, 94n45, 138, 166–72, 183, 187, 202, 204, 218–20, 224, 228, 230–32; dream-, 228, 230, 232, 240n8, 242n24; fulfillment, 219, 226

work, xiii, 58–61, 64, 131, 195, 231–32; of art, 39–49, 95, 96n17, 99n36–38, 100n38, 142; becoming of the, xvi, 87n24; dream-, xxviii, 222, 225–26, 228, 230, 238n9, 239n4, 240n8, 252n108; institution of, xii–xiv, xvii, 10–11, 39–50, 95; of interpretation, xiv, 227; pictorial, xiv–xv, 77, 100n38

Zeitpunkt (point of time), 5, 80n4. *See also* point of time

Zusammenstimmung (disposition of togetherness), 205

Maurice Merleau-Ponty (1908–1961), along with Sartre, introduced phenomenology to France. He held the Chair of Child Psychology and Pedagogy at the University of the Sorbonne, which was later held by Jean Piaget. He was elected to the Collège de France in 1952, holding the Chair of Philosophy.

Leonard Lawlor is Edwin Erle Sparks Professor of Philosophy at Pennsylvania State University. He previously translated Merleau-Ponty's *Husserl at the Limits of Phenomenology* for Northwestern.

Heath Massey is an assistant professor of philosophy at Beloit College.

www.ingramcontent.com/pod-product-compliance
Lightning Source LLC
Chambersburg PA
CBHW032028290426

44110CB00012B/719